LAW AND ECONOMICS IN THE RIA WORLD

LAW AND ECONOMICS IN THE RIA WORLD

Improving the use of economic analysis in public policy and legislation

Andrea Renda

intersentia
Cambridge – Antwerp – Portland

Intersentia Ltd
Trinity House | Cambridge Business Park | Cowley Road
Cambridge | CB4 0WZ | United Kingdom
mail@intersentia.co.uk

Distribution for the UK:
Hart Publishing Ltd.
16C Worcester Place
Oxford OX1 2JW
UK
Tel.: +44 1865 51 75 30
Email: mail@hartpub.co.uk

Distribution for the USA and Canada:
International Specialized Book Services
920 NE 58th Ave. Suite 300
Portland, OR 97213
USA
Tel.: +1 800 944 6190 (toll free)
Email: info@isbs.com

Distribution for Austria:
Neuer Wissenschaftlicher Verlag
Argentinierstraße 42/6
1040 Wien
Austria
Tel.: +43 1 535 61 03 24
Email: office@nwv.at

Distribution for other countries:
Intersentia Publishers
Groenstraat 31
2640 Mortsel
Belgium
Tel.: +32 3 680 15 50
Email: mail@intersentia.be

Law and Economics in the RIA World. Improving the use of economic analysis in public policy and legislation
Andrea Renda

ISBN 978-1-78068-023-1
NUR 823

British Library Cataloguing in Publication Data. A catalogue record for this book is available from the British Library.

In memory of my father

FOREWORD

This book is the result of years of research, consulting, teaching, travelling and sharing ideas with colleagues, friends and students. Given the wide array of memories and anecdotes that populate its pages, I am sure I would have written it very differently when I was 25, and will probably want to rewrite it from scratch when I'm 64. As in Heraclitus' Πάντα ῥεῖ, even if the river is the same, the water will always be new; what's more, I tend to agree with Cratylus, who argued that it is impossible to step into the same river even once. As a matter of fact, even rewriting this book today would probably lead to a different result. The song remains the same, but the mind moves, like in the famous Zen kōan reported by Douglas Hofstädter, in which two monks were arguing about a flag. One said, "The flag is moving." The other said, "The wind is moving." The sixth patriarch, Zeno, happened to be passing by. He told them, "Not the wind, not the flag; mind is moving."

As a son of two professors of human anatomy, specialized *i.a.* in neuropeptides, I always had problems with the basic assumptions of neoclassical economics, which seemed to me too far from reality, and dangerously so. These certainly included the assumptions that income, unlike most goods, features constant marginal returns; and that individual preferences are independent of income and of the context in which they emerge. These two basic tenets – the irrelevance of distributional issues and pure methodological individualism – are heavily challenged in the pages of this work: overcoming them would lead economics – and law and economics along with it – to much higher grounds.

The problem is that the *pars destruens* of behavioral economics has so far been much more convincing than the corresponding *pars construens*: as a matter of fact, it has inflicted a lethal wound to mainstream neoclassical economics, but did not show where to go from there. Truth is that modern neuroscience makes economics even more dismal, by portraying our brain as a lone soldier entrusted with the desperate attempt to reduce complexity, constantly trying to collect all available information that can be found in past experience, external signals, distorted beliefs, anticipated regret, and just a drop of logic – not more than that. This tells us that we are doomed to use proxies in whatever we do. And that we will never be able to fully master the mysterious ways in which humans react to legal rules. I remember a quote my Dad used in his classes on the nervous system: "If the brain were simple enough for us to understand it, we would be too simple to understand it."

This applies also to public authorities, not just to individuals. And it explains why the *ex ante* assessment of the costs and benefits of public policy should be taken as an exercise constrained by the imperfection of our brains: public authorities should be asked to collect and illustrate all available information from past experience, sound scholarly work, external opinions, basic principles and fundamental goals before they decide to intervene; at the same time, they might want to postpone the answer to certain questions, and prioritize certain decisions, just as we do when we just have too much to squeeze in one day. But they cannot be asked to build a crystal ball and predict the future with full certainty, nor they should be required to make their calculations in isolation, such that they would reach the same results under every sky.

Writing this book, I have gradually realized that some social sciences have progressed more than economics in the past few decades. In my opinion, this occurred because economics, unlike these other disciplines, desperately needs to be immediately useful to policy. That's why "we the economists" should learn from what our colleagues in other social sciences can teach us. To paraphrase Bob Dylan in "my back pages", we were much older ten years ago; we are much younger now, and must take action to help policymakers address the huge challenges that they will have to face in the coming years. Even more difficult, we need to reflect further on what does it mean to be "efficient", "fair" and "just", and find new ways of reconciling the three concepts in our approach to public policies. Otherwise we will be forced to accept reality: that we economists are not able to predict crises, we are not helpful in fostering the happiness of the most, and that, when we are particularly smart people prefer to call us philosophers (one easy example: Amartya K. Sen).

Social sciences are like this, after all. The fact that what you are writing about does not exist *in rerum natura* can be overwhelming at times. This reminds me of when I was 22, and I attended one of my first conferences in law and economics in Hamburg, Germany. I sneaked into a room and ended up seating next to a legendary Professor from the University of Manchester, Anthony Ogus, one of the most enlightened fathers of the European Law and Economics movement. When Professor Ogus saw me, he shook my hand and asked me what I was researching on at the time. I said "I am studying fairness". He then smiled, took a while to reflect, and then replied "fairness is a very nice subject… because it doesn't exist!"

My deepest gratitude goes to all those that have directly or indirectly influenced my research over the past years. In the study of law and economics, Roberto Pardolesi and Roger van den Bergh – with whom the first concept of this book was discussed – have taught me how to walk even before I could stand on my own feet. Michael Faure has patiently and quickly read my drafts, and pointed me in the right direction when my mind was drifting apart. Marianne Breijer was of invaluable help during the drafting of this research. In the RIA world, colleagues and friends such as Claudio Radaelli, Scott Jacobs, Bob Hahn, Colin Kirkpatrick, Jacques Pelkmans have shown me the keys of the kingdom. My girlfriend Rosa, my mother Loredana, my brothers Luca and Carlo, Fiorella, Amy, Franca, Jorge and our good old friends have made it possible by giving my boggling mind a compass, a warm shelter, and many things to be proud of.

Rome, 14 February 2011

CONTENTS

1. PROLOGUE: THE BIRTH OF ADMINISTRATIVE LAW AND ECONOMICS

More than three decades ago, lawyers and economists met in Chicago for "the greatest gig in the sky" in the history of law and economics: the Symposium on "Efficiency as a legal concern", where many of the most authoritative law and economic scholars of that time discussed the merit of adopting efficiency criteria in legal adjudication, and ended up digging quite thoroughly into the virtues and hidden traps of the Kaldor-Hicks criterion as a normative basis for deciding about complex and controversial legal issues. That was also the time in which scholars like Richard Posner, William Landes, George Priest and Paul Rubin – all in favor of replacing legal criteria in adjudication with Kaldor-Hicks efficiency – were challenged by others, such as Ronald Dworkin, Richard Epstein, Anthony Kronman, Duncan Kennedy, Charles Fried, Gerald O'Driscoll Jr. and Mario Rizzo, who considered that efficiency criteria could lead to potential distortions in the making of value judgments when adjudicating legal controversies.

One of the most striking result of the Symposium was that economists, not lawyers, were the first to reject the idea that legal adjudication in common law could be based on resourcist efficiency criteria aimed at wealth maximization, such as the Kaldor-Hicks one. For example, Richard Posner stated (and later wrote) that "while Kaldor-Hicks is not a Pareto criterion as such, it will sometimes function as a tolerable, and more to the point, administrable approximation of the Pareto superiority criterion"[1]; whereas the economist Mario Rizzo recalled, from its Austrian School perspective, that "the substantial information requirements that must be satisfied in order to identify efficient legal rules make efficiency impractical as a standard".[2]

The papers presented in the Chicago symposium – later published in the Hofstra Law Review and the Journal of Legal Studies – have eternally marked the law and economics debate in the US, and traces of the battle between efficiency and fairness are still quite visible in the literature, starting from attempts to modify the Kaldor-Hicks criterion "from the inside" (*e.g.*, by adding ethical considerations as well as accounting for behavioral concerns); and ending

1 Posner, R. A. (1980), *The Ethical and Political Basis of the Efficiency Norm in Common Law Adjudication*, 8 Hofstra L. Rev., 1980, p. 487.

2 See Rizzo, M. J. (1980), *The Mirage of Efficiency*, 8 Hofstra L. Rev., 1979–1980, p. 641.

with research streams that depart from resourcist approaches, and increasingly look at utility functions, happiness maximization and even weak paternalistic claims.[3]

The Chicago Symposium was also very topical, as it marked an important schism in the history of law and economics in the US: one the one hand, efficiency criteria failed to become the one and only grounds for adjudication in the US, thus frustrating the alleged "imperialist" attempt of neoclassical lawyers and economists; on the other hand, the Kaldor Hicks criterion entered the stage in US policymaking from another front door: the requirement that Federal agencies perform an *ex ante* appraisal of their major new regulations, which culminated in the introduction of Regulatory Impact Analysis (RIA) as a mandatory procedure. This, in turn, meant that government agencies, such as *i.a.* the Department of Transport, the Occupational Safety and Health Agency and the Environmental Protection Agency, were *de facto* called to apply Kaldor-Hicks in crafting their regulations, and justify them in "net benefit" terms.[4] This trend, strengthened during the Clinton Administration with Executive Order 12,866, later led authoritative commentators to advocate for a "cost-benefit state"[5]; and even to the so-called "Grand Experiment", *i.e.* the compilation of yearly reports to the President of the United States, on the costs and benefits of Federal regulation as a whole.[6] Today, use of net benefits calculations remains at the core of federal regulation in the US, and is ensured by the constant monitoring and operation of a rather "adversarial" gatekeeper – the Office of Information and Regulatory Affairs within the OMB – which secures that agencies perform adequate cost-benefit analysis when taking actions to solve a market failure, and justify that action in net benefit terms, by *de facto* adopting the Kaldor-Hicks criterion of potential Pareto efficiency.[7]

---

3 Zerbe Jr., Richard O., *Justice and the Evolution of the Common Law* (November 2005); Zerbe Jr., Richard O., *Should Moral Sentiments Be Incorporated into Benefit-Cost Analysis? An Example of Long-Term Discounting. Policy Sciences*, available at SSRN: http://ssrn.com/abstract=739804; Kahneman, *Experienced Utility and Objective Happiness: A Moment-Based Approach*, Chapter 37, pp. 673–692, in: D. Kahneman and A. Tversky (eds.), *Choices, Values and Frames*, New York: Cambridge University Press and the Russell Sage Foundation, (2000), etc.; Adler and Posner, *Happiness Research and Cost-Benefit Analysis*, at http://lsr.nellco.org/upenn/wps/papers/167, (2007); Frey and Stutzer (2007), at www.oecd.org/dataoecd/16/36/38331948.pdf. And Cass Sunstein and Richard Thaler, *Nudge. Improving Decisions about Health, Wealth and Happiness*, Yale University Press 2008.

4 U.S. Office of Management and Budget (OMB). (2003). Circular A-4: Regulatory analysis. www.whitehouse.gov/omb/circulars/a004/a-4.pdf.

5 Sunstein, C. R. (2002), *The Cost-Benefit State*, University of Chicago Law School, John M. Olin Law & Economics, Working Paper No. 39.

6 Hahn, R.W. and M.B. Muething (2003), *The Grand Experiment in Regulatory Reporting*, Administrative Law Review, 2003, Vol. 55, No. 3, pp. 607–642.

7 See Renda, A. (2006), *Impact Assessment in the EU*, Centre for European Policy Studies, Brussels.

The different fate of cost-benefit analysis in these two streams of public decision-making – common law adjudication on the one hand, federal regulation on the other – may appear, at first blush, rather odd, and hard to explain. How can one reject efficiency criteria as a "mirage" in common law adjudication, at the same time adopting them as the one and only principle in identifying the alternative to be undertaken in federal regulation? If, quoting again Rizzo, "the substantial information requirements that must be satisfied in order to identify efficient legal rules make efficiency impractical as a standard" in common law adjudication, how could the opposite hold when the public decision-maker is an agency? And how can we reconcile Calabresi's "pointlessness of Pareto" with the almost religious vocation to potential Pareto efficiency of federal agencies in the US? Does a resourcist efficiency criterion such as the "net benefit" one provide a sound basis for regulatory decisions?

1.1. TWINS SEPARATED AT BIRTH?

The three decades that have elapsed since the Chicago symposium on "efficiency as a legal concern" have witnessed a remarkable increase in the use of economic arguments to justify public policy decisions. In academia, the expansionist (many would say, imperialist) tendency of economics has led to the proliferation of movements of all kinds, bringing economics into previously unexplored domains, from marriage and divorce to terrorism and the cold war. At a more political level, fueled by international organizations such as the OECD and the World Bank, the need to introduce forms of *ex ante* policy appraisal has become a recurring *refrain* in the international community, gradually developing into a field of research and professional expertise that meets growing demand in the job market. The most common acronym used to summarize the *ex ante* appraisal of future consequences of policy measures is "RIA", *i.e.* regulatory impact analysis: this acronym, later shortened as "IA" (impact assessment) in the European context, represents a fairly standardized practice in the international community, which follows specific steps to guide policymakers in the evaluation of alternatives and the selection of the most appropriate policy option.[8] As shown in the figure below, today virtually all OECD member countries have adopted a RIA procedure, and many non-OECD countries have done the same, at national and sometimes also sub-national level.[9]

8 See below, Section 2, for a description of the key steps of an impact assessment.
9 An estimated 50 countries today have institutionalized RIA in their legal system.

Figure 1. RIA adoption in OECD countries

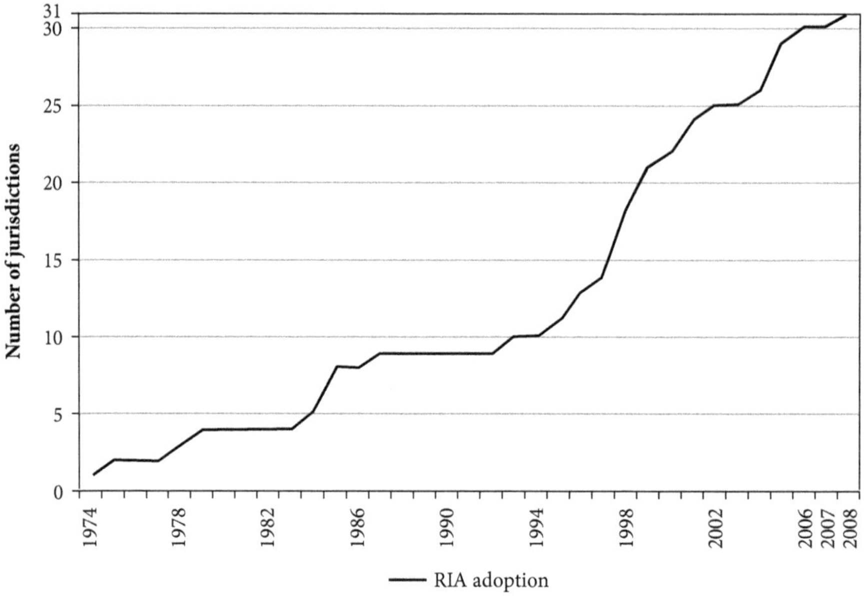

Source: OECD

Despite this apparent success, the use of economics as the main foundation of *ex ante* policy evaluation – albeit not necessarily the only one – is not uncontroversial, for a number of reasons. First, economics in and of itself is not an uncontroversial subject matter: many social scientists have expressed serious doubts on the inherent bias embedded in the use of mainstream economic tools, especially those related to the Neoclassical paradigm that still dominates a large portion of economic studies, as well as the application of economics to public policy. Second, the use of economics from an *ex ante* perspective (*i.e.*, with a normative purpose) has been heavily criticized, since it can lead policymakers into the formulation of rather heroic assumptions when communicating and motivating policy choices: this, in turn, can end up transplanting into policymaking the typical problems attributed to economics, such as the "can opener" problem (over-reliance on assumptions); the "knowing the price of everything, and the value of nothing" problem: and many others.[10] Third, the transparent use of economic analysis to back policy proposals often meets the

[10] See, *i.a.* F. Ackerman, L. Heinzerling and R. Massey, *Applying Cost-Benefit to Past Decisions: Was Environmental Protection Ever a Good Idea?*, Georgetown Public Law Research Paper No. 576161, Georgetown University, August 2004; F. Ackerman and L. Heinzerling, *Priceless: on Knowing the Price of Everything and the Value of Nothing*, New York: The New Press, 2004; and See David Driesen's White Paper, *Is Cost-Benefit Analysis Neutral?*, 2 February 2005 (available at http://ssrn.com/abstract=663602), p. 7. See also Hahn, R.W. (2005), *In Defense of the Economic Analysis of Regulation*, American Enterprise Institute, Washington, D.C., 2005.

fierce resistance of elected political powers. Parliamentarians, for example, typically hate being constrained by any form of objective rationale when voting on policy proposals: rather, they prefer pursuing their own political agenda and strike deals between conflicting and often competing interests.[11] Finally, and perhaps more importantly, the economic analysis of proposed legal rules is normally performed by civil servants in charge of a policy portfolio within a national administration: traditional "Weberian" bureaucrats, however, typically do not possess enough knowledge to perform sophisticated economic analysis, and they, themselves, end up resisting the adoption of these tools. So to say, people normally either love or hate economics, but hate is much easier and way more frequent.

Today, the reluctance to accept the widespread use of economics to back public policy decisions is also rooted in the poor performance exhibited by economic theory in protecting citizens from a number of adverse consequences of human behavior and market interaction. Examples are manifold, and range from collective action problems in taking action against global hunger and climate change to the frequent intrusion of hackers into private computer networks. Economic theory was targeted by even more violent critiques due to the recent, major economic crisis that originated in the sub-prime mortgage crunch in the United States, and later spread like an oil spot in the real economies of most developed countries worldwide.[12] The fact that one of the most deeply researched domains of human interaction – financial markets – ended up being prey of an unsustainable pattern of evolution and eventually crashed without parachute – expressed in terms of legal rules, governance, or even liability – struck the attention and conscience of the public opinion, casting a dark shadow over the soundness of the economics used in support of regulation.

In a nutshell, when it comes to the use of economic theory in support of public policy, we live in an age of distrust. A time like this, however, is also a time of great opportunities for improving our understanding of the economic interactions that form the subject matter of policymaking. After all, economic theory has been on trial before. For example, in the aftermath of the 1973–1975 oil crisis, while receiving the Nobel prize in 1974 Friederich Von Hayek took the opportunity to scream against those economists that tried to "sell" economics as a natural science, just like physics, and against those policymakers that did not

11 See, *i.a.* McCormick, R.E. and R.D. Tollison (1981), *Politicians, Legislation and the Economy. An Inquiry into the Interest-Group Theory of Government*, Boston: Martinus Nijoff; Kau, J.B. and P.H. Rubin (1982), *Congressmen, Constituents and Contributors*, Boston: Martinus Nijoff; Peltzman, S. (1984), *Constituent Interest and Congressional Voting*, Journal of Law and Economics 27, 181–210.

12 See *i.a.*, Posner, R.A. (2009), *A Failure of Capitalism. The Crisis of '08 and the Descent into Depression*, Harvard University Press. Stiglitz, J. *et al.* (2010), *The Stiglitz report: Reforming the World Economy in the Wake of the Global Crisis*, The New Press, New York. And Krugman, P. (2009), *The Return of Depression Economics and the Crisis of 2008*, W.W. Norton & Company, New York.

resist the sirens of such an apparently reassuring practical, easy advice. In short, Hayek meant that public policy was based on obsolete, highly surpassed economics: without a careful updating of the theoretical framework, using economics to inspire public policy becomes a fairly dangerous exercise.

More than three and a half decades after Hayek's speech, and despite the progress made in some domains of economics, most of the rhetoric of public policy is still dominated by a rather unsophisticated Neoclassical approach. During the 1980s and 1990s, international organizations have used that approach to heavily promote privatization and market liberalization in developing countries, creating fragile outcomes that have recently been defined as "gods with clay feet", and thus not very different from the sub-prime mortgage market before the crisis.[13]

Interestingly, while the practice of *ex ante* regulatory impact analysis (RIA) in the United States blossomed at the end of the 1970s as a natural consequence of a period of expansionism of economics into public policy, in those same years the law and economics movement that had changed the mindset of lawyers and policymakers in the 1960s started transforming into the "economic analysis of law" (EAL), *i.e.* a normative version of law and economics that started looking, more than at the way the law *is*, at how the law *ought to be*. The two disciplines overlapped in many respects. EAL essentially looked at how to design and structure legal rules to trigger efficient outcomes, mostly relying on individual and market reaction to the introduction of new policy measures. On the other hand, RIA was meant to guide policymakers in the selection of the policy solutions that fulfilled one given condition, *i.e.* they stood to maximize net benefits and thus social welfare. Even more importantly, both EAL and RIA have until recently been based (at least in the United States) on the application of a specific criterion – Kaldor-Hicks efficiency – that imposes a "resourcist" calculation of net benefits.

Despite this parallelism, which makes them almost "twins" in the landscape of social sciences, EAL and RIA have remained "separated at birth" since the early 1980s. It was only quite recently that the enormous progress made by EAL over time has surfaced again in the aisles of the major institution in charge of RIA in the United States – the Office of Information and Regulatory Affairs. This is due, in particular, to the appointment of one of the most prolific and insightful law and economics scholar of our time, Cass R. Sunstein, as the Head of the OIRA (the so-called "Regulatory Czar") within the Obama administration. From that pedestal, Cass Sunstein is starting to import more modern (behavioral) law and economics concepts into the daily policy activities of the US administration.[14]

---

13 I owe this definition to my friend and colleague Paul Cook, Professor Emeritus of Economics at the University of Manchester.

14 See, for a brief overview of Sunstein's academic work, Wiener, J. (2008), *Best Cass Scenario*, Tulsa L. Rev., Vol. 43, 933–946.

Funnily enough, while early law and economics contributors were mostly considered as conservative Chicagoans, the return of law and economics in RIA after thirty years was received with a degree of skepticism by many commentators, who consider Sunstein – a Chicagoan himself – almost as a dangerous Marxist for his idea of "libertarian paternalism".[15]

The perceived "hybridization" of the established practice of *ex ante* RIA in the US with contemporary law and economics is not, after all, a departure from a state of grace. As a matter of fact, both EAL and RIA are drowning into a deep mid-life crisis. On the one hand, law and economics scholars are struggling with an expansionist movement that willingly neglects every conclusion that does not lend itself to formalization in mathematical terms, to the extent that lawyers – once the driving force of the movement – hardly recognize their original approach, polluted as they are by the streams of propositions and lemmas that populate most of the scholarly papers in the field.[16] In addition, outside the US acceptance of this inter-disciplinary approach has been rather cold: in a recent article, Garoupa and Ulen (2007) observe that "law and economics has been one of the most important developments in North American legal scholarship of the twentieth century but has hardly registered as a scholarly innovation in Europe".[17] Overall, EAL is still perceived in many enlightened academic environments of the Old Continent as a very conservative, pro-market discipline.

On the other hand, it is no mystery that so far the implementation of RIA has been a failure in most countries around the world. In the United States, RIA is under attack mostly for reasons related to the methodology it adopts to reach very socially sensitive conclusions – in particular, I refer again to the use of Kaldor-Hicks Benefit-Cost Analysis in the assessment of so-called "lifesaving regulation", including policy domains related to health care, safety, and the environment.[18] In the EU and elsewhere, critiques of the RIA system currently focus both on issues related to governance and substance. Even if international organizations like the OECD often mention RIA as a practice that has successfully spread in most developed and several developing countries, the reality is that the formal adoption of the model has been followed by very limited

15 Of the several articles appeared in the press, see Benjamin Wallace-Wells, *Cass Sunstein wants to nudge us*, New York Times, 16 May 2010. Interviewed by the NY Times reporter, Saul Levmore – a former Dean of the School of Law at the University of Chicago – observed that Sunstein has "the quintessential University of Chicago habit of mind".

16 See, *i.a.*, Manne, H.G. and J. D. Wright (2008), *The Future of Law and Economics: a Discussion*, George Mason University Law and Economics Research Paper Series n. 08–35.

17 Ulen, Thomas S. and Nuno M. Garoupa (2007), *The Market for Legal Innovation: Law and Economics in Europe and the United States*. University of Illinois Law and Economics Research Paper No. LE07–009. Available at SSRN: http://ssrn.com/abstract=972360.

18 For a definition of lifesaving regulation, See Graham, J.D. (2007), *Saving Lives through Administrative Law and Economics*, University of Pennsylvania Law Review, Vol. 157: 395, at 397. And see Harrington, W., L. Heinzerling and R. Morgenstern (2009) for a discussion of some of the outstanding critiques to the US RIA system, with a focus on the RIA practice of the Environmental Protection Agency.

and often awkward implementation attempts. Today, in virtually no country outside the US RIA can be said to be a success, with the only, very partial exceptions of the European Commission and possibly the United Kingdom, Canada and Australia. This also means that there is no Civil Law jurisdiction where RIA has been successfully mainstreamed into the policymaking process to date.

1.2. MOTIVATION FOR THIS RESEARCH PROJECT

The idea of writing about the relationship between law and economics and RIA came to me back in 2005, when I started researching on the European Commission's impact assessment system and its comparison with the US RIA model. Reading through the impact assessment documents produced by these administrations over time, the absence of a real consideration of individual incentives and market behavior raised my eyebrows, given my academic background in law and economics. I decided to start exploring the missing links between the two disciplines already in a short paper presented at the mid-term meeting of the Erasmus Mundus European Master in Law and Economics in Ghent in March 2008.[19]

Further inspiration came when the European Commission called me to lead a major impact assessment project, on the delicate issue of whether and how to encourage private antitrust damages actions in Europe. Law and economics scholars know well that private enforcement and litigation is one of the fields in which the law and economics movement has provided the most inspiring and revolutionary contributions. The drafting of that report for the European Commission led me to draw several lessons, which I report in some of the sections of this work.[20] Perhaps the most important of all lessons was that, while Commission officials seemed to be chiefly interested in the first part of the report, dedicated to the monetization of the costs and benefits of a "hypothetically more effective" private antitrust enforcement system in Europe, I always thought that the most useful part of the report was the more difficult and sophisticated second part, where our research team was making extensive use of the law and economics approach to show which combination of legal rules would have placed the most efficient incentives on all players involved. It is on this dichotomy that this book is essentially grounded.

Later on, I drew further inspiration from other works carried out for the European Commission: most notably, from the application of the Standard Cost Model in a number of fields (see, in particular, my account of large exposure

---

19 The paper is available at SSRN: http://ssrn.com/abstract=1291032.

20 See Renda *et al.* (2008), *Making Antitrust Damages Actions More Effective in the EU*, at http://ec.europa.eu/competition/antitrust/actionsdamages/files_white_paper/impact_study.pdf.

reporting below, in Section 5.5); and from the study on tying and other potentially unfair commercial practices in retail financial services. In the latter study, again, policymakers cared mostly about the quantification and monetization of impacts, whereas the most relevant part of the work was the attempt to understand the peculiar dynamics of the interaction between consumer and financial services providers, characterized by fiduciary elements and a strong informational asymmetry.

Moreover, the temptation to undertake this work became irresistible when I started discussing with one of the most authoritative experts in the field about the possibility for RIA to address distributional impacts. Opinions are still split: some authors think RIA should stay away from the monetization of impacts, in particular social impacts, that are very difficult to quantify; others propose to depart from Kaldor-Hicks exactly for the purpose of accounting for distributional impacts; and others think Kaldor-Hicks should be at least complemented (if not replaced) by measures of happiness and hedonic values that, in their opinion, provide a better measure of societal improvements than a mere "resourcist" measure of net benefits.[21]

Finally, a decisive element in the decision to carry out this work came from the recognition that the two disciplines analyzed in the following pages are both navigating through rather difficult waters, for different reasons. The temptation of "catching two birds with one stone" by identifying avenues for tighter cooperation between two disciplines is one that scholars normally fail to resist. I am no exception.

1.3. MAIN RESEARCH QUESTIONS

This research project attempts to provide an answer to a number of main research questions, which I illustrate below.

First, should law and economics be more integrated with the practice of ex ante *impact assessment*? This question, in turn, entails a discussion of the main purpose and scope of RIA systems, as well as problems emerged in the implementation of RIA at national and regional level (in particular, in the US and the EU).

Second, *in what ways can law and economics contribute to the quality, usefulness and effectiveness of ex ante impact assessment*? This question looks at the methodological approaches adopted by law and economics scholars, which have led to a more thorough understanding of individual and collective behavior and, more generally, to the development of normative conclusions as to how to design and enforce legal rules.

---

21 I refer, in particular, to Scott Jacobs, John Graham, and Cass Sunstein.

Third, *what does the law and economics literature imply for the design and organization of policy evaluation within government?* Law and economics is not only about policy impacts, but also about the organization of government and the use of better regulation tools to control the bureaucracy. A stronger role for law and economics in RIA systems should not be confined to the substance of RIA, but easily extends also to the design of RIA systems, including the purpose, scope and governance of RIA at national and regional level.

Fourth, *what would a stronger integration between law and economics and RIA mean for the US and EU impact assessment systems?* In particular, given the significant differences in the pattern of adoption and implementation, as well as in the success of both law and economics and RIA on the two sides of the Atlantic, it is important to assess whether the prospects for a stronger interaction between the two disciplines would yield similar results, or whether different conclusions and recommendations should be drawn for the two legal systems.

1.3.1. WHAT THIS BOOK IS NOT

Both law and economics and RIA are complex disciplines, which have been approached from several different perspectives. In particular, RIA has been studied by political scientists, public management scholars, economists and – to a lesser extent – lawyers in different ways.[22] It is thus important to clarify what this research project is not, *i.e.* which of the many perspectives on RIA and law and economics do not form the core subject matter of this volume.

First, this is not a project on regulatory governance and regulatory reform, in the sense normally adopted by international organizations such as the World Bank or the OECD. For perspectives on how to approach RIA within the broader framework of regulatory reform, readers can refer to OECD (1995, 2009); Jacobs (2006); and to several papers written by experts – including myself – for the World Bank.[23]

Second, this is not a project focused on the US and EU better regulation agenda. Although the analysis of RIA systems in the US and EU will necessarily lead me to touch upon several issues related to the future of better regulation tools on the two sides of the Atlantic, the main purpose of this book is to look at RIA from the perspective of institutional mechanisms and methodology, rather than within the broader context of political priorities expressed in these two

22 See, for a description of the literature on impact assessment, Meuwese, A.C.M. (2008), *Impact Assessment in EU Lawmaking*, Kluwer Law International.

23 See, *i.a.* IFC Better Regulation for Growth program, *Regulatory Governance in Developing Countries*, available online at: www.fias.net/ifcext/fias.nsf/AttachmentsByTitle/BRG_PapersWhatisit/$FILE/RegulatoryGovinDevCountries.pdf See also *i.a.* Renda, A. (2010), *The Development of RIA in the European Union*, paper presented at the World Bank Regulatory Reform Conference in Belgrade (Serbia), 13–14 September 2010.

complex legal systems. For more specific literature and my own analysis of this specific perspective, please see *i.a.* Renda (2006, 2008); Renda *et al.* (2009), where the comparison between the US and EU agenda and better regulation strategy is performed more in detail.

Third, this volume is not chiefly aimed at offering an evaluation of the quality of impact assessment in the US and the EU, although the approach adopted is *per se* critical on the specific types of methodology adopted and suggested by current guidelines. For more focused papers on this issue, readers can refer to several papers by Bob Hahn with different co-authors, and to Cecot, Hahn, Renda and Schrefler (2007).[24]

Finally, this research project does not aim at offering a systematic overview of all the vast literature existing both in the law and economics field, as well as in the field of policy appraisal and regulatory reform. The need to allow for a meaningful comparison of the main *tenets* of the two disciplines suggested a degree of parsimony in references to existing literature. This hopefully facilitates the reader in understanding the core messages contained in the text.

1.4. METHODOLOGY

This book looks at the interaction between two already inter-disciplinary fields of research, and as such draws on several different streams of literature in social science. Below, I briefly summarize the different scientific achievements that compose the pantheon of this work.

---

24 See Hahn R.W. and R.E. Litan. (2005). *Counting Regulatory Benefits and Costs: Lessons for the US and Europe*, Journal of International Economic Law, Oxford University Press, vol. 8(2), pages 473–508. Hahn, R.W., *Regulatory Reform: Assessing the Government's Numbers*, AEI-Brookings Center for Regulatory Studies, Working Paper No. 99–06, American Enterprise Institute and Brookings Institute, Washington, D.C., 1999. Hahn, R.W., *In Defense of the Economic Analysis of Regulation*, American Enterprise Institute, Washington, D.C., 2005. Hahn, R.W. and R. Litan, *An Analysis of the Third Government Report on the Benefits and Costs of Federal Regulation*, AEI-Brookings Joint Center for Regulatory Studies, American Enterprise Institute and Brookings Institute, Washington, D.C., 2000. Hahn, R.W., J. Burnett, Chan Yee-Ho, E. Mader and P. Moyle, "Assessing Regulatory Impact Analysis: the Failure of Agencies to Comply with Executive Order 12866", *Harvard Journal of Law and Policy*, 2000, Vol. 23, No. 3. Hahn, R.W. and Cass R. Sunstein, *Regulatory Oversight Takes Exciting New Tack*, AEI-Brookings Joint Center Policy Matters 01–25, American Enterprise Institute and Brookings Institute, Washington, D.C., 2001. Hahn, R. and C. Sunstein, "New Executive Order For Improving Federal Regulation? Deeper And Wider Cost-Benefit Analysis", University of Pennsylvania Law Review, 2002, Vol. 150, No. 1489. Hahn, R.W. and M.B. Muething, "The Grand Experiment in Regulatory Reporting", *Administrative Law Review*, 2003, Vol. 55, No. 3, pp. 607–642. Hahn, R. and P. Dudley, *How well Does the Government Do Cost-Benefit Analysis?*, AEI-Brookings Joint Center for Regulatory Studies, Working Paper 04–01, American Enterprise Institute and Brookings Institute, Washington, D.C., 2004. Finally, see Cecot, Caroline, Hahn, Robert W., Renda, Andrea and Schrefler, Lorna, *An Evaluation of the Quality of Impact Assessment in the European Union with Lessons for the U.S. and the EU* (December 2007). AEI-Brookings Joint Center Working Paper No. 07–09.

First, mainstream law and economics is a key reference of this book, also thanks to the extensive work done by scholars such as Parisi and Mackaay in categorizing the main schools that have made the history of law and economics. Within this domain, I will extensively draw on the contribution of the pioneers of law and economics, and especially Ronald Coase, Guido Calabresi and Richard Posner, but also all the scholars that contributed to the Symposium on Efficiency as a Legal Concern" already quoted in this introductory chapter. In addition, I have found inspiration in the work of more recent contributors, such as Ian Ayres and Lee Anne Fennell, especially as regards the development of optional law.

Another key theoretical framework used in the drafting of this book is the study of theories of justice, especially in the work of John Rawls, David Gauthier, John Braithwaite, John Harsanyi and Amartya Sen. The outstanding quality of their analysis in this domain has left me with a recurring doubt: that economists, when they are really good, tend to become and be called philosophers. The quest for viable definitions of justice, fairness and efficiency has crossed paths with law and economics in several occasions, in the work of Richard Posner but also at a later stage, not least when Louis Kaplow and Steven Shavell tried to reconstruct the view that efficiency also means fairness.

This book also reflects the new paradigms in law and economics that have been brought by the advancement of cognitive sciences, behavioral economics and neuroeconomics, especially through the pioneering work of Maurice Allais and Herbert Simon, and later of Daniel Kahneman, Amos Tversky, Colin Camerer, Christine Jolls, Russel Korobkin, Tom Ulen and Richard Thaler. Their insights are the real beacons of hope towards a better integration of law and economics with more practical policy appraisal.

Besides the contributions of behavioral economics and neuroeconomics, I have been greatly inspired by the literature on methodological individualism and preference-based policy. I refer in particular to the work of Amir Licht (2000), Robert Ahdieh (2002), and above all Herbert Hovenkamp (1994).

At the same time, the "RIA world" has chiefly been a subject matter of political scientists in Europe. I have learned a great deal from exchanges I have had in the past years with some of the best experts in this field. Scholars such as Claudio Radaelli have by far outperformed lawyer-economists in the developing an understanding of "how context matters" in impact assessment, what are the preconditions for its successful implementation, and the key mechanisms that trigger its diffusion in a given legal system including political commitment, actor certification, accountability, the existence of an epistemic community of champions of better regulation.[25] All this elaboration underlies the text of this book, especially in Chapters 2 and 3, where I describe the evolution of the RIA system.

[25] See, for an illustration, Radaelli, C.M. (2005), *How context matters: regulatory quality in the European Union*, Journal of European Public Policy, 12,5, 924-943.

A separate room in my pantheon is inhabited by those scholars that have advanced scientific knowledge in the field of public law and economics. I refer, in particular, to the study of cost-benefit analysis as a tool for procedural efficiency within a chain of delegation and oversight, like *i.a.* Matthew Adler and Eric A. Posner.[26] Their work is also highly indebted with the previous elaboration of scholars that have developed the notion of transaction cost politics, such as Niskanen (1971), and later McCubbins, Noll and Weingast (1986), Dixit (1996), Adler and Posner (2000), Posner (2001) and Epstein and O'Halloran (2003).

Along with the work of political scientists, also economists and practitioners in the field of impact assessment have represented a key reference for this book. I refer, *i.a.* to the work of Scott Jacobs, John Graham and Bob Hahn, Dick Morgenstern and Jonathan Wiener as providing the building blocks of any meaningful economic analysis of a RIA system. Likewise, economists and lawyers that have provided interesting critical views of the US and EU RIA systems in the past decade include Bruce Ackerman, Lisa Heinzerling and Richard Revesz.

Finally, besides the living example of Cass Sunstein, the only attempt to propose a further integration of law and economics with RIA I have found before drafting this book are in the work of Anthony Ogus. I am therefore indebted to his initial intuition, which I hope to have developed in some meaningful direction.

1.5. STRUCTURE OF THE BOOK

This book is structured as follows. The first part of the work sets the scene to help the non-specialized reader get familiar with RIA and its main role in contemporary policymaking. Section 2 explains the context in which RIA developed in the late 1970s in the United States, and explains how the system evolved over time, focusing in particular on the governance arrangements of RIA, the main mechanisms that underpin its functioning and main purpose, and the current debate on the most appropriate methodology to be used to assess both marketable and non-marketable goods. Section 3 contains the story of the adoption of the impact assessment model in the European Union and explains in detail the differences in the scope and methodology used in Brussels compared to Washington DC. This is reflected also in an extensive scorecard analysis of the content of European Commission's impact assessments produced between 2003 and the end of 2009, as well as in a description of the main governance

26 See Adler, M. and E.A. Posner (2006), *New Foundations of Cost-Benefit Analysis*, Harvard University Press. And Adler, M. and E.A. Posner (2007), *Happiness Research and Cost-Benefit Analysis*, U of Penn, Inst for Law & Econ Research Paper No. 07-15; U of Penn Law School, Public Law Research Paper No. 07-29; U of Chicago Law & Economics, Olin Working Paper No. 345. Available at SSRN: http://ssrn.com/abstract=999928.

arrangements currently in place to motivate officials in EU institutions to produce high quality *ex ante* impact assessments. The Section comments briefly also on the failure of RIA adoption in EU member states and in other non-EU countries.

The second part of this work is dedicated to law and economics, and its evolution since the early, seminal contributions of pioneers such as Ronald Coase, Guido Calabresi, Gary Becker, Richard Posner and Oliver Williamson. In particular, Section 4 explores the key insights that can be derived from the main schools of law and economics as described in the mainstream literature – *e.g.* in Mackaay (2000), Medema (2010) and Parisi (2004). The chosen taxonomy of existing schools implies the existence of a "positive" a "normative" and a "functional" school of law and economics, each with peculiar focus and approach to the economic analysis of legal rules. This section also concludes by highlighting the areas of RIA in which the law and economics approach seems to be most useful, and potentially calls for a revision of the current RIA practice. Section 5 then operationalizes these insights by discussing eight case studies.

Finally, Section 6 looks at future developments and provides answers to the main research questions addressed by this book, drawing conclusions also in terms of whether and how should we act to change our RIA systems in the US, and in particular in the European Union.

PART I

THE RIA WORLD

2. RIA IN THE UNITED STATES

Today, Regulatory Impact Analysis is understood as a "family of tools" belonging to the better regulation toolkit, and as a procedural requirement composed by a number of phases. Regardless of the *nuances* featured by a number of national RIA models, it can be safely stated that RIA requires at least the following steps:

- *Problem definition.* This phase normally entails the identification of the problem, *e.g.* a market failure or a regulatory failure, and the identification of the need to intervene.
- *Identification of alternative regulatory options.* Often, available guidelines at international and national level recommend that alternatives to "heavy-handed" regulation, such as light-touch regulation, regulation through information, principles-based regulation, and alternative forms of intervention such as self- and co-regulation are duly taken into account, in order to ensure that the remedy chosen is not disproportionate to the problem at hand.
- *Data collection.* This phase may entail desk research, consultation of stakeholders, and commissioning of external studies.
- *Assessment of alternative options.* This can be carried out through different techniques – the most common being cost-effectiveness analysis (CEA), cost-benefit analysis (CBA), least-cost assessment (LCA) and risk analysis. Options scrutinized typically have to include the so-called "zero option" or "baseline", which corresponds to the option of doing nothing.
- *Identification of the preferred policy option.* Once the available options have been carefully scrutinized, a RIA document normally leads to the identification of the most preferred option. This is not necessarily the options that should be undertaken, as the IA *per se* is only a support to, not a replacement of, the policymaker's role in selecting the most appropriate action.
- *In-depth assessment of the impact of the preferred policy option.* International guidance documents often recommend that the preferred option is subject to a more in-depth assessment, mostly aimed at quantifying the prospective impacts and associated risks, and identifying indicators for monitoring and evaluating the policy action over time.
- *Input to proposal drafting.* At the end of the RIA exercise, a report is released as an input to the policy document to be drafted. Again, the RIA report is not necessarily indicating the "right" way to go, but only the result of an assessment exercise mostly aimed at capturing impacts.

- *Provisions for monitoring and evaluation.* The RIA report should also specify the ways in which the impact of the selected policy action can be monitored over time, and a clear and efficient time horizon for revision of the action in the future. In addition, whenever indicators can be selected at the *ex ante* stage, this facilitates the *interim* and *ex post* evaluation of the selected action, which should follow the *ex ante* phase.

That said, RIA systems worldwide differ widely on a number of key dimensions such as the scope of the procedure, the purpose for which it was adopted, the methodology and the degree of quantification in the analysis of the impacts, the overall governance of the system and the effective volume of RIA documents that have been produced. More generally, RIA systems worldwide differ according to the "context" in which they have been introduced, being sometimes the result of a tendency towards rational policymaking (the United States), a drop in an ocean of symbolic politics (the United Kingdom, the European Commission), or a more pragmatic move towards simplification and deregulation (*e.g.*, Scandinavian countries).[27]

Below, I introduce the non-specialized reader to the RIA world by providing a historical account (Section 2.1) of how the procedure was introduced for the first time in the United States, and with what methodological features (Section 2.2). Then, Section 2.3 concludes and summarizes the main critiques to the US RIA model.

2.1. A HISTORICAL ACCOUNT

2.1.1. THE EARLY YEARS

As already mentioned in the introductory section of this book, the United States were the first country to adopt a RIA model. The earliest evidence of rules requiring the calculation of prospective costs and benefits of new regulations dates back to the Nixon administration, when US firms started complaining about the costs of regulation and uncontrolled 'regulatory creep', mostly as a result of newly passed environmental legislation.[28] The administration reacted with the so-called *Quality of Life Review*, which mandated a preliminary calculation of firms' costs resulting from compliance with new environmental rules as a fundamental pre-condition of good-quality regulation.[29] The Review,

---

27 Radaelli, C.M. and A.C.M. Meuwese (2009), *Better Regulation in Europe: between Public Management and Regulatory Reform*, Public Administration, Volume 87, Issue 3, pages 639–654, September 2009.

28 For a short illustration of the major waves of regulatory reform in the US, see Office of Management and Budget (available at www.whitehouse.gov/omb/inforeg/chap1.html).

29 See the OMB memorandum on "Agency regulations, standards, and guidelines pertaining to environmental quality, consumer protection, and occupational and public health and safety", 5 October 1971 (available at www.thecre.com/ombpapers/QualityofLife1.htm).

conceived as a privileged channel for public consultation, soon ended up enhancing the risk of regulatory capture, leaving legislative initiatives in the environmental field prey to aggressive and well-organised interest groups.[30]

Under the Ford administration, the US government showed an increased interest in promoting the use of cost-benefit analysis in assessing the prospective impact of proposed regulations. Executive Order 11,821, issued in 1974, mandated an Inflation Impact Assessment by federal agencies. Such procedure introduced an *ex ante* assessment of the expected impact of new regulatory measures on the inflation rate.[31] The creation of the Council on Wage and Price Stability aimed at ensuring that proposed regulations that were likely to exert a significant upward impact on nominal prices could be rejected in case they carried an incomplete or insufficient assessment of the inflationary impact.[32]

The Inflation Impact Assessment procedure can indeed be considered as a first version of what would later become the US Regulatory Impact Assessment (RIA) model. As a matter of fact, economists in the Council on Wage and Price Stability gradually transformed the mere estimation of the inflationary impact into a real cost-benefit analysis, to be used as a 'counter-argument' during public consultation processes mandated by the 1946 Administrative Procedure Act.[33] US President Gerald Ford amended the Inflation Impact Assessment model by issuing Executive Order (EO) 11,949, and stating that "[t]he title of Executive Order No. 11,821 of November 27, 1974 is amended to read 'Economic Impact Statements'".[34]

A few years later, during the Carter administration, the 10 most relevant new regulations in each year's US government agenda were made the subject of extended *ex ante* assessment by a specialised *ad hoc* group of economists called the 'Regulatory Analysis Review Group'.[35] But the introduction of a more comprehensive regulatory impact assessment procedure only occurred under the Reagan administration.

---

30 See Rodriguez, L. (1988), *Constitutional and Statutory Limits for Cost-Benefit Analysis Pursuant to Executive Orders 12291 and 12498*, 15 B.C. Envtl. Aff. L. Rev. 505. See also, for a short description, Robert W. Hahn and Robert E. Litan (2005), *Counting Regulatory Costs and Benefits: Lessons for the US and Europe, Journal of International Economic Law*, Vol. 8, No. 2, p. 474.

31 See e.g. M. Weidenbaum, *Regulatory Process Reform from Ford to Clinton*, The CATO Institute, 2000 (available at www.cato.org/pubs/regulation/regv20n1/reg20n1a.html).

32 See J. Morrall III, *Ebbs and Flows in the Quality of Regulatory Analysis*, speech at the Weidenbaum Center Forum on "Executive Regulatory Analysis: Surveying the Record, Making It Work", National Press Club, Washington, D.C., 17 December 2001.

33 See J. Morrall III, *An Assessment of the U.S. Regulatory Impact Assessment Program*, in Best Practices in the Main OECD Countries, OECD, Paris, 1997.

34 See Executive Order No. 11,949 (Economic Impact Statements) of 31 December 1976 (available at www.thecre.com/ombpapers/ExecutiveOrder11949.htm).

35 See Weidenbaum, *supra* note 31.

2.1.2. THE REAGAN AND BUSH (SR.) ADMINISTRATIONS

Under the Reagan administration, with EO 12,291 issued in 1981, federal agencies were obliged to adopt a full-fledged regulatory impact analysis (RIA).[36] The EO mandated a thorough reassessment of the existing regulation in force, for the purpose of identifying norms to be abolished or simplified. The evaluation and oversight of agencies' behavior, previously performed by the CWPS, was taken on by OIRA, Office of Information and Regulatory Affairs, created within the Office of Management and Budget (OMB) for the purpose of implementing the *1980 Paperwork Reduction Act*.[37] OIRA was given the power to suspend regulations by sending them back to the sponsoring agency until a satisfactory cost-benefit analysis was performed. The OMB, as a result, became a sort of regulatory clearinghouse.

Since then, thousands of proposed regulations have been scrutinized by the OMB. Possible contrasts between OMB and agencies were addressed with the help of a new Task Force on Regulatory Relief, chaired by then Vice-President George Bush, Sr.[38] The Task Force was also asked to estimate the savings that could follow from a full implementation of the new RIA procedure. The result was striking: according to the administration, the new procedure produced yearly cost savings as high as $10–20 billion. This calculation, however, was heavily criticized.[39] Similarly, the activity of the Task Force was subject to fierce opposition. The Reagan administration was accused of having drastically reduced the budget and personnel of federal agencies, achieving substantial decreases in the cost of regulation, but also a dramatic reduction in the number

---

36 The text of EO12,291 is available at www.thecre.com/pdf/EO12291.PDF.

37 In 1980 the US Congress responded to the disappointing results contained in the Final Report of the Commission on Federal Paperwork by enacting the *Paperwork Reduction Act* – which required agencies to request OMB approval before collecting information from the public and led to the creation of the Office of Information and Regulatory Affairs (OIRA) – and the *Regulatory Flexibility Act*, which mandated special analysis of rules affecting small businesses and small governments and created the Chief Counsel for Advocacy as a separate, presidentially appointed officer within the Small Business Administration. See the text of the 1980 Paperwork Reduction Act, available online at www.thecre.com/pdf/Carter_PaperworkRedAct1980.PDF; and the 1980 Regulatory Flexibility Act, at www.thecre.com/pdf/Carter_RegFlexAct1980.PDF.

38 The other members were the Secretary of the Treasury, Attorney General, Secretary of Commerce, Secretary of Labor, Director of OMB, Assistant to the President for Policy Development and the Chairman of the Counsel of Economic Advisers. See the White House's Fact Sheet on Reagan's Initiatives to Reduce Regulatory Burdens, 18 February 1981 (available at www.thecre.com/pdf/Reagan_RegainInitiatives.pdf). President Reagan identified regulatory relief as one of the four key elements for the recovery of the US economy. The results were however quite disappointing. See Reagan's Memorandum on the "Comprehensive Review of Federal Regulatory Programs", 15 December 1986; and the commentary by William A. Niskanen, *The Weak Fourth Leg of Reaganomics*, that appeared in The Wall Street Journal on 30 June 1988.

39 See Weidenbaum, *supra* note 31, and Breyer, S. (1990), *Regulation and Deregulation in the United States*, in G. Majone (ed.), "De-regulation or Re-regulation? Regulatory Reform in Europe and the United States", London: Pinter Publishers.

of policy proposals. As a consequence, in 1983, the Task Force was abolished and the OMB was given back its predominant role in the US RIA procedure.[40]

A second Executive Order, in 1985, required agencies to provide the OMB with detailed information on their regulatory agenda at the end of each year. This eventually paved the way for what has been termed the 'grand experiment', i.e. the OMB Report to Congress on the Costs and Benefits of Federal Regulations, a yearly publication that constitutes a unique example of a comprehensive, yearly calculation of total costs and benefits of the *corpus* of existing regulations.[41]

Under the Bush Sr. administration, the role formerly played by the Task Force on Regulatory Relief was assigned to the Council on Competitiveness, chaired by Vice-President Richard Quayle, which was given a mandate to abrogate all federal rules that could hinder the competitiveness of US firms.[42] The main goal was to minimize regulatory burdens faced by the economy. Such a revolutionary attempt was strongly criticized by the Democrats and a number of economists, but also by federal agencies, Congress Commissions and environmentalist associations, which lamented that the OMB (and in particular, the OIRA) exercised an excessive and unchallenged *veto* power on proposed regulations. Some commentators complained that OIRA and the White House had been captured by powerful interest groups, which inspired their intervention to stifle and repeal needed regulations, thus decreasing the transparency and accountability of federal rule-making. Institutional tension reached a peak when Congress refused to confirm a politically appointed agency director.[43]

According to an authoritative commentator, the excess centralization of the RIA procedure and the consequent critiques contributed to an institutional void and a lack of legal certainty that led to an increase in the burden of regulation, particularly in the fields of public health, environment and public safety.[44] At the end of the Bush mandate, the US RIA model appeared at once as a pioneering

---

40 See A. Morrison (1986), *OMB Interference with Agency Rulemaking: The Wrong Way to Write a Regulation*, 99 Harvard Law Review 1059, 1062 (describing Reagan's EO as implicitly designed to ensure that regulation was only a 'last resort' option).

41 See the description provided by Robert W. Hahn and Mary Beth Muething, *The Grand Experiment in Regulatory Reporting*, Administrative Law Review, Vol. 55, No. 3, Summer 2003, pp. 607–642.

42 See Weidenbaum, *supra* note 31.

43 See *e.g.*, the 1992 Report by the OMB Watch and Public Citizen, *Voodoo Accounting: the Toll of President Bush's Regulatory Moratorium*, stating that claims of huge public savings resulting from the announced regulatory moratorium were hardly substantiated. See also B.D. Friedman, *Regulation in the Reagan-Bush Era: The Eruption of Presidential Influence*. Pittsburgh: Pittsburgh University Press, 1995; and B. Woodward and D.S. Broder, "Quayle's Quest: Curb Rules, Leave 'No Fingerprints'", *Washington Post*, 9 January 1992.

44 See R.W. Hahn (1999), *Regulatory Reform: Assessing the Government's Numbers*, AEI-Brookings Center for Regulatory Studies, Working Paper No. 99–06, July 1999. See also W.F. West (2005), "The Institutionalization of Regulatory Review. Organizational Stability and Responsive Competence at OIRA", *Presidential Studies Quarterly*, No. 1, Center for the Study of the Presidency, 2005.

experience worldwide and a problem 'in search of a solution', in strong need of careful redressing, mostly aimed at reducing regulatory burdens for US firms.

2.1.3. RIA UNDER THE CLINTON ADMINISTRATION

A tentative reaction to this *impasse* was the enactment of Executive Order 12,866 in 1993, under the Clinton administration.[45] Within the more general context of 'Reinventing Government' and the National Performance Review, EO 12,886 attempted to 'cut red tape' by providing OMB with the power to syndicate over proposed regulations within a strict 90-day deadline from presentation of the RIA form by the federal agency. If, after the deadline expired, conflict between OIRA and the sponsoring agency had not been solved, the US President or the Vice-President entered the stage to solve the controversy.[46] The unconditioned *veto* power previously awarded to the OMB was then transformed into a conditional opposition with limited potential to infinitely delay entry into force of newly proposed regulations. Furthermore, the Vice-President's power to directly influence administrative policy was replaced with a milder role of 'default' mediator in case the agency and OIRA failed to negotiate a mutually satisfactory solution. This *escamotage* significantly increased the transparency of regulatory reforms in the US.[47]

One of the major problems to be solved was undoubtedly OMB's overwhelming workload in the regulatory review process. Before the Clinton mandate, the OMB, with just 40 employees, had reviewed on average more than 2,200 federal regulations every year.[48] In order to avoid the inevitable inefficiency that followed from such a drastic centralization, EO 12,866 introduced a minimum threshold, specifying that only regulations whose expected impact was greater than $100 million were subject to mandatory *ex ante* impact

45 The text of EO 12,866 is available at http://govinfo.library.unt.edu/npr/library/direct/orders/2646.html.

46 See *ibid.*, at Section 7: "[t]o the extent permitted by law, disagreements or conflicts between or among agency heads or between OMB and any agency that cannot be resolved by the Administrator of OIRA shall be resolved by the President, or by the Vice President acting at the request of the President, with the relevant agency head (and, as appropriate, other interested government officials)."

47 *Executive Order 12866: Regulatory Planning and Review*, Federal Register 58, Washington, D.C.: The White House, 30 September 1993. EO 12866 also required that all written communications to OIRA or the White House from non-governmental parties should be placed on the public record. Moreover, the EO ordered that only the OIRA administrator or the deputy administrator could receive oral communications from parties outside the Government, and mandated docketing of all conversations between OIRA and agencies as well as between White House officials and private interests.

48 See, *inter alia*, the descriptions provided in the OMB's Reports to Congress on the Costs and Benefits of Federal Regulations, (available online at www.whitehouse.gov/omb/inforeg_regpol_reports_congress/).

assessment.[49] In October 1994, OIRA produced a report entitled "The First Year of Executive Order No. 12866", finding that the number of significant rules reviewed by OIRA had fallen to 900 per year, 60% lower than the 2,200 per year average reviewed under the previous Executive Order, and that about 15% of the rules were found to be "economically significant". The report also found that the 90-day review period had been generally respected, and concluded that the new openness and transparency policy had served to defuse, if not eliminate, the criticism of OIRA's regulatory impact analysis and review program.

2.1.4. RIA UNDER GEORGE W. BUSH

During the eight years of George W. Bush, a number of relevant changes have been introduced to the institutional setting of RIA. In particular, these concern the role and powers attributed to the OIRA and the Vice President. As occurred in the EU, the regulatory pendulum in the US evidently shifted in the direction of cutting red tape. First, EO 13,258, issued on 26 February 2002, removed the Vice President from the regulatory review process.[50] Such removal responded to critiques that hinged on the excessive powers granted to the executive in shaping bureaucrats' decisions, as well as to growing concerns that the involvement of the Vice President could significantly raise procedural costs. At the same time, the Bush administration tried to grant enhanced powers to OIRA. Its structure was consolidated to only four branches – Health, Transportation and General Government; Information Policy and Technology; Natural Resources, Energy and Agriculture; and Statistical and Science Policy. OIRA had six branches in 1992, and five under the Clinton administration. Such consolidation was aimed at revitalizing OIRA, as testified by its increased staffing level. OIRA had 90 staff members in 1981, but the size had decreased to 69 under Reagan, 60 under Bush Sr. and 47 during the Clinton administration. The George W. Bush administration started hiring seven new members and is gradually increasing the staff number, hiring also scientists and engineers, and thus bringing skills that OIRA had never had before.[51] OIRA administrator John Graham started issuing 'prompt letters', which suggest that agencies give priority to specific issues – a novelty that was welcomed with enthusiasm by authoritative scholars such as Bob Hahn and Cass Sunstein (who would later become Graham's successor).[52]

49 For a more detailed definition of significant regulatory actions, see Section 2.2.1 below.

50 67 Fed. Reg 9,385 (2002).

51 See West, cit., *supra* note 44.

52 The list of issued Prompt Letters under the George W. Bush Administration is available at www.whitehouse.gov/omb/inforeg/prompt_letter.html. For positive comments on the introduction of prompt letters, see R.W. Hahn and Cass R. Sunstein (2001), *Regulatory Oversight Takes Exciting New Tack*, AEI/Brookings Joint Center Policy Matters 01-25, September 2001.

More generally, the removal of the office of the Vice President from its oversight role seems to have led to a more aggressive confrontation between OIRA and federal agencies. Along with some other commentators, the US General Accounting Office remarked that the role played by OIRA vis-à-vis federal agencies has shifted from a 'collaborative, consultative' role under Clinton to that an 'adversarial gatekeeper' model in the Bush administration.[53] Data on the number of rules returned or withdrawn by OIRA confirm this shift. West (2005) reports that an annual average of 106 rules were either returned or withdrawn during the last two years of the Bush Sr. administration, whereas the corresponding figure was only 20.5 under Clinton and jumped again to 172 during George W. Bush's first year in office.[54]

OIRA's strengthened role also led to increased attention for standards to be applied in performing cost-benefit analyses and to a marked reduction in the estimated dollar cost of new rules. The average annual cost of new rules decreased from $8.5 billion under the first Bush administration to $5.7 billion under Clinton and down to $1.5 billion in the first three years after George W. Bush took office. And, although the total regulatory burden appears to have increased over time, its growth rate appears to have significantly declined over the past few years.[55] This was also the result of the proliferation of government initiatives on administrative simplification, aimed at streamlining the regulatory environment, facilitating dialogue with small businesses and, more generally, cutting red tape.

In 2007, EO 13,422 signed by President Bush extended the provisions of EO 12,866 to guidance documents, together with regulation. In addition, and most notably, the new Executive Order included independent regulatory agencies – previously subject only to part of the provisions of the EO 12,866, and certainly not to centralised review by the OIRA – in its cost-benefit regulatory reports to Congress.[56]

---

53 See the Report by the General Accounting Office on *OMB's Role in the Reviews of Agencies' Draft Rules and the Transparency of these Reviews*, September 2003. See also West (*op. cit.*), finding that the review has become "less invasive and less confrontational". This new pattern of relationships is sometimes referred to as a 'hot-tub approach' after a definition given by Sally Katzen, Clinton's first OIRA administrator.

54 See West, *supra* note 44, p. 19.

55 See e.g. the testimony of James L. Gattuso to the Subcommittee on Energy Policy, Natural Resources and Regulatory Affairs Committee on Government Reform, US House of Representatives, on "What is the Bush Administration's Record on Regulatory Reform?", 17 November 2004 (available at www.heritage.org/Research/Regulation/tst111604a.cfm).

56 As stated in Black and Jacobzone (2009), independent regulatory agencies were subject to part of the Executive Orders. In particular, they had to follow the "regulatory philosophy" and the "twelve principles" of regulation, to conform to the "unified regulatory agenda" and to submit their "regulatory plans". See Black, J. and S. Jacobzone (2009), *Tools for Regulatory Quality and Financial Sector Regulation: A Cross-Country Perspective*, OECD Working Papers on Public Governance, No. 16, OECD Publishing.

2.1.5. RIA UNDER BARACK OBAMA: BACK TO THE FUTURE?

On January 30, 2009, President Barack Obama signed Executive Order 13,497 which revoked Executive Order 13,422, and marked almost a U-turn in the way RIA is overseen by the OIRA in the United States – as a matter of fact, the new Executive Order "restored the regulatory review process to what it had been under Executive Order 12866 between 1993 and 2007".[57] However, a more careful look reveals that the Obama administration has gone beyond a mere "erase and rewind" approach: to the contrary, it marked a potentially thorough change in the approach to RIA, thanks mostly to the appointment of Cass R. Sunstein as the new chairman of the OIRA.[58] As announced by Sunstein himself, the new regulatory philosophy at OIRA is likely to devote more attention to behavioral law and economics and the analysis of individual incentives and consumer behavior, something that is often difficult to reconcile with mere monetization of costs and benefits. Recently, Sunstein referred to this approach as one of "humanizing" RIA, which entails moving in three main directions: accounting for actual human behavior, including bounded rationality and willpower; more accuracy of data beyond mere monetary measures; and democratizing data by strengthening data collection, transparency of government and public participation within a new "open government" initiative.

A first (and already controversial) example of the new approach to RIA at the White House is the first review letter sent by the OIRA under the Obama administration, on 19 March 2010, to the National Highway Traffic Safety Administration (NHTSA) related to the new "Tire Fuel Efficiency Consumer Information Program".[59] The request to analyze more thoroughly consumer behavior and the likely reaction to different forms of labeling has already elicited concerns and critiques, showing that the transition towards the new approach will likely be slow and difficult.

---

57 See OIRA Memorandum M-09-13, at www.whitehouse.gov/sites/default/files/omb/assets/memoranda_fy2009/m09-13.pdf.

58 In a memorandum dated January 30, 2009, President Obama directed the head of OMB, in consultation with representatives of regulatory agencies, to produce within 100 days a set of recommendations for a new executive order on federal regulatory review. The memorandum stated that, among other things, the recommendations should offer suggestions for the relationship between OIRA and the agencies; provide guidance on disclosure and transparency; encourage public participation in agency regulatory processes; offer suggestions on the role of cost-benefit analysis; address the role of distributional considerations, fairness, and concern for the interest of future generations; identify methods of ensuring that regulatory review does not produce undue delay; clarify the role of behavioral science in formulating regulatory policy; and identify the best tools for achieving public goals through the regulatory process.

59 The review letter is available online at www.reginfo.gov/public/postreview/Tire_Fuel_Efficiency_Consumer_Information_Final_Rule.pdf.

2.2. THE US RIA MODEL: MAIN FEATURES

After the historical perspective given in the previous section, it bears looking at the way in which the US RIA model has shaped the creation of a real system of "administrative law and economics". I do this by looking at selected features that will be relevant for the remainder of this book, and in particular at the scope and purpose, the methodology used and the governance arrangements of the US RIA system.

2.2.1. THE SCOPE AND PURPOSE OF RIA IN THE UNITED STATES

A very important feature of the US RIA system is its limited scope. RIA is applied only to secondary legislation, namely agency-made rules. Moreover, RIA is not compulsory for all regulations: since the enactment of EO 12,866 under the Clinton administration, RIAs are mandatory for government agencies only when they refer to 'significant regulatory actions' – *i.e.*, those that: i) have an annual effect on the economy of $100 million or more or adversely affect in a material way the economy, a sector of the economy, productivity, competition, jobs, the environment, public health or safety, or State, local, or tribal governments or communities; ii) create a serious inconsistency or otherwise interfere with an action taken or planned by another agency; iii) materially alter the budgetary impact of entitlements, grants, user fees, or loan programs or the rights and obligations of recipients thereof; or iv) raise novel legal or policy issues arising out of legal mandates, the President's priorities or the principles set forth in EO 12,866.

From the outset, independent agencies and Congress have been left out of the RIA system. This is intimately linked with the overall purpose of the system in the United States: as recalled, *i.a.*, by Matthew Adler and Eric Posner, the system is designed to entail control of specialized bureaucrats by a less informed watchdog[60]: and the requirement to use cost-benefit analysis, as will be explained below in Section 2.2.2.1, is the way in which OIRA (the principal) can control government agencies. Independent agencies were left out of this centralized scrutiny since they were not subject to the provisions on centralized review of regulations by OIRA, which applied only to executive agencies. This choice was heavily criticized by academics, especially those that were advocating the transformation of the United States into a "cost-benefit state" – including Professor Cass Sunstein himself.[61] As

60 See Adler, M.D. and Eric A. Posner (2006), *New Foundations of Cost-Benefit Analysis*, Harvard University Press, 2006; University of Pennsylvania Law School, Public Law Working Paper No. 06–40; University of Pennsylvania, Institute for Law & Economics Research Paper No. 06–23.

61 Pildes, R.H. and Sunstein, C.R. (1995) *Reinventing the Regulatory State*, The University of Chicago Law Review 62: 1–129; and Hahn and Litan (2005), *supra* note 24).

reported by Kagan (2001), President Reagan introduced RIA only for 'his' executive agencies because of the fear of opposition from Congress – opposition raised by the threat of extending Presidential power beyond federal executive agencies. All other Presidents have confirmed the initial choice made by Reagan. *De facto*, the limited scope of RIA (there is no RIA obligation for independent agencies) has created problems in a number of sectors (*e.g.* most financial regulations 'escaped' RIA since they were enacted either by the SEC or by Congress).

Although Congress is not obliged to perform RIA, in the past years the practice of drafting and publishing cost estimates for specific proposals or amendments has become more established. Today, the Congressional Budget Office (CBO) is required to develop a cost estimate for virtually every bill reported by Congressional committees to show how it would affect spending or revenues over the next five years or more. CBO's cost estimates have become an integral part of the legislative process, and committees increasingly refer to them at every stage of drafting bills. Although mostly focused on costs for government, increasingly these documents report also the impact on the private sector.[62]

2.2.2. GOVERNANCE AND PROCEDURAL ASPECTS OF RIA IN THE UNITED STATES

The institutions that are most heavily involved in the RIA procedure are the proposing agencies and the OIRA. RIA is prepared by the analytical office of the federal agency promulgating a rule, and is then submitted to the OIRA for review. During the first phases of RIA drafting, the OIRA acts as a helpdesk to provide feedback and advice before formal review of the RIA is undertaken.[63] The RIA is then published together with the draft rule in the *Federal Register* for a notice and comment period of 60 days. As the OIRA has a veto power over the publication of RIAs where analysis is insufficient, of poor quality, or does not demonstrate that the benefits of the draft rule are likely to justify ensuing regulatory costs, the responsible agency is often called to review the RIA before publication. OIRA's negative comments are included in what are known as 'return' letters. Following the notice and comment period, the RIA is revised and finalized and the OIRA has 90 days to approve or reject the proposed rule on the basis of the quality of the cost-benefit analysis performed by the agency.[64] If the proposal is accepted the process continues; if not, negotiations between the agency and OIRA start and the latter can refuse the rule until a satisfactory analysis is presented (figure 2 and figure 3 below).

62 The CBO's cost estimates are available online at www.cbo.gov/CEBrowse.cfm.

63 See Jacobs, S. (2006), *Current Trends in Regulatory Impact Analysis: The Challenges of Mainstreaming RIA into Policy-making*, Jacobs & Associates, Washington.

64 See Renda, A. (2006) *Impact assessment in the EU. The State of the Art and the Art of the States*, Centre for European Policy Studies, Brussels, 2006.

Figure 2. Phases of the rulemaking process

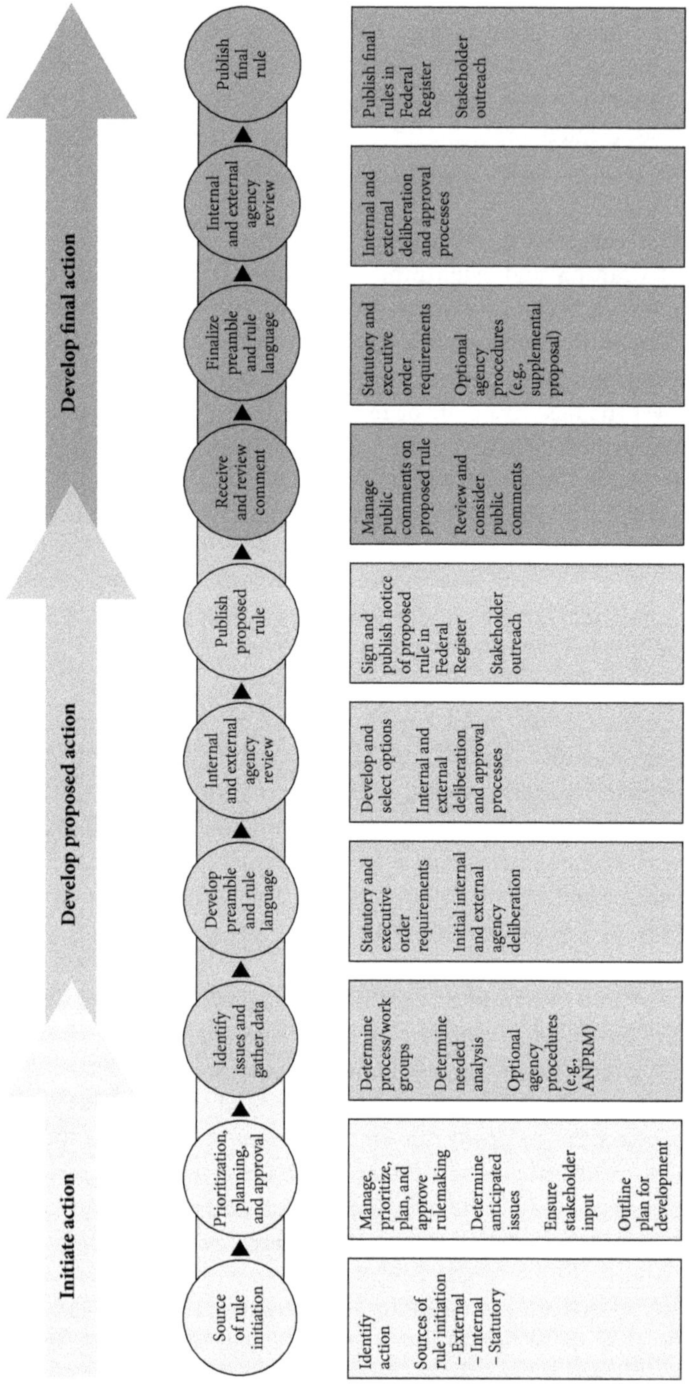

Source: EPA.

As shown in Figure 3 below, in the initial stage the proposing agency drafts a preliminary RIA form, comparing different regulatory options – which must include the so-called 'zero option' (leaving the existing regulation unchanged) – and providing a rough estimation of benefits and costs associated with each alternative option and an indication on the relevance of the expected impact of the proposed regulation, which is the *conditio sine qua non* for the activation of the RIA procedure.[65] The RIA form is then subject to a 60-day notice and comment period, in which interested parties can file their comments and suggestions regarding the regulatory option chosen by the agency.[66] After the notice and comment period, the final RIA form is completed as an obligatory step before a final proposal can be drafted and submitted for approval. At this stage, the OIRA has 90 days to approve or reject the proposed regulation on the basis of the quality of cost-benefit analysis performed by the agency. If the proposal is approved, the proceedings go forward. If not, a negotiation between OIRA and the proponent agency begins.

Figure 3. The US RIA model

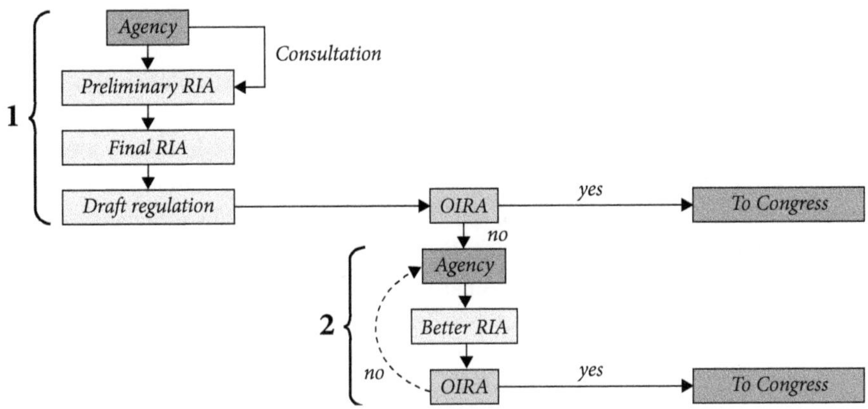

Source: Renda (2006:21).

In fact, OIRA reviews the most significant rules three times: i) at the planning stage during the preparation of the Regulatory Plan that agencies submit to Congress on an annual basis (see below); ii) before the publication in the *Federal Register* for notice and comment; and iii) before the publication of the final rule. Before publication on the Federal register, OIRA can call upon its power to reject

65 See EO 12,866, *supra* note 45.

66 The 1946 *Administrative Procedure Act* already recognized the citizen's right to participate in the consultation process. The 60-day notice and comment period was in any event considered only partially satisfactory, as it often results in a mere procedural step, more than a real opportunity to collect valuable views from the general public and targeted groups. See OECD, *The OECD Review of Regulatory Reform in the United States*, OECD, Paris, 1999.

proposals at will, until the proposal is accompanied by a sufficiently detailed and precise RIA. The number of rules returned or withdrawn by OIRA has dramatically increased under the George W. Bush administration, as a result of the new 'gatekeeper' role assumed by OIRA after the removal of the Vice President's oversight role (now restored by President Barack Obama).

2.2.2.1. OIRA as a watchdog

The US RIA system follows a logic of control of delegated regulatory powers, whereby political principals (the US Congress and the President) need adequate instruments to monitor the regulatory choices of agents (federal departments and agencies) tasked with promulgating federal rules. Although US agencies have multiple principals, the centralized structure of oversight through the Office of Information and Regulatory Affairs (OIRA) – located in the Office of Management and Budget (OMB) – suggests that the balance of power is tilted in favor of the President (Kagan 2001). The OIRA benefits from a strong political support given that the centralized enforcement of regulatory principles and procedures is considered a core ingredient of the US approach to regulatory policy (OECD 2006).

Oversight is attributed to the OIRA that reports to the White House. Under the current system, the OIRA can challenge individual rules by preventing agencies from publishing draft rules if the accompanying RIA does not show that the benefits are likely to justify costs. This amounts, *de facto*, to a veto power on draft regulations, and is viewed as one of the strongest RIA oversight systems currently in place worldwide. In particular, between the Clinton and the Bush Jr administrations the role of the OIRA has been transformed from a "consultant" to the agencies, into a more aggressive "adversarial gatekeeper" (Renda 2006). Accordingly, the OIRA has made more frequent use of its powers, and 20 rules were returned to agencies in the first year of the George W. Bush Administration, more than the total number of rules returned in the previous eight years (see above, section 2.1.4).

Besides issuing RIA guidelines, the OIRA also undertakes studies of the costs and benefits of federal regulations and can suggest review priorities to other departments. Since 1994, OIRA has reviewed between 500 and 700 significant proposed and final rules each year, and can clear the rules with or without changes, return the rules to the agencies for reconsideration, or encourage the agencies to withdraw them. As reported by the OECD (2006) the OIRA currently reviews about 30 to 40 "major" federal initiatives every year and has played for several years a leading role in regulatory innovation, due to the long term RIA experience of the USA. For example, ideas such as the adoption of regulatory budgets to aggregate the impact of regulation across different sectors, the use of quality of life measures, and the introduction of peer review originated in the OIRA. Conversely, the OIRA has been less successful in *ex post* monitoring of regulation, partially because of the reluctance of departments to reopen complex regulatory debates or review rules resulting from a political compromise (OECD 2006).

It should be noted that the OIRA can also issue 'prompt letters' requiring federal departments and agencies to look at a specific policy field and explore whether additional regulation is necessary. This procedure may act as means to overcome the bureaucratic inertia of some agencies (Kagan 2001, Radaelli and De Francesco 2007), and contrasts with the traditional image of the OIRA as an instrument for deregulation (Graham 2007). Past evidence (McGarity 1991, Morgenstern 1997) suggests that OIRA's oversight role was not always transparent: for example, comments on draft RIAs are not publicly available and in some cases this played in favor of the deregulatory/pro-regulatory stance of the Government of the day. This issue was addressed by Executive Order 12,866 promulgated under Clinton that increases the transparency of the oversight process during RIA preparation. The executive order requires OIRA or the rulemaking agencies to disclose certain elements of the review process to the public, including the changes made at OIRA's recommendation.

Besides scrutinizing quality, the OIRA also reviews RIAs to identify rules that are not consistent with the President's policies, principles and priorities; to ensure coordination among agencies; discuss inconsistencies with regulators and suggest alternatives that would be consistent. Recently, the OIRA has increased its scrutiny powers by setting a higher level of data quality standards and by introducing scientific peer review of analyses. Although the OIRA lacks formal powers to oblige an agency not to proceed when a RIA is inadequate (Jacobs 2006), its recommendations and return letters are always taken into account by the agencies.[67]

Additional scrutiny is provided by the presence of a special type of administrative law – the 1946 Administrative Procedure Act (APA) – and by judicial review. Below, we briefly explain the scope of these mechanisms.

2.2.2.2. Quis custodiet ipsos custodes?

Oversight activities introduced during the Clinton Administration were not limited to Presidential oversight. In 1996, the *Congressional Review Act* prescribed that all sponsoring agencies were bound to send their proposals to the Congress for an evaluation, The US Congressional Budget Office can repeal any draft regulation within 60 days from receipt of the proposal.[68] Such an oversight mechanism also extends to Congressional bills, thus completing the framework

---

[67] For a more critical view of OIRA's role as an oversight body, see Bagley, N. and R.L. Revesz (2006), *Centralized Oversight of the Regulatory State*, Columbia L. Rev. Vol. 106, 1260–1329.

[68] The Congressional Review Act is part of the Small Business Regulatory Enforcement Fairness Act of 1996 (available at http://usgovinfo.about.com/library/bills/blcra.htm).

of controls over the cost-effectiveness of federal legislation. Nonetheless, a number of commentators have recently advocated the extension of the RIA model to independent agencies.[69] Given the highly 'political' nature of the US RIA model, however, such an extension would significantly undermine the independence of such agencies from the executive.

As one of the political principals delegating regulatory powers to federal agencies, Congress has a clear interest in scrutinizing regulatory activities, and RIAs are a means to that end. Specifically, the Congressional Budget Office oversees both the quality of regulation and the activities of the OMB. Congress has also responded to Presidential review of regulation by directing the OMB not to interfere with special-interest legislation (Moe and Wilson, 1994: 39) and by securing Senate confirmation of OIRA heads, as well as more public information and precise deadlines on the review process.

Regulatory agencies must send their proposals to Congress for evaluation, and any draft regulation can be repealed within 60 days. This scrutiny also extends to congressional bills. Congress can also commission reports or invite experts to testify on the general RIA system, on presidential Executive Orders, and on specific RIAs.

A degree of oversight on the RIA process is exerted by the CBO through expert reports that look at the activity of specific agencies, for example the EPA.[70] More occasionally, the CBO also reviews the functioning of the RIA system in government agencies. For example, in 1997 a comprehensive analysis of the consequences of RIA for the legislative process was carried out.[71]

Finally, *ex post* scrutiny is performed by the Government Accountability Office (GAO). The GAO has repeatedly observed that presidential oversight of federal regulation, primarily through OIRA, has become well-established under successive administrations over the past 30 years. However, the GAO pointed out that (i) some administrations have been more collaborative and consultative with agencies, while others have assumed more of a "gatekeeper" role when reviewing agencies' draft regulations; (ii) despite executive order requirements under successive administrations to improve the timeliness and documentation of OIRA's regulatory review role, GAO identified significant gaps in the transparency of OIRA's involvement in rule making.

In addition, GAO raised concerns about the extent to which the cumulative procedural and analytical requirements placed on rule-making over the years effectively added value, or instead contributed to the "ossification" of the rule-making process.[72] In addition, according to the GAO several aspects of the OIRA

69 See e.g. Gattuso, *supra* note 55.

70 See *Cost-Benefit Analysis of EPA Regulations: An Overview*, CRS Report for Congress RL30326, 1999.

71 Available at www.cbo.gov/doc.cfm?index=4015&type=0.

72 GAO-07-791, GAO-05-939T. On the concept of "ossification" of rulemaking, see McGarity, T.O. (1997), *The Courts and the Ossification of Rulemaking: A Response to Professor Seidenfeld*,

regulatory review process could be more transparent to better allow the public to understand the effects of OIRA's reviews. In particular, the transparency requirements in Executive Order 12,866 applicable to agencies and OIRA could be redefined to include not only the formal review period, but also the informal review period when OIRA says it can have its most important effect on agencies' rules.

The GAO periodically reviews selected rules as regards the appraisal procedure that take place inside the agencies. A recent GAO report issued in April 2009 reviews 139 major rules including 16 case-study rules, and finds that: (i) OIRA's reviews of agencies' draft rules often resulted in changes (of 12 case-study rules subject to OIRA review, 10 resulted in changes, about half of which included changes to the regulatory text); (ii) Agencies used various methods to document OIRA's reviews, which generally met disclosure requirements, but the transparency of this documentation could be improved; (iii) out of eight prior GAO recommendations to improve transparency OIRA has implemented only one – to clarify information posted about meetings with outside parties regarding draft rules under OIRA review.[73]

2.2.2.3. *Judicial oversight*

The Courts have played a special role by clarifying principles of risk regulation and by developing jurisprudence on risk regulation (Majone, 2002, Vogel, 2003). Although RIA and risk regulation are not the same, it is important to stress that the progress made in relation to issues such as uncertainty, the level of protection, risk-risk analysis, and proportionality in risk reduction have been made because of judicial review and the very active role played by courts. The courts have in fact used the review of agencies' rule to make the principles and practices of risk assessment more explicit and more rigorous.

In the past decades, federal courts have clearly moved from an initial reluctance to accept cost-benefit analysis by federal agencies to an increased recognition of the need for sound *ex ante* assessment of costs and benefits aimed at motivating the need to regulate and the choice of the regulatory option. Eric Posner (2001) quotes cases such as *American Trucking Associations, Inc, v EPA*[74] – in which the D.C. Circuit called on the Environmental Protection Agency (EPA) to provide a quantitative justification of the regulation if it wanted to

75 TEX. L. REV. 525, 528–36; Seidenfeld, M. (1997), *Demystifying Deossification: Rethinking Recent Proposals to Modify Judicial Review of Notice and Comment Rulemaking*, 75 TEX. L. REV. 483, 483–90; Pierce, Jr., R.J. (1995), *Seven Ways to Deossify Agency Rulemaking*, 47 ADMIN. L. REV. 59, 60–62; McGarity, T.O. (1992), *Some Thoughts on "Deossifying" the Rulemaking Process*, 41 DUKE L.J. 1385, 1385–86.

73 See GAO-09-205, at www.gao.gov/highlights/d09205high.pdf.

74 175 F3d 1027 (DC Cir 1999), reviewed in part by *Whitman v American Trucking Associations, Inc*, 2001 US LEXIS 1952.

regulate particulate matter pollution – and *Corrosion Proof Fittings v EPA*[75] – in which the Fifth Circuit heavily criticized the EPA's cost-benefit analysis on the merit.[76]

The relevance and desirability of the judicial review of agency rulemaking has been subject to a lively debate in the United States, not limited to benefit-cost analysis but, even more hectically, in the domain of risk assessment and the use of scientific evidence in support of regulatory decisions. According to some authors, the prospect of transparency (through notice and comment) and subsequent judicial oversight transforms the RIA document into a double-edged sword for regulatory agencies, as the document itself ay serve as a basis for litigation at a later stage.[77] Likewise, other authors have expressed doubts on the courts' ability to scrutinize technical documents such as RIAs, and pointed at an overly strict interpretation of cost-benefit requirements as having caused suboptimal regulatory decisions and too strict standards in regulation in a number of occasions.[78]

2.2.2.4. Transparency and publication requirements

Since 1984, the USA has a regulatory planning process whereby very preliminary RIA summaries are published every six months in the *Unified Agenda of Federal Regulations*, in order to increase transparency on the regulatory activities of federal agencies. Moreover, the review of draft and final RIAs by the OIRA is public as both 'prompt' and 'return' letters are available on its website. This transparent approach in reviewing RIA is unique and is closely linked to the very structure of the US system; the *equilibria* in a parliamentary system would render such transparency much more difficult to achieve.

As explained above, transparency is a core element of the US RIA system and is enacted through a 'notice and comment' procedure. Before a new regulation is adopted in the USA, it must be: (i) published in the Federal Register in proposed form, with an opportunity for public comment and, in some cases, a formal public hearing; and (ii) published again in the Federal Register in final form, with written explanation of any important revisions that have been made and the official response to public comments. As already recalled, the US Congress mandated the process of public comment already in the 1946 Administrative

75 947 F2d 1201 (5th Cir 1991).

76 See Posner (2001), stating *i.a.* that the EPA had discounted costs but not benefits, had used inconsistent valuations for statistical lives, refused to quantify certain benefits, refused to repeat the analysis with better data supplied by industry, etc.

77 Wagner, *The CAIR RIA: Advocacy Dressed Up as Policy Analysis*, in Harrington, W., L. Heinzerling and R. Morgenstern (2009), *Reforming Regulatory Impact Analysis*, Resources for the Future Report, Washington D.C.

78 See *i.a.* Pierce, Jr., R.J. (1991). *The Unintended Effects of Judicial Review of Agency Rules: How Federal Courts Have Contributed to the Electricity Crisis of the 1990s*. Administrative Law Review 43:7.

Procedure Act. This process entails creation of a public docket of information that Federal judges can review if a regulation is challenged through litigation.[79] Relevant studies and data used by the regulator are generally included in the public docket and cited in the Federal Register.

Executive Order 12,866 requires both agencies and OIRA to disclose to the public certain information about OIRA's regulatory reviews. After the regulatory action has been published in the Federal Register or otherwise issued to the public, an agency is required to: (1) make available to the public the information provided to OIRA in accordance with the executive order; (2) identify for the public, in a complete, clear, and simple manner, the substantive changes between the draft submitted to OIRA and the action subsequently announced; and (3) identify for the public those changes in the regulatory action that were made at the suggestion or recommendation of OIRA.

The order also requires OIRA to maintain a publicly available log that includes the following information pertinent to rules under OIRA's review: (1) the status of rules submitted for OIRA review; (2) a notation of all written communications received by OIRA from persons not employed by the executive branch, and (3) information about oral communications between OIRA and persons not employed by the executive branch. After the rule has been published or otherwise issued to the public (or the agency has announced its decision to not publish or issue the rule), OIRA is required to make available to the public all documents exchanged between OIRA and the agency during the review by OIRA. However, as reported by the GAO (2009), "an OIRA official … pointed out that OIRA does not monitor, on a rule-by-rule basis, compliance by rulemaking agencies with their disclosure obligations under Executive Order 12,866".

In 2003, a GAO report found that the transparency of OIRA reviews could be significantly improved. The GAO issued eight recommendations to OIRA, and in 2009 found that OIRA had followed only one (improve the clarity of OIRA's meeting log to better identify participants in OMB meetings with external parties on rules under review by disclosing the affiliations of participants). However, OIRA did not agree with the seven remaining recommendations in the 2003 report and did not implement those recommendations. Accordingly, the 2009 GAO Report reiterated the seven recommendations, which read as follows:

1. Define the transparency requirements applicable to the agencies and OIRA in Executive Order 12,866 in such a way that they include not only the formal review period, but also the informal review period when OIRA says it can have its most important impact on agencies' rules.

[79] See Graham, J.D. (2007). *The Evolving Regulatory Role of the U.S. Office of Management and Budget*, Review of Environmental Economics & Policy, 1:171–191.

2. Change OIRA's database to clearly differentiate within the "consistent with change" outcome category which rules were substantively changed at OIRA's suggestion or recommendation and which were changed in other ways and for other reasons.
3. Re-examine OIRA's current policy that only documents exchanged by OIRA branch chiefs and above need to be disclosed because most of the documents that are exchanged while rules are under review at OIRA are exchanged between agency staff and OIRA desk officers.
4. Establish procedures whereby either OIRA or the agencies disclose the reason why rules are withdrawn from OIRA review.
5. Define the types of "substantive" changes during the OIRA review process that agencies should disclose as including not only changes made to the regulatory text but also other, non-editorial changes that could ultimately affect the rules' application (for example, explanations supporting the choice of one alternative over another and solicitations of comments on the estimated benefits and costs of regulatory options).
6. Instruct agencies to put information about changes made in a rule after submission for OIRA's review and those made at OIRA's suggestion or recommendation in the agencies' public rulemaking dockets, and to do so within a reasonable period after the rules have been published.
7. Encourage agencies to use "best practice" methods of documentation that clearly describe those changes.

2.3. RIA UNDER ATTACK: THE DEBATE ON THE ROLE OF QUANTITATIVE COST-BENEFIT ANALYSIS IN THE UNITED STATES

Perhaps the most well-known feature of the US RIA system is its emphasis on quantitative cost-benefit analysis, which led some authors to advocate the transformation of the US government into a "cost-benefit state".[80] Over time, however, the system has increasingly focused on more sophisticated methodologies, such as risk analysis and uncertainty analysis. Figure 4 below shows the required information for different rules in the US. Decision-making criteria in the US RIA system consist of a broad 'soft net benefit' approach whereby regulatory agencies should choose policy options that maximize net benefits, including potential economic, environmental, public health and safety,

[80] See *i.a.* Cass R. Sunstein (1996), *Congress, Constitutional Moments, and the Cost-Benefit State*, 48 STAN. L. REV. 247, 255; Thomas O. McGarity, *A Cost-Benefit State*, 50 ADMIN. L. REV. 7 (1998); Cass R. Sunstein, *Cost-Benefit Default Principles*, 99 MICH. L. REV. 1651, 1656–63 (2001); see also Amy Sinden, *Cass Sunstein's Cost-Benefit Lite: Economics for Liberals*, 29 Colum. J. Envtl. L. 191, 239 (2004).

and other advantages; distributive impacts; and equity. When assessing possible regulatory alternatives, agencies should also take into account economic incentives to encourage the desired behaviour (*e.g.* user fees, marketable permits, information requirements).

OIRA circular A-4 contains the methodological guidance to government agencies for carrying out RIA. Cost-benefit analysis (CBA) and cost effectiveness analysis (CEA) are the main analytical models for US RIA (See Circular A-4, Section D). The two approaches are required in different circumstances (OECD 2006): CBA is the norm for all regulations, except for health and safety rules where CEA is recommended, as it is believed that decisions in this specific policy area should not be based on cost/benefit considerations. However, for major health and safety rules where monetization of the primary expected health and safety outcomes is possible, CBA should be used. Along the same line of reasoning, CEA can be chosen for non health and safety proposals, whenever the "primary benefit categories" cannot be monetized. Reportedly, the use of CBA in health and environmental regulation has considerably increased in recent years.[81]

Available empirical evidence on the use of analytical methods in RIA shows that there is still room for improvement. For example, Morgenstern, Pizer, and Shih (2001) have assessed the actual relationship between the costs reported in a sample of RIAs and the actual economic costs of a rule, and found that regulatory costs are generally overestimated.[82] This is often the result of the unanticipated use of new technology to comply with regulation, as testified by Harrington, Morgenstern, and Nelson (2000).[83] According to an AEI-Brookings review of RIAs (2004), a significant percentage of assessments does not contain some basic economic information (*e.g.*, net benefits and policy alternatives), and over 70% of the analyses fail to provide any quantitative information on net benefits. Hahn and Tetlock (2008) found that costs and benefits are often poorly estimated but that it is difficult to find clear evidence of systematic biases in RIAs. The authors also conclude that the quality of economic analysis has remained relatively stable across RIAs and tends to be below the standards set in the RIA guidelines. Moreover, it seems difficult to establish a clear link between economic analysis and regulatory output in the USA. However, a marginal effect on the content of final rules is undeniable and this may actually amount to significant cost-savings in the case of major rules. A deterrent effect of RIA and economic analysis on low-quality rules is also plausible, but difficult to establish.

---

81 See Harrington *et al.* (2009), *supra*, note 77.

82 See Morgenstern, Richard D., William A. Pizer and Jhih-Shyang Shih (2001). *The Cost of Environmental Protection,* The Review of Economics and Statistics, 83(4): 732–738.

83 Harrington, W., R.D. Morgenstern, and P. Nelson (2000). *On the Accuracy of Regulatory Cost Estimates*" Journal of Policy Analysis and Management 19(2):297–322, at 314.

Figure 4. Requirements generally applicable to major rules

Source of requirements	Characterization of agencies' responsibilities
Requirements applicable to rules of all agencies	
Administrative Procedure Act	Procedures required for informal rulemaking, also known as notice-and-comment rulemaking
Congressional Review Act	Submission of rules to Congress for review
Endangered Species Act	Analysis of impact on endangered or threatened species
National Environmental Policy Act	Analysis of environmental impacts
National Technology Transfer and Advancement Act	Use of voluntary consensus standards
Paperwork Reduction Act	Analysis of paperwork burden and submission to OIRA for approval of new information collections
Regulatory Flexibility Act	Consideration of regulatory alternatives to lessen the burden on small entities
Requirements applicable to rules of cabinet departments and independent agencies, but not to rules of independent regulatory agencies	
Unfunded Mandates Reform Act	Analysis of costs and benefits of federal mandates and consideration of alternatives
Executive Order 12372	Consultation with state and local elected officials
Executive Order 12630	Analysis of impact on constitutionally protected property rights
Executive Order 12866	Submission of significant rules for OIRA review and analysis of costs, benefits, and regulatory alternatives
Executive Order 12898	Consideration of environmental justice impact on minority and low-income populations
Executive Order 12988	Ensuring clarity of regulatory language regarding legal rights and obligations
Executive Order 13045	Evaluation of environmental health or safety effects on children
Executive Order 13132	Consultation with state and local officials on federalism implications
Executive Order 13175	Consultation with Indian tribal governments
Executive Order 13211	Analysis of effects on energy supply, distribution, or use

Source: GAO.

Of the various procedural and substantive requirements, it bears recalling that risk assessment is required in all cases (OECD 2009) and the RIA guidance mandates the discussion of issues of uncertainty and sensitivity analysis.

Guidelines recommend that RIA authors assume a risk-neutral attitude in their analyses, but also recognize that this may not happen in all cases. The neutral approach to risk validates the use of expected value analysis as the fundamental tool for weighing different alternatives (OECD 2007). Suggested values of a statistical life (VSL) adopt different real and nominal rates in respect to different time horizons. The real rates vary from 3.0% (3 years) to 5.5% (30 years) and are based on the pre-tax rate of return on private sector investments in recent years (OECD 2004). A discount rate of 7% is required together with sensitivity analysis using a discount rate of 3% (OECD 2006).

The strength of cost-benefit analysis in the united States is not unlimited. Harrington *et al.* (2009) explain that when the law and CBA conflict (as it is often the case, *e.g.*, in health and safety regulation), the law prevails. As a result, if Congress states that a specific performance level must be achieved by a given rule, but some monetization can nonetheless be included in the analysis and ends up questioning those targets, the resulting mismatch can lead to legal conflict. Moreover, in some cases CBA has not proven particularly useful as it was applicable only to a limited subset of the costs and benefits, thus leading to the consideration of a limited set of regulatory alternatives. As result, the complex analytical tools included in the RIA turn out to be less informative than simpler techniques. This 'complexity trap' – Harrington *et al.* (2010) argue – can be attributed to the process of judicial review that leads agencies to prepare RIAs for surviving judicial challenges and less as an aid to decision-making.

Nevertheless, several authors have recognized that cost-benefit analysis in support of regulation has gained increasing recognition also in court. However, it is important to recall why cost-benefit analysis has been selected as the common language of regulatory agencies in the US, in order to avoid misunderstandings. The use of cost-benefit analysis has always been under attack in the United States. In methodological terms CBA is under attack because it carries an untenable welfare standard; because it may systematically lead to an undervaluation of environmental and health impacts; because it lends itself badly to the assessment of distributional impacts; and because it is difficult to implement by regulatory agencies, sometimes requiring heroic assumptions at best. To the contrary, defenders of the CBA approach offer mostly pragmatic explanations, by arguing that it minimizes error costs, and overall is preferable to all available alternatives, including *i.a.* feasibility analysis.[84] Finally, Eric Posner (2001) – following previous authors, such as *i.a.* Epstein *et al.* (1999), Mashaw (1997) and Matthew, Noll and Weingast (1987) – argues that the main purpose of CBA is not fairness or any measure of efficiency, but to enable and

---

84 See Masur, Jonathan S. and Posner, Eric A. (2010), *Against Feasibility Analysis*, University of Chicago Law Review, Forthcoming; University of Chicago Law & Economics, Olin Working Paper No. 480; University of Chicago, Public Law Working Paper No. 274. Available at SSRN: http://ssrn.com/abstract=1452984.

facilitate control of the bureaucracy by elected politicians.[85] This statement, however, assumes that CBA is a suitable tool to achieve this result. In section 4.4 below I will get back to this debate to show how law and economics has approached the role of CBA as a tool that facilitates the control of bureaucracy within a principal-agent system.

2.3.1. THE IMPACT OF RIA IN THE US: AVAILABLE EVIDENCE

The introduction of RIA by the Reagan administration was coupled with estimated yearly savings of roughly $10–20 billion. Non-governmental estimates are however very different: according to one authoritative economist, the cost of regulations even increased after the introduction of compulsory RIA for federal agencies, and has never stopped mounting since then.[86]

On the other hand, relevant critiques have been addressed to the current implementation of RIA in the US. As already recalled, a 2000 study by Bob Hahn and Bob Litan found that only in less than one third of the cases agencies had quantified both expected costs and benefits of proposed regulations, only in 63% of the cases the proponent agency calculated all identified costs, whereas only in 28% of proposals had the agency calculated the net present value of the regulatory intervention.[87] More recently, in 2004 Bob Hahn and Pat Dudley analysed 55 cases of RIA performed by federal agencies between the Reagan, Bush Sr. and Clinton administrations, with similar results.[88] Accordingly, economists have stressed the need for more accuracy of cost-benefit estimates by federal agencies as a necessary measure to improve the quality of *ex ante* evaluation. Robert Hahn and Robert Litan have also issued recommendations on how to improve the quality of US RIA, by enhancing the soundness and pervasiveness of the model.[89]

---

85 Posner, E. A. (2001), *Controlling Agencies with Cost-Benefit Analysis: A Positive Political Theory Perspective*, University of Chicago Law Review, Vol. 68.

86 Hahn, R.W. and R. Litan (2000), *An Analysis of the Third Government Report on the Benefits and Costs of Federal Regulation*, AEI-Brookings Joint Center for Regulatory Studies, 2000; and E.A. Posner (2001), "Controlling Agencies with Cost-benefit Analysis. A Positive Political Theory Perspective", *University of Chicago Law Review*, Vol. 68, 2001.

87 *Ibid.*

88 R.W. Hahn and P. Dudley (2004), *How well Does the Government Do Cost-Benefit Analysis?* AEI-Brookings Joint Center for Regulatory Studies, Working Paper 04–01, January 2004.

89 See Hahn, R.W. and R. Litan (2005), *Counting Regulatory Benefits and Costs: Lessons for the U.S. and Europe*, Journal of International Economic Law, Vol. 8, No. 2, 2005, pp. 473–508, see in particular, pp. 496–499 (suggesting that "Congress pass a law requiring that *all* federal regulatory agencies submit annual cost and benefit estimates of major regulations to OMB", and that "OMB issue a scorecard assessing the overall quality of regulation and ask the agencies to complete a scorecard for each major regulation"). See also, for a more recent review, Hahn, R. W. and P. Tetlock (2008), *Has Economic Analysis Improved Regulatory*

Furthermore, besides critiques addressed towards the quality of RIAs performed by federal agencies, some disagreement has emerged as regards the scope of application of the US RIA model. As of today, the US impact assessment procedure only involves federal agencies, not independent authorities, i.e. the authorities that normally deal with the most relevant part of economic regulations.[90] And, while it is certainly true that such authorities ought to be left independent of the executive, many commentators have criticised the decision to limit the application of RIA scrutiny to all new rules except core economic and social rules enacted by giant regulators, such as the FCC, the FTC or the SEC.[91]

Finally, the US regulatory review model has been the subject of extensive study by game theorists and political scientists, as its peculiar institutional setting lends itself to applications of principal-agent models and raises issues of political control over the bureaucracy.[92] For example, Lazer (2004) finds evidence that, although the staff at OIRA has remained quite stable between the Bush Sr. and Clinton administrations, the White House has radically redistributed its attention and political support towards OIRA members with compatible political viewpoints. The appointment of John Graham as the OIRA head and the gradual strengthening of OIRA's role as gatekeeper are seen as consistent with the removal of the Vice President from the review procedure, a solution aimed at ensuring that the White House keeps control over federal agencies and at the same time economizing on its fairly limited capacity to gather information on proposed new rules.

This finding is compatible with a competitive agent model of control, and suggests that, in the regulatory review model adopted in the US, presidential influence is exerted mostly through an institutionalization of the conflict and competition between the anti-regulatory OIRA and activist regulatory agencies, such as the Environmental Protection Agency or the Occupational Safety and Health Administration. In this model, the President has a clear incentive to exert

---

Decisions?, Journal of Economic Perspectives, Volume 22, Number 1, Winter 2008, Pages 67–84.

90 Hahn, R. and C. Sunstein (2002), *New Executive Order For Improving Federal Regulation? Deeper And Wider Cost-Benefit Analysis*, University of Pennsylvania Law Review, Vol. 150, No. 1489; McGarity, T.O. (1987), *Regulatory Analysis and Regulatory Reform*, Texas Law Review, Vol. 65, No. 1243. See also Pildes R.H. and C.R. Sunstein, *Reinventing the Regulatory State*, University of Chicago Law Review, 62, 1, 1995.

91 See e.g. Gattuso, *supra* note 55.

92 See, *i.a.*, Moe, T. (1982) *Regulatory performance and presidential administration*, American Journal of Political Science, 26(2), pp. 197–224; Moe, T. (1985), *Control and feedback in economic regulation: The case of the NLRB*, American Political Science Review, 79, 1094–1016; And Moe, T. (1984) *The new economics of organization*, American Journal of Political Science, Vol. 28, n. 4, 739–777. See also Niskanen, W.A. (1971), *Bureaucracy and Representative Government*, Chicago, IL: Aldine, 1971.

heavy control on the bureaucracy also because the White House competes with Congress in controlling bureaucrats.[93]

Finally, the peculiar structure, scope and governance of the US RIA system seem to have been less widely studied than other features of the system, such as the cost-benefit model used to evaluate all types of secondary legislation within the domain of central government, including lifesaving regulation. However, the existence of several other forms of oversight, transparency and accountability mechanisms is perhaps more important than the methodology used in RIA, as it portrays the nature of a mechanism designed to facilitate delegation and oversight in a presidential system such as the US one. This is essential to evaluate the performance of the system itself, and also to correctly approach the question whether a US-like RIA system can be successfully imported in Civil Law countries, and in parliamentary democracies. I will come back to this issue in Sections 4 and 6 of this volume.

93 See Lazer, D. (1998), *Regulatory Review: Presidential Control through Selective Communication and Institutionalized Conflict*, available at www.ksg.harvard.edu/prg/lazer/control.pdf.

3. EU IMPACT ASSESSMENT: HISTORY, PRACTICE AND OUTCOMES

The European Commission has adopted methods for assessing the impact of its policy proposals since 1986, when the *Business Impact Assessment* (BIA) *System* was launched under the UK presidency. The BIA system, like the UK Compliance Cost Assessment procedure, exhibited a strong focus on the impact of proposed regulations on business enterprises, with no specific emphasis on social welfare as a whole.[94] As such, the BIA procedure elicited strong criticisms for its lack of theoretical soundness and scarce impact on regulatory costs faced by European firms.[95] As a result, the system was gradually integrated with an array of initiatives and projects (such as the Business Test Panel, the SLIM project, etc.), aimed at extending the limited scope of the BIA. Such a hysteresis of initiatives ended up creating an overly confused scenario for EU impact assessment – exactly the regulatory creep that impact assessment was supposed to counter. For such reason, in 2002 EU institutions agreed on the need for new actions in the field of better regulation, with a specific focus on impact assessment.

At the beginning of the past decade, as EU policy-makers were striving to lead Europe away from its disappointing economic performance and back on the Lisbon track, better regulation became a new mantra, and during the Prodi mandate as President of the European Commission the need to strengthen the *ex ante* impact assessment of EU legislation conquered new supporters, who saw it as the philosopher's stone that would improve the quality of EU legislation in the following years. Thus, the better regulation agenda strongly relied on the successful implementation of an ambitious new Integrated Impact Assessment (IIA) model, which entered into force on 1 January 2003 and mandated the assessment of the economic, social and environmental impact of major new initiatives included in the Annual Policy Strategy or in the annual Legislative Work Program.

94 For a description of the UK compliance cost assessment, see Renda (2006), pages 26 ff.

95 See, *inter alia*, the BIA Final Report, *Lessons Learned and the Way Forward*, Enterprise Paper No. 9, 2002, p. 2. The Commission acknowledged that BIA "has not always worked as originally intended… Instead, BIAs are often carried out as an ex-post 'paper exercise' on already finalised proposals, leading to significant drawbacks with regard to both the quality of the analysis made and the possibility of feeding the results into the drafting process". The Final Report also mentioned that "many BIAs are not backed up by objective information and impacts on business are rarely quantified", and that "[t]here is little evidence of an institutional learning process from previous BIAs".

As will be observed in more detail in the next sections, the transition towards a full-fledged impact assessment system in Europe occurred without a thorough reflection on the scope and purpose that this system would exhibit in Europe, especially as opposed to its homologous systems in the US and UK. First and foremost, while in the US the RIA system applies only for secondary legislation proposed by government agencies, and thus is not compulsory for Congress and independent agencies, at EU level the system was adopted for all major new initiatives included in the European Commission's yearly legislative and work program: this means that an impact assessment may be performed on ambitious, cross-cutting pieces of legislation such as the services directive; on pure regulatory decisions such as the technical requirements for narrow tractors or the safety of toys; or on high-level strategy documents such as the i2010 strategy, the thematic air pollution strategy, or even the new legislative framework for mutual recognition of goods within the Internal Market. Needless to say, the emphasis on the monetization of impacts could not be the same as in the US, where specialized regulators are called to perform quantitative analysis on policy proposals that fall entirely in their domain of technical expertise.

Second, the different scope of the IA system in Europe reflects also a different purpose. While the US RIA system is centered around the logic of delegation of powers and oversight, the EU IA system is sometimes presented as a toolkit available to European Commission bureaucrats, to help them learn how to draft good quality policy proposals. As we will see in the following sections, this is probably a very partial explanation of the EU IA system, which was indeed presented to external stakeholders as a tool that would also achieve better regulatory *outcomes*, not only a better quality of the proposals. In addition, the "pure learning" explanation was inconsistent with early developments in EU institutions, such as the 2003 Inter-Institutional Agreement on Better Regulation, in which also the European Parliament and the Council committed to the same IA system adopted by the European Commission, as far as their major amendments on Commission proposals were concerned. This agreement – renewed and strengthened in 2005 under the term "Common Approach to Impact Assessment" – remains to date almost exclusively on paper, as I will explain in more detail in the next sections: this also means that whatever effort the Commission puts on its on Impact Assessment documents, the final piece of legislation, as amended during the co-decision procedure, will never be fully associated with the original IA. In a nutshell, the IA document – which should clearly serve purposes other than mere in-house learning – becomes an extraordinarily short-lived document, with very rapid obsolescence.

Third, the different scope and purpose of the EU impact assessment system inevitably affected also the methodological arrangements adopted by European Commission Directorates General (DGs). However, especially after 2005, and even more with the appointment of the Impact Assessment Board (IAB) in 2006 and the new IA guidelines in 2009, emphasis has been put on the need to quantify and monetize impacts, including in most cases also macroeconomic impacts of proposed EU policies. In this respect, the European Commission seems to be slowly converging with the type of cost-benefit analysis required in the United States: however, this approach seems hardly fit for the peculiarities of the EU impact assessment system, which requires a way more nuanced approach to the methodological choices needed to justify the adoption of a given policy proposal – would you use quantitative cost-benefit analysis to choose the preferred option when deciding between harmonisation of legislation and mutual recognition in the circulation of widgets?

The introduction of Impact Assessment in the European Commission has suffered from this confusion in the scope, purpose and methodology. The situation became even worse when the system was re-launched in 2005 by Commission Vice-President Verheugen, who announced that with impact assessment Europe would gain awareness of "the full costs and benefits of future legislation".[96] Against this background, since 2003 Commission DGs have carried out impact assessment of White Papers, Directives, Regulations, strategy documents, Decisions, expenditure programmes, negotiating guidelines for international agreements and other types of documents, often of a non-binding nature. The system required them to mandate the assessment of the economic, social and environmental impacts of proposed new initiatives, and introduced a number of "screens" – *e.g.* competitiveness, proportionality, subsidiarity, impact on SMEs, macroeconomic impacts, provisions for *ex post* monitoring, etc. – which diluted, to some extent, the efficiency-oriented nature of EU RIA, transforming the system into a sort of panacea, *i.e.* a tool that, rather than containing sound economic analysis, often merely summarizes the interests at stake and tries to find a compromise between political and policy stances advanced by different stakeholders holding an interest in the rules at hand.

After all, the EU impact assessment system soon exhibited the same problems that affected the only available European model, from which the EU system had taken several features: the UK RIA system launched in 1998 soon went into trouble, sometimes turning into a mere box-ticking exercise. In Europe, commentators saw early signs of "plateau-ing" of the EU better regulation agenda, also due to a number of bad episodes (*i.a.*, the REACH regulation, the services directive, and many others) and to a persistent lack of transparency in the final drafting phase of the Commission's policy process, in particular due to the fact that the Commission does not consult on draft Impact Assessment documents.

96 See Verheugen's speech at the UK Presidency Conference on Better Regulation, Edinburgh, 23 September 2005 (available at http://europa.eu/rapid/pressReleasesAction.do? reference=SPEECH/05/543&format=PDF&aged=1&language=EN&guiLanguage=en).

Against this background, it is fair to state that the European Commission has managed to achieve important progress in the quality of its Impact Assessment documents between 2003 and 2010, although a lot seems to depend on the type of proposal and on the policy area where the proposal falls. To be sure, such progress is unmatched in Europe, as neither the other EU institutions, nor Member States have reached any similar result to date. At the same time, it is also true that the "regulatory pendulum" in Europe seems to be gradually shifting towards other tools, and in particular towards the Standard Cost Model for the measurement and reduction of administrative burdens.[97]

In the remainder of this chapter, I illustrate the birth and evolution of the EU impact assessment system, starting with a brief account of the early experience with Business Impact Assessment (Section 3.1.1) and then describing more in detail the scope, purpose and governance of the current system, in place since 2003 (Section 3.1.2). Section 3.2 then looks at the Impact Assessment guidelines of the European Commission, in their current version dated January 2009. Section 3.3 provides evidence of the quality of the Commission IA documents by illustrating the results of a scorecard analysis of the 475 IAs produced by the Commission between 2003 and the end of 2009. Section 3.4 concludes with some insights from the analysis of the EU IA system and the prospect for future reform.

3.1. HISTORY AND EVOLUTION OF THE EU IMPACT ASSESSMENT SYSTEM

3.1.1. THE EARLY YEARS: THE BIA SYSTEM

The EU experience in regulatory impact assessment began in 1986, when the UK took its turn in the Presidency of the Council. For this reason, the impact analysis procedure introduced – called Business Impact Assessment (BIA) – closely echoed the UK model of Compliance Cost Assessment.[98] The BIA Pilot Project aimed at evaluating the impact of a limited number of proposed regulations on businesses, expressed in terms of compliance costs. Since 1989, the procedure has been put under the competency of DGXXIII (DG Enterprise), which coordinated other DGs and selected the proposals included in the Commission's agenda that should be subjected to a BIA test.[99] The BIA Pilot Project led to a selection of draft proposals from DG Enterprise in the fields of detergents,

97 See, for an illustration of the Standard Cost Model, Böheim, Renda *et al.* (2006), *Pilot Project on Administrative Burdens*, Report for the European Commission, DG Enterprise, at http://ec.europa.eu/enterprise/policies/better-regulation/files/pilot-study_en.pdf.

98 See Renda (2006), pages 26 ff. for a description of the UK compliance cost assessment model.

99 See the BIA Final Report, *supra* note 95.

electromagnetic compatibility, environmental impact of electrical and electronic equipment (EEE) and pre-packaging, and concentrated on examining three major elements of the impact assessment process, namely external consultation, economic analysis and organizational structures.

Figure 5 illustrates the essential structure and the critical steps of the BIA procedure. As shown in the figure, DG Enterprise ensured that a limited number of proposals included in the Annual Policy Strategy were scrutinized under the BIA procedure. If a proposal was found to exert a substantial impact on compliance costs, the proponent administration was required to draft a *fiche d'impact*. The *fiche* had a standard form, and was introduced with the aim of representing the likely impact of the proposal at hand on target firms. First, the *fiche* illustrated the main reasons for intervention. Lead DGs were asked to explain the reasons for changing legislation currently in force (or to intervene *ex novo* in unregulated fields). The next step was the identification of businesses that would be affected by the proposed intervention, followed by a list of actions to be undertaken in order to comply with the changing regulatory environment. For each of these actions a cost estimate had to be provided, by specifying bureaucratic costs, taxes, monitoring and reporting costs and other compliance costs.

Figure 5. The BIA system

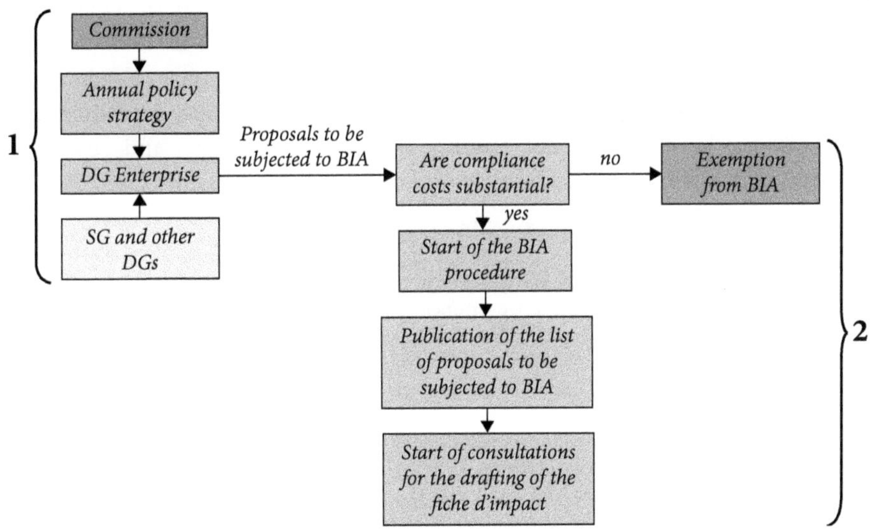

The standard *fiche d'impact* also included an evaluation of the likely macroeconomic effects of the proposed regulation, which in turn incorporated the impact on employment and on the investments and competitiveness of target firms. Finally, the *fiche* should devote specific attention to assessing the expected impact of the proposal on SMEs, in line with the 'think small first' principle already established at that time.[100] While drafting the *fiche*, lead DGs were required to consult interested stakeholders. The final document contained a summary of the opinions expressed during the consultation process.

The BIA system was subject to heavy critiques, mostly related to its incompleteness and uncertain institutional setting. First, as was already recalled, the BIA procedure did not imply the preliminary identification of a range of alternative regulatory options, and only entered the stage after the Commission had identified the preferred option in its yearly regulatory agenda. Secondly, the BIA only contained information on business compliance costs, without considering other cost categories or the social impact of the proposed regulation, often less easily quantifiable and often not subject to market exchange. Furthermore, the EU experience with BIA was characterised by the poor quality of the evaluations performed, which casted heavy doubts on the reliability of such instrument as a support to EU policy-makers.[101] The absence of training initiatives for officials of the DGs in charge of BIA contributed further to generate widespread pessimism over the prospects for improving the quality of performed evaluations in the short run without changing the procedure completely.[102]

For this reason, the Commission decided during the 1990s to add new tools and to launch new projects for the purpose of completing the evaluation of proposals carried out under the BIA system. Such initiatives include the SLIM project (Simplification of the Legislation on the Internal Market), aimed at strengthening the ex post assessment of the quality of regulation; the creation of the BEST (Business Environment Simplification Task Force), in 1997; and the creation of the Business Test Panel in 1998, with the aim of acting as a permanent body for consultation of firms affected by EU regulations.[103] Such a proliferation of initiatives, however, did not produce the desired outcome, and ended up creating an overly fragmented framework for EU impact assessment.

---

100 The 'think small first' principle was included in the European Charter for Small Enterprises, as endorsed by the Heads of State or Government at the Santa Maria da Feira European Council of 19–20 June 2000 (Annex III of the conclusions of the Santa Maria da Feira European Council). Today, the principle is embedded in the Small Business Act, and subject to specific guidance in the European Commission's Impact Assessment Guidelines. See COM(2008)394 A Small Business Act for Europe, and Annex 8 to the IA Guidelines, p. 32, at http://ec.europa.eu/governance/impact/commission_guidelines/docs/iag_2009_annex_en.pdf.

101 See the BIA Final Report, *supra* note 95.

102 Ibid., p. 23, stating the need for a cultural change, both within the institution and in its relationships with the public, through the implementation of a series of straightforward and common-sense adjustments, which are intended to be neither bureaucratic nor complicated to put in place.

103 As regards the SLIM Pilot Project, see the Commission Communication of 6 November 1996, COM(96)559 (available at http://europa.eu.int/comm/internal_market/simplification/docs/com1996-559/com1996-559_en.pdf). The subsequent Commission reports are available at http://europa.eu.int/comm/internal_market/simplification/index_en.htm#slim. For what concerns the BEST project, the Final Report, issued in May 1998, is available at http://europa.eu.int/comm/enterprise/enterprise_policy/best.

This *impasse* led the Commission to issue in 2001 a White Paper on European Governance and the Lisbon Council to mandate the creation of a high-level advisory group (the so-called 'Mandelkern Group') for the drafting of an "action plan for better regulation" and the definition of a new model of impact assessment to be implemented at Community level. The Mandelkern Group was created to "set out by 2001 a strategy for further co-ordinated action to simplify the regulatory environment, including the performance of public administration, at both national and Community level", and after the Ministers for Public Administration from EU Member States had signed the Strasbourg Resolution in November 2000, mandating the advisory group to "develop a coherent approach to this topic and to submit proposals to the Ministers, including the definition of a common method of evaluating the quality of regulation."

Such model was expected to provide a more complete tool for assessing the social, economic and environmental impact of proposed regulations.[104]

3.1.2. THE 2001 WHITE PAPER AND THE MANDELKERN REPORT

The Commission's 2001 White Paper on European Governance clarified the Commission's agenda for the establishment of new better regulation standards in the EU.[105] The preparation of the White Paper was coordinated by the former 'Governance team' chaired by Jerome Vignon. The team organised 12 working groups dealing with six main working areas. Working Group 2c dealt with issues of better regulation and explored possible actions for improving the quality of regulation at EU level as well as the implementation of EU legislation at member state level. Better regulation was defined in terms of seven dimensions, namely proportionality, proximity, legal certainty, coherence, high standards, timeliness and enforceability. The need for action at member state level was stressed during the preparatory work for the White Paper, in stating that "action at Community level alone – and *a fortiori* by the Commission alone – is certain not to succeed".[106] Subsequent developments, unfortunately, confirmed such prophecy.

According to Working Group 2c, BIA was an insufficient tool to appraise the expected impact of a regulation for a number of reasons. First, BIA was "only a

---

104 The Mandelkern Group was made up of representatives of the EU-15 and officials from the Commission's Secretariat-General. An interim report was finalised at the end of February 2001 and considered by the Heads of State and Government at the Spring European Council in Stockholm. The Final Report (so-called 'Mandelkern Report') was published in November 2001; the majority of recommendations were included in the Commission's 2002 Better Regulation Action Plan.

105 See European Commission, White Paper on European Governance, COM(2001)727, 25 July 2001.

106 See the Preparatory Work for the White Paper, European Commission, 2002, p. 119, available at http://ec.europa.eu/comm/governance/areas/preparatory_work_en.pdf.

questionnaire, without a proper process and without guidance".[107] This, according to the opinion expressed by the working group, could lead to significant differences in the quality of the analysis. Moreover, the questions were handled only at a late stage of the regulatory process, when political pressures are expected to be highest.

Finally, BIA was found to be inappropriate since the analysis contained in the *fiche* was presented separately from the tests of subsidiarity and proportionality and the sectoral provisions in the Treaty, leaving stakeholders and policy-makers unaware of the relationship between prospective costs arising from the proposal for businesses and expected benefits to consumers, the environment or SMEs. Accordingly, more sophisticated tools were needed in order to support policy-makers with clearer, more relevant and more comprehensive information on the prospective cost-benefit balance of regulatory proposals.[108]

Importantly, the preparatory report of the working group on evaluation and policy also recommended the use of cost-benefit analysis as the most complete and accurate methodology in the evaluation of proposed legislations, based on the observation of the US and UK systems and the recommendations of the OECD.[109] However, exact economic calculations were considered not to be the most important contributors to regulatory quality. Rather, the working group took a 'lesson-drawing' approach by stating that observing the international experience and undertaking contextualised benchmarking are the most important steps towards a compete understanding of the logic of decision-making. The working group also suggested that monitoring existing EU legislation was at least as important as evaluating the expected impact of new regulation.[110]

The publication of the White Paper on European Governance was followed by a fierce debate and a period of frantic institutional tension. The European Parliament issued a resolution on governance in the wake of the 'Kaufmann Report', in which it criticised the lack of cooperation between the Commission and the Parliament in defining the EU agenda for better regulation.[111] In other words, the Parliament complained that, after stating the need for cooperation at both horizontal (inter-institutional) and vertical (with member states) level, in fact the Commission was 'playing solo' on the reform of European governance. For such reason, the Parliament warned the Commission "against taking measures in the legislative sphere which might affect the roles of Parliament and the Council in the legislative process before Parliament has been fully

107 *Ibid.*, p. 106.

108 See *e.g.*, J. Pelkmans, S. Labory and G. Majone, "Better EU Regulatory Quality: Assessing Current Initiatives and New Proposals", *op. cit.*

109 See Preparatory Work for the White Paper, op. cit., Section 3.2.1, p. 91.

110 *Ibid.*, Section 3.3.3, p. 92.

111 European Parliament, *Report on the Commission White Paper on European Governance*, A5-0399/2001, adopted by the European Parliament on 29 November 2001 (OJ C 153E, 27 June 2002, pp. 314–322).

consulted".[112] The resolution suggested instead the promotion of stronger inter-institutional dialogue on governance reform, and welcomed the establishment of an inter-institutional working group announced by President Romano Prodi on 2 October 2001.

But the Parliament resolution contained other interesting comments on the Commission's White Paper. In particular, the Parliament considered some of the plans formulated by the Commission in the White Paper as patently (and sometimes unnecessarily) ambitious. Instruments such as the "online consultation through the inter-active policy-making initiative" (Section 3.1 of the White Paper) created, in the Parliament's view, the "risk of an escalation in consultation" which would end up being incompatible with the Commission's goal of "reducing the long delays associated with the adoption and implementation of Community rules".[113]

A few months after the publication of the White Paper on European Governance, the Mandelkern Group on Better Regulation published its final report. The report specified some of the features of the prospective new RIA model, suggesting its adoption by the Commission before June 2002 and its application to all Commission proposals with possible regulatory effects.[114] The Mandelkern Group also recommended that the Council and the Parliament should not consider proposals that had not been subjected to the agreed impact assessment system, except in cases of urgency.[115] Furthermore, the Mandelkern Report highlighted the need for increased participation by member states at an early stage of preparation of proposals, as well as the need for each member state to adopt its own impact assessment system "adapted to their circumstances" by June 2003.

As regards Regulatory Impact Assessment (RIA), the Mandelkern Report contained a set of recommendations for an effective implementation of such procedure. These included the following steps:[116]

- Description of the problem or risk to be addressed;
- Description of different options considered;
- Affected parties and at least a qualitative assessment of impact on them;
- Summary of the consultation process undertaken and of its results;
- Estimated lifetime of the policy or options;
- Description of the impact on SMEs or other disproportionately affected group;

112 *Ibid.*, p. 8.
113 *Ibid.*, p. 8.
114 Mandelkern Group, Final Report (available at www.eulib.com/documents/mandelkern_report_en.pdf).
115 On 30 September 2002, the Competitiveness Council stated its intention, in principle, not to consider substantial regulatory proposals not accompanied by proportionate impact assessments.
116 See the Mandelkern Report, *op. cit.*, p. 26.

- Explanation of how the proposal fits with existing rules and policies; and
- Description of the methodology adopted.

The Mandelkern Group also recommended the adoption of a 'dual stage' RIA model, with a preliminary impact assessment devoted to the analysis of alternative regulatory options and an extended impact assessment in which the detailed assessment of the benefits and costs of the preferred regulatory option is performed. However, the Mandelkern Report did not contain any indication on the scope and comprehensiveness of the impact to be assessed.

The recommendations following from the Final Report represented a fairly important input into the Commission's new impact assessment model. But, as will be clearer in the next section, the Commission's new Better Regulation Action Plan and the Communication on impact assessment, both issued in June 2002, went somehow further than what had been envisaged by the Mandelkern Group.

3.1.3. AWAY FROM RIA: BUILDING THE INTEGRATED IMPACT ASSESSMENT

At the European Council meetings of Göteborg and Laeken, the Commission announced its Action Plan for Better Regulation, launched in June 2002. The new impact assessment model was introduced as part of the wider Action Plan, together with a communication aimed at simplifying and improving the regulatory environment and measures aimed at promoting "a culture of dialogue and participation" within the EU legislative process.[117]

The Communication on impact assessment was inspired partially from the activity of the Mandelkern Group, but also from the commitment undertaken by the Commission at the Göteborg Council, to develop a tool for sustainable impact assessment.[118] As a result, the Commission decided to integrate all forms of *ex ante* evaluation by building an integrated impact assessment model, to enter

---

117 During 2002 and early in 2003, the Commission developed its Action Plan through eight targeted Communications, at the same time defining with the European Parliament and the Council an overall strategy on better law-making. The Communications addressed the following issues: 1) General principles and minimum standards for consultation (COM(2002)704); 2) the collection and use of expertise (COM(2002) 713); 3) impact assessment (COM(2002) 276), including internal *Guidelines*; 4) Simplifying and improving the regulatory environment (COM(2002) 278); 5) proposal for a new comitology decision (COM(2002) 719); 6) operating framework for the European Regulatory Agencies (COM(2002) 718); 7) framework for target-based tripartite contracts (COM(2002) 709); and 8) Better monitoring of the application of community law (COM(2002) 725).

118 See Communication COM(2002)276, p. 2. See also the Communication from the Commission to the European parliament, the Council, the Economic and Social Committee and the Committee of the Regions, *Towards a Global Partnership for Sustainable Development*, COM(2002)82, 12 February 2002.

into force on 1 January 2003.[119] Such model bears the heavy responsibility of ensuring that adequate account is taken at an early stage of the regulatory process of both the competitiveness and sustainable development goals, which rank amongst the top priorities in the EU agenda.

The new integrated impact assessment (IIA) model introduced in 2002 – which incorporated not only the economic impact, but also the social and environmental impact of the proposals concerned – adopted a 'dual stage' approach. All Commission initiatives proposed for inclusion in the Annual Policy Strategy or the Commission Legislative and Work Programme and requiring some regulatory measure for their implementation – thus including not only regulations and directives, but also White Papers, expenditure programmes and negotiating guidelines for the international agreements – must undergo a 'preliminary impact assessment'.[120] Moreover, a selected number of proposals with large expected impact, are subjected to a more in-depth analysis called 'extended impact assessment'.

The selection of proposals for extended impact assessment was part of the Commission programming and planning cycle. On the basis of the preliminary impact assessment statement, the Commission was asked to decide in the Annual Policy Strategy or (later) in its annual Legislative and Work Programme which proposals should undergo an extended impact assessment. In deciding, it had to take into account whether the proposal would result in substantial economic, environmental and/or social impacts on a specific sector or several sectors; whether the proposal would have significant impacts on major interested parties; and whether the proposal represented a major policy reform in one or several sectors.

The preliminary impact assessment consisted merely in a short statement containing an identification of the issue at stake, the regulatory options available (including the 'zero option' or 'no policy change' scenario), preliminary indications on the expected impact and an indication of whether an extended impact assessment would be needed. There was no clear identification of the policy option to be preferred, but only a specification of the options that should be excluded at the preliminary stage, taking into account also the subsidiarity

---

119 "Impact assessment is intended to integrate, reinforce, streamline and replace all the existing separate impact assessment mechanisms for Commission proposals." See the Commission's Communication on impact assessment, COM(2002) 276, 5 June 2002, Section 1.3.

120 Proposals that are exempted from impact assessment include: a) Green Papers where the policy formulation is still in process; b) periodic Commission decisions and reports; c) proposals following international obligations; d) executive decisions, such as "implementing decisions, statutory decisions and technical updates, including adaptations to technical progress"; and e) Commission measures deriving from its powers of controlling the correct implementation of Community Law (although the Commission may in some instances decide to carry out an impact assessment). See Communication on impact assessment, COM(2002) 276, 5 June 2002, Section 2 ("Coverage").

and the proportionality principle. Overall, the outline for preliminary impact assessment did not seem to be particularly informative.[121]

The extended impact assessment (ExIA) contained an in-depth evaluation of expected social, economic and environmental impact of the various policy options associated with the proposal and a summary of the consultation activity, which should also focus on political and ethical issues related to the proposal. The Commission also specified that the expected impact should be estimated in qualitative, quantitative and possibly monetary terms. The alternative policy options were to be evaluated according to criteria such as the relevance to the problem, the effectiveness in achieving the objectives, the coherence with wider economic, social and environmental objectives, the interaction with other existing and planned Community interventions, the cost or resources required and the user-friendliness of the regulatory option at hand.

More in detail, the Commission provided a description of what is meant by economic, social and environmental impact:

- The *economic* impact includes both the macro- and micro-economic impact of the selected option, mostly in terms of economic growth and competitiveness, i.e. changes in compliance costs, including administrative burdens to businesses/SMEs and implementation costs for public authorities, impacts on the potential for innovation and technological development, changes in investment, market shares and trade patterns as well as increases or decreases in consumer prices, etc.
- The *social* impact includes the impact of the proposal on human capital, on fundamental/human rights, the compatibility of the proposal with the Charter of Fundamental Rights of the European Union, but also prospective changes in employment levels or job quality, changes affecting gender equality, social exclusion and poverty, impacts on health, safety, consumer rights, social capital, security (including crime and terrorism), education, training and culture, as well as distributional implications such as effects on the income of particular sectors, groups of consumers or workers, etc.
- The *environmental* dimension concerns positive and negative impacts associated with the changing status of the environment such as climate change, air, water and soil pollution, land-use change and bio-diversity loss, changes in public health, etc.

As clearly emerged from these definitions, the IIA model proposed by the Commission appeared as a very complex exercise, aimed at predicting all possible consequences of the enactment of a new regulation, with evaluations that – whether qualitative or quantitative – would certainly be costly, burdensome, highly discretionary and time-consuming for administrations. Furthermore, the

121 See Renda (2006).

often denounced lack of training for EU public officials, which led to obscure and unreliable assessments at a time when the BIA was the prevailing impact assessment tool, were likely to be exacerbated with the entry into force of the new procedure, possibly the most complex model implemented worldwide at the time. It must be recalled that the Commission decided to introduce the new procedure gradually, and expected to reach the planned complexity and comprehensiveness only in 2004. Moreover, in September 2002, the Commission published the first version of its guidelines for the implementation of an impact assessment procedure.

The IIA model introduced by the Commission in 2002 is illustrated in Figure 6. As emerges from the figure, the new procedure permeated the whole Commission's Strategic Planning and Programming Cycle (SPPC), from the definition of the Annual Policy Strategy (APS) to the publication of the Commission's Work Programme (CWP) that leads to inter-service consultation before selected initiatives are undertaken and pursued. Preliminary IAs could be included in the APS, but had to be completed at the latest before the publication of the CWP. The availability of an extended IA (for proposals selected for such a more in-depth analysis) was a necessary precondition for launching inter-service consultation at the beginning of the year in which the regulation will be issued. The ExIA report was then attached to the proposal when it was submitted to the Commission for final adoption and adopted as a working document of the services. After adoption, the ExIA was sent to other institutions along with the proposals and made available online.

Figure 6. The IIA system, 2003–2005

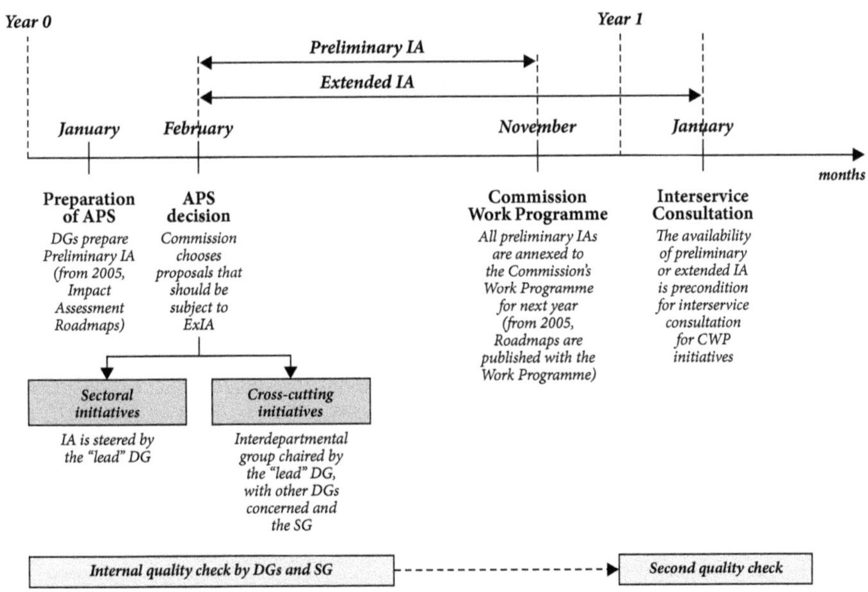

3.1.4. THE RE-LAUNCH OF THE EU IA SYSTEM IN 2005

The Commission assessed the first results of its new Integrated Impact Assessment model in December 2004, by drawing a mixed picture on the progress made in improving the quality of EU legislation. At the time, the worrying signals shown by the mid-term review of the Lisbon strategy in February 2005 called for greater emphasis on fostering employment and growth and reducing the administrative burdens of regulation, shifting the focus from sustainable development to competitiveness, and from integrated impact assessment to economic assessment, when not mere compliance cost assessment.[122]

This was a key passage for the Commission's Impact Assessment system, which led to more evident convergence towards the US model – in 2005, the UK was also revising its RIA system, which resulted however in a dilution of the previous system and the adoption of more pragmatic tools to cut red tape on the stock of existing legislation, rather than on the flow of new proposals. Importantly, this passage also led to abandoning the dual stage system of preliminary and extended IAs, to create a single system dominated by the principle of proportionate analysis. Against this background, a first measure was to request services to establish 'Roadmaps' for the initiatives they have put forward for inclusion in the Annual Policy Strategy (APS) and in the Commission's Work Programme.[123] Roadmaps, now available online at the end of every year, contain indications of the IA activity already carried out, consultation undertaken, options considered and future work to be undertaken.[124]

But several sources of pressure were calling for some major effort from the Commission in order to significantly improve the momentum of better regulation efforts, with specific emphasis on strengthening and improving impact assessment methods. First, the Parliament and the Council were urging the Commission to accept a greater involvement of all EU institutions in the procedure, by extending impact assessment to major amendments and defining common methodologies for carrying out assessments in all three institutions. Moreover, the failure to achieve the goal of achieving a 25% reduction in the volume of the *acquis communautaire* by 2005, stated by the Prodi Commission, suggested the need for new efforts in the field of simplification. Finally, the

---

[122] In its Communication to the Spring European Council on "Working together for Growth and Jobs – A New Start for the Lisbon Strategy", COM(2005)24 of 2 February 2005, the Commission suggested that "[a] new approach to regulation should seek to remove burdens and cut red tape unnecessary for reaching the underlying policy objectives. Better Regulation should be a cornerstone for decision making at all levels of the Union."

[123] See European Commission Staff Working Paper, *Impact Assessment: Next Steps*, SEC(2004)1377, Brussels, 21.10.2004.

[124] See the Roadmaps for every year, available online on the Commission's website, at http://ec.europa.eu/governance/impact/planned_ia/planned_ia_en.htm.

decision to extend the impact assessment procedure to all the initiatives included in the Commission's 2005 Legislative and Work Programme (roughly 100) starkly contrasted with evidence that the scheduled IAs had not been completed and had exhibited significant methodological problems, calling for a refinement of the guidelines and a redress of the proportionality principle.

The Commission took action in March 2005 with a new Communication on Better Regulation for Growth and Jobs in the European Union, defining the achievements of the first years of implementation of the IIA as "first steps in what must be a permanent effort".[125] The communication laid down important changes in the IIA procedure and re-launched the role of IA and better regulation as part of the Lisbon strategy. The Communication's vibrant statement on the need to boost better regulation initiatives at all levels results in the launch of three key actions, to be reviewed in 2007, devoted to: a) the design and application of better regulation tools at EU level; b) a closer collaboration with member states to ensure a consistent application of better regulation principles; and c) a stronger, constructive dialogue with all EU regulator, member states and other stakeholders.

The main features of the Commission's new strategy on impact assessment can be summarized as follows:

- Although the IIA was rooted in the sustainable development principle and its integrated nature was not under discussion, there was an *urge to strengthen the assessment of the economic impact* of proposed regulations - compared to the social and environmental impact assessments - in view of the increased importance of the competitiveness principle.
- The Commission started developing a methodology to better integrate the *measurement of administrative costs* in its IA model, and has launched a pilot project for the quantification of such burdens that will produce the first results in late 2005, together with a trial new methodology named 'EU Net administrative cost model', which later became the EU Standard Cost Model.[126]
- The Commission launched an independent evaluation of the Impact Assessment system, which was then completed by The Evaluation Partnership in 2007.[127]

---

125 See Better regulation for Growth and Jobs in the European Union, European Commission Communication - COM(2005)97 (March 2005).

126 See Commission Staff Working Paper, Annex to the 2005 Communication on Better Regulation for Growth and Jobs in the European Union, *Minimizing Administrative Costs Imposed by Legislation, Detailed Outline of a Possible EU Net Administrative Cost Model*, SEC(2005)175, 16 March 2005. Recall, in addition, that the UK Presidency stated its intention to develop a common methodology on measuring administrative burdens, based on the Standard Cost Model successfully applied in the Netherlands.

127 Communication on Better Regulation for Growth and Jobs in the European Union, *Supra* note 125, p. 6 (emphasis in original).

- The new IA model was extended to the Parliament and the Council, where the co-decision procedure applied, for all major amendments to Commission proposals. This, later, became the "Inter-institutional Common Approach to Impact Assessment".[128]
- Two networks of experts were created. A first network grouped high-level national regulatory experts for the development of a "coherent set of common indicators to monitor progress as regards the quality of the regulatory environment" both at EU and member state level. In addition. another network was created, composed of experts in better regulation issues, including academicians and practitioners from the economic, social and environmental fields, who will be called to advise the Commission on a case-by-case basis as regards the methodology adopted for carrying out the IA.

To those who have followed the debate on the implementation of the Commission's IA model since 2003, these changes came to no surprise. The IA was coming back to the somewhat tighter walls of cost-benefit analysis, compliance cost assessment and simplification, in line with the established experience of other countries, and with the mounting pressure of industry stakeholders. The 'back to basics' hypothesis was supported by the new Guidelines issued by the Commission in June 2005.[129] The Technical Annex to the Guidelines devoted special attention to methods for assessing the economic impact of proposed regulations, in particular the impact on growth, competitiveness and employment. A specific section was also dedicated to the assessment of administrative costs imposed by legislation (Annex 10 to the Guidelines, from March 2006).

3.1.5. EVOLUTION OF THE EU IMPACT ASSESSMENT SYSTEM SINCE 2005

The external evaluation of the Commission's IA system in 2007 concluded that the Commission was making progress, by improving the quality of proposals, providing effective aid to decision-making, and enhancing transparency.[130] The evaluation, however, pointed out the need to clarify the concept of proportionate analysis (see below), to better identify the initiatives to be assessed, to improve the timing of IA, and to reduce the number of impact assessments per policy choice.

---

128 http://ec.europa.eu/governance/impact/ia_in_other/docs/ii_common_approach_to_ia_en.pdf.

129 See European Commission, Impact Assessment Guidelines, SEC(2005)971, 15 June 2005.

130 See http://ec.europa.eu/governance/impact/docs/key_docs/tep_eias_final_report.pdf.

More generally, looking back at the suggestions issued in 2001 by the Mandelkern Group, it is quite clear that many member states have not followed the example of the European Commission, and are still far from adopting a real better regulation strategy, let alone a full-fledged IA system. And even in countries that have made some progress in this respect, the IA systems conceived by national regulators differ so widely that any attempted *reductio ad unum* would inevitably fail.[131]

- The European Parliament and the Council have been increasingly involved in the better regulation agenda, a tendency which culminated in the 2003 Inter-Institutional Agreement on Better Lawmaking and the 2005 agreement on a "common approach" to impact assessment.[132]
- In late 2006, the Commission appointed an Impact Assessment Board (IAB), responding to repeated calls for better quality assurance mechanisms and stronger coordination in the *ex ante* assessment activities carried out by the various DGs.[133]
- In January 2007, the Commission launched its Action Programme for the measurement and reduction of administrative burdens generated by EU legislation.[134] As recalled by Dunlop *et al.* (2009) and by Wegrich (2009), while RIA was the most important instrument in better regulation policies between 1995 and 2005, over the past few years other instruments, such as the standard cost model used for the reduction of administrative burdens, have become more pivotal.
- The European Commission published an updated and improved version of the IA Guidelines in January 2009, followed a few months later by an *ad hoc* guidance document on the assessment of social impacts, an aspect that was perceived to be particularly weak in the IA documents produced by the European Commission.
- A consultation on the future of the smart regulation agenda in the EU was launched in 2010, with a view to collecting stakeholder views on how to improve the system in the years to come.

Today, the Commission IA system is firmly nested into the Commission's policy cycle. The second Barroso Commission has so far placed emphasis on the need to perform *ex post* evaluation before any new IA is undertaken (which reinforces the analysis of the *status quo* and calls for the completion of the policy cycle). The IA procedure, coupled with stakeholder consultation, takes approximately 52 weeks to be completed, before the Commission proposal can indeed be

131 Radaelli (2007), presented at the ENBR workshop in Lisbon.

132 Both documents can be found at http://ec.europa.eu/governance/better_regulation/ii_coord_en.htm.

133 For a short description of the IAB, see http://ec.europa.eu/governance/impact/iab_en.htm.

134 COM(2007)23 final, 24 January 2007.

finalized and sent – where appropriate – to other EU institutions. Figure 7 below shows the Commission policy process and the corresponding timing of IA.

Figure 7. Countdown for preparing IA in the European Commission

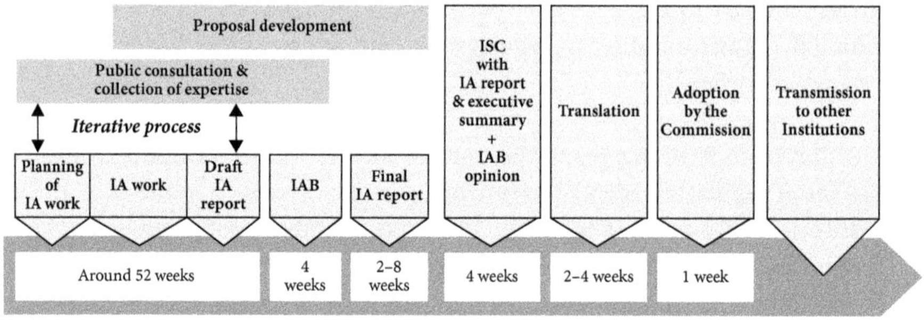

Source: European Commission, Impact Assessment Guidelines, 15 January 2009.

Of the abovementioned changes, perhaps the most important ones – the ones that left a mark on the overall design of the system – are the adoption of the 2009 IA guidelines, the creation of the IAB, and the launch of the Action Programme for the measurement and reduction of administrative burdens. Below, I elaborate briefly on the issue of oversight on the Commission's IA activity. For an account of the relevance and methodological features of the Standard Cost Model, see Böheim, Renda *et al.* (2006), Renda (2008) and Allio and Renda (2010).

3.1.6. THE 2009 IMPACT ASSESSMENT GUIDELINES: FEATURES AND SCOPE OF THE EU IA SYSTEM

Reading the 2009 Impact Assessment Guidelines of the European Commission is an interesting way of discovering the current vision of the Brussels executive on the scope and purpose of the IA document, as well as grasping the differences with the US approach as described in OIRA Circular A-4. In particular, a number of aspects are worth being briefly recalled.

First, the definition of impact assessment in the US and EU differs noticeably. In the US, RIA is defined as "a tool regulatory agencies use to anticipate and evaluate the likely consequences of rules", which "provides a formal way of organizing the evidence on the key effects (good and bad) of the various alternatives that should be considered in developing regulations", and has a main motivation "to (1) learn if the benefits of an action are likely to justify the costs or (2) discover which of various possible alternatives would be the most cost-effective". In the EU Guidelines, IA is "a set of logical steps to be followed when you prepare policy proposals", and "a process that prepares evidence for political decision-makers on the advantages and disadvantages of possible policy options by assessing their potential impacts". This different definition supports the view that impact assessment in the EU is way less geared towards the quantification of impacts and the calculation of net benefits compared to the US one. As the US RIA is tailored to the production of secondary legislation, the element of "informing the legislator" is less present than in the EU, where the first recipients of most Commission IAs are the democratically elected EU institutions that are called to participate in the co-decision process.

Likewise, the EU impact assessment guidelines seem to imply that quantitative cost-benefit analysis or cost-effectiveness analysis are not always needed. For example, the Guidelines state that "[f]ull cost-benefit analysis should be used when the most significant part of both costs and benefits can be quantified and monetised, and when there is a certain degree of choice as regards the extent to which objectives should be met (as a function of the costs associated with the proposed measures)". At the same time, the Guidelines invite services to perform a multi-criteria assessment by keeping the three pillars (economic, social, environmental) separate:

> *As a first step, you should summarise the impacts of each option by area of impact (economic, social, environmental) and even by sub-impacts. In this summary, the impacts should not be aggregated; negative and positive impacts should be stated next to each other. In some cases, it may be possible to assess net impacts per area of impact and to provide an assessment of the overall net impact (positive impact minus negative impact) of each option. However, when this type of cumulative presentation of impacts is made, you should be careful not to give the impression that impacts are zero or low when, in fact, it is a case of significant positive and negative impacts of the same type having simply cancelled each other out.*

However, in another section the Guidelines also state that, in comparing the options, "[t]he aim of all interventions is of course to provide benefits that exceed any possible negative impacts. In the terminology of cost-benefit analysis this means that you should select options that promise the greatest net benefits". Accordingly, there is confusion in the Guidelines as regards the role of net benefits: if full cost-benefit analysis is not always needed and multi-criteria analysis is supposed to keep impacts separate, one could infer that net benefits are not the core of the IA document, and that the document is prepared to inform policymakers about a range of impacts of different kind. However, the need to select options that bring net benefits seems to clash with the previous statement.

The Guidelines are accompanied by as many as 14 annexes, which add a lot of detail to the information available to Commission services and external stakeholders as regards the expected content of an IA document. What seems to be missing in the Annexes – which describe, *i.a.*, several types of impacts and generic regulatory options to be considered – is an attention towards implementation, enforcement and compliance as key elements in the comparison of options. I will come back to this point in Section 4 below, in explaining how law and economics can inform better choices by shifting the focus beyond the formulation of a legal rule, into the effectiveness of its implementation in real life.

3.1.7. THE OVERSIGHT QUERELLE

The problem of strengthening oversight to improve the quality of IAs has long been discussed in Brussels. For example, already in the Final Report on the Business Impact Assessment (BIA) system – the "predecessor" of IA – the Commission had stated that "weaknesses identified in the BIA system, particularly as regards the identification of proposals that should be subject to BIA and the quality check on the analysis carried out, indicate that a dedicated structure is needed to support an impact assessment process. This is also in accordance with international practice." The Commission also acknowledged that such a structure should be given mandate for issuing guidance and checking that the quality of the analysis is satisfactory, and suggested that "[p]referably, it should be situated centrally within the Commission in order to ensure transparency and coordination". Further support to the creation of dedicated oversight bodies came from OECD since the late 1990s. OECD reports have always stated the importance of linking impact assessment to an oversight body as a key enabler of the success of regulatory impact analysis models.[135]

Back in 2005, when the Commission IA system was at the end of its pilot phase, Renda (2006) observed that stronger oversight and quality control was needed at EU level, especially in order to strengthen the incentives of DGs in the drafting of IAs, from a principal-agent perspective. Also scholars like Robert Hahn and Robert Litan were advocating for the creation of a "strong centralized oversight unit to help evaluate significant regulatory proposals" at EU level.[136] Hahn and Litan also specified that the centralized unit should have a status similar to the units it will have to discipline (i.e., lead DGs); that the unit should take on a leadership role in establishing information quality and regulatory guidelines both for EU and member state policymakers; that the unit should be given the power to challenge proposals that do not carry a sufficient or satisfactory estimate of net benefits; that it should publish its findings on the Internet; that it should publish a comprehensive annual report on the costs and

[135] For example, Josef Konvitz recalled that "[t]he relationship between an effective, comprehensive regulatory policy and the existence of a central oversight body appears to be strong." Konvitz, J. (2004), "The Institutional Context for Better Regulation", paper presented at the Conference on Simple is Better: Effective Regulation for a More Competitive Europe, Amsterdam, 7–8 October 2004.

[136] Hahn, R.W. and R.E. Litan, "Counting Regulatory Benefits and Costs: Lessons for the U.S. and Europe", Journal of International Economic Law, 2005, Vol. 8, No. 2, pp. 473–508.

benefits of EU regulation; and that it should be adequately funded in order to provide training for EU regulators and better information to MEPs.

The Commission's reaction was initially negative: internal quality checks through inter-service consultation and the internal coordination function of the Secretariat General were considered to be sufficient to ensure the quality of IAs produced. However, at the end of 2006 things started to change, and eventually an Impact Assessment Board (IAB) was created within the Secretariat General, grouping five top-level officials from the SecGen, DG Enterprise, DG Employment, DG Internal Market, DG Environment – although the members of the Board act in their personal capacity, not representing their own DGs.

3.1.7.1. Intra-institutional oversight: the Impact Assessment Board

The IAB was created with very little resources within the Secretariat general of the European Commission. Its members are essentially five (plus a small secretariat): the Deputy Secretary-General responsible for better regulation and one permanent official at Director level from the Commission departments with the most direct expertise in the three pillars – economic, social, environment – of integrated impact assessment, namely DG ENV, DG ECFIN, DG EMPL, DG ENTR. Interestingly, the DG dedicated to the Internal Market (MARKT) was not included in the IAB. And even more interestingly, the Members of the IAB perform their activity on top of their ordinary professional duties within their Directorate Generals: "members have been appointed in a personal capacity and on the basis of their expert knowledge".[137]

The opinions of the Board are not binding. As in the case of OIRA in the United States, the positioning of the IAB at the centre of government, in a position that is more *super partes* than *inter pares*, makes the binding nature of decisions almost superfluous: more important is the moral suasion that the IAB can exert on the DGs.[138] Ultimately, it is the Commission itself that decides whether or not an initiative should be adopted, and this also on the basis of the IA and the IAB opinion.

Since it began scrutinizing the Impact Assessments prepared by Commission services, the IAB has left a clear mark on the whole IA system in Brussels, also thanks to the energy and competence of its Chairman Alexander Italianer. As I had the chance to experience in several occasions, the principal-agent mechanism established with the creation of an internal oversight body has emerged as one of the key features of the Brussels IA system today, to the extent that Commission

137 See description at http://ec.europa.eu/governance/impact/iab/iab_en.htm.

138 On the differences and similarities in the role played by the OIRA and IAB in the US and EU, respectively, see Wiener, J.B. and A. Alemanno (2010), *Comparing Regulatory Oversight Bodies Across the Atlantic: The Office of Information and Regulatory Affairs in the US and the Impact Assessment Board in the EU,* in Rose-Ackerman, S. and P. Lindseth, (eds.), "Comparative Administrative Law", Edward Elgar.

officials in charge of drafting IA documents eventually do it "for the IAB", rather than for the EU institutions that will have to discuss the proposals. And many of them are indeed terrified by the prospect of having the "fab five" scrutinizing every detail of their IAs.

In the first three years of activity IAB opinions have focused mostly on problems in the analysis of impacts, on the definition of the baseline and objectives, on the identification, analysis and comparison of policy options, as well as on procedural issues and on the content of the executive summary. Overall, the impact of the IAB seems positive, although many commentators and industry stakeholders consider that stronger, possibly independent oversight bodies would be needed at EU level.

However, the level of administrative complexity associated with the creation of a new independent agency in charge of external oversight is certainly high. A suitable alternative to the creation of an oversight body would be an increased transparency of the Commission's policy process – in particular, the Commission could publish draft IAs for consultation before the IAB opinion, so that the industry could be given the chance to comment on the quality of the data, on the selection of policy options, and on the analysis itself, before the IAB gives its opinion on the quality of the document. This would also be important since the IAB, even if composed by very experienced members, cannot possess the knowledge needed to scrutinize the quality of the substantial analysis provided by Commission DGs in their IAs; and also since the limited staff available to the IAB, according to a recent draft report circulated by the European Court of Auditors, leaves its Members an average four person/days to read each draft IA and comment.[139]

So far, so good. However, as the Commission's effort towards expanding the use of IA becomes stronger, and the number of IAs produced every year increase at breakneck pace (see *infra*, Figure 8), the sustainability of the IAB model as it is already comes into question: could such a small body sustain the review of so many IAs per year? Is it efficient and cost-effective to have the IAB scrutinize each and every IA, and would this have an impact on the quality of the individual opinions issued by the IAB? In some respects, this recalls the situation of the OIRA in the US before the Clinton administration decided to introduce a minimum threshold for mandatory RIA. Before Executive Order 12,866, issued in 1993, with just 40 employees, the US central oversight body had reviewed on average more than 2,200 federal regulations every year, and could not sustain the burden anymore without losing quality. In the case of the IAB, with an equivalent of 15 full time staff, scrutiny of a draft impact assessment has to be finalized within an average of 3–4 weeks, and in case of urgency, this has been shortened to 5–7 working days in 2007. This also means that the IAB has to work in parallel at least on 2–3 IAs to evaluate the quality of all IAs foreseen for 2008.

[139] See the Report of the European Court of Auditors, *Impact Assessment in the EU Institutions: do they support decision-making?*, Special Report 3/2010.

Apart from sustaining such a mounting workload, the internal oversight model chosen by the Commission only ensures, to some degree, quality control. This, looking at the IAB's opinion issued so far, mostly revolves around whether all impacts have been adequately taken into account, whether the IA at hand followed the guidelines, whether case-by-case adjustments are needed, and whether more quantification would be appropriate.[140] As reported by the IAB, in 2007 the most common recommendations referred to the selection and/or analysis of the policy options; the need for reinforcement of the analysis of social impacts and distributional impacts, as part of a more balanced approach to the three pillars of impact assessment (economic, social, environmental); the need to substantiate the tests of whether the principles of subsidiarity and proportionality are respected; and the need for analysis of simplification potential, presentation of corresponding benefits and calculation of impact on administrative burden (including measurement with the EU Standard Cost Model, whenever administrative burden impacts are likely to be significant).

This also means that the IAB performs only some of the key functions that could be assigned to an oversight body to ensure the quality of lawmaking, *i.e.* guidance, consulting, challenge, coordination of existing activities and yearly reporting. The IAB does very little on advocacy, training and keeping institutional relations. Of these, the advocacy role seems particularly crucial, and could be conferred with more emphasis on the IAB, especially at the early stage of the policy process, in which the depth and scope of analysis, together with compliance with the principle of subsidiarity, should be thoroughly assessed. Advocacy may also include the increased use of (variants of) tools such as "prompt letters", such as the ones issued by the OIRA in the US, or "Legislative Reform Orders" in the UK.

The "missing functions" of the IAB as an oversight body are mostly related to the often recalled problem of the lack of "identity" of the EU IA system. This question can also be translated into the usual *querelle* on who controls the policy process in the EU. This problem, originally mentioned already by Giandomenico Majone in 1999 and recently highlighted also by Radaelli and Meuwese (2008), remains one of the key pending issues within the whole better regulation agenda of the European Union. As will be argued in Section 4 below, the answer most probably lies in the delicate balance between; (i) the need to empower the IAB with the more concrete role of translating Council priorities into proposals for concrete action; (ii) the need to expand the Commission's competencies throughout the co-decision procedure, especially in the revision of IAs that are severely amended by the Parliament and/or the Council; and (iii) the need for more control over a more powerful Commission.

140 See the Report of the Impact Assessment Board for 2007, available online at http://ec.europa.eu/governance/impact/docs/key_docs/sec_2008_0120_en.pdf.

3.2. EVALUATING THE PRACTICE OF IMPACT ASSESSMENT IN EU INSTITUTIONS: A LOOK AT THE EVIDENCE

The EU experience with IA is considered as being fairly successful, but margins for improvement certainly exist. As confirmed also by the 70 opinions gathered by the Commission during the consultation on the future of smart regulation that ran between 23 April and 25 June 2010, the issues to be tackled in the years to come include the need to improve the methodology and soundness of the economic analysis, the efficient use of resources devoted to Impact Assessment and ex post evaluation in the European Commission, the urge to involve other EU institutions and national governments in the drafting of IAs, etc.[141] These views also echo the comments formulated over the past years by a number of commentators, which were a bit less generous than the *ex post* evaluation carried out for the Commission by TEP. For example, in 2006 Ragnar Löfstedt argued that the EU better regulation agenda, after reaching a peak, had eventually "plateau-ed", after attempts to fully transform it into a paradigm for EU policymaking.[142] Wiener (2007) suggested a number of changes in the EU better regulation agenda – on which he expressed a positive overall judgment – entailing the adoption of strategies such as "enlarging the scope of impact assessment and benefit-cost analysis toward a broader, 'warmer' and more even-handed application of these tools", "moving beyond a narrow focus on cutting administrative costs or simplification for their own sake, toward criteria that address benefits as well as costs" and "centralizing expert oversight so that impact assessments actually influence decisions, both to say 'no' to bad ideas and 'yes' to good ideas". In 2008, the final policy paper of the EU-funded EVIA project suggested, *i.a.*, that "IAs should support the decision-making throughout the whole policy cycle", and that "it seems useful to define an overall broad scope, but to implement it through targeted analytical methods and tools". Finally, Radaelli and Meuwese (2008) argued that the future of IA in the European Commission still faced a number of hard questions, mostly related to the need to define who controls the policy process at EU level.[143] In several papers, Claudio Radaelli (together with several co-authors) argued that the IA system in the EU should be more targeted, as it eventually applies to too many policy proposals, of

---

141 The consultation document and opinions expressed can be found at http://ec.europa.eu/governance/better_regulation/smart_regulation/consultation_en.htm.

142 See Löfstedt, R. (2007), *The 'Plateau-ing' of the European Better Regulation Agenda: An Analysis of Activities Carried out by the Barroso Commission,* Journal of Risk Research, vol. 10 (4), 423–447.

143 See Radaelli, C.M. and A. C. M.Meuwese (2010), *Hard questions, and equally hard solutions? Proceduralization through impact assessment in the European Union,* West European Politics 33, 136–53.

which only a few would actually deserve an IA.[144] Likewise, Meuwese (2008) makes the case for IA as a tool to inform the policymaker, but with an elusive meaning – in some cases taking the form of "speaking the truth to power", in others as "letting stakeholders have a say in the policy process".[145] Finally, suggestions for reform of the IA system in the EU are also contained in Renda (2008) and Renda *et al.* (2009).

One methodology that is frequently used to assess the quality of IAs – better, their completeness and their respondence to the IA guidelines – is the scorecard analysis introduced in this field by Robert Hahn.[146] Below, I describe some of the early attempts to provide a scorecard analysis of Commission IAs, and then provide an updated scorecard on all the IAs published by the Commission between 2003 and 2009, with the ultimate purpose of tracking progress and identifying weaknesses in the current system.

3.2.1. PREVIOUS SCORECARDS AND EVALUATIONS

Scholars that have undertaken a tentative assessment of the first IAs undertaken by European Commission's DGs have reported quite puzzling results. For example, Lee and Kirkpatrick (2004) have scrutinized the first six Extended IAs (as they were called at that time) completed by the Commission in 2003, reporting a number of weaknesses and an overall heterogeneity in the quality of the assessment performed. Methodological weaknesses included an unclear description of the problem, obscure ranking of the objectives, a relatively narrow range of alternative policy options considered, an unbalanced coverage of different types of impact (*e.g.* economic, social, environmental), unreliable assessment findings, deficiencies in the presentation of report findings, insufficient time and resources available to complete a sufficiently detailed analysis, lack of transparency in the process and inadequate arrangements for external consultation.[147]

---

144 Radaelli, C.M. and A.C.M. Meuwese (2009), *Better Regulation in Europe: Between Public Management and Regulatory Reform*, Public Administration 87, 639–54. Radaelli, C.M., F. De Francesco and V.E. Troeger (2007) *The implementation of Regulatory Impact Assessment in Europe*, Paper presented at the European Network for Better Regulation, Workshop on Regulatory Quality: Developing tools, approaches and sources for research on impact assessment, University of Exeter, Exeter 27 and 28 March 2007.

145 More in detail, Meuwese (2008) distinguishes between four different meanings of RIA as "instrument that informs the decisionmaker": (a) to speak the truth to power; (b) to use RIA to highlight trade-offs in lawmaking; (c) to provide a forum for the input of a wide range of stakeholders; and (d) to give reasons for legislative decisions. Meuwese then argues that there is no agreement among EU institutions about which notion is really predominant, which lead RIA to constantly fluctuate in search of an identity. See Meuwese (2008), *supra* note 22.

146 See *supra* note 24 for an extensive list of references.

147 Lee, N. and C. Kirkpatrick (2004), *A Pilot Study of the Quality of European Commission Extended Impact Assessments*, IARC Working Paper Series No. 8, 2004, p. 27.

Similarly, Vibert (2004) analyzed the first 20 Extended IAs performed by the Commission, by applying a scorecard approach similar to that developed by Robert Hahn.[148] Out of 20 Extended IAs, only 10 quantified (and only 9 monetized) costs and benefits, only 11 carried data on market alternatives and only 2 contained a provision for peer review. Finally, all 20 proposals subjected to IA were finally approved, and 10 were re-designed as a consequence of the results obtained in the IA process. The author concluded that the EU IA model deserved a positive initial evaluation, in particular because it added a lesson-learning dimension to the formulation of Commission's legislative initiatives. However, the unreliability and heterogeneity of the cost-benefit analysis severely undermined the actual contribution that the new procedure can provide to EU competitiveness and sustainable development in the medium range.

Other early scorecards include Opoku and Jordan (2004), who analyze all the 41 Extended IAs completed by lead DGs in 2003 and 2004, by focusing in particular on the consideration of the external dimension and on the detailed scoring of a more limited set of ExIAs, related to the sugar regime, the tobacco regime, the REACH Directive, the Kyoto Protocol, the 'Youth in Action' program and the 'Lifelong learning' program. They concluded that a number of measures would be required to improve the consideration of the external dimension in Extended IAs. These included "updating the guidelines with more explicit instructions to consider the external dimension in all sections of the IA; the clarification of which aspects of the guidelines are mandatory and which are discretionary; the allocation of resources for undertaking the IAs; the clear application of selection criteria for choosing policy proposals to undergo an extended IA; and also the thorough consultation of all interested parties including DGs and outside actors (especially NGOs)."[149]

Lussis (2004) applies a check-list model for the purpose of comparing 13 Extended IAs completed between 2003 and 2004. He finds that "most of the ExIA define policy alternatives and assess them. However, there is obviously a 'methodological hole' in the areas of impact identification, prediction and

---

148 F. Vibert (2004), *The EU's New System of Regulatory Impact Assessment – A Scorecard*, European Policy Forum, London. See also Robert W. Hahn and Patrick M. Dudley 82004), *How Well Does the Government Do Cost-Benefit Analysis?*, Working Paper No. 04-01, AEI-Brookings Joint Center for Regulatory Studies, Washington, D.C.; Hahn, R.W. and R.E. Litan (2005), *Counting Regulatory Benefits and Costs: Lessons for the U.S. and Europe*, Journal of International Economic Law, Vol. 8, No. 2, 2005, pp. 473–508; and, for a more recent comparison of scorecards for US and EU, see Cecot, C., Hahn, R.W., Renda, A. and Schrefler, L. (2008), *An Evaluation of the Quality of Impact Assessment in the European Union with Lessons for the U.S. and the EU*, Regulation & Governance, Vol.2, No. 4, December 2008, pp. 405–424(20).

149 See C. Opoku and A. Jordan (2004), *Impact Assessment in the EU: A Global Sustainable Development Perspective*, paper presented at the Berlin Conference on the Human Dimension of Global Environmental Change, 3–4 December 2004 (available at www.fu-berlin.de/ffu/akumwelt/bc2004/download/opoku_jordan_f.pdf).

assessment. In addition, ... most ExIAs do not bring up a clear comparison of the alternatives regarding the impact assessment."[150]

More recently, Renda (2006) compared empirical results on the first 75 IAs completed by the Commission in 2003–2005 with the expectations raised at political level, and concluded that the first years had resulted in a "sea of disappointment". The same paper concluded that the system had to be revised, *i.a.* by strengthening central oversight. Similar results were found in more recent years by Cecot, Hahn, Renda and Schrefler (2007), who draw some lessons for the US from a scorecard analysis of Commission IAs completed between 2003 and 2006.

3.2.2. AN UPDATED SCORECARD

The European Commission has achieved significant results in mainstreaming IA into its policymaking process, though important margins for improvement remain. At the end of 2009, the European Commission had completed 475 IAs, distributed as in Figure 8 below.

Figure 8. Number of IAs per year at the European Commission, 2003–2010

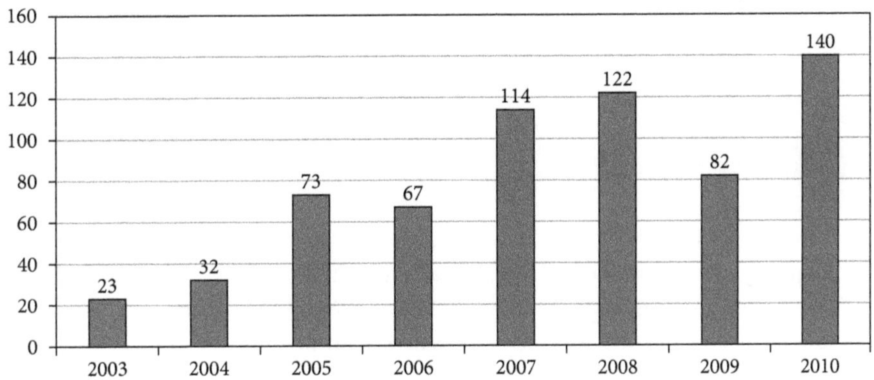

Source: Author's elaboration (2010 data estimated from Commission roadmaps).

The number of IAs has been increasing significantly since 2006, although 2009 marked a slow-down due mostly to the transition towards a new European Commission and a new European Parliament. In 2010, at least 140 IAs are expected according to the available 2010 roadmaps.[151]

---

150 See B. Lussis (2004), *EU Extended Impact Assessment Review*, Institut pour un Développement Durable Working Paper, 9 December 2004 (available at http://users.skynet.be/idd/documents/EIDDD/WP01.pdf).

151 See http://ec.europa.eu/governance/impact/planned_ia/roadmaps_2010_en.htm.

However, not all Commission DGs have been involved in the process in the same way. Figure 9 below shows that some DGs – *i.e.* Transport and Energy (TREN), Environment (ENV), Justice Liberty and Security (JLS), Enterprise and Industry (ENTR) and Internal Market (MARKT) – completed more than 60% of all Commission IAs, and other DGs only performed a few IAs over the 2003–2009 timeframe.

Figure 9. Number of IAs per DG, at December 2009

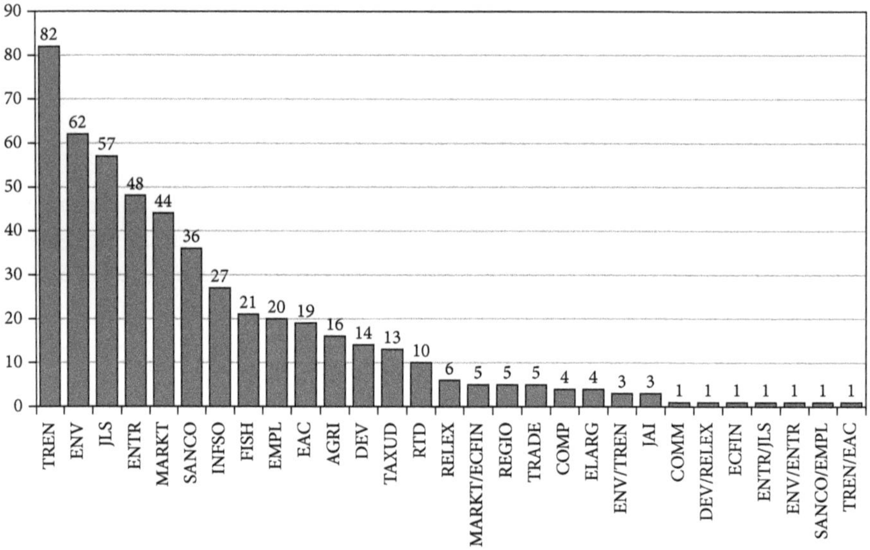

Source: Author's elaboration.

In any event, available data confirm that the Commission IAs have become more complete and transparent over time. In particular, a scorecard recently completed by the Centre for European Policy Studies (unpublished) on the 475 IAs completed between 2003 and 2009 revealed a number of interesting insights, which are summarized below.

3.2.2.1. *Types of proposals*

An analysis of the types of initiatives subject to IA in the European Commission in the period 2003–2009 reveals that, with the increase in the volume of IAs performed, the percentage accounted for by cross-cutting policy proposals (CC) has been decreasing. Figure 10 below shows that, on the contrary, non-binding communications (COM) and narrow policy initiatives (NA) account for the lion's share of Commission's impact assessments. This is particularly important, especially as regards the application of the principle of proportionate analysis and the consequence depth of analysis and degree of quantification to be expected.

Figure 10. Type of initiative subject to IA, 2003–2009

(a) Type of proposal

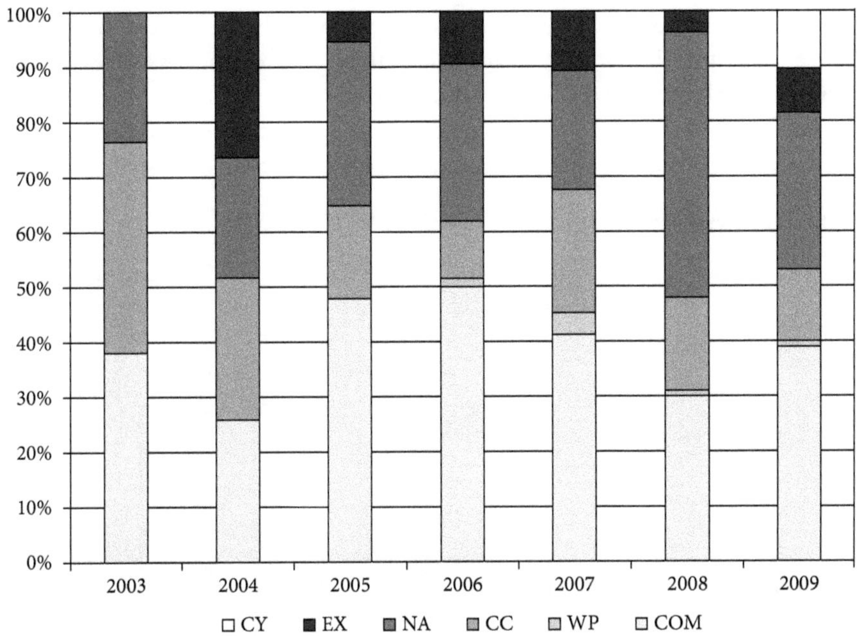

(b) Type of binding proposal

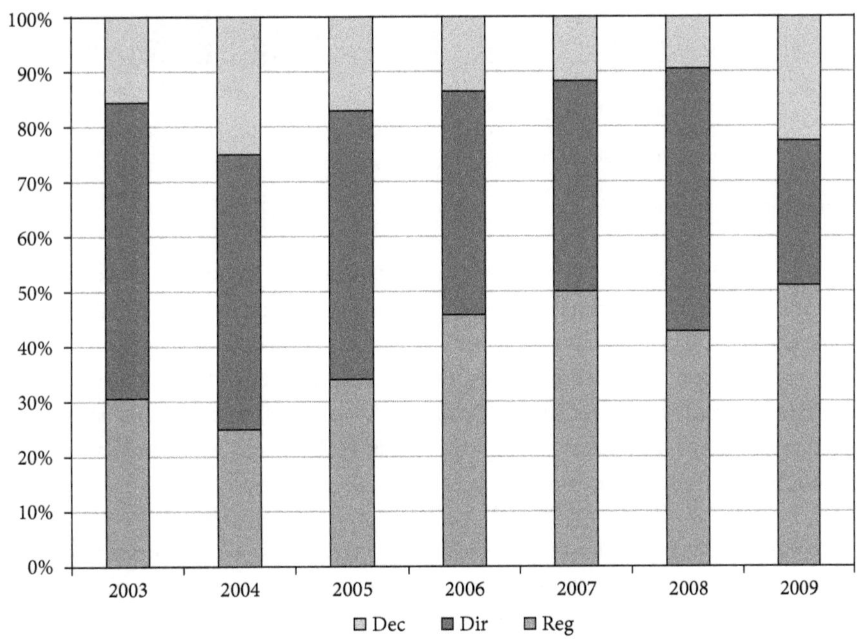

Source: Author's elaboration.

3.2.2.2. *Assessment of impacts*

The assessment (qualitative or quantitative) of economic, social and environmental impacts has become more systematic between 2003 and 2009. Figure 11 below shows that in 2005, less than 30% of the IAs assessed the environmental impact, whereas economic and social impacts were considered in less than 70% of the IAs. In 2009, environmental impacts were assessed in 60% of the IAs and economic and social impacts were assessed in almost all IAs.

Figure 11. Assessment of impacts, Commission IAs, 2003–2009

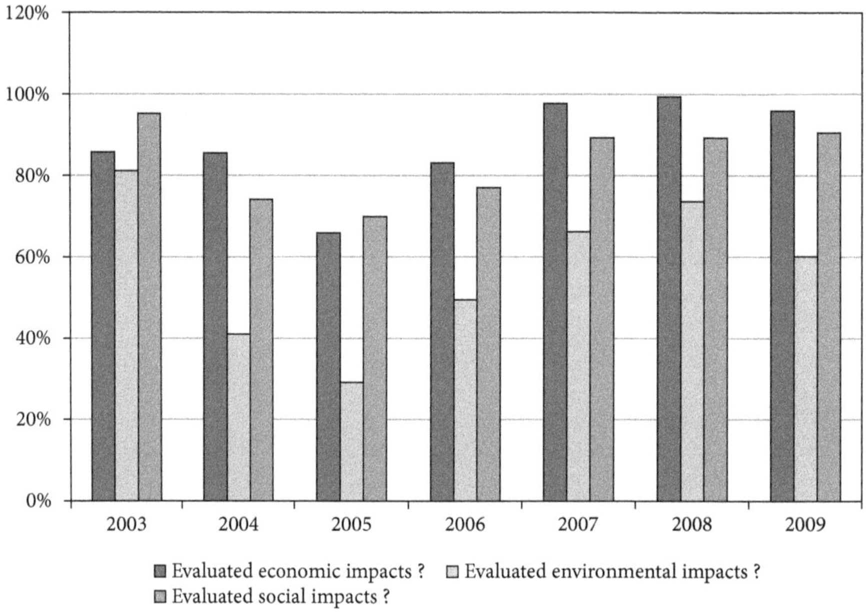

Source: Author's elaboration.

More in detail, figure 12 below shows some data on the frequency of assessment of economic impacts, including the impact on competitiveness, on SMEs, on the single market and the macroeconomic impacts of the proposal. The figure shows some remarkable improvements in the completeness of IA documents: for example, the fact that more than 60% of all IAs on binding proposals carried an assessment of the impact on competitiveness is, by itself, a remarkable result, although the quality of such assessment is not always superb.

A similar trend is visible looking at social impacts, as in figure 14. Impacts such as health, employment, social inclusion and fundamental rights are increasingly considered by the European Commission DGs when drafting Impact Assessments.

Figure 12. Frequency of assessment of specific economic impacts

(a) – All IAs

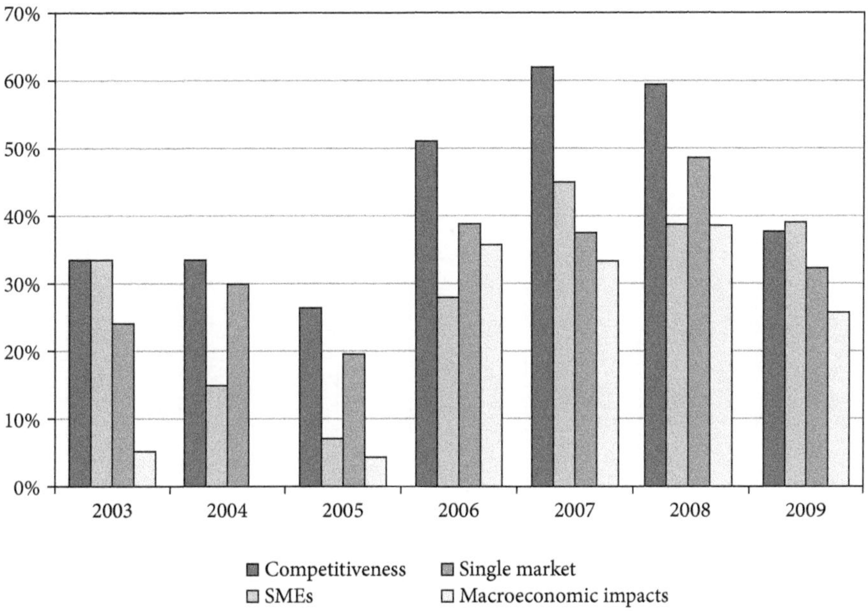

(b) only IAs on proposed binding policy initiatives

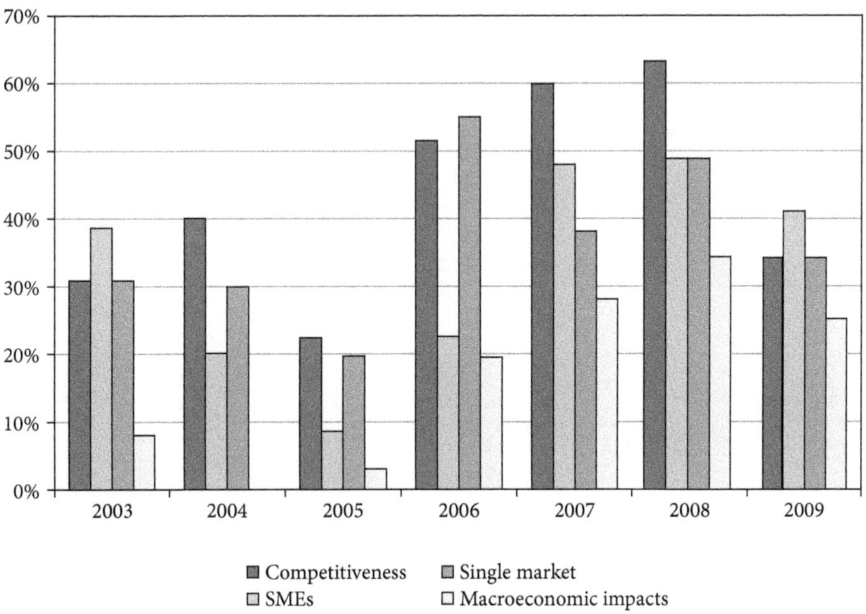

Source: Author's elaboration.

Figure 13. Frequency of assessment of specific social impacts

(a) – All IAs

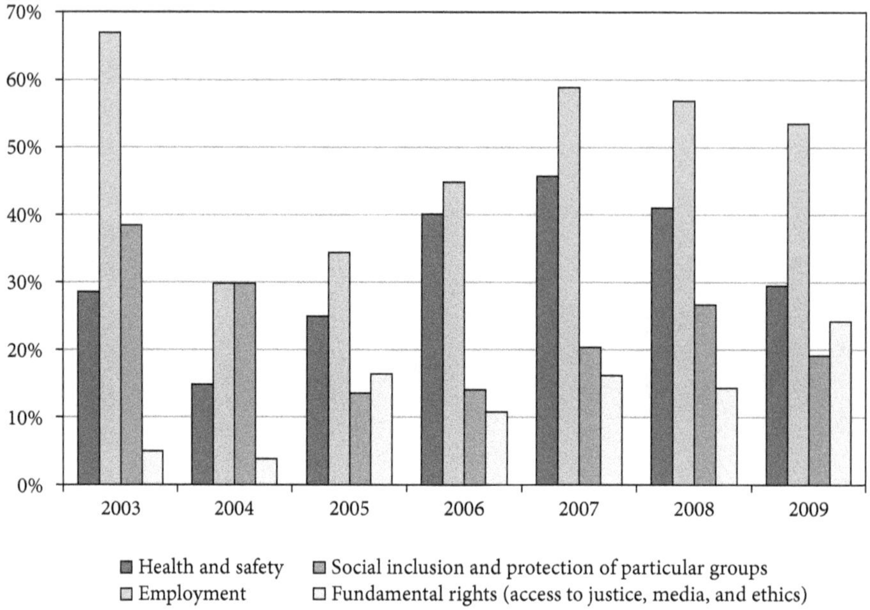

(b) only IAs on proposed binding policy initiatives

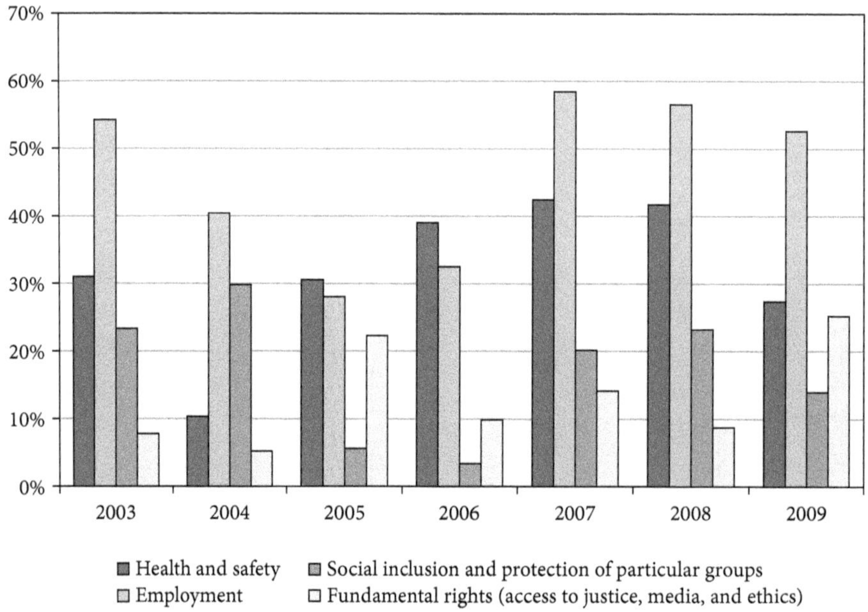

Source: Author's elaboration.

Finally, environmental impacts have also become more frequently assessed by the Commission DGs, although the trend towards greater frequency of assessment is less evident than for economic and social impacts.

Figure 14. Frequency of assessment of specific environmental impacts

(a) – All IAs

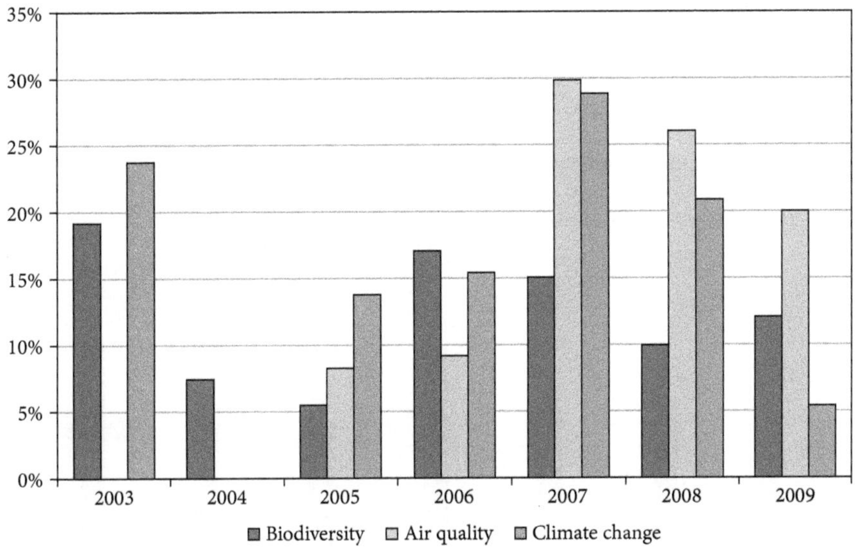

(b) only IAs on proposed binding policy initiatives

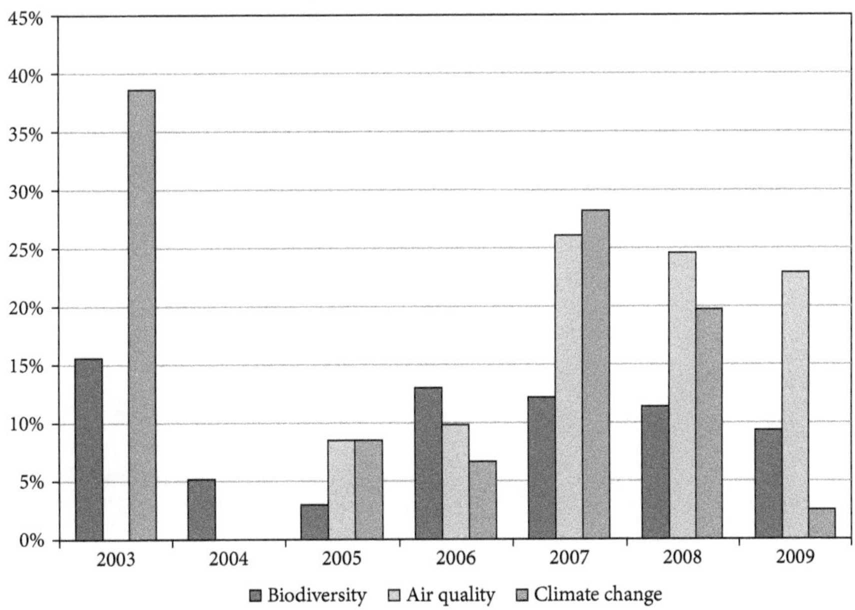

Source: Author's elaboration.

3.2.2.3. *Assessment of alternatives*

The assessment of alternatives seems to have become more systematic. As shown in figure 15 below, the costs and benefits of alternative policy options are more frequently quantified and monetized in Commission IAs, especially compared to the 2004–2005 period, in which the assessment of alternatives was very limited. Today, in approximately 30% of the cases the European Commission provides an indication of the net benefits or cost-effectiveness of the policy options considered – a figure that must be appraised also in light of the fact that not all Commission IAs are related to binding policy actions.

Figure 15. Assessment of alternative policy options, Commission IAs, 2003–2009

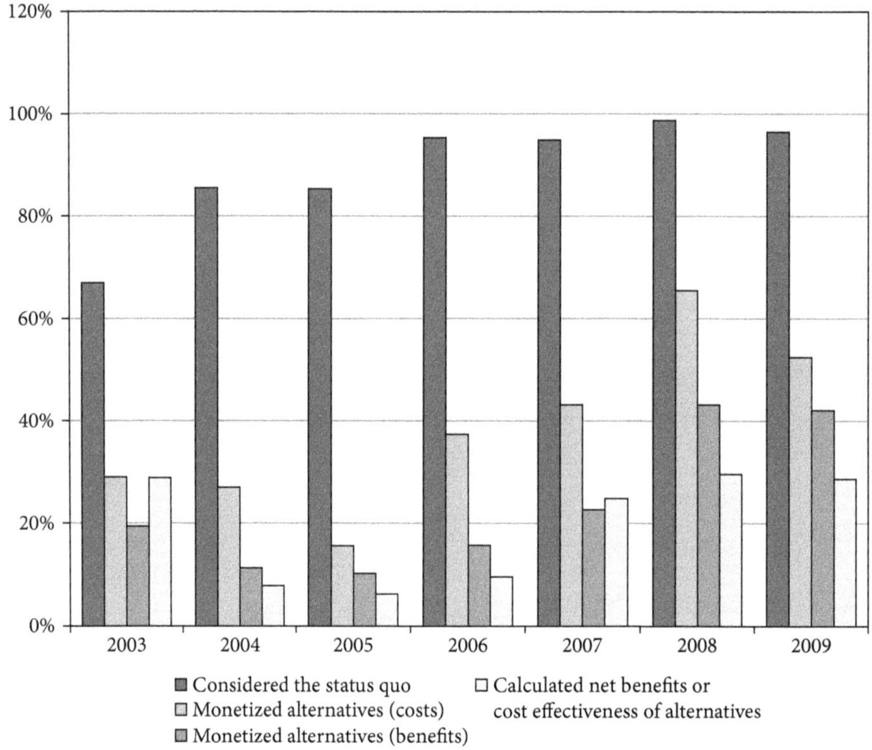

Source: Author's elaboration.

3.2.2.4. *Methodology*

Available data confirm that the Commission IA system is less geared towards cost-benefit analysis and the adoption of similar (but simpler) methodologies such as cost-effectiveness analysis.

Figure 16. Net benefits and cost-effectiveness calculation

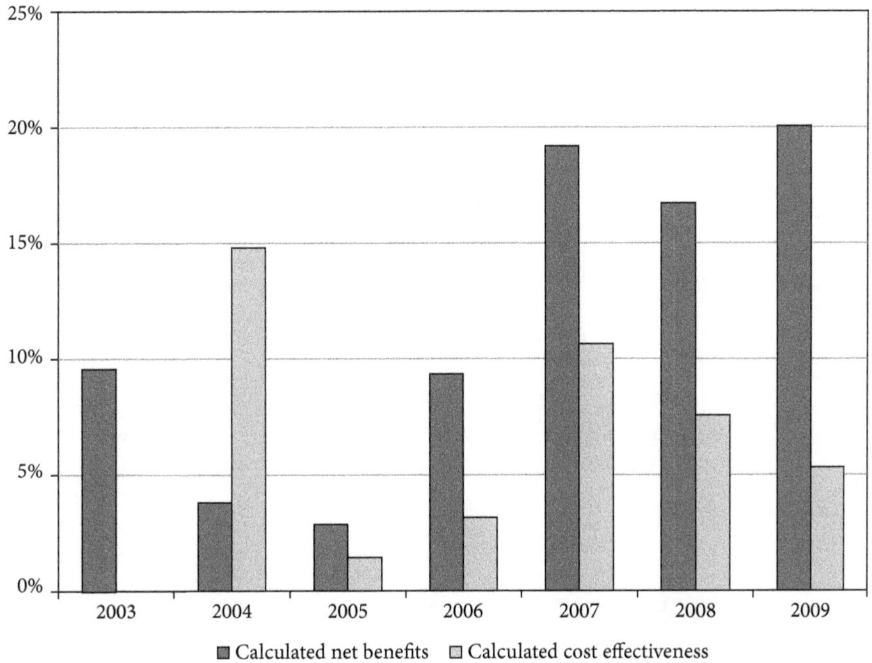

Source: Author's elaboration.

The degree of sophistication of Commission IAs is anyway on the increase. Figure 17 shows the number of IAs that embarked in difficult economic analyses such as the calculation of the number of lives saved by a given policy option is increasing year on year. At the same time, the Commission makes more use of discount rates when assessing future impacts; performs risk assessment more often; and offers a sensitivity analysis to check the robustness of its assumptions.

Figure 17. Sophistication of Commission IAs, 2003–2009 (selected indicators)

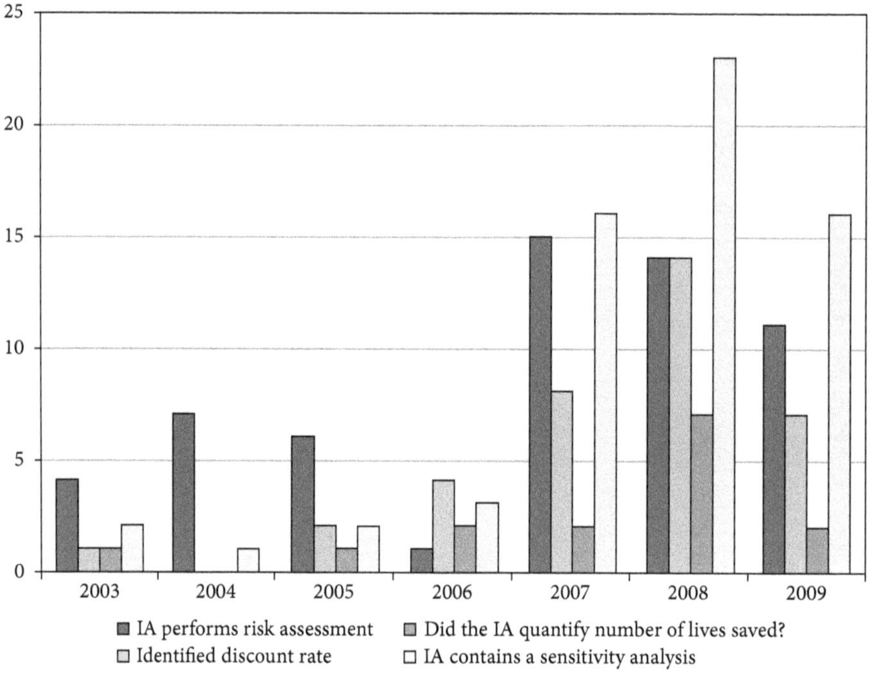

Source: Author's elaboration.

3.2.3. OTHER EU INSTITUTIONS

While the European Commission has managed to make systematic use of IA tools, it is no mystery that other EU institutions such as the European Parliament and the Council have largely failed to achieve the objective of performing assessments on their major amendments on Commission's proposals, despite their commitments expressed in the 2003 "Inter-Institutional agreement on better lawmaking", and in the 2005 "Common Approach to Impact Assessment". This also means that European Commission IAs, once the proposal is amended during the co-decision procedure, lose their representativeness and their usefulness for potential users such as national governments.

The European Parliament has gradually replaced the practice of IA with the commissioning of external background studies and briefing notes, which normally are not linked with the original Commission IA, and do not feature the structure of an IA document. The Council is reportedly making more use of Commission IAs, but after a pilot project on a limited number of amendments back in 2004, has dropped completely the production of IAs.

In a recent publication, Renda *et al.* (2009) debate whether the failure of the Common Approach to IA should lead to a new approach to inter-institutional dialogue at the EU level.[152] Below, we briefly discuss this issue together with the other emerging trends in EU impact assessment.

3.3. EU IMPACT ASSESSMENT: TOWARDS REFORM?

The trajectory of Impact Assessment in the European Union is at least tortuous, and a mix of success and failure. The main success lies in the fact that Impact Assessment is – at least partly – changing the way in which bureaucrats in Brussels think about policymaking and the need to motivate the need for policy action, and the form of action that is preferable to others. Only partly, because instances of IAs that fall randomly on the shoulders of unaware officials who have little or no knowledge of economics, as well as cases in which IA is done with a passive box-ticking attitude are still frequent in many DGs. In addition, the fact that certain DGs (MARKT, ENTR) are working on their own version of the guidelines to improve the quality of their own IAs is symptomatic of a drive towards improvement and increased IA quality.

The main problem that remains inside the European Commission's IA system is the lack of a clear focus. Being clear that the EU IA system does not follow the same logic of the US one, and is less geared towards the monetization of all impacts through Kaldor-Hicks cost-benefit analysis, it remains unclear whether the IA document produced by Commission DGs and validated by the Board should abide by any specific methodology or need for quantification. In other words, it is unclear what is the benchmark when the IAB scrutinizes IAs, if not the (still quite generic) IA Guidelines. Perhaps, given the fact that the European Commission has several goals and a generalized lack of policy coordination across different actions, the lack of focus of the IA document simply reflects the lack of policy coherence in Brussels.

To be sure, the IA document, far from being a panacea, let alone a piece of highly scientific analysis, is now becoming a sort of synecdoche, a document that contains a summary of all the competing and contrasting interests that surround the formulation and discussion of the policy proposal. This, in turn, makes it very difficult to distinguish the IA document from an explanatory memorandum, even if decorated with tables, some numbers and bit more structure. The fact that the IA document does not adopt a clearly recognizable viewpoint – for example, the result of a quantitative cost-benefit analysis – weakens the process irremediably.

---

[152] Renda, A. *et al.* (2009), *Policymaking in the EU; achievements, challenges and proposals for reform*, Centre for European Policy Studies, Brussels.

In addition, the fact that the IA system is still relatively weak in Brussels reflect the fact that the European Commission is still relatively weak from an institutional perspective. If the IA could be used by the Commission to resist amendments imposed by the Parliament and the Council, which clearly go against the economic evidence, then the role of the Commission would partly become that of real "guardian of the Treaty", and at the same time watchdog in charge of monitoring the behavior of other EU institutions and ensure that, whenever they seriously amend a Commission proposal against the evidence, they do it by taking full political responsibility for such choice.

Finally, the European Commission needs to re-organize its IA system to make sure it uses resources efficiently, and possibly in a more targeted way. The increased amount of IAs that are being produced by Commission DGs threatens the sustainability of the IAB: in addition, the principle of proportionate analysis seems to be followed very imperfectly, and Commission IAs do not seem to respond to the well-know adagio of "asking the right things, at the right time, in the right sequence" that was mentioned already in the Mandelkern Report. More in detail, the sequence of questions that the Commission asks during the policy cycle (from the impact assessment of the White Paper through to the IA on a framework directive, and the IAs on implementing regulations) sometimes translates into overlapping questions and cases in which the Commission, after having gone through a full-fledged RIA in an early stage, reinvents the wheel in subsequent stages.

The Commission seems to have taken action to solve some of these problems with the Communication on Smart Regulation in the European Union, adopted in October 2010.[153] There, the Commission announces its intention to "close the policy cycle" by providing for *ex post* evaluations of existing legislation before any new *ex ante* IA can be performed. Likewise, the Commission plans to strengthen the ex ante consideration of transposition, implementation, enforcement, and make use of implementation plans at national level. At the same time, the Commission wishes to move beyond the narrow focus of current IAs, which necessarily refers to individual policy initiatives, and engage more in "fitness checks" covering entire policy domains – the first ones were launched in the fields of environment, transport, employment/social policy and industrial policy, but new areas will be identified in 2011.

But obviously, the real problem with impact assessment does not reside in Berlaymont or Charlemagne, but rather inside Justus Lipsius. The fact that the IA document is never updated during the co-decision procedure is a major obstacle to the development of multi-level evidence-based policymaking in the EU. And this is also a major challenge for the Barroso Commission in the years to come.

153 COM(2010)543, 11 October 2010.

In Section 6 I will come back to some of these problems to offer a solution that is grounded in law and economics, as well as in past experience with the IA system in Europe. Section 3.4 below briefly illustrates the current state of Impact Assessment development at national level in EU member states.

3.4. RIA IN EU MEMBER STATES: EMERGING TRENDS

In the international regulatory reform community, as well as in many circles of political science, Regulatory Impact Assessment (RIA) is considered as one of the most useful and effective tools for the scrutiny of the flow of regulation, as well as a powerful regulatory governance instrument. Several countries around the world feature some form of RIA, which may serve different purposes depending on the context in which the procedure is introduced. Compared with other tools such as the increasingly widespread measurement of administrative burdens, consultation procedures or *ex post* monitoring and evaluation, RIA appears to require a more profound change in the culture of public administrations and bureaucrats, and has therefore encountered significant problems in its implementation around the world. From an international perspective, the first countries that managed to mainstream RIA into their policymaking process were notably common law countries, especially within the broader context of public management reforms – *e.g.* the New Public Management wave in the UK, the Reinventing Government in the United States.[154] Other countries, in particular civil law countries, have committed resources to the development of *ex ante* RIA practices, but for many years have failed to fully implement RIA for a substantial part of their flow of legislation. Accordingly, a conspicuous adoption-implementation gap has emerged, as observed by several scholars in the past few years.[155]

Against this background, the international RIA landscape appears more like a patchwork of very different experiences and alternate fortunes, rather than a consistent and parallel development. One scholar has compared the practice of comparing RIA systems around the world to that of comparing apples and pears, given the existing divergence in the way national governments have attempted to mainstream this procedure in their policymaking process.[156]

More in detail, RIA systems differ according to a number of characteristics, including the following:

---

154 See Renda, *Impact Assessment in the EU*, Centre for European Policy Studies, Brussels (2006).

155 See Radaelli, De Francesco and Troeger, *supra* note 144. And Radaelli, C. M. (2005). *Diffusion without convergence: How political context shapes the adoption of regulatory impact assessment*. Journal of European Public Policy, 12(5), 924–943.

156 Radaelli, C. M. (2009). *Desperately seeking regulatory impact assessments: Diary of a reflective researcher*. Evaluation, 15(1), 31–48.

- *Scope*. Some countries have introduced mandatory RIA only for secondary legislation (*e.g.* the United States), whereas other legal systems require it also for primary legislation or even for non-binding policy documents (*e.g.* the European Union). Some countries limit RIA to certain sectors (*e.g.* network industries, or proposals to implement EU legislation), whereas others apply them to all the new legal proposals. Some countries have enacted thresholds to select the proposals that should undergo RIA (*e.g.*, the US, the UK), whereas in other systems there is no such threshold, and the selection follows other principles, including that of proportionate analysis (*e.g.* the EU).
- *Purpose*. In some countries RIA serves the main purpose of enabling the monitoring of the performance of bureaucrats, within a principal-agent scheme between the government and its administration (*e.g.* the United States). To the contrary, in other legal systems the main purpose has been in-house learning (the EU), or specific targets to contrast poverty (Ireland), reduce administrative burdens (the Netherlands, Germany), allow for dialogue with the business sector (Sweden) or even the reduction of corruption through greater transparency and accountability (as in several developing countries).
- *Methodology and quantification*. Different scopes and different purposes are also reflected in a different emphasis being placed on the quantification and monetization of impacts in different countries. Eastern European countries, such as Poland and in particular Ukraine, have traditionally placed more emphasis on RIA as an explanatory document, and as such have made limited use of quantitative cost-benefit analysis in their RIA documents; on the other hand, the United States have devoted growing efforts to the monetization of impacts, including non-market goods such as biodiversity or the value of human lives, in order to increase the transparency of decision-making and the measurability of impacts over time. Also the European Commission has strengthened the emphasis on quantitative analysis since 2005, and later with the appointment of the Impact Assessment Board.
- *Governance and oversight*. In several countries there is a single, dedicated unit nested in the centre of government, with the role of consultant, advisor and/or adversarial gatekeeper for the departments, ministries or other bodies in charge of drafting the RIA document. In some countries the whole RIA process is managed by the Cabinet Office (*e.g.*, the UK, Italy), in others by the Ministry of Economy or Finance (*e.g.*, the Netherlands, Slovakia), in others by the Ministry of Justice (*e.g.*, Hungary) or the Ministry of Interior (the Czech Republic), depending on the purpose and scope of the RIA system. In addition, some countries have appointed *ad hoc* external oversight bodies in charge of monitoring the RIA activity performed by the government: in most cases these bodies – such as Actal in the Netherlands, the *Normenkontrollrat*

in Germany or the Regulatory Policy Commission in the United Kingdom – have a more specific mandate confined to the measurement of administrative burdens or the compliance costs of legislation. Finally, in some countries other bodies, such as courts of auditors, perform an *ex post* oversight function (*e.g.* the NAO in the UK, the GAO in the US, the Dutch Court of Audit, the European Court of Auditors, etc.).

- *Effective implementation.* Past research projects such as the European Network for Better Regulation (ENBR) have shown that, despite a general trend towards the adoption of the RIA system, only a fistful of European countries have effectively reached a significant number of RIAs published (see Section 3 below). Cases in which RIA has emerged as a key step in the policy process include to some extent the United Kingdom and non-EU countries such as Ukraine. In all other countries, the situation was less encouraging, although the past 2–3 years have shown some sign of development in countries like Sweden, Ireland, the Netherlands and, most recently, France.

Compared to the progress achieved by the European Commission in *ex ante* impact assessment, most EU Member States appear to significantly lag behind. While one country, the UK, clearly took the lead in Europe, significantly determining the launch of the IA system in Europe, to date in several Member States IA is still on paper, or has even not been launched. A snapshot of the current adoption-implementation gap is provided by the comparison of Figure 18 and Figure 19 below. In Figure 18, the results of the OECD "government at a glance" in 2009 are reported, with specific focus on explicit requirements for RIA processes in Central government. These variables describe the extent to which RIA is sponsored and formally adopted in central governmental structures.

Figure 18. Requirements for RIA in central governments, with sensitivity analysis, 2005 v. 2008

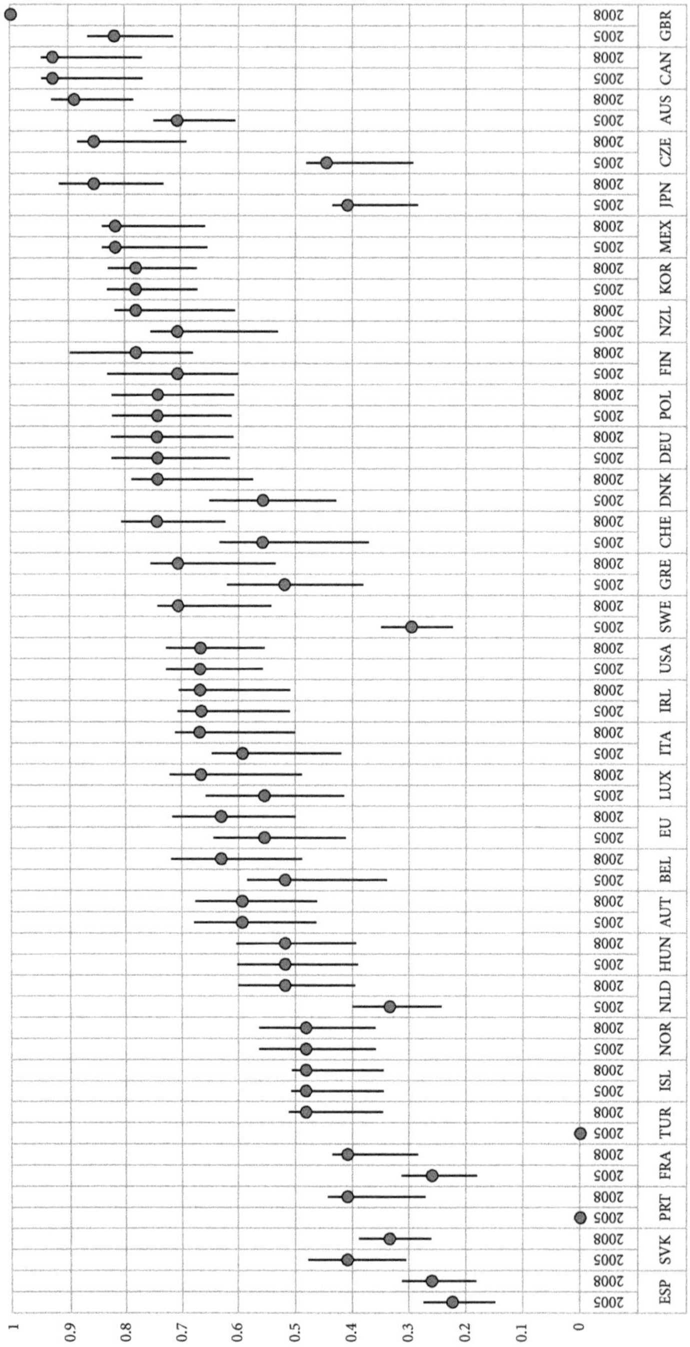

Source: OECD, Government at a glance, 2009.

When looking at the actual implementation of RIA in practice, it is important to define RIA in the first place. The ENBR project back in 2005 hosted a discussion between experts on what can constitute a valid definition of RIA. According to ENBR experts, a RIA has four components (ENBR Handbook on Methodology 2006:6):

1) *A systematic, mandatory, and consistent assessment of aspects of social, economic, or environmental impacts such as benefits and/or costs.* This means that an IA is part of a system of impact analysis based on clear scope and directions. The scope can be narrow or broad, but it is clear that an IA is not an intermittent or voluntary effort to examine impacts.
2) *Affecting interests external to the government.* The purpose of IA is to expand the range of impacts relevant to decisions to external impacts. An assessment only of fiscal or government budget implications is an input into traditional fiscal policy, and is not IA in the modern sense.
3) *Of proposed regulations and other kinds of legal and policy instruments.* Governments use many policy instruments to implement policy, and *ex ante* assessment of impacts can be used for most or all of those instruments.
4) *To i) inform policy decisions before a regulation, legal instrument, or policy is adopted; or ii) assess external impacts of a group of laws or regulations to support reforms; or iii) assess the accuracy of an earlier IA.*

This definition, in and of itself, led ENBR researchers to exclude many documents published by national governments, which appear to lack some of the typical features of a RIA. This already created concerns in the real nature of the documents being produced by national governments in Europe, which are termed as RIA, but in fact are something different from a systematic requirement to perform *ex ante* impact assessment of proposed legislation.

Figure 19 below shows the number of actual IA documents produced by governments that matched the ENBR definition illustrated above at the end of 2008, for each of the countries covered by the ENBR DIADEM database. As shown in the picture, only the UK, Ukraine and the European Commission could be said to have reached a sufficient level of RIA documents – with many differences – among the countries covered.

Figure 19. Impact Assessments in the DIADEM database, end of 2008

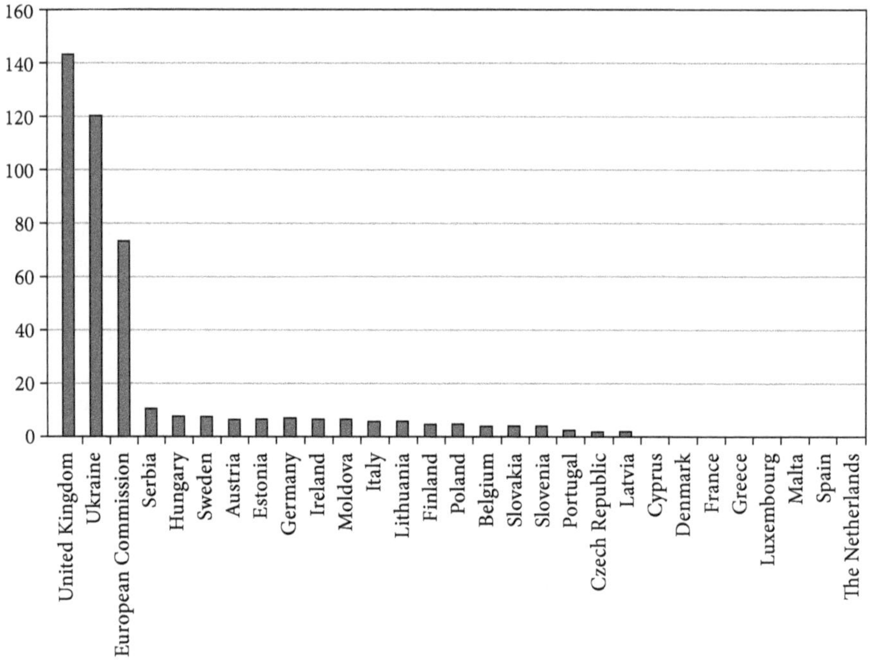

Source: DIADEM database, www.enbr.org.

Interesting and more updated results were found, for a more limited number of countries, by Staronova (2010) for the Central and Eastern European Countries, and by the OECD EU15 project.[157] Overall, the review of better regulation in the 15 countries has revealed the existence of a number of problems in the implementation of *ex ante* impact assessment, including, most notably, the need to clarify the link between IA and administrative burden reduction programmes, which appear more widespread and more strongly implemented at national level. The reason for this may well be that the Standard Cost Model (SCM), on which burdens reduction programmes are based, is a less intrusive model as it does not require a real change in the culture of public administrations; and also because it is easier to communicate to stakeholders, as it leads to clearly identifiable reduction proposals. At the same time, however the SCM has a much narrower scope than *ex ante* IA, since it only looks at administrative burdens and can potentially extended to compliance costs, but does not look at the benefits of legislation in place or alternative policy options.

Looking at the EU27 landscape, it is possible to distinguish different types of countries as regards their experience on IA procedures.

---

157 See Staronova, K. (2010), *Regulatory Impact Assessment: Formal Institutionalization and Practice*, Journal of Public Policy, 30, 1, 117–136. And the main report of the OECD EU15 project at www.oecd.org/dataoecd/20/14/45115076.pdf.

- *Pioneers*. As already explained, one country – the **UK** – can be defined as pioneer in Europe, having experimented with IA practices since the 1980s and with a more full-fledged IA since 1998. Other countries, *i.e.* Denmark, Germany, Hungary, the Netherlands, and Sweden have been defined as pioneering countries, since they formally adopted RIA before the OECD agreement on regulatory reform. However, in none of these countries RIA has been successfully implemented in the policy process.
- *CEE countries*. Finally, some Central and Eastern European countries – also pushed by the OECD Sigma project – have launched RIA pilots back in the 1990s. This is the case, in particular, of **Hungary** and **Estonia**, which started experimenting with RIA in 1994 and 1999, respectively (Staronova, 2010); in the **Czech Republic**, the Legislative Rules of Government introduced a RIA requirement in 1998 but it only entered into force in 2007. In **Slovakia**, requirements for RIA were introduced in November 2001 via an amendment of the Legislative Rules of the Government, following recommendations by the Audit of State Administration. In 2004, the **Slovenian** government signed The Act on Cooperation between the National Assembly and the Government in EU Affairs, which obliges the Government to carry out assessments of the impact and implications of draft EU-related measures. In **Poland**, already at the end of 2001 IA became compulsory for all the legislative drafts adopted by the Council of Ministers, and a Department for impact assessment was established at the Government Legislation Centre. Early starters have, however, faced several difficulties in effectively implementing RIA in their policy cycle. For example, Hungary, despite its early attempt in 1994, has never managed to produce good quality RIA documents over time, and reportedly lags behind other CEE countries in several respects, including consultation, the identification and analysis of impacts, and the overall quality of the assessment. Estonia, on the other hand, has gradually managed to improve the system and was later joined by the Czech Republic, where only a few, high quality RIAs have been produced to date.[158]
- *Late adopters* often have the advantage of learning from other countries' mistakes, and can achieve better outcomes within a lower time frame. A first consequence of this has been the emergence of a group of *successful late adopters* in the EU27. For example, **Ireland** has abandoned its fragmented system that entailed separate assessments of various impacts (including poverty impact assessment) to launch a more comprehensive RIA system in 2007. Similarly, the government of **The Netherlands** is considering the launch of a comprehensive RIA system that replaces the previous three-pronged *ex ante* assessment model, based on business impacts, environmental impacts and the practicability and enforcement assessment in use since 1994. **Sweden** has made enormous progress in its adoption and implementation of RIA, and

[158] Staronova, K. (2010), *supra* note 157.

in December 2007, the Government issued a Regulatory Impact Assessment Ordinance, which supersedes the Ordinance on Special Impact Assessment of the Effects of Rules on Conditions for Small Enterprises, which previously regulated IA work. The new Ordinance states that IA must now be carried out for every new or amended regulation. The watchdog set up by the business confederation, the NNR, has observed that in the past eight years IA has progressed noticeably in Sweden, but also stated that too few good RIAs are being produced. Finally, after years in which the RIA system had faced significant adoption problems, let alone implementation, **France** has launched a new system of impact studies since 1 September 2009: the system possesses a unique feature in Europe, as impact studies have been made a constitutional requirement. Absent a (sufficiently detailed) RIA document attached to bills sent by the Government to parliament, the Speakers of either of the two assemblies may refuse to place the related policy item on the agenda, including if they find it inadequate.

- *Countries dominated by the "cutting red tape" agenda.* There is a clearly emerging group of countries where the better regulation rhetoric has evolved into a de-regulation and simplification one, leading to the blossoming of programs aimed at cutting red tape, and to gradually shift the focus towards administrative burdens reduction, and away from more full-fledged RIA. These countries certainly include **Germany**, where the formal adoption of RIA – very much in line with the original OECD approach – never led to a real implementation of RIA in practice, while the Standard Cost Model has successfully permeated the regulatory agenda, and is currently being revised to cover, more generally, regulatory costs to businesses. Similar developments can be observed in **Denmark**, due to an early and very successful implementation of the SCM; in **Finland** and in **Austria**, where business associations and a fistful of courageous academics are trying to create momentum for RIA in an environment in which the dominant form of policymaking does not accommodate for real transparency.[159]
- Finally, a group of *laggard countries* seems to face important problems in mainstreaming RIA into their often complex policymaking process. **Italy**, for example, adopted the RIA procedure quite early (in 1999), but has never managed to really implement it to date, if not limited to one independent sectoral regulator and a fistful of regional governments – the regulatory framework to support RIA adoption in Central Government was completed

---

159 See Weigel, W. (2008), *The Standard Cost Model – A Critical Appraisal.* 25th Annual Conference of the European Association of Law and Economics, 2008. Available at SSRN: http://ssrn.com/abstract=1295861; Biegelbauer, P. and S. Mayer, (2007), *RIA or no RIA: the Dialogue Between Policymakers and Stakeholders in the Regulatory Process in Austria*, ENBR Working Paper No.10; and Biegelbauer, P., and S. Mayer, (2008), *Regulatory Impact Assessment in Austria: Promising Regulations, Disappointing Practices*, in: Critical Policy Analysis 2(2), 118–142.

only in the spring of 2009. On the other end of the spectrum, **Greece** decided to start experimenting with RIA in 2007, but launched an overly ambitious project, which ended up almost impossible to take up all at once.[160] Finally, **Bulgaria, Romania, Lithuania, Latvia, Spain** and **Portugal** seem light years away from a successful implementation of RIA. Similar issues could be said about **Luxembourg, Malta** and **Cyprus.**

Table 1 below summarizes my conclusions in terms of grouping of countries according to their RIA implementation. It bears observing, in this respect, that implementation should not be equated with success, but only with the achievement of a regular production of RIA documents as a mandatory requirement, supported by guidance on how to produce the analysis, and subject to scrutiny and internal or external quality control. Examples of countries that have adopted RIA but not implemented it are, unfortunately, abundant; in addition, countries that have indeed implemented RIA have sometimes failed, sometimes only partly succeeded: the example of the UK, where efforts to mainstream RIA in the policy process have led to overlapping generations of regulatory reforms, patchy and fragmented implementation, tendency towards box-ticking, limited quantification of impacts, and finally a remarkable shift towards the reduction of administrative burdens generated by the stock of legislation is not necessarily the most successful case study one can think of.

Table 1. Groups of countries according to effective implementation of RIA

Pioneers	CEE countries with RIA development	Late adopters	Red-tape-dominated	Laggards
United Kingdom	Czech Republic, Estonia, Hungary, Poland, Slovakia, Slovenia	France, Ireland, The Netherlands, Sweden, Belgium *(Flanders)*	Austria, Belgium *(Central gov)*, Denmark, Finland, Germany	Bulgaria, Greece, Italy, Lithuania, Latvia, Luxembourg, Malta, Portugal, Romania, Spain Cyprus

Source: Author's elaboration from several sources.

Notwithstanding the rather depressing picture that emerges from the current implementation of RIA in the EU27, several lessons can be drawn from the experience of past research projects, direct field experience, academic literature and reports by international organisations such as the OECD and the World Bank. I try to briefly summarise them below.

160 Hatzis, A.N. and S. Nalpantidou (2007), *From Nothing to Too Much: Regulatory Reform in Greece*. Available at SSRN: http://ssrn.com/abstract=1075963.

- *Political commitment remains essential.* Typical examples are those of France and The Netherlands, where comprehensive RIA systems have been or are being launched as a result of a solid demand for regulatory governance and reform. Where commitment has been limited or absent (*e.g.* Italy, Poland, Germany), even the most ambitious RIA strategy has failed.
- *Oversight and coordination.* The invaluable role of central watchdogs has led several countries (but also the European Commission) to recognise the need for a centralised gatekeeper entrusted with the task of managing the RIA process and its development. Even where this has happened, the level of commitment and investment has markedly differed: Radaelli *et al.* (2007) reported that in four countries (Germany, Hungary, the Netherlands and Spain) the number of employees dedicated to RIA is unknown notwithstanding the presence of a central unit; whereas Ireland and Italy have a very light central unit with 1.5 employees respectively. To the contrary, larger units exist in Czech Republic (9 employees), Poland (10), Sweden (12), and Belgium (20); whereas the UK stands as an outlier with approximately 70 employees.
- *Hierarchy.* Another important lesson that can be drawn is related to the relative positioning of the central coordinating body *vis à vis* administrations in charge of RIA. In countries where the oversight unit has been put at the same level of administrations in charge of producing RIAs, as *unus inter pares*, the moral suasion impact of its decisions has been limited.[161] To the contrary, where the watchdog acts from the centre of government, with a somewhat superior authority, there is often no need to grant the watchdog powers to formally reject proposal: as in the case of the US OIRA and the EU IAB, moral suasion is enough, no administration would dare to neglect the gentle advice of the watchdog.
- *Expectations.* Some national governments have made the mistake of launching an overly ambitious RIA system, and/or raised too high expectations among stakeholders. Examples, as already mentioned, include the European Commission (due to initial promises of full quantification), Italy, and Greece. Given that RIA takes several years to produce meaningful results, including *i.a.* enhanced predictability, transparency and accountability of policymaking, as well as greater policy coherence, it is important that reforms are communicated with a word of caution and by keeping in mind a reasonably long time horizon. Otherwise, the first episodes of disappointment among stakeholders may jeopardize the entire process.
- *Gradual introduction v. big bang.* Connected to the problem of expectations is the problem of how and when to introduce RIA. The experience of countries such as the UK, France and the Netherlands suggests that it may take several years before a system of partial, narrower-scope assessments can generated

161 Staronova (2010), *supra* note 157.

momentum and demand for a more comprehensive RIA system. Also the European Commission has gone through years of separate assessments (the BIA, the environmental and sustainability impact assessments developed by different DGs) before moving to an integrated system: and yet it took several years before the Commission services got used and acquainted with the specifics and the technicalities of IA.

- *Exploit the link with the Standard Cost Model (SCM) for the measurement of administrative burdens.* Faced with problems in generating the cultural change needed in public administrations, several governments have opted for reforms related to simplification and the reduction of administrative burdens. Given the political commitment required for the implementation of the SCM – *i.e.* the *ex ante* commitment to reduce burdens by a given percentage *before* actually measuring them – the SCM has proven easier to communicate to business stakeholders. At the same time, the SCM does not require revolutionary changes in the way bureaucrats behave, as most of the process is carried out in conjunction with external consultants and is aimed at the stock, rather than the flow of legislation. That said, once administrative burdens have been measured, reduction proposals must be assessed as regards their potential costs and benefits for society as a whole. As explained in Allio and Renda (2010), IA procedures are required to successfully complete the implementation of the SCM: accordingly, a new momentum for introducing a comprehensive IA system may emerge in all those countries – practically, all EU member states – that have decided to embark in the measurement of administrative burdens, especially after the Spring Council in 2007.

PART II

LAW AND ECONOMICS: POSITIVE, NORMATIVE AND FUNCTIONAL APPROACHES

4. *EX ANTE* POLICY APPRAISAL: INSIGHTS FROM POSITIVE, NORMATIVE AND FUNCTIONAL SCHOOLS OF LAW AND ECONOMICS

In the first part of this work, we have analyzed the evolution and current features of *ex ante* policy appraisal in two of the world largest legal systems, the United States and the European Union. What emerged from that account of the "RIA world" is that, although with substantial differences, in both cases the practice of *ex ante* impact analysis is subject to fierce criticisms both in terms of their methodological shortcomings and for reasons related to governance. Overall, it comes to no surprise that authors have hardly managed to demonstrate that RIA makes a difference in terms of legal quality, but also in terms of growth and competitiveness around the world, despite attempts (especially by the OECD) to prove that countries that have undergone regulatory reform grow faster than countries that don't: this may be true for regulatory reform, it is not for RIA – at best, there is no conclusive evidence.[162]

Against this background, there is an obvious appeal to the idea of putting in place a system aimed at improving the quality of legal rules through the provision of detailed, inspired economic analysis. In principle, RIA should become the engine of a more transparent policymaking process, and possibly also a more participative, efficient and effective one. So, why has RIA failed in most countries so far? Well, one could say that the introduction of this tool is relatively recent in many countries, and thirty years ago even budgeting was hardly known and accepted in government administrations, whereas today bureaucrats have learned how to live with it, and happily. Will the same happen to RIA in the next decade or so?

One way of looking at current RIA practice, which may help in the understanding whether current systems are headed in a satisfactory direction, is to go back to the roots of the academic elaboration on the economic analysis of legal rules, and assess whether current RIA practice conforms with the key

[162] Hahn and Tetlock (2008) do not find sufficient evidence to conclude unambiguously that RIA has an effect on economic outcomes such as growth. Hahn, R.W. and P. Tetlock (2008), *Has Economic Analysis Improved Regulatory Decisions?*, Journal of Economic Perspectives, Volume 22, Number 1, Winter 2008, Pages 67–84. See also Baldwin, R. (2005), *Is better regulation smarter regulation?* Public Law (Autumn), 485–511.

insights that decades of law and economics scholarship have developed and brought to the attention of field experts and scholars. Accordingly, this section attempts to build a bridge between theory and practice by describing some of the main insights developed by the law and economics literature in the past decades, and their possible applications as improvements of the current economic analysis provided in RIA documents in the US and the EU.

This Section contributes to the main research questions of this book by describing the many ways in which law and economics can inspire a more informed and thorough *ex ante* policy appraisal. More in detail, the aim is to inform the discussion of the *an* (should we use more law and economics in RIA?), *quomodo* (how can we apply law and economics in RIA) and *quantum* (when and to what extent should we apply law and economics in RIA).

Section 4.1 below provides a brief introduction to the history and evolution of law and economics. Section 4.2 then explores the main achievements of "positive" law and economics, mostly focusing on the understanding of individual and collective rationality, the functioning of markets and market-based instruments and the allocation of legal entitlements. In other word, the section addresses the issue whether, given a defined set of goals that the legal system is supposed to pursue, it is possible to design legal rules in a way that effectively achieves those goals. Section 4.3 discusses the "normative" version of law and economics, which looks at the way in which legal rules *should* be designed, or, as often mentioned, what the law "*ought to be*", rather than what it is: in particular, the section focuses on the evolution of the debate on the role of wealth maximization as an "ancillary paradigm of justice" and, more generally, of the legal system as a whole; in addition, the section explores the various interpretations that have been given to the goals of the legal system, including various efficiency criteria, as well as theories of justice. Section 4.4 then analyzes the "functional" school of law and economics, in particular as regards the view of RIA and cost-benefit analysis as procedural mechanisms aimed at facilitating control of bureaucrats under a system of delegation and oversight; and as a way to "nudge" both administrations and citizens to induce the achievement of desired policy outcomes. Section 4.5 briefly concludes by summarizing the main lessons learned from this chapter.

4.1. FROM BENTHAM TO SUNSTEIN: A BRIEF, "INSTRUMENTAL" ACCOUNT OF THE EVOLUTION OF LAW AND ECONOMICS

The law and economics movement has been defined as one of the "greatest intellectual triumphs of social science", and "the foremost intellectual movement in law in the last half century".[163] Especially in the US, the subject matter is now deeply entrenched in university faculties and in courts, in particular in domains such as contracts, torts, property, but also competition and regulation.[164]

The idea that the body of (mostly neoclassical) economics could be the foundation for a more thorough understanding of how legal rules are formulated has been gaining adepts in fields such as property law, contract law and the law of torts. In particular, the first contributions of modern law and economics originated in the Chicago School since the 1940s, thanks to the work undertaken by Aaron Director and others. At that time, the scope of the analysis was chiefly aimed at demonstrating that the Common Law system was oriented towards the selection of efficient rules. In doing this, Chicagoans mostly adopted Marshallian price theory and relied on theories of public intervention that were rooted in the work of economists such as Pigou.

4.1.1. THE PIONEERS

From a very general – and certainly overly simplified – perspective, law and economics has always been characterized by its instrumental vision of the law.[165] More precisely, traditional law and economics views law as functional to the definition of relative prices that affect the choices made by rational decision-makers, be they individuals, groups, corporations, or even governments. Given its instrumentalist approach, the law and economics movement has been traced back to the early contributions of philosophers such as Cesare Beccaria, David Hume, Jeremy Bentham, Nicolò Macchiavelli and Henry Sidgwick.[166] In particular, the utilitarian nature of human behavior as portrayed in the law and economics literature inevitably led to identifying Bentham as a prominent and influential ancestor of modern legal economists.[167] The links between utilitarianism and law and economics became evident when, at the beginning of the 1960s, the seminal contributions of Ronald Coase (1960), Guido Calabresi

---

163 See Andrei Shleifer and Richard Posner, respectively, on the back cover of Steven Shavell's *Foundations of Economic Analysis of Law.*

164 In a recent contribution, Stephen Medema measures the success of the economic approach to law by observing the gradual decline and fragmentation of its most important challenger, *i.e.* the Critical Legal Studies movement. See Medema, S.G. (2010), *From Dismal to Dominance? Law and Economics and the Values of Imperial Science*, in Hatzis, A. (ed.), "Norms and Values in Law and Economics". London: Routledge, forthcoming 2011.

165 See K.N. Hylton (2004), *Calabresi and the Intellectual History of Law and Economics*, Working Paper Series Law and Economics 04–04, Boston University, School of Law (2004).

166 See Posner, R. A. '*The Law and Economics Movement: From Bentham to Becker*', in F. Parisi and C.K. Rowley (eds.) *The Origins of Law and Economics: Essays by the Founding Fathers* (Cheltenham, U.K. and Northampton, MA: Elgar 2005) 328.

167 Ibid.

(1961) and Gary Becker (1968) paved the way for the development of contemporary law and economics.[168]

4.1.1.1. Coase, Calabresi, Becker

At the outset, law and economics was essentially "positive", meaning that it implied the use of economic theory – mostly rooted in Neoclassical, "Marshallian" price theory – to predict the effects of various legal rules and assess whether the legal system was automatically geared towards the selection of efficient rules. This stream of law and economics was essentially assuming that individuals would behave rationally, and would then decide whether and how to comply with legal rules after a thorough, informed cost-benefit analysis. The allocation of entitlements and resources followed from the meeting of the minds of rational players. For example, the "strong" version of the Coase theorem highlights the irrelevance of the initial allocation of entitlements whenever transaction costs are equal to zero.

However, in recognizing the importance of legal remedies when transaction costs are significant, Ronald Coase already made the case for a normative version of law and economics, moving from a descriptive version of his theorem to a prescriptive one, which pointed at the need to formulate legal rules in a way that minimizes the impact of transaction costs on the final allocation of rights.[169] This recognition that "legal rules do matter" is indeed the foundation of the normative version of law and economics, which does not aim at describing how the rule *is*, but rather looks at how the law *ought to be* in order to generate certain efficient outcomes.

The contribution of Ronald Coase – himself a student of Pigou – to the analysis of the *sein* and the *sollen* of legal rules marked a departure from the "Pigouvian" approach to public policy, which relied on taxation as the most important tool for policymakers wishing to achieve income redistribution. As in his 1959 paper on "The Federal Communications Commission", in which he effectively paved the way towards modern spectrum policy in telecommunications, with "The Problem of Social Cost" Coase managed to shift the attention towards public policy as a way to eliminate obstacles for private individuals and firms to freely exchange entitlements in the marketplace, which according to Coase represented the most expedite way to achieve allocative efficiency (Coase, 1960). In doing this, he managed to achieve a twofold result: placing emphasis on private players and their interaction in markets as actors of public policy, but also

168 This is what Posner defines as the "second wave" of law and economics. For a more extensive account of the history of law and economics, see Mackaay (2000); Parisi (2004); Medema (2010); Hylton (2004); and Veljanosky (1982).

169 See *i.a.* Cooter, R. and T. Ulen (2004), *Law and Economics*, 4th edn, Addison-Wesley Longman.

equating market efficiency with morality, at least under certain circumstances. The former insight, however, ended up being more fortunate than the latter.[170]

At the same time, in his parallel work to that of Coase, Guido Calabresi had the enormous merit of showing how tort law can be framed in economic terms, by accounting for the incentives of individuals to take due care under different liability regimes, and providing guidance on how to select a legal regime that minimizes the cost of accidents, regardless of the fairness of the system in legal terms. Again, Calabresi's early work was already deep into normative analysis. Very much rooted in Bentham's utilitarianism, Calabresi was essentially advocating for the replacement of the negligence regime for tort law with strict liability, subject to certain conditions.[171] The idea of the "cheapest cost avoider", who would be called to bear the direct burden of a strict liability regime, was very much in line with Bentham's proposition that rules had to be chiefly simple and easy to comply with. In the following years, Calabresi became a pioneer in the economic approach to legal remedies, in particular to designing legal rules that achieve a "shift" in the timing of the allocation of rights, as well as in the choice of the decision-maker (see Section 4.4 below).

Calabresi (with Douglas Melamed) later overlapped with the Coasian research track by adding to the Coase theorem a brilliant analysis of the choice of legal remedies, which illustrated the conditions under which a property rule would be superior to a liability rule in the resolution of controversies over incompatible uses.[172] This seminal work – perhaps one of the most quoted in the history of law economics – has ramifications into several subsequent contributions, from Ian Ayres' "optional law" to access policy regimes in network industries. As will be shown in the next chapters, it can also inform the choice and design of market-based instruments as a policy option in several regulatory contexts. Calabresi's view of economic efficiency was far more *nuanced* than the one exhibited by Coase and other prominent scholars in the field: the idea that justice should be achieved as a major goal, taking precedence also on efficiency, exposed Calabresi to major critiques from his fellow lawyer-economists. At the same time, Calabresi was often critical of the Coase theorem, in particular as

170 Coase's conclusion that market outcomes are always efficient, and that economic efficiency should be the ultimate goal of public policy is neither straightforward nor easy to digest for many scholars. On the one hand, the "Coase theorem" carried an underlying assumption, that policymakers and judges should not care about the outcomes of market exchanges, as markets "know best" how resources should be allocated. This assumption elicited substantial criticism among legal and economic scholars: the so-called Critical Legal Studies movement represented *i.a.* by the work of Duncan Kennedy is a good example of disagreement with Coase's reasoning. See also Arcuri (2002). See Hovenkamp (1994), stating that "Coase's extreme faith in private bargaining blinded him to the problems of bargaining in two-person markets that Pigou saw quite clearly and that remain with us to this day". Hovenkamp, H. (1994), *The Limits of Preference-Based Legal Policy*, 89 Northwestern University Law Review 4.

171 See Hylton (2004), *supra* note 165.

172 See Calabresi, G. and A. Douglas Melamed (1972), *Property Rules, Liability Rules, and Inalienability: One View of the Cathedral*, 85 HARV. L. REV. 1089.

regards its applicability to contexts with positive transaction costs: Calabresi's view of the formulation and selection of legal rules appeared from the outset to be more complex, articulated, and at the same time less immediately prescriptive than the one adopted by Coase and, later, by Richard Posner. In the early years of law and economics, Calabresi had already explored at length the roles of efficiency, justice, inalienability and (weak and true) paternalism as co-existing principles within the same legal system, and was advocating the use of "conjectures" by the policymaker in order to arrive to an informed judgment over the optimal alternative among the ones on the table. In this respect, as will be recalled again in Section 4.4 below, Calabresi was a precursor of those "nudging" approaches that are pervading the US RIA system under the guidance of Cass Sunstein.[173]

Finally, Gary Becker was a pioneer in advocating for the use of economics in the analysis of non-market behavior. As will be argued in more detail below, his writings on the economics of crime and punishment still lie at the core of the formulation of legal rules, especially as regards the incentive to comply with the law – often a neglected aspect of RIA – and the possibility of effective enforcement. Authoritative scholars have highlighted the decisive contribution of Gary Becker in the expansion of economic analysis into previously untouched domains, including charity, love, addiction, crime, racial discrimination, marriage and divorce, etc.[174] More malicious commentators charge him with the accusation of having fostered the "expansionism" or even the "imperialism" of economic theory, *i.e.* the tendency to apply economics to a range of other disciplines, gradually cannibalizing their scientific method and traditional tools. And again, Becker's work on crime and punishment – one of the reasons why he was awarded the Nobel Prize for economics in 1992 – was deeply normative, as it described *i.a.* how sanctions should be designed in order to trigger efficient behavior in criminal law, but also in other fields such as tort law.

Now, it is true that much of the conclusions drawn in this initial pieces of literature has been surpassed by follow-up contributions, especially those that have revisited the concept of rationality to introduce the findings of cognitive science in the analysis of human behavior. However, these law and economic lessons – that under some conditions markets work better than command and control regulation; that legal rules do matter for allocative efficiency; that remedies should be designed according to the expected level of transaction costs; and that enforcement should take into account the perspective of the would-be infringer – still remain among the most insightful contributions that a lawyer-

173 For a very interesting account of Calabresi's life and contribution, see Grembi, V. (2005), *Guido Calabresi e L'Analisi Economica del Diritto*, Siena Memos and Papers in Law and Economics, 41/05, at www.unisi.it/lawandeconomics/simple/041_Grembi.pdf.

174 MacKaay, E. (2000), *History of Law and Economics*, 1 Encyclopedia of Law and Economics (Cheltenham, U.K.: Edward Elgar Publishing).

economist can bring to the policymakers' table. I will then get back to them in Section 4.4 below given their egregious normative power.

4.1.1.2. Richard Posner and "Efficiency as Justice"

During the 1970s, the expansion of law and economics and its ambition to transform the way traditional legal scholars think about law became the subject of hectic counter-attacks. Ronald Coase himself had stated that "much, and perhaps most, of legal scholarship has been stamp collecting. Law and economics, however, is likely to challenge all that and, in fact, has begun to do so".[175] As explained, *i.a.*, in the preamble to the Hofstra Law Review's special issue on "Efficiency as a Legal Concern" in the spring of 1980,

> *The operative definition for the economic analysis of law rests on the concept of efficiency ... as economic analysis explored new avenues and sought to bring an increasing number of formerly distinct legal areas within its ambit under a unified analysis, this definition proved too crude. While it provided a convenient standard for approaching such diverse topics as property rules, discrimination, breach of contract, and civil procedure, its simplicity left it open to attack on descriptive grounds. On a normative level, it failed to provide more than the most basic justification for its existence. In addition whatever moral claims it had rested largely on the strength of utilitarianism, a theory generally viewed as bankrupt. It was in part to flesh out the definition and to firmly anchor the theory on defensible normative grounds that scholars began addressing the justification for economic analysis of law. This has opened a new debate on the theory's philosophical underpinnings and spurred fresh examinations, albeit often implicitly, on the question what is law.*

The first and most committed of those attempts to justify the economic analysis of law on ethical and philosophical grounds was celebrated with the prolific work of Richard Posner.[176] Posner, almost a mythological character in the history of law and economics, attempted to strengthen the link between Bentham's utilitarianism and modern law and economics. While earlier Chicagoans generally recognized their limits in developing prescriptive recommendations for legal reform, with Posner, law and economics becomes normative, and known as the economic analysis of law (EAL).[177]

---

175 Coase, R. (1993), *Law and Economics at Chicago*, 36 Journal of Law and Economics 239 at 254 ('Ernest Rutherford said that science is either physics or stamp collecting, by which he meant, I take it, that it is either engaged in analysis or operating a filing system. Much, perhaps most, legal scholarship has been stamp collecting. Law and economics is likely to change all that'.

176 See Harnay and Marciano (2009), *Posner, Economics and the Law: from Law and Economics to an Economic Analysis of Law*, Journal of the History of Economic Thought, Volume 31, Issue 02, pp 215–232.

177 See Parisi, F. (2004), *Positive, Normative and Functional Schools in law and Economics*, European Journal of Law and Economics Vol. 18, n. 3, December 2004.

More in detail, the idea that common law was essentially aiming towards efficient solutions – typical of the Chicago School since the early 1960s[178] – was operationalized by Posner into a rather different concept: that in all areas of common law, including legal adjudication, but also government regulation, the real objective should be wealth maximization; that economic efficiency is the natural way to achieve wealth maximization; and that this goal is justified on moral grounds as it is a measure (better, an "ancillary paradigm") of justice.[179] The direct consequence of the Posnerian view of efficiency was that efficiency criteria *à la* Pareto (including potential Pareto efficiency, or Kaldor-Hicks efficiency) could be justified on ethical grounds.

The explanation is relatively simple: moving from an ethical justification of the outcome of market transactions on grounds of contractual autonomy and individual freedom – a conclusion developed by authors such as Nozick and Epstein following a Kantian approach, rather than a utilitarian one *à la* Bentham – Posner developed an idea of justice and happiness as wealth maximization, based on individual consent. Since it is impossible to measure individual utility and compare utility between individuals, the only possible basis for judging on the impact of a given allocation of resources is indeed individual consent: if individuals express their agreement to a given reallocation of resources, it must mean that the new state of the world makes them happier. Since this result is obtained in Pareto efficiency – especially when parties agree on a given transaction – then efficiency is a measure of justice, and it should be pursued systematically when crafting and enforcing legal rules.

It was clear, however, that moving from the Pareto criterion to the Kaldor-Hicks Potential Pareto Superiority would not be easy to justify on ethical grounds. As a matter of fact, the Kantian explanation of universal consent as the basis for identifying improvements in social welfare did not hold under Kaldor-Hicks, where individuals that are left worse-off by a given reallocation of resources have not expressed any consent to such reallocation.[180] According to Posner, however, also the Kaldor-Hicks principle could be justified on ethical grounds, since individuals would give their *ex ante* consent to wealth maximization as a paramount principle in policies that reallocate resources among individuals. This has very important normative implications: for example, as explained in Posner (1980), if a negligence system for the case of road traffic accidents is cheaper than strict liability (counting both the costs of precaution and insurance premiums), then if all individuals have the same preferences everybody would prefer the former system to the latter. It does not matter, Posner

---

178 *Ibid.*, quoting, *i.a.* the so-called "efficiency of the common law hypothesis", as described and discussed in Ehrlich and Posner (1974), Rubin (1977) and Priest (1977).

179 See Klick and Parisi (2003), *Functional Law and Economics: The Search for Value-Neutral Principles of Lawmaking*, George Mason University Law and Economics Working Paper Series, 03–39.

180 See *infra*, Section 4.3.2 for a more detailed discussion.

said, if individuals have not given their *express* consent: from the standpoint of law making and legal adjudication, as a matter of fact, what matters is that every citizen – or a majority of citizens – would have agreed *ex ante* to institutions that regulate in favor of wealth maximization, whatever the final outcome in terms of resources allocation. This idea is grounded in what economics call *ex ante* compensation: for example, the uncertainty on future states of the world is already discounted by individuals when concluding market transactions – so to say, individuals most often self-insure by imposing an adjustment in market prices: if I expect a 10% likelihood that someone will build a house between my balcony and a gorgeous view, I'll take this into account before I buy it. Likewise, if there's a chance that I'll end up in the losers' group after a Kaldor-Hicks-superior move, I'll adjust *ex ante*.

Posner's idea of efficiency as justice was very influential in the United States in the mid-1970s, and originated from an attempt to transform the Kaldor-Hicks principle into a more universally accepted principle of justice. In more philosophical terms, Posner's elaboration drew its origins on Kant and Bentham – in that it was elaborating on the idea of individual autonomy and looked at a measure of happiness and pleasure as expressed by individual preferences – but was also close to the work of John Rawls, in that it looked for a measure of efficiency based on *ex ante* consent; and shared some similarity to the work of John Harsanyi (1953) on cardinal utilities in welfare economics, where the future Nobel laureate hinged on the notion of *ex ante* commitment to average utilitarianism. As recalled years later by Jules Coleman (2003) the idea of an *ex ante* commitment to a maximization of utility is the inevitable consequence of how the notion of rationality is defined: with the possibility of measuring individual utility, from an *ex ante* perspective rational individuals may choose to maximize average utility, just as under the Rawlsian "veil of ignorance". As in Coleman (2003), "one would then have to show what moral value, if any, is embodied in this particular conception of rationality".[181]

In any event, at the end of the 1970s Posner's view of wealth maximization as a paradigm of justice was gaining ground among scholars and policymakers. This over time evolved as a defense of the Kaldor-Hicks principle as a criterion to be used in drafting and enforcing legal rules. As will be shown in the next sections, it would be incorrect to state that the economic analysis of law really adopted this view outside the work of Richard Posner and a few other scholars. However, when the "schism" between EAL and the administrative law and economics took place at the end of the 1970s, the latter domain incorporated Kaldor-Hicks efficiency as a dominant paradigm. As I will explain in the next sections, while the regulatory review model adopted in 1980 under the Reagan administration looked very much in line with Posner's original claim that wealth

181 See Coleman, J. (2003), *The Grounds of Welfare*, Review of the article "Fairness versus Welfare by Kaplow, L. and S. Shavell, The Yale Law Journal Vol. 112, No. 6 (Apr., 2003), pp. 1511–1543.

maximization and the Kaldor-Hicks criterion were the way to justice and happiness, since then law and economics scholars (including Hicks and Posner) have refined their view of the Kaldor-Hicks criterion, and have mostly rejected its universal application. They started doing it already in 1980, on the pages of the Hofstra Law review and in the Journal of Legal Studies: and they continued since then, by developing schools of thought that promise to subvert the role of Potential Pareto Superiority as a dominant paradigm for federal regulation, and for RIA as a whole.

4.1.1.3. The "greatest gig in the sky"

In the Symposium on "Efficiency as a Legal Concern", recalled at the beginning of this book, many of the most authoritative law and economic scholars of that time discussed the merit of adopting efficiency criteria in adjudication, and ended up digging quite thoroughly into the virtues and hidden traps of the Kaldor-Hicks criterion as a normative basis for deciding about complex and controversial legal issues. That was also the time in which scholars like Richard Posner, William Landes, George Priest and Paul Rubin – all in favor of replacing legal criteria in adjudication with Kaldor-Hicks efficiency – were challenged by others, such as Ronald Dworkin, Richard Epstein, Anthony Kronman, Jules Coleman, Duncan Kennedy, Charles Fried, Gerald O'Driscoll Jr. and Mario Rizzo, who considered that efficiency criteria could lead to potential distortions in the making of value judgments when adjudicating legal controversies.

Reading the contributions to that Symposium, the most striking result was that the economists were the first to reject the idea that legal adjudication in common law could be based on strict efficiency criteria such as the Kaldor-Hicks one. For example, Richard Posner stated (and later wrote) that "while Kaldor-Hicks is not a Pareto criterion as such, it will sometimes function as a tolerable, and more to the point, administrable approximation of the Pareto superiority criterion"[182]; whereas the economist Mario Rizzo stated – almost in the form of a *mea culpa* – that "the substantial information requirements that must be satisfied in order to identify efficient legal rules make efficiency impractical as a standard".[183]

Developments in the law and economics literature since that famous Chicagoan symposium have moved in the direction of finding a suitable alternative to the – rather rough – potential Pareto superiority criterion. To be sure, the law of decreasing marginal utility already condemned the Kaldor-Hicks criterion from the outset, by suggesting that net benefit calculation is not as decisive as the identity and wealth condition of winners and losers in determining

182 Posner R.A. (1980), *The Ethical and Political Basis of the Efficiency Norm in Common Law Adjudication*, 8 Hofstra L. Rev., 1980, p. 487.

183 See Rizzo, M.J. (1980), *The Mirage of Efficiency*, 8 Hofstra L. Rev., p. 641.

whether a change in the rules of the game should be considered as an "improvement" or the achievement of a "bigger pie".[184] In other words, economists have discovered over the past decades that the way in which the pie is distributed affects dramatically the size of the pie; whereas the Kaldor-Hicks criterion looked only at the size (in "resourcist" terms) by leaning on a mere "potential" for leaving each and every individual with at least the same slice he or she had before.

Secondly, developments in behavioral law and economics, neuroeconomics and (more generally) cognitive sciences have gradually led to reconsidering the idea that a change in an individual's endowment of resources, as well as an individual's willingness to exchange the *status quo* for a different mix of goods and money is not as straightforward as one would expect. Theoretical achievements such as Brian Arthur's "path dependence" in human behavior, the contributions of Maurice Allais and Herbert Simon on bounded rationality, the development of "prospect theory" and the application of cognitive sciences to economics (*e.g.* by Daniel Kahneman and Amos Tversky) potentially leave the Kaldor-Hicks criterion down on its knees, both in common law adjudication and in regulatory decision-making. Law and economics scholars have made important steps forward, for example by conceiving ways of "de-biasing through law".[185] Measures of the potential other-regarding behavior of individuals in some settings have led many economists to depart from the stereotype of *homo oeconomicus* when modeling human behavior.[186]

Thirdly, the use of Cost-Benefit Analysis (CBA) in regulatory decisions has been strongly criticized in the economic literature over the past years. Some commentators have gone back to decisions taken by the Environmental Protection Agency in the "pre-RIA" age, and found that CBA would have led to highly undesirable conclusions.[187] This critique was lately extended to a number of other regulatory initiatives in the environmental policy field, such as the US Clean Air Act, for which the EPA used CBA, but ultimately was glamorously captured by partisan interests.[188] This stream of the debate has culminated in Bob Hahn's recent work in defense of the economic analysis of regulation, which

184 Bebchuk, L.A. (1980) *The Pursuit of a Bigger Pie: Can Everyone Expect a Bigger Slice?*, in Symposium on Efficiency as a Legal Concern, 8 Hofstra Law Review 671–709.

185 See Jolls, C. and C.R. Sunstein (2006), *Debiasing through Law*, Journal of Legal Studies, Vol. 35, 1.

186 See, *i.a.*, Itoh, H. (2004) *Moral Hazard and Other-regarding Preferences.*

187 See F. Ackerman, L. Heinzerling and R. Massey, *Applying Cost-Benefit to Past Decisions: Was Environmental Protection Ever a Good Idea?*, Georgetown Public Law Research Paper No. 576161, Georgetown University, August 2004; F. Ackerman and L. Heinzerling, *Priceless: on Knowing the Price of Everything and the Value of Nothing*, New York: The New Press, 2004; and See David Driesen's White Paper, *Is Cost-Benefit Analysis Neutral?*, 2 February 2005 (available at http://ssrn.com/abstract=663602), p. 7.

188 See *i.a. Polluted Logic. How EPA's ozone standard illustrates the flaws of cost-benefit analysis in regulatory decision making*, Report by OMB Watch, available online www.ombwatch.org/files/regs/PDFs/PollutedLogic.pdf.

adopts the rather "Posnerian" – and also hardly contestable – view that CBA is often *le meilleur des mondes possibles*, as no suitable alternatives have been proposed to date in the economic literature.[189]

The split between law and economics and RIA practice is evident also in recent literature: for example, in 2000 Matthew Adler observed rather bluntly that "Kaldor-Hicks efficiency should be removed from our normative vocabulary. It lacks the basic status of Pareto efficiency, overall well-being, distributive considerations, deontological requirements, and (perhaps) perfectionist value."[190] Adler was not alone: suffice it to look at the way in which Jules Coleman (2003) reviewed Louis Kaplow and Steven Shavell's "Fairness v. Efficiency" a few years ago: "

> *"the book openly endorses precisely the imperialistic claims with which others have saddled the law and economics movement, often in an effort to discredit it as inadequately catholic or, in the extreme, uncivilized. Whereas the vast majority of law-and economics scholars have been trying to make the case for including efficiency among the factors suitable to assessing legal reform proposals, the entire point of the Kaplow and Shavell argument is that the* only *considerations that can figure in a rational reform policy are those of human welfare – or efficiency properly construed."*[191]

Coleman also added that there is no way of justifying the adoption of a Kaldor-Hicks efficiency criterion on the basis of the fact that it can be seen as a Potential Pareto Superiority test: "That they are potentially Pareto superior has as much bearing on how they should be treated as the fact that I am potentially President of the United States has on how I should be treated now".[192]

4.1.2. SCHOOLS OF LAW AND ECONOMICS TODAY

Since the 1970s, the law and economics movement has gradually split into a number of different schools and approaches, mostly distinct as far as the theoretical background in economics and the propensity to formulate prescriptive policy suggestions are concerned. A good introduction to this increasingly complex galaxy is offered *i.a.* by Mackaay (2000), Medema (2010)

---

189 Hahn, R.W. (2005), *In Defense of the Economic Analysis of Regulation*, American Enterprise Institute, Washington, D.C., 2005. Later, however, Hahn wrote a more sophisticated paper arguing that refinements in the traditional cost-benefit analysis methodology can significantly improve the informative contribution of this tool. See Hahn, R.W. (2008), *Designing Smarter Regulation with Improved Benefit-Cost Analysis* (September 8, 2008). Reg-Markets Center Working Paper No. 08–20.

190 Matthew D. Adler (2000), Beyond Efficiency and Procedure: a Welfarist Theory of Regulation, 28 Florida State Univ. L. R.

191 See Coleman (2003), *supra* note 181.

192 *Id.*, at 107.

and Parisi (2004). Below, I offer a brief description of the main schools of law and economics that emanated from the work of the early pioneers, with no ambition to develop a comprehensive analysis. A full account would indeed fall outside the scope of this study: to the contrary, I will focus on streams of literature that may be considered particularly interesting for the future of *ex ante* policy appraisal. Posner and Parisi (1996) and Parisi (2004) recall the fundamental distinction between (i) a "positive" school of law and economics rooted mostly in the Chicago school; (ii) a "normative" school of law and economics that can be attributed mostly to Yale scholars; and (iii) a "functional school", which originated from the Virginia School of Political Economy.

More in detail, the positive school distinguishes itself for the emphasis placed on individual economic agents as key players that decide whether and how to comply with legal rules on the basis of a rational decision. This stream of law and economics has often been reluctant to enter normative discussions, although the normative implications of their main tenets are self-evident: if individuals act rationally and – along with the Coase theorem – can enter Pareto-efficient transactions to reallocate entitlements and resources up to the level that is allocatively efficient, then the role of legal rules is mostly confined to the removal of obstacles to those transactions, *i.e.* the removal of (the impact of) transaction costs. In this respect, Chicagoans have been very normative in their rejection of public command and control intervention in certain markets – the best proof being the impact of the Chicago school on antitrust law and economics.

The faith in the market exhibited by Chicagoans has been criticized on several grounds. This led the positive school of law and economics to take on board new concepts and refine its original assumptions. A rough way of describing this move revolves around the concept of error. As a matter of fact, Chicago scholars had to revisit their theories on the basis of evidence that: (i) individuals err in their judgment; and (ii) judges and regulators err in their implementation of the law. This, in turn, has led to important developments in the field of behavioral law and economics, on the one hand; and the so-called "neo-Chicago" approach centered on error costs in the formulation and implementation of legal rules.[193]

At the same time, the Yale school developed a much stronger skepticism on the role of markets and that of efficiency as the ultimate goal of a legal system, both in legal adjudication and in regulation. Following the statement of Guido Calabresi (1980), that "an increase in wealth cannot constitute a social improvement, unless it furthers some other goal, such as utility or equality", Yale scholars have significantly expanded the array of circumstances under which markets fail, and there is potentially a need for government intervention to achieve more socially desirable outcomes. The reasons for this include, again, the

193 See Padilla, A.J. and D.S. Evans (2005), *Designing Antitrust Rules for Assessing Unilateral Practices: A Neo-Chicago Approach*, University of Chicago Law Review, Vol. 72.

findings of behavioral (law and) economics, especially as factored into the analysis by authors such as Christine Jolls and Cass Sunstein, but also Thomas Ulen and Russel Korobkin. Sunstein himself stated clearly that "there is no plausible argument that WTP is important in itself. If policymakers should attend to it, it is because of its connection to welfare".[194]

Finally, a sophisticated hybrid between the Chicago and Yale schools is the functional "Virginia" school, which adds public choice theory to law and economics. Rooted in the seminal contribution of James Buchanan, the Virginia school rejects the efficiency-as-justice paradigm proposed by Posner and postulates that the outcome of policy processes must be appraised in light of the interaction between institutions and the rent-seeking behavior of political actors and stakeholders.[195] This so-called "functional" school of law and economics bears important consequences on the possibility for economics to become the dominant paradigm in policymaking and politics. A notable application of this public law and economics perspective, rooted in the application of game-theoretical concepts such as principal-agent models, is the development of transaction cost politics by early authors such as Niskanen (1971), and later by McCubbins, Noll and Weingast (1986), Dixit (1996), Adler and Posner (2000), Posner (2001) and Epstein and O'Halloran (2003). According to this stream of literature – very closely related to public choice and positive political theories – the role of *ex ante* policy appraisal as a mandatory administrative requirement must be seen as a "lubricant" in the decision, by Congress or by the central administration, to delegate certain courses of action to specialized agencies. This form of "make or buy" decision emerges since: (i) the centre-of-government does not possess all the skills and resources to regulate in all domains of policymaking; and (ii) in some cases, the centre of government does not want to take ultimate political responsibility for taking regulatory actions in certain fields, and prefers to leave the blame (if any) to agencies. The framing of the delegation and oversight decisions as "make or buy" decisions allowed these scholars to draw extensively on previous law and economics literature on transaction and administrative costs, starting with Coase (1937) and continuing most notably with Oliver Williamson (1979); Klein, Crawford and Alchian (1978); and Grossman and Hart (1986).[196]

---

194 Sunstein, C.R. (2007), *Willingness to Pay v. Welfare*, 1 Harvard Law and Policy Review.

195 Parisi and Klick (2003), *supra* note 179.

196 See Williamson, O.E. (1979), *Transaction Cost Economics: The Governance of Contractual Relations*, Journal of Law and Economics, XXII, 233–261; and Williamson, O.E., *The Economic Institutions of Capitalism* (New York: The Free Press, 1985); Grossman, S.J., and O.D. Hart, *The Costs and Benefits of Ownership: A Theory of Vertical and Lateral Integration*, Journal of Political Economy, XCIV (1986), 691–719; and Klein, B., R.G. Crawford, and A.A. Alchian, *Vertical Integration, Appropriable Rents, and the Competitive Contracting Process*, Journal of Law and Economics, XXI (1978), 297–326.

To sum up, the historical development of law and economics testifies of lively and insightful developments in the understanding of individual behavior in response to the enactment of legal rules; in the design of legal rules themselves; and in the understanding of the governance mechanisms that operate behind the choice to introduce administrative procedures such as RIA as a way to control the effort and behavior of specialized bureaucracy – *i.e.* controlling agencies not based on the *outcome* of the regulatory process, but on the *way* in which the outcome was chosen.[197] Sections 4.2, 4.3 and 4.4 below explore in more detail the substantive contribution that these streams of law and economics literature can provide to the understanding, framing and implementation of legal rules and *ex ante* policy appraisal.

4.2. POSITIVE LAW AND ECONOMICS: INSIGHTS FOR *EX ANTE* POLICY APPRAISAL

Positive law and economics, in its mainstream definition, looks at human behaviour in response to law and the explanation for the law *as it is*, rather than *as it ought to be*. In this section, I focus in particular, on the former aspect – human behaviour – to explain why the advent of behavioral theory had changed substantially the perspective of scholars in this field, leading in particular Chicago scholars to reconsider many of their original tenets. Section 4.2.1 focuses on individual decision-making, whereas Section 4.2.2 deals with collective decisions.

4.2.1. UNDERSTANDING HUMAN BEHAVIOR: FROM *HOMO OECONOMICUS* TO NEUROECONOMICS

Neoclassical economic theory inspired most of the early contributions in law and economics, and still permeates most of law and economics papers. The key insights of these early writings were that legal rules had a major impact on individual incentives, rather than regulatory outcomes. Given the legal rules in place, perfectly rational individuals would then decide whether and how to comply with legal rules. In other words, rules – in the minds of lawyer-economists – became the starting point of individual negotiation: once the rule provided the setting and the allocation of property rights, private individual agents would sort out the most efficient allocation by acting rationally and trading rights. For example, in the famous theory of efficient breach in contract law, an individual party that committed to perform a contractual obligation

[197] See Epstein, D. and S. O'Halloran (1999), *Delegating Powers. A Transaction Cost Politics Approach to Policymaking under Separate Powers*, Cambridge University Press.

decides rationally to breach his or her own promise to attain a more rewarding outcome.[198] The breach is efficient whenever the "price" of that breach – *i.e.* the damage compensation imposed by the judge for breach of contract – is high enough to compensate the counter-party for the case of non-performance. Given that individuals act rationally and are perfectly informed as regards their own valuation of different states of the world, whenever damage compensation is set at the efficient level (in the simplest scenario, at expectation damages), the final outcome of human interaction will be Pareto efficient.

Likewise, in tort law, the superiority of strict liability over negligence in certain domains was explained on the basis of a key assumption – that private agents act in a perfectly rational way, and are more informed on the overall cost to society of their conduct than judges defining the optimal level of diligence *ex post*. Or, in property law, the Coase theorem relies on private parties as rational decision-makers and postulates that the lawmakers should limit themselves to minimizing the impact of transaction costs, thus unleashing the full potential of rational decisions taken by the agents involved.

So far, so good. However, already back in the mid-20th century some economists had started to challenge the paradigm of a perfectly rational *homo oeconomicus* and the Neoclassical belief in the self-healing virtues of market forces. In particular, since the early writings of Maurice Allais (1953), economic theory had been struggling with the idea that the proxy chosen for human behavior, that of perfect rationality, may not be a good one. The pioneering work of Herbert Simon in those same years confirmed that the human brain was structurally different from the brain of a *homo oeconomicus*, and this bore epochal consequences for the models used in law and economics – although many scholars preferred to ignore those findings for more than two decades. In particular, as recalled by Camerer (2007), the "ignorance of psychology" postulated by Pareto was strengthened by Chicago scholars such as Milton Friedman (1953), who developed the so-called "positive economics".

From a logical and chronological perspective, a first important finding that threatened the perfect rationality assumption was the relevance of some types of transaction costs for the outcome of otherwise rational decisions. For example, in the field of consumer protection, the notion of *rational ignorance* developed following the work of George Stigler (1960) led to a reconsideration of the idea that weaker contractual parties could be asked to become perfectly aware of all the content and consequences of the contract clauses they sign. As a matter of fact, since the marginal benefit of acquiring information on a given contractual document are often decreasing, whereas the marginal cost of acquiring additional "units of information" are increasing, even perfectly rational consumers will decide not to become perfectly informed before deciding. Especially in business-to-consumer (B2C) transactions, this meant that more informed and specialized

---

198 See, *i.a.* Posner, R.A. (1973) *Economic Analysis of Law*, Boston: Little Brown (1st edition).

businesses and professionals will always, inevitably, hold an informational advantage over their counter-parts, and may be able to exploit that advantage to extract more surplus from consumers, leading them into transactions that are not even Pareto-efficient from them. This finding – which stands at the core of public intervention to protect consumers in B2C transactions, as translated into legislative initiatives such as the German AGBG in 1976, the French "Loi Scrivener" in 1978 and later EU initiatives such as *i.a.* the Directive on Unfair terms in Consumer Contracts and the Unfair Commercial Practices Directive – already questions the belief that, when let alone, individuals enter transactions also when they are Pareto-efficient.[199]

After all, the theory of rational ignorance echoed earlier contributions such as the Popperian *statute de rationalité*, in which Karl Popper defends the act of the fool as being perfectly rational *given the context in which it was undertaken.*[200] Even more closely, rational ignorance echoes the findings of Herbert Simon as regards the fact that human beings do not take perfectly rational decisions, but only *satisficing* decisions.[201] This means that, faced with a reality that is too complex to be fully elaborated and understood, our brains collect "proxies" (as economists would call them) that enable them to adopt a reasonably informed decision, and stop collecting and elaborating information the moment this activity becomes too lengthy and cumbersome to enable any timely course of action. As a matter of fact, Simon's *satisficing* behavior did not question the perfect rationality of individuals: more precisely, it questioned the rationality of the outcomes of their decisions, given the constraint represented by the resources available to our brain.

Even more importantly, Simon drew from his study of the human brain the conclusion that the proxies that we collect to be able to make decisions in a world that is too complex for us to understand are a mix of past experience and external signals. This, in turn, means that our expectations partly govern our future actions, and our representation of reality is inevitably path-dependent. In this respect, the work of Simon can be closely associated with that of Brian Arthur, who – from a completely different perspective – argued that individual and

---

199 See the French Law 78–22 of 10 January 1978, on the protection and information of consumers; German *Gesetz zur Regelung des Rechts der Allgemeinen Geschäftsbedingungen* (AGBG); Council Directive 93/13/EEC of 5 April 1993 on unfair terms in consumer contracts; and Directive 2005/29/EC of the European Parliament and of the Council of 11 May 2005 concerning unfair business-to-consumer commercial practices in the internal market and amending Council Directive 84/450/EEC, Directives 97/7/EC, 98/27/EC and 2002/65/EC of the European Parliament and of the Council and Regulation (EC) No 2006/2004 of the European Parliament and of the Council.

200 On the relevance of context, see Korobkin, R.B. and T.S. Ulen (2000), *Law and Behavioral Science: Removing the Rationality Assumption from Law and Economics.* California Law Review, Vol. 88, at 1102 ff.

201 Simon, H.A. (1956). *Rational Choice and the Structure of the Environment*, Psychological Review, Vol. 63 No. 2, 129–138.

collective human behavior exhibit strong path-dependence, mostly due to the switching costs associated with changing course of action, as well as to the economizing activity of our brain, which "cuts corners" and takes shortcuts in making decisions. An ancillary finding of this stream of cognitive science is that, in their effort to collect proxies that enable them to take decisions, human beings are often affected by the observation of what other people do. This effect, sometimes termed "herd behavior" or "bandwagon effect" in economics, does not surface only along with direct network externalities: it is an important element in many important decisions individuals take every day.[202]

The work of pioneers such as Allais, Simon and Arthur constituted a first, major attack at the foundations of neoclassical economics and its faith in market outcomes. The idea that rationality could be bounded, *i.e.* prey of an array of diverse constraints that limit the potential of individual decision-making, was at once devastating and thrilling for economists, and showed that economics was not rocket science, since the individual dimension of decision-making made an exact forecast of future outcomes impossible. For example, in 1974, while receiving the Nobel Prize for Economics, Friederich Von Hayek denounced the flaws of neoclassical (macro)economists, who had failed to predict the major economic crisis of the early 1970s. In doing so, he reminded the audience that economics is not like physics: it is a social, not a natural science, and its usefulness and soundness crucially depend on the underlying assumptions that are used to approximate and simplify the complexity of the outside world. In doing this, he was pointing the finger at economists like Paul Samuelson, who looked at physics as the science for economics to emulate.[203]

Subsequent years have led to a major reconsideration of the features of human decision-making and its impact on market outcomes. The research on the so-called "prospect theory" by Daniel Kahneman and Amos Tversky, awarded the Nobel prize in 2002, was an essential step towards operationalizing the findings of cognitive psychology into the portrayal of an array of situations in which humans will indeed err, and will do it systematically. Since then, the tenets of Neoclassical economics have gradually tumbled down. Examples are manifold. Take the so-called "endowment effect" elaborated by Richard Thaler back in 1980 and extensively studied in modern neuroeconomics[204]: the fact that people attach an asymmetric value to gains and losses based on the situation that they consider to be the "default state" challenges several insights from early Chicago law and economics, including the theory of efficient breach and the idea of liability rules as Pareto-Superior solutions, and extends beacons of skepticism over the whole

202 See, *i.a.* Rohlfs, J. (1974) *A Theory of Interdependent Demand for a Communications Service*, Bell Journal of Economics 5, 16–37.

203 See, *i.a.* Lo, A.W. and M.T. Mueller (2010), *Warning: Physics Envy May be Hazardous to Your Wealth!* (March 12, 2010). Available at SSRN: http://ssrn.com/abstract=1563882.

204 Thaler, R. (1980). *Toward a positive theory of consumer choice.* Journal of Economic Behavior and Organization, 1, 39–60.

approach to damage compensation. Empirical evidence that individuals systematically under-estimate risk in certain circumstances, and over-estimate risk in others, bears significant consequences in several areas of legislation, in which the optimality of individual decision-making had been an essential feature of policy advice. Moreover, "regret theory" shows that individuals may prefer courses of actions that minimize their regret, compared to other options that, though potentially more rewarding, can also lead to missed opportunities.[205]

The relevance of behavioral and cognitive studies for several social sciences was so strongly felt that some economists decided to go deeper in the analysis of the human brain and started testing the major structural biases in human rationality through Magnetic Resonance Imaging and similar tools. The branch of neuroeconomics has today advanced to the study of neurotransmitters such as dopamine as key factors that determine the outcome of individual choices.[206] The findings of cognitive sciences and neuroeconomics have recently become subject to livelier interest in the policy community. On the one hand, competition authorities and consumer protection bodies are trying to incorporate these insights in their overall policy approach. At the same time, international organizations such as the OECD (2008) have devoted conferences to the understanding of the impact that behavioral biases may exert on the design and on the effectiveness of policies. The most studied impacts include the following[207]:

- *Choice/information overload*: economic models suggest that the benefits from extra choice and information are unbounded. Even the theory of "bounded rationality" does not suggest that extra choice and information is detrimental. Market research however, in products as diverse as jams and retirement savings, suggests that past a point, when provided with more choice and information, we either walk away from markets, choosing not to choose, or we choose randomly.
- *Endowment bias*: What one has is valued more than what one might have. Consumers are often reluctant to switch suppliers because of a loyalty, which may be misplaced, to existing suppliers. This is particularly evident in telecommunication and financial services.
- *Overconfidence*: in many situations, consumers are overconfident in their abilities and in their future fortunes. For example, many people invest, believing that they can beat the stock market, or they underestimate the risk that illness or unemployment may cause difficulty in repaying a loan. Again, this bias is important in financial services.

205 In this respect, regret theory is very related to Rawls' idea of maximin. See below, Section 4.3.3.2.

206 See *i.a.* Camerer, C., G. Loewenstein and D. Prelec (2005), *Neuroeconomics. How Neuroscience can Inform Economics*. Journal of Economic Literature 43, 1, 9–64.

207 Source: OECD 7th Global Forum on Competition, Introductory Note, February 2008.

- *Framing biases*: Consumers are influenced not only by the objective information provided by suppliers, but also by the "frame" of that information. For example, a claim "92% fat free" elicits a different response than "8% fat."
- *Difficulty in handling uncertainty and risk*: The frame in which choices are considered influences consumer's perceptions of the consequences of uncertain outcomes. When gambles (such as insurance choices) are considered in isolation, consumers tend to be irrationally risk averse. When consumers consider themselves to be in a loss situation (such as becoming heavily overcommitted on a credit card) they tend to behave recklessly. Furthermore, consumers often have difficulty in thinking rationally about possible outcomes with very low probability.
- *Mis-evaluation of future benefits and costs (hyperbolic discounting, myopia)*: Consumers do not rationally weigh up present against future benefits and costs; rather they put too much weight on the immediate. This bias is manifest in outcomes such as low retirement savings in the absence of compulsion.

The example of retail financial services is perhaps the most intuitive, when it comes to explaining the impact of these decision-making biases. For example, in a recent paper on consumer investment decisions, Oehler and Kohlert (2009) comment on the information overload effect by arguing that

> "*The sheer amount of information the customer has to perceive and to process means a high grade of complexity on its own. The number of options and corresponding attributes inherent in this quantity of information clarifies that. If the individual investment types and products, respectively, are considered decision options, the client is confronted with about five options alone at the investment type level (e.g., liquidity, bonds, stocks, insurance, funds) with different subgroups each (e.g., money market funds, bond funds, equity funds, real estate funds) of which each again has a much higher number of corresponding attributes. The multiplicity of attributes can be clarified by considering different attribute levels (e.g., level 1: cost, level 2: purchase cost, level 3: indirect cost, level 4: kick-back payments). Furthermore, the information the client receives during an advising session are highly interrelated... If we consider that humans cannot simultaneously process more than nine information units, even less in the case of complex problems... it is unavoidable that the majority of the clients who have little or no knowledge and experience in the investment area will suffer from information overload*".[208]

In addition to this account of rational ignorance, several papers in behavioral economics and neuroeconomics illustrate individuals' decision-making bias

---

208 Oehler, A., and D. Kohlert. (2009), *Financial Advice Giving and Taking – Where are the Market's Self-healing Powers and a Functioning Legal Framework When We Need Them?*, Journal of Consumer Policy 32: 91–116., at 103.

when facing ambiguous or risky situations.[209] The main prescriptive result of this literature is that financial intermediaries have several options to engage in misleading conduct such as steering or churning, and will use their informational advantage to extract as much surplus as possible from less informed customers.[210]

More generally, the law and economics of human behavior has converged on three different types of bounds on otherwise rational behavior. First, individuals exhibit *bounded rationality*, which means that their mental resources are limited and individuals make judgment errors and systematically depart from the expected utility theory. In addition, humans display *bounded willpower*, which captures the fact that people sometimes make choices that are not in their long-run interest, and often feature a "multiple-selves" problem.[211] Finally, *bounded self-interest* incorporates the fact that humans are often willing to sacrifice their own interests to help others – *i.e.* other-regarding behavior is part of decisions taken by individuals.[212]

In the field of law and economics, some scholars have attempted to translate these findings into concrete prescriptive solutions. After the more "exploratory" nature of papers such as Ulen and Korobkin (2000), some scholars have

---

209 See Barberis, N. and R. Thaler (2002), A Survey of *Behavioral Finance*, available at http://ssrn.com/abstract=327880 or doi:10.2139/ssrn.327880; Bossaerts, P. L. (2009), *What Decision Neuroscience Teaches Us About Financial Decision Making*, Annual Rev. Fin. Econ. 2009.1:383–404; Camerer, C. (2008), *The Case for Mindful Economics*, in Caplin, A., and Schotter, A. (ed.), Foundations of Positive and Normative Economics (New York: Oxford University Press, 2008); Camerer, C., G. Loewenstein, and D. Prelec (2004), *Neuroeconomics: Why Economics Needs Brains*, Scandinavian Journal of Economics, 106(3), 2004, 555–579; and Camerer, C; G. Loewenstein, and D. Prelec (2005), *Neuroeconomics: How Neuroscience Can Inform Economics*, Journal of Economic Literature, 43, March 2005, 9–64.

210 See Renda *et al.*, (2009), *Tying and other potentially unfair commercial practices in retail financial services*, final report for the European Commission, Dg internal Market and Services, available online at http://ec.europa.eu/internal_market/consultations/docs/2010/tying/report_en.pdf.

211 See, for an early contribution, Posner R.A. (1997), *Are We One Self or Multiple Selves? Implications for Law and Public Policy*, in Legal Theory, 3, pp. 23–35. More recent elaborations on the multiple selves problem include Rasmusen, E. (2008), *Internalities and Paternalism. Applying the Compensation Criterion to Multiple Selves across Time*, Indiana University, Kelley School of Business, Department of Business Economics and Public Policy Working Paper No 2008-13.

212 In the definition given by Jolls, Sunstein and Thaler (2001), that people display bounded rationality is linked to the fact that they suffer from certain biases, such as over-optimism and self-serving conceptions of fairness; they follow heuristics, such as availability, that lead to mistakes; and they behave in accordance with prospect theory rather than expected utility theory. Bounded willpower means that they can be tempted and are sometimes myopic. Finally, they are boundedly self-interested, which means that they are concerned about the wellbeing of others, even strangers in some circumstances, and this concern and their self-conception can lead them in the direction of cooperation at the expense of their material self-interest (and sometimes spite, also at the expense of their material self-interest). See also Jeffrey J. Rachlinski, *The "New" Law and Psychology: A Reply to Critics, Skeptics and Cautious Supporters*, 85 Cornell L. Rev. 739, 761 (2000).

attempted to illustrate ways to achieve "de-biasing" through law. For example, Sunstein and Thaler (2003), Jolls and Sunstein (2005) and Jolls (2006) analyze the impact of behavioral law and economics on traditional ways of appraising and justifying policy. Jolls (2006) brings examples related to distributional impacts in legal rules, discovery rules in litigation, the business judgment rule in corporate law, rules on contractual renegotiation and specific rules in consumer protection laws. The de-biasing approach implies that policy actions do not try to "protect legal outcomes from the effects of the errors", but instead "by operating directly on the errors and attempting to help people either to reduce or to eliminate them".[213]

The consequences of realizing that human behavior systematically diverges from the prototype of *homo oeconomicus* are far-reaching, especially when we consider cost-benefit analysis as grounds for justifying policy actions and the choice of a preferred action over alternative, as done in RIA. This, in turn, shows that the evolution of the "positive" school of law and economics" bears important normative consequences. At a minimum, it seems fair to state that the Coase theorem should be redefined to accommodate the role of legal rules in minimizing the impact of behavioral biases.[214] But the potential impact of behavioralism is more pervasive: suffice it to mention that, according to Sunstein and Thaler (2003), in the presence of the endowment effect a "cost-benefit study cannot be based on willingness to pay (WTP), because WTP will be a function of the default rule". Even outside the realm of cost-benefit analysis *per se*, consequences may be significant: according to Jolls, depending on the circumstances, de-biasing can and should be obtained through substantive law, through procedural law, or a blend of both. A similar approach to de-biasing through law is adopted by Sunstein (2009) in developing the concept of "nudging". Section 4.3.6 below explores the potential consequences of adopting a behavioral approach to the design and enforcement of legal rules by describing what "nudging" may mean for the design and implementation of RIA practice, and how nudging can be usefully introduced in a RIA exercise.

213 Jolls, C. (2007), *Behavioral law and economics*, Chapter 4 in in Diamond, Hannu Vartiainen and Yrjö Jahnssonin säätiö (eds.), *Behavioral economics and its applications*, Princeton, N.J.: Princeton University Press, at 34–35.

214 Some authors have expressed themselves for a "de-Coasing" of law and economics, at least in the environmental field. See Arcuri, A. (2005), *A Different Reason for de-Coasing Environmental Law and Economics*, European Journal of Law and Economics Volume 20, Number 2, 225–246.

4.2.2. NORMS, GROUPS AND INSTITUTIONS: CHALLENGING METHODOLOGICAL INDIVIDUALISM

Traditional law and economics basically rested on two key assumptions: perfect rationality of individual agents, and methodological individualism. As explained in the previous section, law and economics scholars have come to grips with cognitive sciences and neuro-anatomy by developing new approaches known as behavioral law and economics and neuroeconomics. However, the attacks to the neoclassical paradigm do not end there. The second key assumption of traditional neoclassical (law and) economics has been subject to less well-known, but perhaps more pervasive and disruptive criticism, which bears important consequences for our understanding of how modern law and economics can contribute to the *ex ante* appraisal of policy.

Methodological individualism can be defined in non-technical terms as the assumption that individual preferences are dependent on each individual's specific situation, and not on external constraints. More precisely, under a methodologically individualist approach marginal utilities – and thus individual preferences in market and non-market contexts – "do not depend on what society as such has, but on what individual members have". Following Schumpeter (1909), "nobody values bread according to the quantity of it which is to be found in his country or in the world, but everybody measures the utility of it according to the amount that he has himself, and this in turn depends on his general means".[215] Chicago-style law and economics fully adopted this approach due to its deep roots in neoclassical economics. Even more generally, the study of economics has most often adopted individuals as the basic unit of analysis.[216]

As illustrated by authors such as Hovenkamp (1994), Udehn (2002), Hodgson (2007), and Ahdieh (2009), reliance on methodological individualism is the key pillar on which economics builds the analysis of social outcomes, and in particular the aggregation of individual preferences into the public good as "spontaneous" order. As succinctly put by Robert Ahdieh (2009), "in a methodologically individualist approach ... analysis of the social must occur by way of the individual". Departing from this assumption, therefore, also means

215 Schumpeter, J. (1909) *On the Concept of Social Value*, 23 Q.J. ECON. 213, 231 (1909). Even before Schumpeter, the elaboration of methodological individualism can be traced back to the work of Ludwig Von Mises and Carl Manger, but also in Jeremy Bentham, John Locke, and John Stuart Mill. See Ahdieh, R.B. (2009), *Beyond Individualism in Law and Economics*. Emory Public Law Research Paper No. 9–78; Emory Law and Economics Research Paper No. 09–48.

216 See, *i.a.*, Arrow (1994) (stating that "it is a touchstone of economics that all explanations must run in terms of the actions and reactions of individuals. Our behavior in judging economic research, in peer review of papers and research, and in promotions, includes the criterion that in principle the behavior we explain and the policies we propose are explicable in terms of individuals, not of other social categories").

undermining the true foundations of the method used by economics to formulate normative prescriptions. To the contrary, it leads economic analysis closer to the findings of sociology, typically rooted in the study of social phenomena from a non-individualist perspective.

Relaxing methodological individualism to embrace "holism" means departing from the assumption of subjectivity of preferences. At a minimum, this means that social constraints – including, in particular, social norms and herd behavior – shape individual preferences and provide the framework in which such preferences are formed. A direct consequence is that one cannot defend the rationality of an individual choice on the basis of the subjectivity of preferences and the impossibility to calculate utility and engage in inter-personal utility comparison. Rather, it is the recognition of the inter-dependence of individual preferences that determines an important scholarly conclusion: that contrary to the dictates of methodological individualism, the idea of aggregation of preferences is misleading, and "the phenomena to be explained involve interdependence of individuals' actions, not merely aggregated individual behavior".[217]

An important consequence of this debate is that, according to psychologists, socio-economists and a growing number of lawyer-economists, the way in which economics has been aggregating preferences for decades – including, most notably, through the Kaldor-Hicks calculation of net benefits in terms of money – is flawed, approximate and incomplete. Far from occurring exclusively in the economic agent's mind, the formation of preferences becomes subject to important external constraints, up to the point where it originates from a "social mind". The key examples are the role of social norms and that of network effects, or – to avoid confusion with market effects depicted in network industries – "herd behavior" phenomena in several markets.

4.2.2.1. Social norms and the law

Social norms are relevant to the understanding of several aspects of the formulation and implementation of legal rules. First, if we accept that social norms exert a constraint on individual preferences and choice, the natural consequence will be that the same legal rule may exert a different impact depending on the type of social context in which the decision to comply will be formulated. A similar effect was defined, though in a different stream of academic literature, as the "compliance trap". According to Christine Parker (2006), the compliance trap occurs "where there is a lack of political and cultural support for the moral seriousness of the law it must enforce". When this is the case, any attempt to enforce the law in a formalistic way is doomed to failure, unless the

217 See Udehn, L. (2002), *The Changing Face of Methodological Individualism*, 28 Annual Review of Sociology 479, 484.

policymaker can promote the "moral" content of the law in a way that directly changes the social norms behind it.[218] The strength of social norms can be so decisive that in some environments social norms definitely trump legal rules whenever a conflict arises. Examples are manifold, and range from the implementation of the ban on smoking in public places (*e.g.*, in Jordan) to pooper-scooper norms (Cooter, 1996[219]) to compliance with the law in post-communist countries, and to the violations of copyright in cyberspace.[220] In this respect, perhaps the Internet is the most intuitive example: so far, changing the *netiquette*, which perceived file sharing as perfectly legitimate although often illegal, has proven prohibitive through legal means and any attempt at changing social norms. Legislators around the world are now trying with technology, *i.e.* changing the constraints on individual choices by changing the architecture of the IP-based environment in which they operate. In this respect, this confirms what Lessig (1999) stated about law in cyberspace: that *code*, not law, defines what's possible and acceptable.[221]

When social norms diverge from the scope and content of a legal rule, the latter's effectiveness can be significantly undermined. Enforcers will find it often inappropriate to apply the rule to a full extent, as they themselves do not share the policymaker's judgment on the morality of the law; recipients will face a collective action problem in deciding to comply: since, when everyone complies the cost of compliance is lower and the benefit of compliance is greater, the individual act of complying creates positive externalities that are never fully internalized until others behave similarly.[222]

The study of social norms and their interaction with legal rules has been subject to an extensive stream of literature in social science. Notable contributions include the work of Karl Polanyi on forms of exchange, which shed light on the emergence of interactions that take non-contractual forms (*e.g.* reciprocity), which are potentially applicable to contemporary phenomena that are hard to categorize under standard law and economics – *i.a.*, open source software.[223] Stewart Macaulay's classic article "Non-Contractual Relations in Business" investigated the contrasting roles of legal and non-legal norms in business

218 See, *i.a.* Braithwaite (2002). And Ayres and Braithwaite (1992).

219 Cooter, R.D. (1996). *Decentralized Law for a Complex Economy: The Structural Approach to Adjudicating the New Law Merchant*, 144 University of Pennsylvania Law Review 1643–1696. And Scott, R.E. (2000). *The Limits of Behavioral Theories of Law and Social Norms*, 86 Virginia Law Review 1603–1647.

220 Galligan, D. (2003), *The Failure of Law in Post-Communist Countries: A Study of Law and Social Norms*, in Galligan and Kurkchiyan (eds.) Law and Informal Practices in Post-Communist Societies (Oxford UP, 2003).

221 See *i.a.* Renda (2009), *Achilles and the Turtle (Akilles och sköldpaddan)*, in "Gratis? Om kvalitet, pengar och skapandets villkor" (ed. Strömbäck, Per), Stockholm: Volante QNB, 2009) (in Swedish language). Information available at http://bokengratis.se/utdrag-andrea-renda/.

222 See Cooter, R.D. (2000), *Three effects of social norms*, Oregon Law Review Vol. 79.

223 See Polanyi, K. (1944) *The Great Transformation*, New York: Farrar & Rinehart.

relationships, showing that the enforceability of contracts under certain circumstances was not seen as a major problem by businessmen due to the existence of strong social norms.[224] Similar studies are the ones that focus on *guanxi*, *i.e.* connections and family ties in Chinese culture as non-legal forms of contractual commitment. Reputational effects, repeated game effects, and the availability of non-legal sanctions dramatically affect the effectiveness and enforceability of commitments, together with the need for strong contractual remedies.[225]

Closer to the law and economics movement, the work of Douglass North (1990) gave rise to a burgeoning literature in New Institutional Economics by defining institutions as "the rules of the game in a society or, more formally, ... the humanly devised constraints that shape human interaction".[226] According to North, this theory of institutions based on the foundation of individual choice potentially reconciles the differences between economics and other social sciences. This also means that integrating individual choices with the constraints institutions impose on choice sets is a major step toward unifying social science research. Recently, Amir Licht (2008) criticized this approach in the Review of Law & Economics exactly by stating that methodological individualism is an incomplete approach to the complexity of institutions and their impact on human behavior.[227]

The relevance of social norms in the study of the impact of legal rules has surfaced in the law and economics literature thanks to the work of Oliver Williamson (2000). This elaboration implies a taxonomy of levels of social institutions. Williamson observes that "Level 1" mostly consists of social institutions, including social norms, which lay the foundations for their layers and deeply affect their working. "Level 2" contains formal legal rules that realize the allocation of entitlements, including most notably property. The next level (3) deals with the transfer of entitlements and governance of economic relationships, including in particular contract law. Finally, level 4 contains the so-called marginal analysis, *i.e.* everything that governs the formation of market outcomes. It is not the purpose of this work to discuss in-depth Williamson's taxonomy: suffice here to recall that, according to Williamson, the first level of analysis, thus the one dedicated to informal institutions and social norms, is normally taken as a given in law and economics, whereas a deeper analysis of that level would

224 Macaulay, S. (1963), *Non-Contractual Relations in Business: A Preliminary Study.* 28 American Sociological Review 1963, 55–67.

225 See Winn, J. K. (1994), *Relational Practices and the Marginalization of Law: Informal Financial Practices of Small Businesses in Taiwan.* 28 Law and Society Review 1994, 193–241.

226 North, D. (1990): *Institutions, Institutional Change, and Economics Performance.* Cambridge University Press, Cambridge 1990.

227 Licht, A. (2008), *Social Norms and the Law. Why Peoples Obey the Law,* Review of Law and Economics, 4:3, 715.

enrich our understanding of the effectiveness and actual interpretation of legal rules in property and contracts, as well as the birth of formal institutions.

The real problem, however, is not solved by Williamson's taxonomy and a greater awareness of the existence of social norms. As a matter of fact, the birth of institutions implies the formulation of some sort of social preferences, that are the result of social interaction that cannot be explained by keeping the individual as the sole unit of analysis. The real obstacle for economists is easily referred to Arrow's impossibility theorem, which draws on an earlier intuition of Condorcet (1792) and postulates the impossibility of aggregating individual preferences into coherent societal ones.[228] Authors such as James Buchanan and Amartya Sen also expressed serious doubts on the possibility to aggregate individual preferences into some notion of societal preference.[229] In a nutshell, while law and economics scholars have recognized the need to expand their analysis into social norms and institutions to achieve a better understanding of human and social behavior as a response to legal rules, they have not tackled the problem of how to aggregate individual preferences into meaningful indicators of societal good. Arrow's impossibility theorem and Sen's Paradox stand on their way to such an achievement, casting dark shadows on the prospects of neoclassical economics in this very complex endeavor.

4.2.2.2. Network effects and herd behavior

Similarly to social norms, network effects and herd behavior are typical cases in which the inter-dependence between individuals and their dynamic interaction makes it impossible to follow a mathematical aggregation of individual preferences as in neoclassical economics. Different levels of interaction between individuals, moreover, imply that coordinated social outcomes will exhibit multiple equilibria, something that economics can hardly cope with due to the excessive number of variables.[230] This general finding is mirrored in the fact that games such as the Prisoner's Dilemma have attracted much more attention than others – *e.g.* the hawk-dove game – which, although very important for the understanding of human interaction, display a multiplicity of potential

---

228 Arrow's impossibility theorem states that, when voters have three or more discrete alternatives (options), no voting system can convert the ranked preferences of individuals into a community-wide ranking while also meeting a certain set of criteria. These criteria are called unrestricted domain, non-dictatorship, Pareto efficiency, and independence of irrelevant alternatives. See the proof of the thorem in Kelly J. (1988), *Social Choice Theory: an Introduction*, Springer.

229 Licht (2008) observes that Lewin (1996) traces this problem, which is also dubbed "Sen's paradox," to the historical roots of the relations between economics and psychology during early 20th century (see Rabin, 1998, for an influential review).

230 See Ahdieh, R. B. (2004), *Law's Signal: A Cueing Theory of Law in Market Transition*, 77 Southern California Law Rev. 215.

equilibria.[231] Coordination games, which stand at the core of the study of social interaction and the emergence of social norms – are not the easiest of fields for law and economics.

One additional feature of phenomena such as herd behavior and bandwagon effects is their reliance on external constraints. More precisely, while direct and indirect network externalities observed in industries such as electronic communications have their roots in straightforward functions of the value and utility of a given product (*e.g.*, the value of a telephone to its user increases exponentially as the number of reachable users increase linearly, and the value of a phone to a user when there is no other user around is close to zero); in other cases the bandwagon effect originate directly from the observation of social, external behavior. For example, if Alice observes that a crowd of people is trying to enter Bob's Restaurant, whereas Charlie's Diner right across the street is empty, she will infer that Bob's has better food. In this case, the need to collect information *ex ante* on an experience good leads Alice to draw on external signals sent by the majority of people she can observe.[232] In other cases, this observation is coupled with some form of external recognition – take the case of fashion products, which lose value as the critical mass of consumers move to another product, even if there is no intrinsic reason why demand should oscillate so significantly.

In all those cases, collective action and individual emulation evolve and interact, forming social phenomena that are difficult to explain by simply relying on the individual's mere endowment. A large portion of these effects can indeed be dealt with by economics. What economists have failed to take into account, however, is that the happiness or satisfaction of a given individual is most often dependant on that individual's relative, rather than absolute well-being. This, as I observe in Section 4.3 below, casts doubts even on the least disputed of welfare-maximization criteria used in economics: Pareto efficiency.

---

231 The Hawk-Dove game was illustrated by John Maynard Smith and G.R. Price. In this game, two individuals compete for a resource of a fixed value V – *e.g.* their survival or fitness. One players (hawk) behaves aggressively, not stopping until injured or until one's opponent backs down; whereas the other (dove) retreats immediately if her opponent initiates aggressive behavior. Over time, the division of roles leads to a stable equilibrium between hawks and doves. this is why this repeated game has been one of the bases for developing evolutionary game theory. The game is also known as the "chicken game". See Maynard Smith, J. and G.R. Price (1973), *The Logic of Animal Conflict*, Nature 246, 15–18.

232 See, for a definition of experience goods, Nelson, P. (1970), *Information and Consumer Behavior*, Journal of Political Economy, 78 – (March-April), 311–29. Nelson, P. (1974), *Advertising as Information*, Journal of Political Economy, 83 (July-August), 729–54. And Darby, M.R. and E. Karni (1973), *Free Competition and the Optimal Amount of Fraud*, Journal of Law and Economics, 16 (April), 67–88.

4.2.2.3. *Concluding remarks*

The consequences of the literature on social norms on mainstream law and economics seem, at first blush, less revolutionary than what claimed by some scholars. As a matter of fact, it is true that economists have regularly downplayed the non-individual aspects of human choice; at the same time, the fact that external constraints shape individual preferences is already accounted for in the behavioral law and economics literature, which draws on the concept of bounded rationality. As I explained in section 4.2.1.1 above, studies of the human brain confirm that the observation of other's behavior is an important source of inspiration for human decision-making, which compared to the one of the *homo oeconomicus* takes the even-more-dismal form of having to cope with an overly complex world with very limited resources. At the same time, the studies on the role of "mirror neurons" in human behavior lay the foundations for "bounded self-interest" as defined in the previous section, *i.e.* the fact that we are anatomically geared towards empathy, and that other-regarding behavior is an integral part of the formation of our individual preferences.[233] David Hume and Adam Smith already referred to sympathy and fellow-feeling as shaping human behavior, and the consequences of these sentiments on human behavior and on the inter-personal comparison of utility have been studied, *i.a.* by Fontaine (2001).[234]

So far, so good: the need to account for social norms and methodological holism can in principle be reconciled with the behavioral critique to neoclassical tenets of economics.[235] But there seems to be more in the critique of methodological individualism, which attacks the true foundation of mainstream law and economics as we use to define it. It shows that the "Posnerian" economic analysis of law – and at the same time, the use of economics to shape legal rules and determine the ultimate goal of the state – is more limited in scope than has been stated in the past decades, and that economics has to come to grips with equally important social sciences such as psychology and sociology, which have gone further in adopting a methodologically holistic approach that accounts for

233 See, *i.a.* Kirman A. and M. Techl, *Selfish or selfless? The role of empathy in economics*, Phil. Trans. R. Soc. B 2010 365, 303–317. And Fontaine, P. (2001), *The changing place of empathy in welfare economics*. Hist. Polit. Econ. 33, 387–409.

234 See also Khalil, E. (2007), *The Mirror-Neuron Paradox: How Far is Sympathy from Compassion, Indulgence, and Adulation?*, MPRA Paper No. 3961.

235 See, on methodological holism (or collectivism), Parker, W., *Methodological Individualism v. Methodological Holism. Neoclassicism, Institutionalism and Socioeconomic Theory*, available online at www.socionomics.org/pdf/neoclassicism_institutionalism.pdf. For a complete bibliography on the debate between methodological individualism and holism in social sciences, see Lukes, S. (1973), *Individualism*, reprinted by ECPR Press, Colchester, 2006.

the social good as something different from the mere sum of its parts – *i.e.* the aggregation of individual preferences.[236]

At the same time, it also means that policymaking should be made dependent on something else than what Hovenkamp (1994) critically defines as preference-based (or "subjective") welfare judgment. To the contrary, there is room for so-called "objective welfare judgment", *i.e.* the determination of welfare goals and the social good with means other than mere reliance on subjective preferences. As we will see in Section 4.4 below, this at once determines the limit of the expansionist trend of economics into law and other social sciences; and the potential justification of "nudging" and intermediate forms of "libertarian paternalism" as ways to affect people's preferences and choice to steer them towards "socially desirable" outcomes as defined by policymakers themselves.

4.3. NORMATIVE LAW AND ECONOMICS: HOW THE LAW *OUGHT TO BE*

The attacks to traditional law and economics based on the critique to rationality and methodological individualism were thorough and almost undisputable ones: the predictive power of economics seemed essentially rooted in a methodological mystification. As a matter of fact, early Progressives such as John Dewey and Clarence Ayres seemed aware of the fact that the key pillars of economics were a double-edged sword[237]: on the one hand, individualism and rationality allowed economics to develop a consistent set of principles and an appearance of scientific soundness, which ended up being very powerful and appealing for policymakers. Economists such as Milton Friedman (1957) explicitly treated the problem and rejected any further sophistication of neoclassical economics, which would have undermined its phenomenal predictive power. Richard Posner entirely followed this approach in proposing an economic analysis of the law, which would basically draw on neoclassical economics to create a fictional world in which individuals always express their preference through market acts.

However, by striking this Faustian deal with the "neoclassical devil", law and economics also had to leave something aside. In particular, the neoclassical fiction could not support any conclusion as regards three of the fundamental

236 See Philippe Fontaine's explanation of Mancur Olson's *Logic of Collective Action*. In Fontaine, P. (2007), *From Philanthropy to Altruism: Incorporating Unselfish Behavior into Economics*, 1961–1975, History of Political Economy 2007 39(1):1–46.

237 This is why both Dewey and Ayres agreed that economics should cooperate with other social sciences, in a *continuum*. See, *i.a.* Tilman, R. (1990), *New Light on John Dewey, Clarence Ayres, and the Development of Evolutionary Economics*, Journal of Economic Issues Vol. 24, No. 4 (Dec., 1990), pp. 963–979; and Campbell, D. (1994), *Ayres versus Coase: An Attempt to Recover the Issue of Equality in Law and Economics,* Journal of Law and Society Vol. 21, No. 4 (Dec., 1994), 434–463.

issues policymakers have to address when crafting policy: happiness, distribution of wealth, and money. These three issues are so important for understanding the limits of today's RIA practice, that the whole result of *ex ante* appraisal may be meaningless if the fallacies concerning them are not fixed.

First, although neoclassical economists generally consider themselves as descendants of Jeremy Bentham, Bentham's vision of the role of public policy was one aimed at maximizing "happiness", rather than "utility" or "welfare". The impossibility of directly measuring happiness, however, led economists to rely on proxies such as "revealed preferences": as a matter of fact, since the direct measurement of happiness, as well as the interpersonal comparison of utility, are not technically possible, one could either rely on some form of introspection (as some psychologists have tried to advocate[238]); or revert to external manifestations of individual perceptions, such as market behavior. Accordingly, if Alice decides to buy a widget for $100, she is implicitly signaling that her willingness to pay for the widget is higher than $100. And if Alice and Bob enter a contract whereby Bob will purchase the widget from Alice at a price of $120, this means that Bob values the widget at least $120 and that the transaction is Pareto efficient, since both parties have *spontaneously* decided to conclude it. Accordingly, parties reveal their preferences by acting on the marketplace, and all successful negotiations lead to a tentative mapping of the parties' preferences through express consent.

However, revealed preferences exhibits important shortcomings. First, observation of (and reliance on) market behavior inevitably carries a bias in favor of those transactions that are actually concluded. The fact that Alice would have bought a widget for $100, but the market price was higher than her willingness to pay is not taken into account by economics in treating revealed preferences. But even more importantly, revealed preferences crucially depend on an individual's willingness *and ability* to pay – if Alice is poor, she may not wish to buy a widget for $100, even if she really likes widgets. Now, if she would have valued the good but could not buy it because of insufficient income, should we care when crafting policy?

Put differently, the use of revealed preferences implies reliance on external manifestations of individual preferences such as the willingness to pay (WTP). But WTP measures exhibit a number of important shortcomings, including *in primis* the dependence on the level of income.[239] Accordingly, a low WTP for a widget does not necessarily signal a low interest. Alice may be highly interested in buying the widget, and the possession of the widget may prospectively make

238 See James, W. (1890), *The Principles of Psychology*, also available online at http://psychclassics.yorku.ca/James/Principles/.

239 See, *i.a.* Heinzerling and Ackerman (2008), on the difference between WTP and ability to pay (ATP).

her very "happy", but if she does not have enough money to spend her WTP for the widget will inevitably remain limited.

Moreover, following the "prospect theory" developed by Nobel laureates Daniel Kahneman and Amos Tversky, an individual WTP for a widget is often very different from the individual's willingness to accept compensation (WTA) for being deprived of the same widget. Accordingly, assessing the impact of redistribution or reallocation of resources in a society is very difficult, if not impossible, as individuals will not converge on a single valuation of a good. Taking the widget from Bob and reallocating it to Alice for a given price *x* may leave Bob unhappy (since his WTA is higher than the price *x*) and at times Alice also unhappy (if price *x* is higher than her WTP). Likewise, the efficient resource reallocation through private bargaining postulated by the Coase theorem may not hold – as demonstrated by Hovenkamp (1994) – whenever the parties do not find a price at which a potentially efficient transaction may take place.

This discussion is related to a *querelle* that has never been resolved in economics. Chicago economists are almost silent on distributional issues: and for good reasons, since they know that their efficiency criterion – mostly Paretian – has nothing to say about distribution. If a cake falls like manna from heaven, and Alice and Bob share it, the neoclassical economist has nothing to say on how big should the share be for each of them. Likewise, in deciding whether the state should transfer a given amount of money to the poor by taxing the wealthy, neoclassical economists are at best agnostic on the overall impact of that transfer. If anything, if the transfer implies some cost, the overall welfare impact will be negative. This is due to the fact that the Pareto criterion looks exclusively at the "size of the pie", rather than at the distribution of the shares. I will come back to this issue in the next section.

At the same time, the discussion calls into question another of the key shortcomings of neoclassical economics: that criteria such as Pareto efficiency and Kaldor-Hicks efficiency essentially work whenever we are dealing with *spontaneous* transactions; however, when we are using the same criteria for forced redistribution of resources, the absence of *consent* leaves no way of demonstrating that the reallocation is increasing or decreasing the size of the pie. As will be shown in the next section, Posner tried to overcome this problem by assuming that the Kaldor-Hicks criterion is rooted in a general principle of justice that is accepted *ex ante* by citizens in a given society. Accordingly, if they could choose which criterion will apply in the future in the making of public policies, they would accept a Kaldor-Hicks one.

Finally, and perhaps most importantly, Chicago economists are incapable of dealing with distributional issues because they assume that money is worth to people independently of how much income they are endowed with. This aspect of Chicago economics is striking: as a matter of fact, economists such as Marshall and Pigou knew perfectly that income, like any other good, exhibits decreasing marginal returns. This means that – with some *caveats* – one could presume that transferring money from a rich to a poor person (who, as Pigou stated, has a similar temperament) would increase the size of the pie. But the Chicago economists that inspired themselves from the work of these enlightening pioneers forgot to follow this precept. This is why these economists have absolutely nothing to say about the redistribution of resources: a cent of Euro is worth to rich Bob as much as it is to poor Alice. And this is quite strange, as the available empirical evidence testifies in favor of decreasing marginal returns of income.

4.3.1. EFFICIENCY, FAIRNESS, MARKET OUTCOMES AND DISTRIBUTION: A SIMPLE NUMERICAL EXAMPLE

The impact of happiness, distributional issues and the returns on income on the neoclassical cathedral is devastating, and casts serious doubts on the possibility of approaching policy-making with the limited and misleading toolkit that Chicago law and economics has provided us with. Accordingly, economists and philosophers are today split between different visions of the role of the policymaker, which involve combinations of efficiency criteria, attitude towards redistribution of income, justice goals and happiness metrics. To introduce the reader into this quagmire, let me start with a simple account of the "ultimatum game" in game theory. Imagine that Alice and Bob are two cousins that live in Europe and are informed that a distant uncle from the United States died. In his testament, the generous uncle leaves a sum of $100,000 to the two cousins, with the sole condition that they, themselves, agree on how to divide the sum. If they fail to agree, none of them will get anything out of the $100,000. A particular fact in this story is that, while Bob is a very rich man, Alice is so poor that she has to play hide and seek with her creditors every morning.

In such context, it is important to answer a number of questions. First, what allocation of the $100,000 sum maximizes the utility of this money? Second, what allocation would be "fair"? Third, what is the allocation that maximizes the happiness of the two cousins? Fourth, what is the allocation that will result from the negotiation between Alice and Bob?

The first question already creates problems in economics. As a matter of fact, as mentioned above, for Chicagoans such as Posner all distributions of the $100,000 sum are (Pareto) efficient, as they leave the two cousins better off. There is no way of ranking various scenarios, and even the case in which negotiation fails – if the sum is reallocated to, say, a charity – is equivalent to all other outcomes, since in all cases there will be a mere reallocation of an existing sum from an individual (the uncle) to someone else (Alice, Bob and maybe the charity). But for early neoclassical economists, as well as many contemporary philosophers and economists, the allocation of the sum makes a difference in terms of maximization of the sum's utility. Even more, as observed *i.a.* by Easterlin (2005), "Few generalizations in the social sciences enjoy such wide-ranging support as that of diminishing marginal utility of income".[240] Accordingly, for many economists a way to maximize the overall utility of the $100,000 sum would be to allocate the lion's share to Alice (the exact amount would depend on assumptions on the shape of each cousin's utility curve and their starting financial endowment).

Second, when it comes to fairness, a "resourcist" principle would look for a 50:50 allocation, which would leave Alice and Bob each with $50,000.[241] However, according to alternative theories of fairness the distribution should be such as to provide each cousin with the same "utility", rather than the same amount of money. This would, again, leave Alice with a larger share than Bob (again, the exact distribution depending on the shape of the utility curves). Moreover, according to other commentators the "fair" allocation of the sum would be the one chosen by an impartial spectator, or by the two cousins in a sort of "original" position, *i.e. before* knowing whether they will be the rich or the poor in this situation.[242]

Third, when it comes to maximizing the happiness that the sum can bring to the two cousins, again if we assume that happiness is positively correlated with income, but that it displays decreasing marginal returns on income, then the allocation of the sum should mostly focus on Alice, for which every cent is useful to repay her debts.

Finally, when it comes to market outcomes, the result is very different. Although neoclassical economics normally places significant emphasis on the efficiency of market outcomes and the results of the spontaneous negotiation of the parties, in this case the possibility of strategic behavior would tilt the balance towards Bob. The reason is that Bob can easily threaten to abandon the negotiation table in case Alice proposes to allocate the $100,000 sum efficiently, or fairly. To use an acronym proposed by Ayres and Nalebuff (1997), Bob's BATNA (best alternative to negotiated agreement) is much better than Alice's: this means that Bob enjoys a superior bargaining power over Alice, also linked to the fact that the marginal utility of the additional portions of income that would accrue to Bob as a result of the agreement with Alice are lower than they are for Alice. Alice is likely to be terrified by the threat of a negotiation breakdown, and this "advantage of threat" will likely lead Bob to appropriate the largest share of the $100,000 sum.

---

240 Easterlin, R. A. (2004), *Diminishing Marginal Utility of Income? A Caveat.* Social Indicators Research. Available at SSRN: http://ssrn.com/abstract=539262.

241 This is the so-called "resource egalitarianism". See Dworkin, R., (1981a), *What is Equality? Part 1: Equality of Resources*, Philosophy and Public Affairs, 10: 185–246. And Dworkin, R., (1981b) *What is Equality? Part 2: Equality of Welfare*, Philosophy and Public Affairs, 10: 283–345.

242 See below, Section 4.3.3.2.

This example shows that, when it comes to policy decisions, it makes a difference whether the policymaker seeks to maximize efficiency, fairness, happiness; or – given that observing individual utility and happiness is very difficult – whether the policymaker is endorsing whatever market outcome individuals will reach by spontaneously behaving on the market. In the next sections, I will explain in more detail Pareto and Kaldor-Hicks efficiency criteria, their most powerful critiques and most recently proposed refinements, and then proceed to briefly explain why fairness, happiness and the orientation of people's preference can affect the basic assumption that *de gustibus non est disputandum*.[243]

4.3.2. EFFICIENCY AND WEALTH MAXIMIZATION: FROM BENTHAM, TO BENTHAM?

Economists have started thinking about how to judge policy outcomes long before Vilfredo Pareto proposed its efficiency criterion. For example, Jeremy Bentham equated the goal of public policy as "the greatest happiness for the greatest number", paving the way for the development of modern theories of welfare and well-being. As already explained, given the impossibility of measuring directly well-being, neoclassical economists started using resourcist efficiency criteria as proxies for the maximization of utility since the end of the 19th century.[244]

Under the Pareto criterion, a public policy is efficient if, as a result of its introduction, at least one member of society is better-off, whereas the policy leaves nobody worse-off compared to the *status quo ante*. When this happens, there is a net increase in wealth, which does not disadvantage any member of a given society. The first Theorem of Welfare Economics postulates that any market will reach a Pareto optimal point, regardless of the initial distribution of goods: this means that the market alone can reach a situation where any further reallocation of resources would not meet the Pareto efficiency conditions. Likewise, the law and economics of contracts and individual negotiation – including the Coase theorem – justified the superiority of private bargaining on the grounds that it systematically achieves Pareto-optimal results.

One of the critiques that have been moved to the Pareto criterion looks at the "moral neutrality" of the criterion. Pareto efficiency has long been considered as the only morally neutral litmus test economists could use to justify public policy choices. However, if one relaxes a number of rather unrealistic assumptions, it

243 Becker and Stigler (1977), *De Gustibus Non Est Disputandum*, The American Economic Review Vol. 67, No. 2 (Mar., 1977), pp. 76–90.

244 See Robbins, L. (1932), *An Essay on the Nature and Significance of Economic Science*, (holding that economists, as scientists, could say nothing about the relative pleasures of a Brahmin and an untouchable).

becomes self-evident that the Pareto criterion is far from being morally neutral. Firstly, as explained in the previous section, several social sciences and the advancement of behavioral economics unanimously point at defining individual well-being not only as a function of one's own endowment of resources and income, but also looking at the relative endowment compared to other members of the society.[245] The fact that an individual that earns a $10,000 yearly salary in a company where everybody earns $10,000 yearly may be happier than an individual that is paid $11,000 when her peers earn $15,000 is widely tested in the literature on psychology and cognitive sciences. Accordingly, it is not automatically true that a situation in which Pareto efficiency is realized will always make everyone happier: this is like stating that welfare – interpreted as the endowment of specific resources in absolute terms – is not always a good proxy for happiness.

Secondly, and relatedly, the Pareto criterion implies that the welfare of all members of a society can be measured by simply summing up the welfare of all its members, as expressed by their revealed preferences. As observed in Section 4.2.2. above, the methodological individualism that lingers on all neoclassical economics finds its limit exactly in this assumption. Not only, on the one hand, the observation of preferences through market behavior hides important constraints such as the limited availability of income, which in turn affects the WTP of individuals on the market; and not only does bounded rationality limit the individual's potential appreciation of the value of a marketed (and worse, of a non-marketed) good[246]; in addition, differences between WTP and WTA and the relevance of other-regarding behavior in the formation of people's preferences and in the determination of people's happiness play a decisive role that Pareto efficiency will never be able to catch.

So far, nothing really worrisome: in applying Pareto efficiency and optimality, one would only need to accept the fact that there is no easier and cheaper way to approximate human well-being than to use welfare as an imperfect proxy. Besides those critiques, however, the Pareto criterion faces two insurmountable and intimately connected problems, related to distributional issues and to the criterion's pointlessness for policy purposes. On the first issue, suffice it to quote what Amartya Sen write in its essay on ethics and economics back in 1987: "A state can be Pareto optimal with some people in extreme misery and others rolling in luxury, so long as the miserable cannot be made better off without

245 See Easterlin, R.A. (1995), *Will Raising the Income of All Increase the Happiness of All?*, 27 J. Econ. Behav. & Org. 35, 39.

246 The application of the Pareto criterion relies *i.a.* on the assumption that preferences are based on full information about the known and possible consequences of regulation. See Graham (2008), *supra* note 19, at 408, stating that "individuals are assumed to have the cognitive capacity and resources required to process such information and to rationally determine their preferences".

cutting into the luxury of the rich"[247] In other words, the Pareto criterion cannot be applied independently of the starting distribution of income to which we apply it. Once we start from an initial uneven distribution of income, the effect of adopting a Pareto efficiency test would be to crystallize that uneven distribution as long as all redistribution efforts would make the rich worse off. Only when income can be provided to the poorest category in a population without depriving the rich of some resources, Pareto would baptize the change.

Relatedly, no one can save the Pareto criterion from another critique, which refers to its "pointlessness" for public policymakers, as defined by Guido Calabresi on the Yale Law Journal in 1990.[248] This critique mostly hinges on the fact that the Pareto criterion is the equivalent of a unanimity requirement for any public intervention, and as such is of very little use for policy purposes: as a matter of fact, all public policies imply some form of reallocation of resources, which are likely to leave some groups worse-off and others better-off. Accordingly, relying only on Pareto as a justification for public intervention means shrinking the role of public policy down to almost nil. This, as will be explained below, led economists to move towards the application of a variant of Paretian efficiency, the so-called "potential Pareto superiority", or Kaldor-Hick test.

4.3.2.1. The Kaldor-Hicks or "net benefits" principle

The Kaldor-Hicks efficiency criterion can be defined also as the "potential Pareto efficiency" criterion since, in the form in which it is normally known and applied, it requires – just like the Pareto one – that a given policy change increases overall welfare measured as the aggregation of individual preferences and by summing up the endowments of society members in terms of resources, not happiness or well-being.[249] The difference between the Pareto and the Kaldor-Hicks criteria is that in the latter, the possibility that someone is left worse-off after an "efficient" policy change is explicitly contemplated. The necessary condition is that it would be in principle possible, for those who gain from the policy change, to compensate the losers. Accordingly, if a given policy

---

247 Sen, A.K. (1987), *On Ethics and Economics*, Basil Blackwell Oxford, 32.

248 See Calabresi, G. (1991), *The Pointlessness of Pareto: Carrying Coase Further*, 100 Yale Law Journal, 1211–1237; see also Adler, M.D. and E.A. Posner (1999), *Rethinking Cost-Benefit Analysis* (April 1999). University of Chicago Law School, John M. Olin Law & Economics Working Paper No. 72.

249 The Kaldor and the Hicks criteria were indeed two different tests. As recalled by John Graham: The Hicks version of the test is the flip side of the Kaldor version. Hicks gives the presumption to the lifesaving regulation and asks whether the ex ante losers from the rule would be willing to compensate the ex ante beneficiaries for not having the rule. Since in some situations the Kaldor and Hicks tests might give different answers, it has been suggested that a rule should have to pass both the Kaldor and Hicks tests in order to be considered efficient. See Hicks, J.R. (1939), *The Foundations of Welfare Economics*, 49 ECON. J. 696; and Kaldor, N. (1939), *Welfare Propositions of Economics and Interpersonal Comparisons of Utility*, 49 ECON. J. 549.

change increases the welfare of group A in a society by $100 million and decreases the welfare of group B by $90 million, the policy change is an improvement since, in principle, group A members could compensate group B members, and this would still leave the former better off by $10 million. When this side payment actually takes place, the policy change gets back to a state of Pareto efficiency. However as stated by Niklas Kaldor, whether such compensation should take place "is a political question on which the economist, qua economist, could hardly pronounce an opinion".[250]

As mentioned already in the introductory section of this book, the Kaldor-Hicks principle is the polar star of current impact assessment practice, especially in the United States, where major secondary legislation adopted by government agencies is subject to scrutiny according to the ability of those agencies to show that their proposed policy actions maximize "net benefits". Accordingly, it is very important to discuss potential shortcomings of this principle in light of its relevance for the whole *ex ante* policy appraisal that takes place in the US and elsewhere.

Needless to say, the Kaldor-Hicks principle features most of the limits and problems that the Pareto principle displays. In particular, it is based on the assumption that welfare can be a good proxy for well-being and is rooted in methodological individualism. A difference between the two criteria is that Kaldor-Hicks is not "pointless" for policy purposes. To the contrary, the test provides a relatively easy benchmark for policymakers wishing to ensure that their actions are not decreasing overall welfare for society. To say it with John Graham (who was the Chairman of the OIRA for the 2001–2006 period), the test is considered to possess attractive features since it considers the preferences of each individual in society, it accounts for the intensity of individual preferences and provides an explicit account of the weights attributed to opposing preferences in a way that is "explicit, calculable, and scrutable".[251] In addition, as Graham states, "if adequate information is available on the consequences of a rule and the preferences of each citizen, the [Kaldor-Hicks] test is also determinate (with regard to efficiency)".[252] Finally, the test does not require the inter-personal comparison of utility. For those reasons, Kaldor-Hicks is a formidable test for policymakers, as it gives them the sensation of being able to master the effects of policy.

However, this advantage, which of course determined the success of the Kaldor-Hicks test in economics and policy, is also the most dangerous limit of the criterion itself. As a matter of fact, by endorsing policy changes that lead to an increase in overall welfare (resource-based) for society, the Kaldor-Hicks principle uncovers one of the most disquieting aspects of neoclassical economics

250 Kaldor (1939), *supra* note 249, at 550.
251 See Graham (2008), *supra* note 19.
252 *Id.*

as interpreted in the "welfarist revolution" of the 1950s: the assumption that a cent of Euro is worth to every person the same – *i.e.* that income does not exhibit decreasing marginal returns.[253] Indeed, Kaldor-Hicks justifies a policy change that increases the wealth of the wealthy more than it increases the poverty of the poor. More concretely, Kaldor-Hicks would justify a policy intervention that makes the richest group of a society richer by $100 million while depriving the poorer group of $90 million. No compensation (if not a potential one) is actually required. In this respect, the test violates the so-called Pigou-Dalton Principle in economics, which stipulates – as described by Adler (2008) – that shifting utility from someone at a higher utility level to someone at a lower level, without changing total utility, must increase the value of the [social welfare function").[254]

Even more basically, the Kaldor-Hicks criterion is subject to the so-called "Scitovsky Paradox", which shows that two states of the world can be Kaldor-Hicks efficient to one another.[255] This means that, as Jules Coleman once observed, "Kaldor-Hicks is not even a weakly transitive ordering relationship".[256] This also means that it can hardly be defended on utilitarian grounds, nor does it lend itself to Kantian or "pre-constitutional" explanations such as the one offered by Richard Posner.

Needless to say, also based on what we explained above, the Kaldor-Hicks test faces more insurmountable technical and moral problems than the Pareto ones: in particular, the impossibility of inter-personal comparisons of utility; the consequent impossibility of preference aggregation and thus the impossibility of relying only on methodological individualism; the impossibility of using welfare as synonymous of (or proxy for) well-being and happiness; the test's agnosticism on the utility function of income[257]; and its compatibility with very uneven distributions of wealth.

Furthermore, the Kaldor-Hicks test approximates individual preferences based on market behavior, and thus relies on revealed preferences as the benchmark for judging the effects on policy decisions. This aspect already creates problems from the standpoint of bounded rationality (*i.e.* people do not always know what's best for them, nor they know how to maximize their utility[258]): combined with the possibility of imposing losses on some members of society, it also calls into question the findings of "prospect theory" as illustrated by Daniel

253 See above, Section 4.3.

254 Adler, M.D. (2008) *Risk Equity: A New Proposal*, 32 HARV. ENVTL. L. REV. 1, 27.

255 Scitovsky, T. (1941). *A Note on Welfare Propositions in Economics*, 9 REV. ECON. STUD. 77 (1941).

256 Coleman (2003), *supra* note 181.

257 Note that this aspect also affects the possibility for the monetary metrics of WTP used in Kaldor-Hicks to capture the intensity of preferences. If WTP is heavily affected by the availability of income, there is no way of measuring actual preferences with precision by simply relying on revealed preferences that result from market transactions.

258 See Thaler and Sunstein in "Nudge" (describing Humans v. Econs), *supra* note 3.

Kahneman and Amos Tversky: if, as already explained, WTP and WTA normally differ for any individual, then the amount of compensation that may be required to restore the position of a given loser after a policy change will often be higher than the loss imposed. Imposing a loss and then (potentially) compensating it is not an automatic way to reach Pareto. This issue was solved in modern interpretations of the test by imposing that gains are measured by WTP, and losses by WTA.

A related issue, perhaps the most controversial of the Kaldor-Hicks test, is that the test is not based on any workable notion of *consent*. While Pareto could potentially be framed in terms of consent, as all the outcomes of market transactions are the result of consent and are Pareto efficient, the Kaldor Hicks test sacrifices Pareto's unanimity requirement on the altar of the test's prescriptive power. This problem was very well-known to Richard Posner, who tried to frame the Kaldor-Hicks test as a basic principle of justice on which individuals beyond a veil of ignorance would give their consent.[259] To put it differently, if asked *ex ante* to which rules should their ideal society confirm, individuals would award their preference to a system governed by a net benefits principle, regardless of whether the losers will be compensated for the loss sustained, because from an *ex ante* perspective they would feel that the application of that principle would leave them better-off over time.[260] This almost "Rawlsian" attempt to save the Kaldor-hicks principle by using what Graham defined as a "pre-constitutional" or "social contract" viewpoint did not lead Posner to gain particular reputation in the fields of economics and philosophy: as a matter of fact, his defense of the Kaldor-Hicks principle as an ancillary paradigm of justice was never convincing for lack of intuitiveness and theoretical grounds.[261] To the contrary, contemporary scholars who have focused on cost-benefit analysis have observed and extensively proven that "the Kaldor-Hicks test should be removed from our normative vocabulary".[262]

It came to no surprise, thus, that in his late years John Hicks himself discarded the validity of his own test by showing his skepticism on the whole idea of cost-benefit analysis. In 1983, Hicks declared that *"[i]t is a besetting vice of*

---

259 See below, at Section 4.3.3.2.

260 According to Graham (2008), *supra* note 19, "When citizens evaluate the test in the pre-constitutional (original) position, behind a veil of ignorance, the case for KH is stronger". However, this rational can be defended only if one adopts methodological individualism and accepts that *ex ante* WTP is a good measure of individual preference, which – as we recalled before – is not uncontroversial.

261 But see Leonard, H.B. and R.J. Zeckhauser, *Cost-Benefit Analysis Applied to Risks: Its Philosophy and Legitimacy*, in VALUES AT RISK 31, 47–48 (Douglas MacLean ed., 1986) (providing an ethical defense of "hypothetical consent" to BCA on the ground that "most individuals, in forming their social contracts," would accept society's need to make uncompensated transfers).

262 *Id.*

economists to over-play their hands ... [and] to claim more for their subject than they should." In stating this, Hicks observed that the role of economist is to:

> *"estimate, so far as he can, the gains and losses that are likely to accrue, to various classes, or sections of the population, from the proposed action... It is not his business, I would now maintain, to weigh up those gains and losses against each other. He can, nevertheless, most usefully, take advantage of his estimates to suggest improvements in the proposal with which he is confronted. Formally, that is to say, he can suggest a second plan, which he thinks will have a prospect of offering smaller losses, and larger, or not much smaller gains, so that in comparison with the first, it has some claim to be more attractive. He cannot prescribe this second plan; arts of persuasion will still be required; but he has some grounds for his persuading".*

Looking more carefully into neoclassical economics, more truth surfaces through the lines of early scholars. Just as Marshall and Pigou never defended the invariance of the marginal utility of income, early neoclassical economists – say, during the first two decades after the development of the Kaldor Hicks test in 1939 – did not advocate Kaldor-Hicks as a necessary and sufficient condition for endorsing a given public policy either.[263] Almost half a century later, Hicks himself seemed to downplay its importance for public policy. Then, one might wonder what happened during the 1960s and the 1970s, which led to embedding the logic of Kaldor-Hicks wealth maximization as the logic of public policy action?

4.3.2.2. The practice of cost-benefit analysis today: the endless quest for prices

Regardless of the problems identified in the application of the Kaldor-Hicks efficiency test, the powerful prescriptive power of the test has led to a widespread diffusion in governments and regulatory agencies, in particular in the United States. This has led to a "routinization" of the application of cost-benefit analysis in day-to-day regulatory appraisal, and consequently to the proliferation of standard methods and steps to go through the analysis. Most importantly, this evolution led to the development of different estimation approaches, which try to solve a single problem: how to monetize the un-monetizable.

As a matter of fact, a full-fledged cost-benefit analysis can be provided only when all costs and benefits of a given piece of regulation are quantified and monetized. This is what is usually referred to as "hard cost-benefit analysis", and is increasingly sought by some US government agencies. The need to quantify

---

263 See, *e.g.*, Arrow, K.J. *et al.* (1996), *Is There a Role for Benefit-Cost Analysis in Environmental, Health, and Safety Regulation?*, 272 Science 221, 222 ("Although formal benefit-cost analysis should not be viewed as either necessary or sufficient for designing sensible public policy, it can provide an exceptionally useful framework for consistently organizing disparate information").

and monetize all impacts faces inevitable problems: as a matter of fact, some impacts are easier to monetize than others. More in detail, some cost and (less often) benefit items can be derived from the observation of market prices or market behavior. For example, if a regulation will force company X to buy a new type of equipment to comply with more stringent emission limits, this additional cost may be quantified in terms of market prices, if the equipment is already sold on the marketplace. If personnel at X has to be trained to use the new equipment, the cost of training services and opportunity cost of the time spent in the training course can all be rather easily quantified based on market prices and productivity data. Likewise, benefits that accrue to a firm or a citizen in terms of cost savings or time savings are normally easily quantifiable – this is often done through the Standard Cost Model in most European countries, when costs are due to red tape and the need to comply with information obligations contained in the legislation.

However, the more policy proposals depart from standard market regulation, the stronger is the need to start quantifying non-market goods. Policy domains such as those summarized by Graham (2008) as "lifesaving regulation" – including health, safety, environmental regulations – are often fraught with impacts that are not related to any marketable good. For example, impacts on mortality and morbidity in health and environmental regulations, impacts on biodiversity, impacts on subjective well-being due to enhanced safety and all impacts related to "risk regulation" (from food standards to critical infrastructure protection) are very difficult to quantify. This is why modern cost-benefit analysis has gradually become a quest for prices, be they explicit or only "implicit" prices.

Table 2 below shows some of the most common estimation approaches currently used in modern cost-benefit analysis, with focus on the estimation of benefits. As shown in the table, in some cases the quantification and monetization effort is objectively determined through the observation of market prices (*e.g.* replacement costs, service values, property values); but for several benefits the need to build implicit prices by relying on subjective preferences is evident.

Now, how safely can we rely on the use of these estimation techniques? To be sure, the need to build implicit prices often leads economists in a neoclassical trap, in which they have to purify stated preferences and WTP-based measures from the impact that income endowments exert on their estimates. The fact that a given individual may be less willing to pay for a given environmental impact is, in economics, an indication of a lower intensity of preference for that specific impact: however, as explained in the previous sections, this is not always true due to the fact that individuals with lower income will also have a lower WTP for certain societal and private benefits.[264]

264 See Heinzerling and Ackerman (2007), on the distinction between WTP and ability to pay (WTA). And Sunstein, C.R. (2007) *Willingness to Pay vs. Welfare*, 1 Harv. L. & Pol'y Rev. 303, 304 (2007).

Table 2. Estimation approaches for different categories of benefit

Benefit category	Estimation approach
To individuals	
Mortality	*Wage compensation; stated preferences; averting behaviour; human capital (foregone earnings); VSL and VSLY*
Morbidity (acute, chronic)	*Stated preferences; cost of illness (medical earnings, pain and suffering, avoidance); averting behaviour; QALYs; DALYs*
Production/consumption	
Crops/forests/fisheries	*Consumer plus producers surplus*
Water-using industry	*Consumer plus producers surplus*
Municipal water supply	*Opportunity cost (alternative aquifer)*
Authorities	*Service replacement (municipal treatment, bottled water)*
Economic assets	
Materials (corrosion, soiling)	*Replacement cost, service value, household production function*
Property values	*Hedonic price models*
Environmental assets	
Recreational use	*Unit day, stated preference, property value, travel cost, random utility, hedonic prices, travel cost, service replacement costs*
Other use (visibility)	*Stated preferences, property value*
Passive use (non-use)	*Stated preferences*

Source: adapted from Greenman (1993).

Secondly, the current practice of cost-benefit analysis has evolved as an aggregation of individual preferences. This is particularly important when we deal with public resources such as the environment, safety and public health: in these domains, simply aggregating individual preferences would systematically fail to capture the externalities produced by individual policy actions, which are conducive to an improvement of the environment also for future generations and also in portions of the territory that are not regularly inhabited by human beings. Against this background, the methodological individualism on which neoclassical economics is built is also a key precondition for modern cost-benefit analysis: no use of objective value judgments is made, and this according to many authors is a guarantee that the analysis remains impartial, and can be used to "inform" policymakers, rather than to mandate any policy conclusion.

Thirdly, the current analysis seems to overlook, in most cases, the ability of markets and individuals to adapt to changing legal environments. Not only do many policy appraisals assume 100% compliance (this is true, *i.a.*, also for the

Standard Cost Model). Available literature suggests a rather intuitive finding, that non-compliance is more likely when compliance costs imposed by a given piece of legislation are very high.[265] As will be observed in Section 5 below, compliance is also more likely when the technology and mechanisms chosen are easier to enforce. Moreover, the dynamic interaction between policymakers and target groups is increasingly considered as a key factor in determining the impacts of specific policy options. In particular, the possibility for individuals and firms to adapt to legal changes is often overlooked in cost-benefit analysis, both from a psychological and purely physiological standpoint. Examples of reactions to these problems are two different U-shaped curves: Daniel Kahneman's proposed a U-index curve that reflects the time spent in a given state of dissatisfaction;[266]; and the debate on the role of hormesis in public policy (implying a U-shaped dose-response function for exposure to toxic substances) as animated *i.a.* by Calabrese and Baldwin (2001, 2003a, 2003b) and Wiener (2004).[267]

Fourthly, modern analysis still faces problems in the comparison of costs and benefits, as well as in the definition of the baseline. In particular, even if one ignores all theoretical limitations (*e.g.* the impossibility to aggregate individual preferences), reasonable cost-benefit analysis should entail the use of WTP-based measures for the gainers, and WTA measures for the losers. However, the practice has shown that obtaining reliable WTA measures is a nightmare, and that in most cases the figures obtained are greatly exaggerated. In other cases, it is virtually impossible to disentangle the added value of a given legal change as a discrete departure from the baseline.

Looking at the literature on cost-benefit analysis, the "immateriality" of the exercise and the increased sophistication in the use of non-market techniques such as econometric estimations of WTP and hedonic pricing models has led to a split in the academic community: on the one hand, some commentators consider that more sophistication in neoclassical cost-benefit analysis will lead to a better approximation of well-being through measurement and aggregation of individual preferences; others argue that too sophisticated analysis cannot save Kaldor-Hicks from an inevitable death in public policy. Below, I elaborate further on this split.

---

265 See, D.A. Farber, *Taking Slippage Seriously: Noncompliance and Creative Compliance in Environmental Law*, 23 Harv. Envtl. L. Rev. 297, 301–11 (1999).

266 See Kahneman, D., A.B. Krueger, D.A. Schkade, N. Schwarz and A.A. Stone (2006): *Would You Be Happier If You Were Richer? A Focusing Illusion*, Science 312, 1908–1910. And Kahneman, D. and A.B. Krueger (2006): *Developments in the Measurement of Subjective Well-Being*, Journal of Economic Perspectives 20, 3–24.

267 Calabrese E.J. and L.A. Baldwin (2001), *The frequency of U-shaped dose responses in the toxicological literature*. Toxicol. Sci. 2001; 62(2):330–338; Calabrese E.J. and L.A. Baldwin (2003a). *Hormesis: the dose-response revolution*. Annual Rev. Pharmacol. Toxicol. 2003, 43:175–197; and Calabrese E.J. and L.A. Baldwin (2003b). *Peptides and hormesis*, Crit. Rev. Toxicol. 2003;, 33(3–4):355–405. Finally, for a critical view, see Wiener, J. (2004), *Hormesis, hotspots and emissions trading*, Human & Experimental Toxicology 23: 289–301.

4.3.2.3. *Pricing the priceless?*

In the past decade, defenses of the use of cost-benefit analysis as a way to inform policy decisions have been more numerous, testifying of an increased pressure on what seems to be a very weak set of arguments in favor of Kaldor-Hicks. The most notable examples are Bob Hahn's 2005 pamphlet "In defense of economic analysis of regulation", and Cass Sunstein's portray of Paretoville in a 2007 article on WTP and welfare, in which he conceded that welfare, rather than wealth, should be the ultimate objective of public policy.

In particular, while Hahn (2005) discusses mostly the anti-regulatory bias many critics attach to current practices in cost-benefit analysis, Sunstein depicts what he himself defines as a "fairy tale", *i.e.* the city of Paretoville inhabited only by *homines oeconomici* in the pure neoclassical meaning. Now, without any doubt Sunstein is aware of the fact that Paretoville does not exist: where he disagrees with some of his critics is in the usefulness of the Paretoville metaphor to inform real-life policymaking. Just like perfect competition does not exist *in rerum natura*, but is used as an ideal market structure that may inform the choices of competition policymakers, Paretoville may represent an ideal place for those that want to study policy *in vitro* before applying it in reality. The problem is that, for both perfect competition and Paretoville, the time seems ripe in economic theory to start reconsidering whether the metaphor is a good one, and a useful one.

In a vibrant response to Sunstein, Lisa Heinzerling and Frank Ackerman (2007) recently argued that Paretoville should be taken as an almost negligible spot in our rearview mirror, rather than something to tend to.[268] In particular, the idea that WTP measures can ever inform policymakers about any future state of the world is fiercely challenged by Heinzerling and her past co-authors, mostly on the basis of the impossibility of measuring and aggregating individual preferences, the undesirability of using them as a proxy for well-being, and the fact that WTP-based measures grossly ignore behavioral misperception and the ability to pay of targeted stakeholders. In this respect, in a series of publications Heinzerling echoes what Hovenkamp (1994) defines as "egregious systemic errors" of the neoclassical approach.[269]

Among the most recurring critiques moved by authors such as Lisa Heinzerling (and her co-authors, including most notably Frank Ackerman) in a number of publications, the following are worth being stated. First, Heinzerling has repeatedly argued that policymakers place too low a value on human life by

268 L. Heinzerling and F. Ackerman, *Wasting Away in Paretoville*, 1 Harv. L. & Pol'y Rev. 363–370 (2007). And see Sunstein's reply, *On Fairy Tales*, 1 Harv. L. & Pol'y Rev. 371–374 (2007).

269 See Hovenkamp, H. (1994), *The Limits of Preference-Based Legal Policy*, 89 Northwestern University Law Review 4, at 6.

adopting a WTP-based measure – the so-called value of a statistical life (VSL).[270] Second, policymakers ignore the virtuous effects of investing in public goods overtime and "shrink the future" enormously in their analyses by applying a high inter-temporal discount rate that depresses the estimated benefits of investing in environmentally-friendly policy. Third, it is impossible to value a shared resource such as the environment, fraught with positive externalities, by simply asking individuals how much they would be willing to pay to preserve it, or how much they would be willing to accept as compensation for being deprived of it.

All these arguments, in my opinion, have merit and are fully in line with my analysis of the flaws in neoclassical economics, and particularly in law and economics scholarship from Coase to Posner. What is missing is a precise research agenda for the future, *i.e.* a clear-cut indication of the direction that public policy appraisal should take absent a requirement for cost-benefit analysis. To be honest, Ackerman and Heinzerling seem to have more than an idea in this respect: her belief in the fact that cost-benefit analysis is deeply flawed leads to advocating a different course of action, such as the introduction of more objective welfare judgments and the replacement of money with expected facts and scientific evidence.[271] In section 4.4 below, I will get back to this proposal to test its relevance under the more procedural view of RIA, which takes cost-benefit analysis as a pure way to trigger a virtuous principal-agent process of delegation and oversight, as well as possible judicial review of the agencies' activity.

4.3.3. ALTERNATIVES TO THE "EFFICIENCY AS JUSTICE" PARADIGM

Faced with the objective unacceptability of Kaldor-Hicks, recently economists, lawyers and philosophers have gotten back to efficiency and justice principles to refine the previously used efficiency tests in the direction of more ethically defendable criteria. The dominant *refrain* in this attempts is that whatever principle is used to identify policies that increase overall well-being (not necessarily the same as economic welfare), such principle cannot ignore the ethical or distributional impacts of a given policy. According to many of these theories the identity of the winners and losers should be taken into account to avoid that the poorest group in a society is put at a further disadvantage after the enactment of a new policy. After this first, basic pillar of distributive justice,

270 For a recent discussion, with a comparison between the VSL concept and quality-adjusted life years, see Karapanou, V. and L.T. Visscher (2010), *Quality Adjusted Life Years as a Way Out of the Impasse between Prevention Theory and Insurance Theory*, Rotterdam Institute of Law and Economics (RILE) Working Paper No. 2010/06.

271 See, *i.a.*, Ackerman, F. *et al.* (2005), *Applying Cost-Benefit to Past Decisions: Was Environmental Protection Ever a Good Idea?*, 57 Admin. L. Rev. 155, 186 (2005).

authors differ as to what kind of criterion should guide the visible hand of the policymaker. Below, I quickly illustrate the main theories that have been proposed as a refinement of (or an alternative to) the Kaldor-Hicks test.

4.3.3.1. Refining Kaldor-Hicks to incorporate equity and fairness

Some authors have tried to solve the evident problems of the Potential Pareto efficiency test from the inside. For example, in several publications Richard O. Zerbe Jr. *et al.* (2005) attempted a revision of the Kaldor Hicks test, aimed at correcting its complete and explicit ignorance of ethics.[272] In doing so, Zerbe Jr. was implicitly trying to solve a problem embedded in mainstream neoclassical economics: that individual preferences never account for bounded willpower, and in particular all the other-regarding behavior that he defines as "moral sentiments" – a rather interesting feature, since Adam Smith himself treated this type of behavior as a complement to rationality in all his work, and in particular in the "Theory of Moral Sentiments" published in 1759. According to Zerbe's view, moral sentiments should be taken into account when choosing between alternative policy options, and this would solve also the problem of aggregate welfare values, by including also morality and altruism. However, Zerbe's solution appears circular, as moral sentiments are calculated as long as there is a WTP for them: this leads us back to the problem of revealed individual preferences, to the difficulty of calculating WTP for non-market values, to the problem of preference-based policy and methodological individualism described in the previous sections, and ultimately in the feasibility of the test in practice. The KHM (Kaldor-Hicks and Moral sentiments) test proposed by Zerbe, thus, appears to share many of the inconsistencies of the original test, but adding an element of complexity and nebulosity that may end up being unacceptable for policy purposes.

More recently, Graham (2008) provided a thorough analysis of the use of Pareto and Kaldor-Hicks principles as the basis for what he calls "lifesaving regulation", *i.e.* mostly environmental, health and safety regulation. According to Graham, the pre-constitutional perspective – which, as observed by Polinsky, transforms "certainty in likelihood" in applying Kaldor-Hicks – adds significant value to the application of this test. On the one hand, it captures the long-term impact of applying the test to every lifesaving decision, which may lead individual members of a society to be sometimes gainers, sometimes losers, with an overall balancing effect that would most often lead them better off in the long run. At the same time, Graham acknowledges that even in the long run the Kaldor-Hicks test might generate some losers, and that this may warrant a corrective screen

272 Zerbe Jr., R. O., Y. Bauman and A. Finkle, *An Aggregate Measure for Benefit Cost Analysis.* Ecological Economics, Forthcoming. Available at SSRN: http://ssrn.com/abstract=855384.

that aims at avoiding nefarious impacts on the poorest groups in society.[273] His idea is not entirely new in economic theory, having been the subject of analysis by other economists such as Harberger (1978) and Ng (1984): however, Graham acknowledged that several problems remain as regards the identification of the members of the category of "poorer" individuals that would deserve a specific screen in cost-benefit analysis. This step may not require simply drawing a line close to the poverty threshold, but also more complex scrutiny of other attributes, including consumption, life expectancy, exposure to serious risk, etc.

While it is important to observe that one of the most authoritative scholars in the field of cost-benefit analysis in the United States (and a former OIRA Chairman) considers the Kaldor-Hicks test as deserving some corrections in the direction of accounting for distributional impacts, it must be recalled that any *ad hoc* screen included in the Kaldor-Hicks test would increase its complexity, and would not contribute to solving the most evident and disruptive problems faced by the test, such as the ones related to methodological individualism and the aggregation of preferences. This is why the need for some "objective" welfare judgment may still surface in a world where specific pro-poor screens are included in the cost-benefit test.

4.3.3.2. "Pre-constitutional approaches"

Graham's perspective on cost-benefit analysis, like Posner's one, have the merit of attempting to "purify" the neoclassical cost-benefit analysis by introducing forms of *ex ante* consent. While their theories are still well rooted in the neoclassical approach aimed at achieving welfare maximization, other authors have departed from efficiency-oriented analysis to propose more justice-oriented tests. In particular, John Rawls has proposed a theory of justice based on the so-called "original position". According to this theory, a just distribution of resources is the one that would be selected by individuals *before* knowing whether they will end up in a "particular" situation – for example, before knowing whether they will be rich or poor. In such a situation, according to Rawls, individuals would choose to minimize the risk of extreme poverty, pain and suffering, and will then choose principles and rules that, as a basic consequence, improve the situation of the poorest individuals. This idea led Rawls to advocate for a specific screen in cost-benefit analysis, which can be termed as "lexicographical order". Under this approach, any rule proposed should first of all satisfy a basic criterion: that the poorest individuals in society are not left worse-off; then, Rawls does not push his argument as far as proposing fully egalitarian solutions. Accordingly, his view is in principle compatible with

273 See Graham (2008), *supra* note 19. at 111. (stating: "*I favor an ex ante version of welfarism, in which BCA is used as a surrogate for welfarism but is qualified by an equity-inspired concern for the welfare of society's poorest citizens*").

the one proposed by John Graham, which entails running and satisfying two Kaldor-Hicks tests (one for the poorest, one for society as a whole). However, Rawls does not propose a preference-based Kaldor-Hicks test for the poorest groups, but instead advocates for a *maximin* rule that is based on a more "objective" moral judgment – *i.e.* the judgment that would be formulated behind a "veil of ignorance".

Another authoritative commentator, Herbert Hovenkamp (1994) proposed a similar approach, by showing that a pre-constitutional approach should at least award priority to improving the situation of the poorest. These views echo an early observation by John Harsanyi (1955), who proposed a "requirement of impartiality" that reflects the policy option an individual would choose "if he did not know what his personal position would be in the new situation chosen".[274] Hovenkamp proposes a utility function for policy purposes, depicted in Figure 20 below, which introduces a discontinuity in correspondence to the point where individuals have satisfied their primary needs. According to the author, the left part of the graph should be subject to objective welfare judgments, rather than merely prey of subjective ones: this would be similar to introducing an element of inalienability in the principle that every individual should be protected as far as the basic primary needs and respect of fundamental rights are concerned.

Figure 20. Hovenkamp's utility function

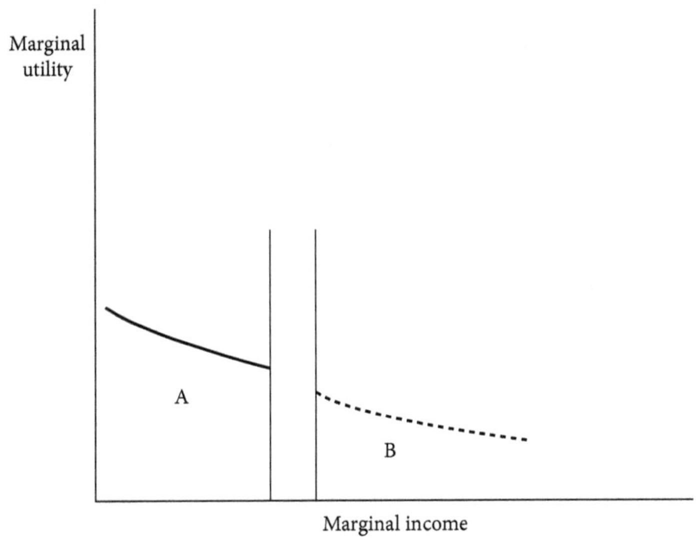

Source: Hovenkamp (1994), Figure 1, at 42.

274 Harsanyi, J.C. (1955), *Cardinal Welfare, Individualistic Ethics, and Interpersonal Comparisons of Utility*, 63 J. Pol. Econ. 309.

Other theories do not even refer to the parties involved in any transaction or policy option, regardless of whether the viewpoint adopted is an *ex ante* or an *ex post* one. These approaches reflect the position of an "impartial spectator" – a metaphor already used by Adam Smith – and aim at incorporating individual preferences for overall happiness in society. For example, Layard (2005) observed that an impartial spectator would surely care more about what happened to the miserable person than to the person who was already happy. He would therefore give a different 'weight' to changes in happiness according to how happy the person was already".[275]

Finally, in a recent contribution Amartya K. Sen (2009) has at one praised and criticized Rawls's theory of justice, arguing that its most serious flaw was its "transcendental institutionalism", *i.e.* its focus on an ideal, perfectly just society, which provides little guidance in terms of how to rank suboptimal situations and how to conclude that a real-world change has indeed made society more just. At the same time, Sen argued that Rawls's most fragile assumption was the uniqueness of the basic principles of justice on which Rawls grounds his whole theory of justice, defined by as principles on which everybody would agree if in a pre-constitutional position. To the contrary, Sen argued in favor of a concept of justice that allows comparisons between sub-optimal states of the world, thus helping the achievement of a more just society through the formulation of public policies.[276] This approach might one day lead to convergence of administrative law and economics towards the prescriptions of moral philosophy, which have so far remained too abstract to be applied in practice – a good example of "moral philosophy in the RIA world".

4.3.3.3. *Welfare as happiness: back to Bentham?*

The need to refine the analysis and understanding of well-being has led in more recent times to a re-discovery of the original quest for "happiness" predicated by Bentham himself. In the past decade, development of economic and statistical tools to measure subjective well-being have led to promising avenues of research in the field of policy evaluation, although it would be exaggerated to state that this stream of literature today constitutes a credible alternative to cost-benefit analysis *à la* Kaldor-Hicks. The underlying idea of hedonic measures is not different from the one of revealed preferences, since both rely extensively on subjective preferences as the basis of public policy. What differs is the proxy that these theories use to describe the impact of policy changes: while mainstream

275 Layard, R. (2005), *Happiness: Lessons From A New Science*, The Penguin Press, at 122. See also Adler, M.D. (2003), *The Puzzle of "Ex Ante Efficiency": Does Rational Approvability Have Moral Weight?*, 151 U. PA. L. REV. 1255 (2003) (questioning the view that *ex ante* efficiency is morally relevant).

276 Sen, A.K. (2009), *The Idea of Justice*, the Belknap Press of Harvard University Press, Cambridge, MA.

neoclassical economics uses willingness to pay and market behavior as proxies for individual well-being and wealth maximization as a proxy for welfare maximization, happiness research seeks the maximization of composite indexes of quality of life and overall satisfaction as proxies for welfare maximization.[277]

There are pros and cons in this evolution of economic analysis of subjective well-being. The added value of happiness research is rooted in the fact that it is way less reductionist than neoclassical WTP-based measures, and aims to take into account the real factors that shape individual happiness and well-being according to a broad spectrum of social sciences. In doing this, it is rapidly evolving towards a very sophisticated portfolio of methods to estimate the impact on different individuals and social groups.[278] One of the key differences between this stream of literature and mainstream economics is that the direct relation between income and well-being is relaxed in favor of a more complex function of individual satisfaction.

On the other hand, just as in the case of behavioral economics, it must be recalled that hedonic measurements are often way more complex and lengthy than standard cost-benefit analysis. As recalled by Richard Posner, "it is easier to guess people's market preferences in areas where the market cannot be made to work than to guess what policies will maximize happiness".[279] Also Graham (2008) observes that, though promising, this line of research "raises as many questions as answers".[280]

To be sure, the literature on the measurement of subjective well-being is advancing. For example, Dolan and Metcalfe (2008) compare WTP-based measures with subjective well-being measures and find that the former are systematically greater than the latter. They argue that WTP responses may be affected by loss aversion in the presence of mental accounting and ambiguities about the time frame over which individuals assess their life satisfaction. However, that of happiness-based metrics is a challenge brought to the mainstream cost-benefit analysis methodology from the inside – *i.e.*, whether WTP-based measures should be replaced by subjective well-being indicators and life satisfaction surveys does not change the overall approach, focused on methodological individualism and the aggregation of individual preferences.[281] If anything, this approach has the merit of highlighting the potential for rational biases to distort some measurements of non-market goods through WTP-based measures, and the need to avoid problems of mental accounting, loss aversion and other imperfections of rationality by devising more sophisticated measures of analysis.

---

277 See Bronsteen *et al.* (2010) *Welfare as Happiness*, Georgetown L. J. Vol. 98, 1583.

278 Kahneman, D. *et al.* (2006), *Would You Be Happier if You Were Richer? A Focusing Illusion*, 312 Science 1908, (finding a "weak relation" between income and "experienced happiness").

279 See Posner R.A. (1981), *The Economics Of Justice*, Harvard University Press, at 79.

280 Graham (2008), *supra* note 19.

281 It may, as a matter of fact, also solve the problem of social values, to the extent that they are incorporated in life satisfaction indicators.

4.3.4. RIA AND DISTRIBUTIONAL CONCERNS: INTO THE WILD

The previous sections have shown that the case for Kaldor-Hicks cost-benefit analysis based on revealed preferences of individuals is increasingly weaker in academia. That said, Adler and Posner (2000) are right in stating that this growing discontent among scholars is striking in light of the increased success of cost-benefit analysis in RIA systems in the US and around the world.[282] The list of challenges and complaints is getting longer every day, and touches upon several complementary issues, from the basic approach based on methodological individualism and perfect rationality, to the methodologies used to collect and elaborate data. However, it would be too optimistic to state that a comprehensive, well-thought and consistent alternative paradigm has emerged in the past few years: as occurred in other fields of economics, perhaps the degree of agnosticism instilled by the study of behavioral biases has created more problems than it has so far contributed to solve. Only time will tell if a more sophisticated and holistic type of economic analysis of law can rise from the ashes of Chicago law and economics.

Many of the critiques moved to the US RIA system can, with a degree of over-simplification, be related to the fact that cost-benefit analysis touches upon impacts that affect individuals with different income levels, and that accordingly the "one cent is a cent is a cent" assumption of neoclassical economics will end up biasing regulation against the poorer groups in society. In this respect, scholars have been fighting for decades over one single question, which I still consider as unsolved as it is fundamental: should *ex ante* policy appraisal deal with distributional issues?

Countless authors have attempted to give an answer to this question. In early neoclassical economics, the view that the legal system would be less efficient than income taxation in redistributing resources prevailed. This view – endorsed by authors such as Pigou – was later challenged by Chicago law and economics, and in particular by Ronald Coase, who claimed that the market would be able to reallocate resources in an efficient – better, Pareto-efficient – way. Richard Posner also has repeatedly stated that distributional issues should not be the primary concern for cost-benefit analysis. In his famous justification of cost-benefit analysis, Kornhauser (2000) also stated that "[c]ost-benefit analysis does in fact ignore distributional concerns, but one might argue that administrative agencies that regulate health and safety ought not to take such distributional concerns into account; these concerns should be left to the relevant redistributional

[282] Adler and Posner (2000), *Implementing Cost-Benefit Analysis when Preferences are Distorted*, Journal of Legal Studies, vol. 29, issue 2, pages 1105–47.

institutions in the society".[283] Similar and even stronger statements are also found in Frank (2000), where ignorance of distributional effects is explicitly advocated, provided that other means of compensation are used.[284]

But law and economics went much further than this. Two prominent scholars such as Kaplow and Shavell provided an extensive analysis of the relative efficiency of income taxes and the legal system in redistributing income. They went as far as claiming that the economic notion of welfare already encapsulates fairness concerns of the individuals, and that any attempt to conflate standard cost-benefit analysis with objective welfare judgments oriented at achieving some form of justice would decrease overall welfare; what's more, in some cases everyone will be made worse-off by such a methodological arrangement. Kaplow and Shavell continue by arguing that welfare analysis should not be contaminated by social values or any other contingent value that generates notions of fairness; these values are socially generated and mutable in time, and consequently would dilute the "purity" of welfare analysis as a guide to policymakers.[285] All this leads to the development of perhaps the most expansionist – or "imperialist" – attempt that law and economics has conceived to the detriment of fairness, and consequentialism at the expense of deontologism. The attempt was so extreme that even some lawyer-economists decided to express their dissent.[286] Jules Coleman vehemently stated that

> *whereas most deontologists are likely merely to dismiss Kaplow and Shavell as unsophisticated and their arguments as inadequately nuanced, the majority of law-and-economics scholars are anxious to dissociate themselves from a thesis they are convinced is dangerous to the cause. Why? The answer is that the book openly endorses precisely the imperialistic claims with which others have saddled the law and economics movement, often in an effort to discredit it as inadequately catholic or, in the extreme, uncivilized.*[287]

Out of the rhetoric and haste that surrounded the debate over Kaplow and Shavell after their claim that welfare should be the one and only goal of public policy, the merit of this and other claims as regards the superiority of the tax

283 Kornhauser, L.A. (2000), *On Justifying Cost-Benefit Analysis*, 29 J. Legal Stud. 1037, 1054 (2000).

284 Frank, R.H. (2000), *Why Is Cost-Benefit Analysis So Controversial?*, 29 J. Legal Stud. 913, 917 ("*We can employ unweighted willingness-to-pay measures without apology, and use the welfare and tax system to compensate low-income families ex ante for the resulting injury*").

285 See Dorff, M.B. (2002), *Why Welfare Depends on Fairness: a Reply to Kaplow and Shavell*, 75 S. Cal. L. Rev. 847. (Challenging this view and comparing the Kantian argument for individual autonomy against utilitarianism with the mirroring arguments put forward by Kaplow and Shavell).

286 Chang, H.F. (2000a), *A Liberal Theory of Social Welfare: Fairness, Utility, and the Pareto Principle*, 110 Yale L.J. 173. Chang, H.F. (2000b), *The Possibility of a Fair Paretian*, 110 Yale L.J.251.

287 Coleman (2003), *supra* note 181.

system over the legal system in achieving redistribution must be seen on the merits. In this respect, several considerations can be put forward. First, any redistribution that employs the tax system after legal rules have been enacted (arguably with uneven social impacts) would be an *ex post* attempt to restore situations that may have been altered in a very complex way: for example, a rule may have had a different impact on different social groups, territories, age groups, etc.; and the tax system may not be the most precise policy tool to single out those that have to be compensated. Second, any compensation would have to take into account the fact that WTP and WTA are different measures, and any attempt to measure the amount to be compensated would require anyway a careful measure of WTA. Third, tax redistribution cannot easily solve *ex post* problems of uncertainty and risk exposure, where the WTA of "losers" is such that compensation would approximate infinite values.[288] Fourth, *ex post* tax redistribution may fall short of the behavioral responses of individuals to the substitution of the tax.[289] Fifth, and more generally, behavioral responses may affect the outcome of legal rules anyway, if affected individuals anticipate the fact that there will be redistribution *ex post*. The list of potential arguments is virtually endless, in the law and economics literature as well as in philosophy.

In summary, there seems to be abundant evidence against the idea that welfarism should survive the evolution of economic theory and legal scholarship in the past decades. To put it simply, every single recent development in social sciences points against the persistence of an exclusively pro-efficiency stance in the formulation of legal rules. And all developments in this stream of law and economics literature in the past decades, after the first Posnerian attempt to prove the relevance of efficiency as justice, have not helped law and economics in coming closer to the complexity and sophistication of other social sciences. That said, the fact that a strong *pars destruens* can be built against welfarism does not mean that we can avail of a more practical alternative in procedural terms: it may well be that all alternatives proposed by scholars would be too costly and sophisticated to be transformed into a procedural requirement to be followed by government agencies, such as RIA is in the US. In the next section, I explore cost-benefit analysis under a different lens, *i.e.* the proceduralist stance of cost-benefit analysis as an ingredient of a system of delegation and oversight.

288 Adler, M.D. and C.W. Sanchirico (2006), *Inequality and Uncertainty: Theory and Legal Applications*. University of Pennsylvania Law Review, Vol. 155, p. 279.

289 Sanchirico, C.W. (2001), *Deconstructing the New Efficiency Rationale*, Cornell Law Review 86(6): 1003–1089.

4.4. FUNCTIONAL APPROACHES: EMERGING PATTERNS IN PUBLIC LAW AND ECONOMICS

The third school of law and economics that we have introduced at the beginning of this Section 5 is the so-called "functional" school, intimately related with the birth of public choice and the seminal work of James Buchanan and Gordon Tullock.[290] Although some authors would not classify this as a real "law and economics" school, the combination of individual incentives and governance structures into a vision of public law and economics makes it a very important stream of literature for the study of RIA systems, with important interactions with positive political theory and regulatory governance studies. Below, in Section 4.4.1, I illustrate the explanatory and prescriptive power of adopting a more "macro" approach to cost-benefit analysis and RIA; Section 4.4.2 then assumes that public policymakers can finally avail of some objective welfare judgment, and explore the potential for law and economics insights to inspire the selection of regulatory alternatives by means such as time-shifting, mechanism choice, framing of individual incentives, and others.

4.4.1. NUDGING ADMINISTRATIONS: RIA AS A MEANS

Cost-benefit analysis is not only the subject of endless discussions between economists, philosophers, environmentalists, legal scholars and many other social and also natural scientists. Cost-benefit analysis (as the basis of RIA systems) is indeed an explicit procedural requirement for government agencies in the US and increasingly for ministries and sometimes also Parliaments in a number of other countries. It is sponsored by international organizations as an instrument of transparency, effectiveness, efficiency and accountability of policymaking. It leads countries to improve their ranking in OECD measuring government and reviews of regulatory reforms every year; it even leads to becoming top reformers in the World Bank's Doing Business if coupled with business simplification.

The procedural aspect of cost-benefit analysis has been analyzed in the law and economics literature, and in particular within the so-called "public law and economics" stream of literature that some authors have broadly equated with the Virginia "functional" school of law and economics.[291] From this perspective, cost-benefit analysis must be framed within the more general system of delegation and oversight that constitutes a landmark of the US organization of

---

290 Buchanan, J. and G. Tullock (1962), *The Calculus of Consent*, Ann Arbor, University of Michigan Press.

291 See Parisi, F. (2004), *supra* note 177.

government.[292] Under a system that features delegation of powers, Congress and central government may have strong incentives to delegate the discretionary power to regulate certain policy areas to specialized agencies – be that due to lack of information and skills, or to the need to avoid responsibility for unpopular choices. In this respect, legislative powers have to solve a "make or buy" dilemma that is very similar to that described by Coase and later Oliver Williamson in describing the nature of the firm, the relevance of transaction costs in the setting up of administrative structures such as a corporation and the outcome of decisions such as the externalization of phases of the value chain. This led some scholars to coin the term "transaction cost politics" to mirror the relevance of those arguments in the context of legislative delegation and oversight.[293]

The basic theoretical framework in which the use of cost-benefit analysis can be framed is thus one of principal-agent relationships between central government and delegated powers (the bureaucracy). Within this framework, the role of RIA is similar to that of several other tools that have been introduced during the New Public Management reforms that blossomed from the UK during the 1980s, and the Reinventing Government initiative launched by the Clinton administration in the early 1990s in the US. The idea that bureaucrats should be kept under control in order to avoid excessive regulatory creep and legislative inflation (the "regulators like to regulate" adagio) was translated into performance-based contracting, increased use of rewards for productivity, efforts to change the culture of administrations and even regulatory budgets made dependant on the adoption of specific indicators, such as the cost reductions achieved. Authors such as Niskanen (1971) paved the way towards an economic analysis of the behavioral incentives of bureaucrats: for example, Niskanen argued that, absent strong monitoring and sanction/reward mechanisms, bureaucrats would have an incentive to inflate their budget in a way that principals would not be able to detect.

In the past decade, authors such as Matthew Adler and Eric Posner have extensively analyzed the role of cost-benefit analysis as a way to monitor the effort of bureaucracies and avoid bureaucratic drift in the daily operation of governments, with focus on the US administration, where cost-benefit analysis has become increasingly widespread in agencies in the past years. In particular, Eric Posner (2001) observes that cost-benefit analysis should not be considered "as a normative criterion but as an analytic concept in a positive analysis".[294] Assuming self-interested actors in the delegation and oversight game, it is possible to conclude that cost-benefit analysis may become something else than

292 For a comprehensive account, see Epstein and O'Halloran (1999), *supra* note 197; and Eric Posner (2001), *supra* note 86.

293 See also Williamson, O. (1999). *Public and Private Bureaucracies: A Transaction Cost Economics Perspective*, 15 J.L. Econ & Org. 306.

294 Posner, E.A. (2001), *supra* note 86, at 10.

an instrument of efficiency, with mixed results for the desirability of RIA-based monitoring.

The argument proceeds as follows, with two actors that, for simplicity's sake, I call Central Government (CG) and delegated agency (DA). Since both CG and DA are self-motivated, they may have goals that differ from that of achieving efficient outcomes (for example, CG may look at re-election or pursuing some social or economic agenda, DA may seek more regulation, including inefficient regulation, to strengthen its power). Absent any other form of control, CG may find it useful to mandate cost-benefit analysis as a backing of rules proposed by DA for several reasons. First, since it is CG's prerogative to sanction DA for insufficient or flawed cost-benefit analysis, CG may decide to support also badly justified rules that converge with its own agenda. In any event, if the analysis will be recognized as flawed in the future, responsibility will fall on DA rather than on CG, since the former was the more specialized agency in charge of producing economic analysis. Accordingly, as stated by Eric Posner, "government principals who are interested in goals other than efficiency will in many situations want agencies to perform cost-benefit analysis, even though cost-benefit analysis evaluates projects on the basis of efficiency or a close approximation".[295]

Paradoxically, this finding may even be less undesirable than it appears at first blush. In a world with imperfect information, and given that cost-benefit analysis in and of itself is an imperfect way to select optimal policy, one could defend the narrowing of procedures induced by the mandatory adoption of RIA as a way to achieve policy coherence and dynamically align the goals of CG and DA even without adopting a pure welfarist approach to government.[296] In other words, to the extent that RIA rooted in cost-benefit analysis proves to be the cheapest way to exert a disciplining effect on bureaucracies and realize virtuous results in terms of policy coherence, then even the most neoclassical approach to cost-benefit analysis may be seen as a desirable procedural requirement. The introduction of models borrowed from positive political theory and public choice, such as interest group competition, produces similar outcomes as clarified by Becker (2000).[297]

Under this different lens, the relevance of a RIA system crucially depends on the system of checks and balances that are established in a given government

295 *Id.*

296 See Adler, M.D. and E.A. Posner (2000), *Implementing Cost-Benefit Analysis When Preferences are Distorted*, 29 J Legal Stud 1105, 1116–25.

297 Becker, G.S. (2000), *A Comment on the Conference on Cost-Benefit Analysis*, 29 J Legal Stud 1151–52 (discussing cost-benefit analysis as it applies in the interest group competition model of political choice). There is also an extensive literature on the selection of types of regulatory remedies and solutions out of the policymaker's toolbox, related to positive and normative mechanisms choice. For an extensive overview, see Wiener, J.B. and B.D. Richman, *Mechanism Choice* (July 1, 2009). Public Choice and Public Law, D.A. Farber and A.J. O'Connell, eds., Forthcoming; Duke Law School Public Law & Legal Theory Paper No. 250. Available at SSRN: http://ssrn.com/abstract=1408163.

setting.[298] The results obtained by Eric Posner (2001) may be significantly altered when draft RIAs are published for consultation before CG can scrutinize their content and decide about their quality: this actually happens in the US, where the 1946 Administrative Procedure Act mandates that notices of proposed rulemaking be submitted for notice and comment before being approved. The internal dialogue and commingling of interest between CG and DA may be fundamentally altered by the visibility of the draft RIA on the stakeholder side: well-organized stakeholders may denounce bad RIAs before they are finalized, and call on CG to impose their revision. This is one of the reasons why the transparency of RIAs and the availability of consultation *before* the oversight body reaches a final decision is perhaps the most fundamental ingredient of a sound RIA system. That said, if the result is to *de facto* bind policy decisions to Kaldor-Hicks cost-benefit analysis, such an efficient RIA system may perform worse than a more hidden system in which DA anticipates the will of CG and both players act strategically to strengthen their position in the policy cycle. In any event, my preference always goes to a better-quality cost-benefit analysis, which overcomes the countless problems faced by pure welfarist models and moves in the directions outlined in the previous sections *and* is made transparent to stakeholders to strengthen the commitment of both DA and CG to high quality *ex ante* policy appraisal.

In addition, this analysis also reveals that in political contexts such as the US one, the delegation and oversight mechanism can be "lubricated" through the introduction of governance mechanisms such as *ex post* oversight by a third body (*e.g.* the CBO, the GAO). This is what increasingly happens in the US, as observed *supra* in Section 2.2.2. At the same time, this specific analytical perspective can inspire judgment on what "type" of watchdog would be most appropriate in a quality RIA system. Evidence that OIRA in the US has been "changing skin" during different administrations, transforming itself from consultant to adversarial gatekeeper may suggest that the task delegation game has turned into a closer oversight aimed at achieving the goals pursued by central government, rather than strengthening the powers of the agencies. The revival of return letters and the introduction of prompt letters between 2001 and 2006 confirms this view of a stronger OIRA in the US, which – again – may lead to more quantified costs and benefits in legislation, but does not necessarily guarantee high quality, distribution-aware cost-benefit analysis.[299]

---

298 For a sophisticated analysis of the mechanisms at play within RIA systems in four jurisdictions, see Radaelli *et al.* (2010), *How to Learn From International Experience: Impact Assessment in the Netherlands*, study for the Dutch government, available at www.eerstekamer.nl/behandeling/20100527/how_to_learn_from_the/f=/vifklgll6miz.pdf.

299 See Graham, J. (2007), *The Evolving Regulatory Role of the U.S. Office of Management and Budget, Review of Environmental Economics and Policy.* No. 1: 171–191. S.E. Dudley and A. Antonelli, *Congress and the Clinton OMB: Unwilling Partners in Regulatory Oversight?*, Regulation, Fall 1997, at 17–18.

The "functional" approach to RIA sheds light on a number of other aspects of the RIA system, especially related to the EU context. First, as will be illustrated in more detail in Section 6 below, the quality and usefulness of the EU impact assessment system is deeply jeopardized for two essential reasons: (i) the principal and the agent are the same political actor, with strong incentives to achieve alignment of final decisions; (ii) the absence of consultation on draft IAs makes it impossible for stakeholders to put pressure on the oversight body (the Impact Assessment Board) to induce improvements in the quality of analysis, and even the consideration of policy alternatives that have been unduly discarded. In addition, other aspects of the system are significantly under-researched: the specific constraints exerted by other institutions (the High-Level Group on administrative burdens, the European Court of Auditors, the European Parliament and the Council of the EU) are in most cases still being defined and shaped; the fact that the EU IA system is not primarily rooted on cost-benefit analysis, and is not only focused on secondary legislation, may dilute the signaling nature of RIA as well as the monitoring capabilities of the central oversight body (due to the absence of a clear standard on which to base the assessment); and the fact that IA is applied also outside binding regulation – *i.e.*, it is an IA and not a RIA system – may lead to imperfect signals between the principal, the agent, and stakeholders, as well as cast doubts on the usefulness of cost-benefit analysis when it is required – as increasingly occurs.

The current OIRA administrator Cass R. Sunstein argued back in 2000 that cost-benefit analysis may be justified because its narrow procedures help overcome the cognitive biases of the public and of administrative officials, in particular by helping administrations to better focus on their priorities and also overcome collective irrationality by providing stronger arguments in favor of apparently nonsensical legislation.[300] In this respect, even more than its "functional" role, RIA may become useful mostly due to its "persuasive" role. Also from this peculiar viewpoint, transparency and public consultation become essential, especially due to the fact that the added value of RIA (and the time and money spent on it) becomes otherwise almost impossible to communicate.

4.4.1.1. *The architecture of RIA: a "behavioral" approach*

Looking at the RIA system and the use of cost-benefit analysis from a functional perspective allows a different use of behavioral biases applied to public authorities. If one considers investing in RIA as a costly exercise – often requiring hundreds of thousands of dollars and several person/months for bureaucrats, consultants and oversight bodies – as well as a fact-finding exercise on the way towards more informed decision-making, then the question of the *an*, the *quantum* and the *quomodo* of engaging in policy appraisal becomes essential. In

300 Sunstein, C. R. (2000), *Cognition and Cost-Benefit Analysis*, 29 J Legal Stud 1059, 1060–61.

this respect, the same behavioral analysis that is applied to individuals can *mutatis mutandis* be also applied to public bodies. In particular, one can approach the development of policy solutions from the standpoint of rational ignorance and bounded rationality as described in Section 4.2.1 above. Below, I sketch a sort of meta-RIA, in order to find out when the RIA system would be an efficient option compared to "no RIA".

The question "if" policymakers should engage in RIA for a given policy proposal can indeed be governed by a cost-benefit comparison: if the expected benefits of having a RIA on that given policy proposal are likely to more-than-compensate the cost of undertaking the exercise, then RIA should be carried out. However, this decision is more complex that it might appear at first blush. In particular, the benefits can be seen as a function of the importance of the proposal *per se*; of the quality of the prospective analysis; of the controversial nature of the proposal (is it merely a minor revision of a previous regulation? Is there an umbrella regulation shaping already the direction and operational toolkit of this piece of legislation? Are stakeholders likely to complain if there will be no RIA supporting the proposal? Are there important implementation modalities or specific key impacts to be ascertained? At the same time, the costs depend on the depth of the analysis, and this may be kept as a fixed variable (as in the US), or left to the decision of the body that supervises the process (as in the EU).

As a matter of fact, the two legal systems analyzed in this work – the US and the EU – have solved the problem in a completely different way. On the one hand, the US feature a system where RIA is almost invariable in terms of depth, and the criteria to select proposals that should undergo RIA are set.[301] In the EU, the set of proposals is much broader, there is not basic requirement – as a matter of fact, even the focus on initiatives included in the Commission legislative and work programme is virtually ignored – but the principle of proportionate analysis described in the IA guidelines should guide the official in charge in selecting the prospective depth of the IA to be undertaken. Especially in the case of the EU, the refinement of this set of criteria seems necessary, as will be explained in more detail in part III below.

Another important aspect of this question is how much to invest at each stage of the policy cycle. In the US this choice is a pure dichotomy between the *ex ante* preparation and the *ex post* evaluation of the same regulation, and the focus is

301 Proposals with annual effect on the economy of $100 million or more or adversely affect in a material way the economy, a sector of the economy, productivity, competition, jobs, the environment, public health or safety, or State, local, or tribal governments or communities; proposals that create a serious inconsistency or otherwise interfered with an action taken or planned by another agency; proposals that materially alter the budgetary impact of entitlements, grants, user fees, or loan programs or the rights and obligations of recipients thereof; or proposals that raise novel legal or policy issues arising out of legal mandates, the President's priorities, or the principles set forth in EO 12,866.

clearly placed on the *ex ante* phase due to the strong principal-agent nature of the system.[302] In the EU, to the contrary, IA can be performed as many as three times on the same proposal at different stages – white paper, communication, proposed binding legislation – and then evaluated *ex post* before a new proposal is tabled. Accordingly, the question of what to ask at what stage becomes even more complicated: as I will explain below in Part III of this book, the European Commission has not satisfactorily solved this puzzle to date.

The issue of "asking the right question, at the right time, in the right sequence" was already mentioned in the Mandelkern Report back in 2001. In my opinion, this is essentially a matter of allocating resources efficiently. Our brain does it all the time, after all. Evidence that human beings only take *satisficing* decisions can be applied also to public officials in charge of RIA: asking them to collect all relevant information on all consequences of a regulatory decision beforehand is as illogical as asking consumers to read and understand all contract terms when dealing with standard form contracts or click-wrap licenses. To the contrary, it would be more efficient to collect and analyze evidence up to the point when the marginal social benefit of such an exercise equates the marginal cost: the problem is that such a choice cannot be left to the private individual, as the marginal private benefit of performing RIA will likely be much lower that the social one. In Part III below, I propose a "staged approach" to IA in the European Union that responds to the need to allocate resources efficiently.

4.4.2. NUDGING PEOPLE: LAW AS A MEANS

In Section 4.4 above, I have explored the issue of whether public policymakers should aim at the achievement of certain goals in society, which are not automatically selected by citizens in their daily interactions. Pure welfarism would suggest that such goal is wealth maximization, and this is what citizens want – some say that they want it *ex ante*, meaning that individuals would choose to live in a world where policymakers seek to maximize average utility by approximating it with wealth – the size of the pie. However, we have found out that in many circumstances mere reliance on individual preferences would lead to an unduly reductionist and profoundly mistaken approach, especially when public goods and externalities are at play.

Now, forget about this *querelle* for a second, and imagine a policymaker that has an objective that market behavior by itself would not be able to reach. This may be a simple case of market failure, or a case in which the policymaker indeed wants to impose a given policy outcome, even against the will of its constituency.

---

302 For example, of the more than 100 major rules issued by EPA from 1981 to 1998, only five were subject to *ex post* evaluation (GAO 1999).

How can legal rules be framed in a way that minimizes the intrusive nature of such policies, without undermining their effectiveness?

As a matter of fact, many commentators have realized that it takes much less than a fan of planned economies to advocate for objective welfare judgments in public policy. Individuals act irrationally in most circumstances; and markets follow the same track (think about herd behavior effects during the recent financial crisis); compliance with legislation often requires such a coordinated collective effort than no one wants to make the first move; social norms often work against the achievement of given social changes for the good. At the same time, a policymaker may want to achieve a given outcome, but may have too little resources, information, time or capacity to be able to impose individual behavior and enforce it throughout the territory on which she has authority. And after all, people hate being told what to do – in political, economic and philosophical terms, dictating behavior is at once ineffective and dangerous.

However, a policymaker with a clear objective can still use the law as a means. In particular, as a means to provide individuals with incentives to behave in a way that ultimately achieves the pre-determined objective or makes it more likely. In other words, it can make the visible hand of the government invisible enough to leave individuals still free to choose. From this standpoint, law and economics has proven of invaluable help in offering policymakers guidance on how to shape legal rules "as means". Below, I illustrate some of the most insightful ways in which law and economics scholars have helped in the understanding of incentives and how to frame individual decision settings. All these tools can be in principle framed within a logic of libertarian paternalism – *i.e.*, cases in which the law is conceived to steer individual behavior towards given directions, be them efficiency or distributive goals. In particular, I refer to "time-shifting", "mechanism choices", "framing of individual incentives", "debiasing through law"; "reliance on technology", and "nudging".

4.4.2.1. *Overcoming informational deficits in policy: time-shifting rules, optional law, and "pragmatic libertarianism"*

In traditional top-down, "command and control" policymaking the legislator is assumed to possess reasonable information about the most appropriate allocation of entitlements, *i.e.* which rights should be assigned, and how should they be protected. In this over-simplified view of lawmaking, a legislator chooses outcome x based on a mix of legal tradition, ideals of justice and – when appropriate – economic or social policy, and proceeds to impose the selected outcome on citizens.

In law and economics, the view is completely different. First, lawmakers are assumed not to possess sufficient information to be able to impose given market outcomes from the outset: therefore, relying on their ability to do so would be hazardous at best. Second, individuals do not take legal rules as given: they can bargain around legal rules in order to achieve Pareto improvements over the initially set allocation of entitlements. Third, and consequently, legal rules may not have as their primary goal the identification of the best solution *tout court*, but the creation of an environment in which parties can easily bargain on their entitlements and reach superior results due to their superior awareness of the contingent circumstances, compared to the policymaker. Put differently, it is possible to devise mechanisms to make sure that the most informed parties eventually decide on which entitlement should be protected, and how. Since the most informed parties are in most cases the ones that will actually experience situations in which legal entitlements are at stake, it is efficient to leave them with as much discretion as possible to reach a final solution on the allocation of those rights.

A situation in which the lawmaker chooses the initial entitlement to protect and leaves as much discretion as possible to private players on the best way to solve inter-individual negotiation is what I define as "time-shifting": as a matter of fact, part of the decision on how the entitlement will be protected is postponed to the moment in which individuals will experience a relevant situation of conflicting rights. As I will briefly explain in this section, time-shifting can take several forms, mostly related to the introduction of liability rules as opposed to property rules as alternative ways to protect given entitlements.

Perhaps the most well-known example of time-shifting in early law and economics scholarship is the "*ex ante* view of the cathedral" that Guido Calabresi and Douglas Melamed described back in 1972. One of the key insights of this seminal paper was that, when transaction costs are low, the best way to protect an entitlement is to delegate the choice of its allocation to private negotiation: this means that – in line with the Coase theorem – a legislator may allocate the entitlement also to the person that deserves it less, since private parties will be able to reach a final allocation through mutually beneficial transactions. The relevance of the initial allocation of the entitlement would, then, be limited to the final distribution of the surplus from negotiation – *i.e.* the party protected by the legal rule will be able to capture a larger share of the surplus. Accordingly, and very much in line with Calabresi's view of *justice before efficiency*, the allocation of entitlements should reflect *in primis* principles of justice and the identification of the allocation that minimizes transaction costs. Likewise, in his analysis of the cost of accidents, Calabresi explained that the choice between strict liability and negligence should not be guided by the desire to impose liability based on principles of justice; to the contrary, the overall cost of the legal system of accident liability should be minimized by attributing liability to the so-called "cheapest cost avoider" or the "superior insurer". As recalled *i.a.* by Faure (2008), Calabresi offers a few hints on how to identify the mythical figure of the cheapest cost avoider. Well aware of the behavioral consequences of legal rules, Calabresi argued in favor of an initial *rough guess* aimed at ruling out from the potential loss bearers activities that could reduce the costs being allocated only at great expense.[303] In addition, lawmakers should seek the allocation of responsibility that achieves the maximum degree of internalization of costs. Overall the choice has to be made in order to minimize the sum of social costs arising from accidents, the costs of precaution and the cost of administering the rule.[304]

When put into practice, the cheapest cost avoider principle has proven superior to alternative models such as the polluter-pays-principle in environmental regulation. In particular, the *ex ante* determination of the cheapest cost avoider is what matters in terms of minimization of the overall cost of the legal system. Under this approach, "if either of two parties can reduce the occurred damage, the party which is able to do so with the lowest cost should act, as long as this cost is lower than the benefit".[305] This requires following four discrete steps: (i) identifying the possible actors who can influence the outcome (*e.g.* polluters, the pollutees, or a third party, like government); (ii) identifying alternative ways in which the outcome can be altered; (iii) assessing the minimum costs of the various methods figured out; and (iv) identifying the least cost method and the actor connected to it, which is indeed the cheapest cost avoider.

Similarly, in cases of strict liability for dangerous activities or liability for third party damages, the behavioral response of targeted agents is taken into account. Calabresi himself has shed light on the role of the "superior insurer" or "deep pocket" in securing efficient strict liability in these circumstances. The time-shifting effect here rests in the decision by the legislator to refrain from seeking the efficient outcome from the outset; to the contrary, the legal rule only looks at ways to minimize the total cost of the legal rule, and delegates to those private parties that can do it in the most effective way the decision to purchase insurance to limit their exposure to risk.

Even more interestingly, an important corollary contained in the paper written by Calabresi and Melamed on the "cathedral" is that, when transaction costs are likely to be high, insisting on protecting the entitlement through a property rule will not achieve the desired result, as parties will fail to negotiate to reach the Pareto frontier. This view of the cathedral is perhaps the most useful for modern law and economics scholars, as it can potentially host consideration of all the limits to human rationality and the bounded willpower that are

303 Calabresi, G. (1970), *The Costs of Accidents. A Legal and Economic Analysis*, New Haven: Yale University Press.

304 According to Calabresi, if there is uncertainty about who is the cheapest cost avoider, accident costs should be charged to the person who can enter into transactions more cheaply: what Calabresi refers to as 'the best briber'.

305 Schmidtchen *et al.* (2008), *The Internalisation of External Costs in Transport: From the Polluter Pays to the Cheapest Cost Avoider Principle*, German Working Papers in law and Economics, Paper 1.

considered to draw the line between *homo oeconomicus* and *homo sapiens*. Under this view, liability rules can be efficiently used to avoid that the parties engage in costly and unfruitful negotiation to change an initial allocation of entitlements. Here, a real time-shifting effect occurs, together with a sort of "Kantian" revolution, in which the decision on the final allocation is moved from the observation (or prediction) of reality to the mind of the non-entitled party, who has to decide whether to exercise an option to "buy" the entitlement at a given (regulated) price. Whenever the circumstances suggest that the choice by the non-protected party is likely to be a reasonably informed one, and the price set by the policymaker is such that it reasonably reflects the WTA of the party protected by the entitlement, this time-shifting effect can prove more efficient and desirable than any top-down imposition of resource allocation.[306]

The view of liability rules as *call options* (*i.e.*, options to buy an entitlement without having to negotiate the purchase) elicited insightful elaborations in the law and economics literature, and bears still under-researched applications in practical policy. In terms of subsequent literature, the study of liability rules as options has been advanced significantly by authors such as Lucien Ayre Bebchuk, Ian Ayres, Eric Talley, Louis Kaplow, Steven Shavell, James Krier, Stewart Schab and Lee Ann Fennell.[307] I will only refer to three of these contributions below, as dealing with the issue in-depth would deserve a separate volume.

306 Note, in addition, that in proposing the use of liability rules whenever transaction costs are significant, Calabresi and Melamed (1972) are already one step away from the notion of mutual consent that has shaped the idea of Pareto efficient negotiation between private parties in Coase's *The problem of social cost*. In this respect, the use of liability rules is potentially compatible with objective judgments, and "nudging".

307 The literature blossomed from the Calabresi-Melamed paper is so numerous that even Guido Calabresi declared himself surprised. Relevant papers include Ayres, I. (1998), *Protecting Property with Puts*, Valparaiso University Law Review 32:793; Ayres, I. (2005), *Optional law: the structure of legal entitlements*, Chicago: University of Chicago Press; Ayres, I. and J.M. Balkin (1996), *Legal Entitlements as Auctions: Property Rules, Liability Rules, and Beyond*, Yale Law Journal 106 (3):703–50; Ayres, I. and P.M. Goldbart (2001), *Optimal Delegation and Decoupling in the Design of Liability Rules*, Michigan Law Review 100 (1):1–79; Ayres, I., and P.M. Goldbart (2003), *Correlated Values in the Theory of Property and Liability Rules*, Journal of Legal Studies 32 (1):121–51; Ayres, I. and E. Talley (1995), *Distinguishing between Consensual and Nonconsensual Advantages of Liability Rules*, Yale Law Journal 105 (1):235–53; Ayres, I. and E. Talley (1995), *Solomonic Bargaining: Dividing a Legal Entitlement to Facilitate Coasean Trade*, Yale Law Journal 104 (5):1027–1117; Epstein, R.A. (1997), *A Clear View of The Cathedral: The Dominance of Property Rules*, Yale Law Journal 106 (7):2091–2120; Epstein, R.A. (1998), *Protecting Property Rights with Legal Remedies: A Common Sense Reply to Professor Ayres*, Val. University Law Review 32:833; Farnsworth, W. (1999), *Do Parties to Nuisance Cases Bargain after Judgment? A Glimpse inside the Cathedral*, The University of Chicago Law Review 66 (2):373–436; Fennell, L.A. (2005), *Revealing Options*, Harvard Law Review 118 (5):1401–1488; Kaplow, L., and S. Shavell (1996), *Property Rules versus Liability Rules*, Harvard Law Review 109:713; Kornhauser, L.A. (1986), *An Introduction to the Economic Analysis of Contract Remedies*, University of Colorado Law Review 57 (4):683–725; Krier, J.E. and S.J. Schwab (1995), *Property Rules and Liability Rules: The cathedral in another light*, New York University Law Review 70 (May):440; Krier, J.E., and S.J. Schwab (1997), *The Cathedral at Twenty-Five: Citations and Impressions*, Yale Law Journal 106 (7):2121–47.

Perhaps the most insightful re-elaboration of the Calabresi-Melamed framework is Ayres' idea of optional law, where the legendary "four rules" identified by Calabresi and Melamed in a standard nuisance context – two property rules and two liability rules, protecting either the polluter or the pollutee – are redefined and expanded. In particular, Ayres (2005) explains that if liability rules that imply an option to purchase an entitlement can be interpreted as *call options*, then there might be also a way to protect entitlements through a *put option*, which gives the party protected through an entitlement the option to force its counter-party to purchase the entitlement at a pre-determined price, *i.e* an option to sell one's own alienable right. When the legislator aims at protecting one of the parties in a specific situation, but wants to make sure that the protection does not crystallize inefficient allocations of entitlements due to prohibitive transaction costs, then the choice of one of these optional rules may be warranted.[308] And indeed, the effort by some academics to trace in common and civil law jurisdictions legal rules that correspond to Ayres' rule 5 and 6 has led to very interesting results in the past few years.[309]

Another important development in the literature has been the attempt by Lucien Bebchuk (2002a, 2002b) to approach the cathedral from an *ex ante* perspective, by looking at the potential impact of the "grid of rules" elaborated by Calabresi and Melamed on the parties' incentives to invest in given economic activities – the approach is easily extended also to the other rules identified a few years later in Ayres (2005). Bebchuk (2002a) suggests that the choice of the rule that will govern the interaction between individuals in contexts with conflicting uses of property can be inspired by the legislator's desire to encourage either of the uses, or to place the decision on the prevailing use on the entity that can reach the most efficient decision most cost-effectively. In my opinion, future elaboration of these theoretical insights will lead to a better framing of regulatory problems such as blocking patents, access policy in network industries, or the resolution of conflicting uses of spectrum, as will be shown in Section 5 below. Even more broadly, fiercely debated issues such as *i.a.* investment in next-generation access network in telecommunications, network neutrality on the Internet, refusal to grant interoperability with *de facto* industry standards, the governance of patent pools, the reallocation of airport slots, access to essential drugs and the compulsory licensing of climate-friendly technologies can be usefully and decisively inspired by this type of approach.[310]

308 Ayres, I. (2005), *Optional Law: the Structure of Legal Entitlements*, University Of Chicago Press; 1 edition (June 15, 2005).

309 Nicita, A., R. Pardolesi and M. Rizzolli (2005), Le Opzioni nel mercato delle regele, SIDE Working Paper, available at www.side-isle.it/wp/05/nicita-pardolesi-rizzolli.pdf.

310 See, *i.a.*, Merges (1996) and Castro (2010).

Finally, Lee Ann Fennell (2005) has provided a useful refinement to the framework of optional law by discussing behavioral rules that do not even require that the legislator possesses sufficient information to be able to set the price of the call and put options in a way that triggers efficient decisions by the private players involved. In certain circumstances, according to Fennell, parties can be put in the same situation of the players in the "cake slicing" game, which closely recalls the pre-constitutional approaches proposed (in a different context and with different features) by Rawls, Harsanyi and Posner. The cake-slicing game is a simple theoretical setting in which a self-motivated young kid is asked to cut the cake in two slices, but is also warned that his little sister will be the one choosing which slice to eat. Under these conditions, the little kid does not know whether he will end up being the giver or the taker of the slice he is cutting, and is therefore in a sort of "original position": then the best thing he can do as a self-motivated player is to cut the cake in two equal pieces – *i.e.* under those conditions the best way to behave selfishly is to adopt what will appear as a very cooperative move. Fennell uses this metaphor to propose a "Texas shoot-out rule" for given situations of conflicts in property uses.[311]

All these are very good examples of insights offered by the law and economics literature on how to efficiently allocate decision-making responsibility between the legislator and private parties to create a suitable setting for reaching efficient results. As a matter of fact, these rules obviously face the problem of self-valuation by private parties, which may incur in behavioral problems such as those described in Section 4.2.1 of this book. Accordingly, these rules must be appraised also in light of the potential biases that may emerge in the formulation of private judgments.[312] In all those rules, and even more evidently in the case of Fennell's Texas shootout rule, important features are the emphasis on what happens *after* the rule is enacted; and the creation of mechanisms in which private parties can be induced to the selection of a desirable course of action. This insight, as will be clarified in the next section, has evolved into more comprehensive policy approaches in the literature, including the creation of choice architectures and the nudging of private actors in the direction of socially desirable behavior.

311 The example reported by Fennell refers to a simple two-partner setting, in which partner P1 must name a price for her share of the partnership venture, whereas partner P2 can choose to pay that price to acquire P1's share of the venture or can instead require P1 to buy out his share (that is, P2's own share) at that same price. See also Renda (2006), *L'Importanza di Essere Onesto. Come Trasformare un Benthamiano in un Rawlsiano*, Rivista della Scuola Superiore dell'Economia e delle Finanze, 2006, Issue 3, at 175.

312 See, broadly, Arcuri, A. (2002), *supra* note 214.

4.4.2.2. *Enforcement and compliance: exploring the missing link*

As explained by Anthony Ogus back in 1998, the "original sin" of regulatory appraisal, and its missing link with law and economics, are related to the fact that contemporary RIA applies to legal initiatives the same set of principles that are normally applied to *ex ante* project evaluation. However, while project evaluation often revolves around assessing whether the value of assets would change following a certain event, "the first-order effects of legal reform depend primarily on the level of compliance by private actors".[313] This is a key problem in regulatory appraisal, which has hardly been tackled, let alone solved, by current RIA practices.

As already mentioned in Section 4.1.1.1 above, one early contribution of law and economics scholars in the field of contracts and torts is the development of theories of optimal deterrence due to the seminal work of Gary Becker (1968). The idea that the deterrence effect obtains by applying sanctions that multiply the expected damage by the inverse of the likelihood of being caught has spurred endless refinements in the literature, which cannot be fully analyzed in this work.[314] Suffice it to recall, in this context, that several rules are still analyzed and compared in RIA documents with very little attention to fundamental questions such as who is going to enforce them, at what cost, and with what degree of effectiveness. For example, as will be illustrated in more detail in Section 5 below by means of examples, rules on financial monitoring and large exposure reporting in the EU Basel II framework, as well as *i.a.* tort rules and antitrust law in EU member states suffer from the very limited attention placed by public authorities on the actual degree of deterrence these rules foster. Furthermore, the popular Standard Cost Model used to assess the administrative burdens generated by existing and prospective legislation in the EU and practically all its member states assumes 100% compliance without even approaching the problem.

The key to solving this puzzle is again formulating assumptions on the incentives that will be faced by private actors when confronted with the decision

313 See Ogus, A. (1998), *Regulatory Appraisal: A Neglected Opportunity for Law and Economics*, European Journal of Law and Economics, Volume 6, Number 1, July 1998, pp. 53–68(16).

314 See the seminal contributions of G.S. Becker, (1968), *Crime and Punishment: An Economic Approach*, Journal of Political Economy, Vol. 76. Pages 169–217. G.S. Becker and G.J. Stigler, (1974), *Law Enforcement, Malfeasance and Compensation of Enforcers*, Journal of Legal Studies, Vol. 3. Pages 1–18. W.M. Landes and R.A. Posner (1975), *The Private Enforcement of Law*, Journal of Legal Studies, Vol. 4. Pages 1–46. D.D. Friedman, (1984), *Efficient Institutions for the Private Enforcement of Law*, Journal of Legal Studies, Vol. 13, 379–397. A.M. Polinsky and S. Shavell (1999), *The Economic Theory of Public Enforcement of Law*, Journal of Economic Literature, forthcoming. For a literature review, see Renda *et al.* (2008), *Making private antitrust damages actions more effective in Europe*, Report for the European Commission, DG Competition, http://ec.europa.eu/competition/antitrust/actionsdamages/files_white_paper/impact_study.pdf.

whether to comply with the rule. In line with the developments in law and economics scholarships described in the previous sections, also in this case behavioral law and economics profoundly affected the prescriptive power of early contributions. However, in the case of the theory of optimal deterrence these critiques do not shake the foundations of the overall approach: rather, they inform the work of the policymaker in a way that better approximates reality.[315]

Even more broadly, when looking at the effectiveness of enforcement under the lens of behavioral biases, it is important to consider that, as recalled by Nuno Garoupa (2003), "once criminals are not fully rational, so are not victims, enforcers, and politicians". In a recent review of the literature, McAdams and Ulen (2008) show, *i.a.* that potential victims of criminal acts may feature over-optimism and thus adopt insufficient precaution; policemen, inspectors and judges may be constrained and affected by "implicit bias" as well as "hindsight bias", which determines the path-dependency of legal adjudication beyond the merits of the individual case at hand[316]; and the costs of litigation may very often lead to settlement, which in turn dilutes both the prospective cost of infringing the law on the side of the would-be infringer, and the benefit of suing for damage compensation on the side of the victim. Finally, any well-designed rule in many fields in which damages actions and injunctive relief are key elements of litigation must control for the incentive of non-victims to strategically use the legal system in order to secure strategic settlements for undeserving (frivolous) lawsuits.[317]

Realizing that the implementation phase of a legal rule is as important as its implicit design is key to the development of effective policy options. A rule may appear optimal in theory but may be very difficult to correctly implement in practice: examples certainly include the EU Markets in Financial Services Directive (MiFiD), which imposed an exchange of information and extensive profiling and disclosure between the financial intermediary and its customers, in a context in which asymmetric information is so deeply entrenched in the relationship that any form of steering and churning may nevertheless take place.[318]

---

315 See *e.g.* Sunstein, C.R., D. Schkade and D. Kahneman (1999), *Do People Want Optimal Deterrence?* University of Chicago Law School, John M. Olin Law & Economics Working Paper No. 77.

316 See McAdams, R.H. and T.S. Ulen (2008), *Behavioral Criminal Law and Economics*, U of Chicago Law & Economics, Olin Working Paper No. 440; U of Chicago, Public Law Working Paper No. 244; U Illinois Law & Economics Research Paper No. LE08–035. Available at SSRN: http://ssrn.com/abstract=1299963. And see also Sunstein, C.R., D. Kahneman, D. Schkade and I. Ritov (2002), *Predictably Incoherent Judgments*, Stan. L. Rev. 54, 1153; Jolls, C. (2004), *On Law Enforcement With Boundedly Rational Actors*, Harvard L&E Discussion paper No. 494; and Jolls, C. and C.R. Sunstein (2006), *The Law of Implicit Bias*, Cal. L. Rev., 94, 969–996.

317 See *i.a.* Bebchuk, L.A. (1998), *Negative Expected Value Suits*, NBER Working Paper No. W6474.

318 See Directive 2004/39/Ec of the European Parliament and of the Council of 21 April 2004 on markets in financial instruments amending Council Directives 85/611/EEC and 93/6/EEC and Directive 2000/12/EC of the European Parliament and of the Council and repealing Council Directive 93/22/EEC.

Finally, as already recalled in Section 4.2.2.1 above, policymakers should gauge the likelihood of compliance also on the basis of existing social norms – *i.e.* not only the "deterrence trap", but also the "compliance trap" may emerge as a result of a badly conceived rule.[319] Policymakers that have dealt with cyberspace in the past few years, including those that have tried to criminalize illegal music downloads through the 1998 Digital Millennium Copyright Act and those that are trying to implement the HADOPI law in France know well how difficult it is to overcome social norms.[320] Close to this approach is the extensive literature on responsive regulation as originally defined by Ian Ayres and John Braithwaite (1992), who build a model in which regulators interact with regulated firms by using various regulatory measures from the least to the most intrusive, and are called to investigate first of all on the reasons for non-compliance before moving to pure deterrence-based approaches.[321] The domain of responsive regulation and its relatively more recent branches of smart regulation and risk-based regulation, mostly originating in the UK debate over regulatory reform, offer a more nuanced menu of tools compared to the standard Beckerian dichotomy between compliance and deterrence.

The combined result of these streams of literature is that any well-conceived RIA guidance around the world should devote an extensive section to nudge proponent administrations to ask the preliminary question "how is this regulatory option going to be enforced? And with what expected results? How can we avoid the deterrence trap and the compliance trap? Why has compliance been so low in the past?" In certain fields of law, answering such a question may lead to U-turns in the way legal rules are conceived.

4.4.2.3. "De-biasing through law" and libertarian welfarism theories

Laws that directly affect individual behavior often display varying degrees of effectiveness due to the behavioral response of individuals. In particular, rules that try to promote healthy or safe behavior such as refraining from smoking, getting vaccination or wearing helmets while riding motorbikes have often failed to achieve full compliance due to the difficulty of convincing individuals to adapt their behavior. This is often due to both individual behavioral biases and social norms. The literature on "de-biasing through law" looks mostly at the former type of distortions, and tries to devise strategies to limit the impact of behavioral

---

319 See, *i.a.* Parker, C. (2006), *The Compliance Trap: The Moral Message in Responsive Regulatory Enforcement.* U. of Melbourne Legal Studies Research Paper No. 163; See also Braithwaite (2002); and Ayres and Braithwaite (1992).

320 See Section 5.8 below for a more detailed description of the French HADOPI law and similar initiatives on the protection of copyright in cyberspace.

321 Even this stream of literature has moves towards behavioral studies. See *i.a.* Baldwin, R. and J. Black (2007), *Really Responsive Regulation*, LSE Law, Economy and Society working Papers 15/2007.

biases in the decision to comply – *i.e.* it takes the imperfections of our brain as a given, and tries to minimize their impacts just as Coase advocated the minimization of the impact on transaction costs.

The simplest version of de-biasing through law is through educational and informational campaigns, the simplest ones being pure messages sent to the eye of the individual at the right moment (such as Sunstein's example of the "look right" message shown on boardwalks in the UK to avoid that tourists cross the street looking left as in their own countries[322]). In crafting more sophisticated campaigns, messages may be framed in a way that captures the attention of the individual and affects her own mental accounting and risk expectation.[323] A vast literature has blossomed in the past few years on how to inform consumers in a way that pushes them to change their behavior. I will show a similar example in Section 5 below.

However, when pure informational remedies are not sufficient, de-biasing may act in other ways. For example, a typical de-biasing form of regulation is the introduction of default rules, which change individuals' focal point when negotiating contracts, providing them with an easy reference on potentially reasonable clauses. Korobkin (2009) observes that, as a result of the *status quo* bias, more people are likely to choose an option if they consider it a constituent part of the *status quo* than if they view it as inconsistent with it. However, this and other similar options discussed by Korobkin (2009) – such as frame alteration tools – already fall in the realm of paternalism, since they presuppose that the policymaker wants to nudge consumers towards the adoption of a given behavior.

Another well-known set of rules that aim at de-biasing individual choice is consumer protection. Today, there is very little disagreement on the fact that behavioral law and economics should be the foundation of a well-designed consumer protection strategy. International organizations such as the OECD, the European Commission, competition authorities such as the OFT in the UK, the FTC in the US and many other institutions have dedicated studies and workshops to the issue of behavioral tools to achieve better consumer protection. This approach bears the heavy responsibility of saving the whole consumer protection movement from its evident failures in the past decades. For example, in a restrospective analysis of the famous *Williams v. Walker-Thomas Furniture* case addressed in 1965 by the US Supreme Court, Korobkin (2004) explains the different results that unconscionability analysis yields if observed under the lens of behavioral law and economics compared to the original approach adopted by the Court.[324] Likewise, recent analyses of early attempts to protect consumers

322 See Sunstein and Thaler, *Nudge*, *supra* note 3.

323 See *e.g.* Jolls (2010), *Governing America: the Emerging of Behavioral Law and Economics.*

324 Korobkin, R.B. (2009), *A 'Traditional' and 'Behavioral' Law-and-Economics Analysis of Williams v. Walker-Thomas Furniture Company.* University of Hawaii Law Review, Vol. 26,

from abusive behavior of their professional counter-parties in contracts of adhesion have rejected previous remedies based on the provision of information, and considered more aggressive strategies aimed at banning certain clauses and framing consumer decisions in a way that triggers better awareness.[325] The future of consumer protection is likely to involve more "structural" remedies such as banning of certain behavior and adoption of default rules, rather than disclosure obligations that fall on contract terms that would take a "three day seminar" to be fully understood by the average consumer. Similarly, a behavioral approach to cooling-off periods must necessarily take into account the fact that consumers, once they have purchased, may be less willing to change their mind, as their mindset and their perceived *status quo* has already changed.

As long as the rules analyzed do not challenge established social norms, but simply aim at correcting behavioral biases towards the adoption of spontaneously efficient decisions, it is fair to state that we are located in that area of law that Korobkin (2009) has defined "Libertarian welfarism". Very close to traditional law and economics, libertarian welfarism is a milder form of departure from mainstream neoclassical economics, of which it can be considered as a mere refinement.

4.4.2.4. Libertarian paternalism: who's afraid of "nudge"?

A different approach to policymaking that draws on behavioralism, but recognizes the need for weak paternalism and objective judgments is what Cass Sunstein and Richard Thaler have termed "Libertarian Paternalism", and is similar to what Camerer *et al.* (2003) call "asymmetric paternalism".[326] Sunstein and Thaler, in particular, have used this overall approach to justify policy intervention aimed at nudging individuals towards choices that correspond to desirable outcomes in the mind of the policymaker. The term libertarian refers to the fact that individuals are merely nudged, but they can still choose whether to follow the nudge, or make their own choice.

The nudging approach is particularly important for a number of reasons. First, because it is advocated *i.a.* by the scholar that is now holding the post of "regulatory czar" in the Obama administrations. Second, because it is the result

---

p. 441, 2004; UCLA School of Law, Law & Econ. Research Paper No. 03–24. Available at SSRN: http://ssrn.com/abstract=471961 or doi:10.2139/ssrn.471961.

325 See, *i.a.* Renda *et al.* (2009), "Tying and Other Potentially Unfair Commercial Practices in Retail Financial Services", Final Report for the European Commission DG MARKT, at http://ec.europa.eu/internal_market/consultations/docs/2010/tying/report_en.pdf; And see Becher (2008), at http://onlinelibrary.wiley.com/doi/10.1111/j.1744–1714.2008.00068.x/abstract.

326 Sunstein and Thaler, *Libertarian Paternalism is not an Oxymoron*, ... Camerer et al. (2003), *Regulation For Conservatives: Behavioral Economics And The Case For "Asymmetric Paternalism"*, U. Penn. L. Rev. 151: 1211.

of a long elaboration in law and economics, which has gradually opened the door to objective judgment and to partly abandoning the methodological individualism and the preference-based approach that have characterized neoclassical and Chicago law and Economics for many decades, towards some recognition of the social good and the need to gently steer individual autonomy towards that goal. Third, because it aims at helping individuals solve problems of externality and collective action (such as compliance with the law) through behavioral means, and as such can lead law and economics into higher ground. Fourth, because it respects – or tries to respect – the individual freedom to choose the course of action that she deems more appropriate and maximizes her subjective expected utility, of course within the boundaries of imperative norms. In other words, the nudging approach appears at first blush as the perfect summary of everything that law and economics has learnt since 1960 (and – incidentally – that Guido Calabresi seemed to know from the very beginning).

However, there are still some doubts as to how prominent nudging will become as a regulatory approach in the years to come, and whether such an approach would face problems of application. In particular, the focus of nudging is clearly on individual behavior, and as such appears way more suited for health and safety regulation than it would be for the regulation of market behavior by companies, or environmental protection (even though Sunstein and Thaler use cases on environmental policy in their book). In this respect, future research might usefully bridge "nudging" in certain areas of law with "responsive regulation" in market regulation and the related enforcement: such a combination of virtually homologous enforcement strategies may lead to a more complete and consistent policy framework for future generations.

At the same time, nudging has been criticized because it presupposes that the "nudgers" are well informed about what is good and what is bad.[327] This "indeterminacy" problem (not knowing exactly "what to nudge for") may lead to inconsistent and suboptimal policy. Personally, I consider this to be a minor critique, as in many cases the policymaker will indeed be nudging individuals to avoid immediate loss ("look right"); towards compliance with under-enforced rules (the "pooper-scooper" rule); towards behavior that scientific research has shown to be healthier (as in Sunstein and Thaler's example of the Cafeteria in "Nudge"); or in any event towards the preservation of a public good in cases where externalities and collective action determine a discrepancy between individual expected utility and the social optimality of certain behaviors.

327 Korobkin, R.B. (2009), *Libertarian Welfarism*. California Law Review, Vol. 97, No. 6, 2009; UCLA School of Law, Law-Econ Research Paper No. 09–09.

4.5. NON-CONCLUDING REMARKS: THE RESIDUAL ROLE OF LAW AND ECONOMICS IN *EX ANTE* POLICY APPRAISAL

Back in the 1970s, during the "expansionist" period of the law and economics movement, the Chicago school had developed an apparently solid and holistic approach to the making and implementation of the law, which seemed to stand as a fully alternative paradigm to traditional scholarship and established practice. This is also the time in which the US decided to create the RIA mechanism as a way to support delegation and oversight within government, and decided to base it on the Kaldor-Hicks criterion as the dominant litmus test to decide if a course of regulatory action would be viable or not.

Years after this decision, the law and economics movement appears to have developed more sophisticated, nuanced, and potentially insightful results. However, at the same time, the advent of behavioralism and a significant degree of relativism as regards the actual impact that rules will have on individual market and non-market interactions seems to cast a dark shadow on the potential for law and economics to deliver answers to the most pressing regulatory and policy questions. In a nutshell, diluting the Neoclassical paradigm has made law and economics dangerously agnostic. This is due to the undeniable fact that most of the original *tenets* of the Chicago school proved wrong, and mostly due to the reconsideration of the initial faith in individual rationality and (consequently) in the self-healing virtues of market forces.

As was observed by some scholars, including Richard Posner himself, the problem with behavioralism is that it never evolved into a consistent theoretical framework, and still relies mostly on individual findings from cognitive sciences, which may guide the legislator, at best, under rather restrictive conditions.[328] Behavioral (law and) economics has been extremely powerful in showing that, contrary to what the Neoclassical view of *homo oeconomicus* postulated, individuals make systematic mistakes and markets follow those imperfections by reflecting systematically sub-optimal outcomes. However, behavioralists have so far failed to produce a comprehensive agenda for reform, and this is indeed their major challenge for the years ahead.

This section has reached a number of findings. First, the evolution of law and economics condemns current cost-benefit analysis as obsolete and methodologically flawed. This is due to assumptions of perfect rationality, but most importantly to the reliance on methodological individualism and the comparison and aggregation of individual preferences.

---

[328] See Hayden, G.M. and S.E. Ellis (2007), *Law and Economics After Behavioral Economics*, University of Kansas Law Review, 55:3 (April 2007): 629–675.

Second, law and economics seems to be converging towards the conclusion that cost-benefit analysis should account for distributional issues. Although the influence of Chicago is still pervasive in the literature, for the reasons discussed above the approach that is more likely to survive the next generation is Calabresi's *justice before efficiency* rather than Posner's *efficiency as justice.* And even Coase's departure from the original ideas of Pigou, in retrospective, seem hardly justified on the basis of economic theory.[329]

Third, since law and economics is drowning in behavioralism and in the decline of neoclassical economics, only methodological holism and a more nuanced and humble approach to other social sciences and policy goals other than efficiency and wealth maximization can save law and economics in the years to come.[330] In this respect, it is fair to state that the age of the expansionism of economics to the detriment of other social sciences has come to an end. Since this means that law and economics will inevitably become more "agnostic", its predictive power is likely to decline in the years to come, in exchange for more methodological soundness.

Fourth, modern law and economics can justify resourcist cost-benefit analysis only as a procedural requirement to "nudge" government agencies, or better to keep them under control. However, it remains to be ascertained whether using Kaldor-Hicks cost-benefit analysis as a signal and a monitoring tool within the delegation and oversight structure of policymaking is likely to distort the incentives of involved players and create equally distorted expectations on external stakeholders.

Fifth, where law and economics can still be of invaluable help for the policymaker is in a number of phases of RIA, where law and economics can often enlighten the identification, analysis and comparison of options. The areas in which this is more likely to occur are: (i) the definition of rules that overcome the policymaker's informational deficit (such as time-shifting rules, optional law, and "pragmatically libertarian rules"); (ii) the analysis of enforcement and compliance (including developments in the analysis of responsive regulation; (iii) the behavioral approaches aimed at de-biasing through law; and (iv) the "nudging" approach developed by Sunstein and Thaler, but also by authoritative scholars in the field of neuroeconomics.

Finally, it is very likely that future approaches to better regulation will indeed reflect a mix of the four abovementioned areas of development. Social sciences in general seem to be moving, in any event, towards a broader acceptance of weak forms of paternalism in the development and enforcement of public policy. Whether this approach will come to dominate the scene also in law and economics – perhaps, also due to the heavy legacy of the current financial and economic crisis – only time will tell.

---

329 Hovenkamp (1994), *supra* note 269.

330 See, for a similar position, Arcuri, A. (2008), *Eclecticism in Law and Economics.* Erasmus Law Review, Vol. 1, No. 3.

5. INFORMING RIA THROUGH SOUND LAW AND ECONOMICS: MISCELLANEOUS EXAMPLES

In the previous section, I have discussed the potential for law and economics to inform the *ex ante* impact assessment of proposed policy initiatives. The main finding is that law and economics can prove particularly useful in suggesting efficient policy solutions that affect individual incentives, but so far largely failed in its attempt to provide adequate tools and criteria to assess the expected impact of policies in terms of social welfare. This section is based on the previous discussion on "if" law and economics can be helpful for *ex ante* policy appraisal (*i.e.* the *an*), and provides concrete examples of "how" law and economics can help, *i.e.* of the many ways in which law and economics can inform a better impact assessment of public policies (the *quomodo*). The specific examples are briefly illustrated in order to avoid imposing undue burdens on the reader: references are provided in order to ensure that the reader can easily find more food for thought on each of the issues presented.

5.1. THINKING "OUTSIDE THE BOX" WITH LAW AND ECONOMICS: OPTIONAL LAW IN SPECTRUM POLICY

The management and allocation of radio frequencies for the supply of electronic communications services is today a very prominent policy issue, worth at least 2.5% of GDP in the EU. Communicating data over the ether has become so important in the age of smartphones, wi-fi connections and digital television, that ensuring an efficient allocation of a scarce resource such as suitable spectrum bands has become a key policy priority. Reaching allocative efficiency in spectrum allocation is made even more difficult by the fact that the bands that can be used for electronic communications (say, from 30Mhz to 30 GHz) are not created equal: generally, lower frequencies imply a higher coverage of antennas; to the contrary, higher frequencies allow greater capacity to transport data. In addition, as technology advances, relatively low frequency bands can be used also for bandwidth-intensive uses, such as Internet connections.[331] In summary, identifying the best uses of each of the suitable spectrum bands is a complex exercise for a public authority, as the "best" use changes along with frequencies and with time.

Against this background, since the birth of modern communications, spectrum policy has always implied a top-down allocation of licenses by administrative authorities for the provision of specific services in specific frequencies. Such a "command and control" policy approach was chiefly dictated by the need to avoid interference between conflicting uses. In this respect, use of the spectrum, especially at certain frequencies, can create situations of "nuisance" very similar to those that arise in property law. Based on these potential interference problems, until the 1950s there was very little debate on the ways in which spectrum could be allocated: given the relative under-development of wireless communications and the existence of (mostly state-owned) monopolies in telecommunications and audiovisual services, regulators simply decided "who" should use "which" portion of the spectrum, to deliver "what" services, and "how" (*i.e.* with what technology).

During those years Leo Herzel (1951) started questioning this approach.[332] In 1959, Ronald Coase wrote an important article, simply titled "The Federal Communications Commission", where he argued in favor of a market for trading property rights on the radio spectrum. Knowing what Coase wrote only one year later in "The Problem of Social Cost", it is easy to understand what he was proposing in his paper on the Federal Communications Commission: compared to a scenario in which the state allocates spectrum rights with a top-down, command and control procedure, market forces can perform better due to superior information. Since the government is not expected to have enough information to understand who will be able to use each portion of the spectrum most efficiently, and how this changes over time, reliance on market forces to achieve allocative efficiency would have been the best way to unleash the extraordinary economic potential of the airwaves. As is well-known, Coase's argument was not welcome by regulators: asked to testify at a hearing, he was greeted by a member of the Commission: "Good morning, Professor Coase. Please tell us, is this all a big joke?"[333] Today, spectrum markets are at the core of the policy agenda in at least some industrialized countries (*e.g.*, US, UK, EU).[334]

---

331 See, *i.a.*, Bohlin, E., C. Blackman, S. Forge and A. Renda (2008), *A Common European Spectrum Policy: barriers and prospects*, study for the European Parliament, ITRE Committee, January 2008, available at www.europarl.europa.eu/meetdocs/2004_2009/documents/dv/itre_st_2007_spectrum_poli/ITRE_ST_2007_SPECTRUM_POLICY.pdf.

332 See Herzel, L. (1951), *"Public Interest" and the Market in Color Television Regulation*, 18 Univ. Chi. L. Rev. 802.

333 See Hazlett, T. (2002), *Washington Wireless Wars*, Washington Institute Forum, August 2002. Available online at www.manhattan-institute.org/pdf/mif2.pdf.

334 See Bohlin, Blackman, Forge and Renda (2008), *Supra* note 331.

Coase's article on the FCC was almost as influential as "The Problem of Social Cost", but it took several years before public authorities decided to open up the airwaves to market mechanisms. However, although several economists had hailed the advent of "propertized" spectrum as the beginning of a more efficient way of approaching spectrum policy in key bands, the results were disappointing. The volume of spectrum trading observed was very low in pioneer countries such as New Zealand, Australia, the US and more recently the UK. Nevertheless, the European Commission since 2005 started advocating for secondary trading of spectrum rights and flexible market-based mechanisms as the recipe for unleashing the potential of spectrum in the modern digital economy.[335] A study carried out for the Commission on spectrum trading back in 2004 estimated that for the EU and the EEA Member States the net gain resulting from the introduction of spectrum trading combined with flexible usage rights would amount to € 8–9 billion per year.[336] Spectrum-dependent technologies are now estimated to account for as much as 2.2% of the EU GDP, or € 250 billion. None of these benefits have materialized to date, and this also due to the fact that the European Commission never managed to really affect spectrum policy in Member States. The latest attempt to launch a five-year spectrum policy plan to help the EU27 achieve the ambitious goals set in the digital agenda is still pending in the European parliament, and most importantly still far from being approved by the Member State governments.

The policy problem is easily identified: spectrum has always been considered as a scarce resource, but for any given moment of time, only approximately 5–10% of it is used, whereas the rest remains idle. Moreover, spectrum policy has normally been carried out to avoid interference between uses rigidly allocated by the government. Against this background, the most important problem of the introduction of market based mechanisms in spectrum policy is not that markets have to fully experiment with it; the real problem is that market-based mechanisms simply haven't worked so far. This suggests that the reliance on market forces exhibited by Ronald Coase in his 1959 and 1960 scholarly papers was excessive.[337] Several aspects of the foreseen market transactions make them unlikely to happen on a mass scale. First, selling a usage right on a given

---

335 See Communication COM(2005)400 final from the Commission to the Council, the European Parliament and the European Economic and Social Committee and the Committee of the Regions – A market-based approach to spectrum management in the European Union.

336 Study "Conditions and options in introducing secondary trading of radio spectrum in the European Community", by Analysys, Dotecon and Hogan & Hartson, available online at http://ec.europa.eu/information_society/policy/ecomm/radio_spectrum/_document_storage/studies/secondary_trading/secontrad_final.pdf.

337 See Hazlett, T, (2001), *The Wireless Craze, the Unlimited Bandwidth Myth, the Spectrum Auction Faux Pas, and the Punchline to Ronald Coase's "Big Jokes": An Essay on Airwave Allocation Policy*, Harvard J. Law & Tech, 14(2), Spring, 335–545.

frequency means, for the seller, either abandoning the market completely, or creating a competitor.[338] This, in turn, means that the opportunity cost of selling a spectrum usage right is prohibitive, and creates an obstacle to the reallocation of resources to the highest-value users. Second, this same situation creates a problem in terms of divergence between the willingness to pay of a potential buyer of spectrum usage rights, and the willingness to accept compensation of the potential seller. This also means that there may not be a price at which the parties will decide to conclude an efficient transaction and reallocate the usage right. Finally, spectrum trading mechanisms should always be accompanied by rules on interference, and the potential for technologies to interfere with each other depends enormously on the type of frequency, the type of technology, and the type of service provided with that technology. Absent a top-down control by the state, it is difficult to rely exclusively on market forces, at least for valuable frequencies such as the ones between 30MHz and 3GHz, and in particular the UHF band.

To be sure, Coase's insight is essential to understand spectrum policy as it stands today. But law and economics has gone much further than Coase, as recalled in the previous sections. In particular, the idea that assigning entitlements protected by a property rule is the most efficient way to reach an efficient allocation of scarce resources has been refined by many authors since Calabresi and Melamed's "View of the Cathedral", but also at a later stage, by Ayres and Talley (1995), Bebchuk (2004), and Ayres (2005).[339] Many of these papers elaborate on the concept of property v. liability rules, and conclude that under certain circumstances transaction costs would be prohibitively high, and that as a consequence trading of property rights would not lead to a sufficient volume of exchanges to enable efficient allocation of resources. In the spectrum world, this would simply mean that rigidities in the market trading and, more generally, high transaction costs are often an obstacle to reaching an efficient spectrum allocation, and that market-based mechanisms would fail to enable spectrum usage to adapt to the evolution of technology overtime. This mostly depends on the fact that giving away spectrum often bears a significant opportunity cost, and can lead to the creation of undesired competitors: strategic bargaining and divergence of valuations and interests can also lead to the failure of some otherwise efficiency-enhancing transactions. This, at the same time,

338 The rationale is similar to the one developed for Airport slots. See the UK Civil Aviation Authority, *Property Rights in Airport Slots. A Discussion paper*, at www.caa.co.uk/docs/5/ergdocs/slotsnov01.pdf.

339 Ayres, I. and E. Talley (1995), *Distinguishing between Consensual and Nonconsensual Advantages of Liability Rules*, Yale Law Journal 105 (1):235–53; and Ayres, I. and E. Talley. 1995, *Solomonic Bargaining: Dividing a Legal Entitlement to Facilitate Coasean Trade,* Yale Law Journal 104 (5):1027–1117.

leads to a situation in which the initial allocation of entitlements is not irrelevant both from an efficiency and a distributional perspective.[340]

To the contrary, when transaction costs are high, a liability rule is normally seen as more efficient than a property rule. It may sound rather straightforward for a law and economics student: it is not, for a spectrum policymaker. For this reason, a RIA on spectrum policy today would simply revolve around the three main modes of spectrum assignment: (i) the "command and control" approach; (ii) the market-based, "Coasian" approach; and (iii) the commons approach, where no entitlements are allocated.[341]

Are there alternative policy options that such RIA would overlook? Yes. Take, as an example, the literature on conflicting uses of property, which was elaborated initially with reference to nuisance law. Interference between uses of adjacent spectrum bands is, for a law and economics scholar, very similar to nuisance in property. But it exhibits some important features as regards transaction costs, as testified by the fact that spectrum trading, though allowed in some national jurisdictions, has yielded rather disappointing results. The law and economics literature would thus recommend the addition of a number of policy alternatives to the policymaker's initial battery. Authoritative scholars such as Ayres (2005) have shown that standard liability rules – *i.e.* allocating the entitlement to the right owner in a given band, but with a call option held by other players, that can exercise the right to buy the entitlement at a regulated price – can prove superior to property rules when transaction costs are high, as they economize on information costs and leave (at least one of) the parties involved with the possibility to choose at a later stage whether to exercise an option or not.

In the case of spectrum, however, this option may prove difficult, as the related uncertainty it would engender could jeopardize incentives to invest in a given band. And choosing the right option price may also reproduce the difficulties of command and control regimes, as it would leave government with the task of identifying the "right" value of the band.[342] However, the law and economics literature has gone even further than this. The literature on optional law has, at least partially, solved the problem of option prices. In the *Texas Shootout Rule* described by Fennell (2004), one of the players (the spectrum licensee) would be called to set a price for the band she is using, whereas other

340 See also *infra*, Section 5.2, on the importance of the initial allocation of allowances in the emissions trading regime.

341 The "commons" option is increasingly advocated by engineers and also economists. However, the commons (or unlicensed spectrum) is more appropriate for relatively high frequencies, *i.e.* portions of spectrum in which the coverage of individual antennas is not too wide. Key examples are remote controls, intelligent parking sensors on cars, and also wi-fi hotspots. In the future, it is more likely that the portion of spectrum that will be left to a commons mechanism will expand, as agile radio technologies and cognitive radio develop.

342 See, for a brief application of the Calabresi-Melamed framework to spectrum policy, Lemley, M.A. and P. Weiser (2007), *Should Property or Liability Rules Govern Information?*. Texas Law Review, Vol. 85, p. 783.

players could be called to choose whether to leave the band to the licensee (put option), or to buy it from her (call option). This way, the spectrum holder would have to choose the price without knowing whether she will ultimately act as a buyer or a seller, and accordingly will simulate a collaborative outcome without having to negotiate with any other player. This outcome – similar to the outcome of the more famous "cake slicing game", replicates in practical terms the Rawlsian concept of "veil of ignorance" – in other words, it simulates a fully cooperative outcome without imposing cooperation on the parties.[343] Finally, the law and economics literature has made very important steps in understanding mixed forms of governance between the commons and property rights, such as "mini-commons" and "semi-commons" theories that perfectly match the spectrum world.

Is any of these policy choices currently reflected in the way spectrum policy is being approached by policymakers? Certainly not in Europe. In the US, where the law and economics literature is more integrated with policymaking, the concept of "easement" in spectrum usage can be said to reflect, at least to some extent, the concept of a permanent, limited call option assigned to non-licensees.

In summary, in our example of spectrum policy, whereas policymakers are still trying to get to grips with Coasian insights on the functioning of private bargaining, the L&E literature is so far ahead that it would take decades, for administrations, to catch up. And meanwhile, many important opportunities for efficient and effective policymaking would be lost. Against this background, it would be very interesting to see the European Commission studying and discussing mechanisms aimed at ensuring that spectrum is not fully propertized, but is subject to regular reallocation based on optional rules similar to Fennell's "Texas shoot-out": although a full analysis of the potential impacts would fall outside our scope, the potential inspiration that law and economics scholarship may offer in terms of helping administrations "think outside the box" would be remarkable.

5.2. EMISSIONS TRADING: A TALE OF SERENDIPITY AND OPPORTUNITY COSTS

When policymakers opt for a market-based mechanism, mainstream economists always celebrate. Just like in the case of spectrum (see Section 5.1 above), a trading system was also advocated by lawyer-economists for CO2 emissions: the main reason for claiming the superior efficiency of this system over traditional environmental taxes or standards is that, since the optimal level of pollution in a society is inevitably above zero, an emissions trading

343 See *supra*, Section 4.3.3.2.

mechanisms can ensure that, for every particle of greenhouse gas (GHG) emitted, the social value of production will be maximized.[344] More precisely, since the first experiments with pollution permits in the United States, the underlying rationale for trading emissions is that, the more a business is willing to pay to buy a pollution permit, the higher the social value associated with the pollution that will be generated by the firm. At the same time, given that pollution permits are costly, businesses will have an incentive to invest in environment-friendly technologies to be able to minimize their need to purchase permits in the marketplace. In a nutshell, emissions trading leads to allocative efficiency: to believe in emissions trading, you must believe in the market mechanism, just like Ronald Coase did.

In 2005, the EU launched an Emissions Trading System (ETS) that now operates in 30 countries (the 27 EU Member States plus Iceland, Liechtenstein and Norway), covering CO_2 emissions from installations such as power stations, combustion plants, oil refineries and iron and steel works, as well as factories making cement, glass, lime, bricks, ceramics, pulp, paper and board.[345] The EU ETS works on a "cap and trade" basis – *i.e.* there is a "cap", or limit, on the total amount of certain greenhouse gases that can be emitted by the factories, power plants and other installations in the system. Within the cap, businesses receive emission allowances that they can trade on the marketplace. The limit on the total number of allowances available corresponds to the level of pollution desired. At the end of each year each company must surrender enough allowances to cover all its emissions, otherwise heavy fines are imposed. The number of allowances is reduced over time so that total emissions fall. For example, the European Commission announced that in 2020 emissions will be 21% lower than in 2005.[346]

An important feature of the EU ETS is that it was originally based, just like the US SO2 trading system, on a grandfathering rule: polluters received most emission rights free of charge based on their historical emissions, so that they did not have to buy those rights in an auction. In the EU, every Member State allocated at least 95% of its allowances free of charge in the period 2005–2007 and at least 90% in the period 2008–2012.[347] This choice, though evidently

344 See, for an enlightening illustration, Pearce, D.W. and R.K. Turner (1990). *Economics of Natural Resources and the Environment,* Hemel Hempstead: Harvester Wheatsheaf.

345 Nitrous oxide emissions from certain processes are also covered. Between them, the installations currently in the scheme account for almost half of the EU's CO2 emissions and 40% of its total greenhouse gas emissions. Airlines will join the scheme in 2012. The EU ETS will be further expanded to the petrochemicals, ammonia and aluminium industries and to additional gases in 2013, when the third trading period will start. At the same time a series of important changes to the way the EU ETS works will take effect in order to strengthen the system.

346 See http://ec.europa.eu/clima/policies/ets/index_en.htm.

347 See Woerdman, E., A. Arcuri and S. Clò (2007), *Emissions Trading and the Polluter-Pays Principle: Do Polluters Pay under Grandfathering?.* Available at SSRN: http://ssrn.com/

increasing the political acceptability of establishing an ETS, was fiercely criticized by field experts on the basis that it would run contrary to the well-acknowledged polluter-pays-principle, which is considered as the basis of the internalization of externalities and the correct attribution of incentives, and is now even rooted in the EU Treaty since the creation of a separate chapter on climate change in 1986 with the Single European Act. The rationale is apparently crystal clear: if polluters don't pay, they will not internalize the negative externalities they impose on society, and will thus tend to produce above the socially optimal level; at the same time, given the existence of the EU ETS, they may even have an incentive to pass-on downstream the value of the emission allowance, thus even profiting from the existence of the ETS without paying for it.

In light of this problem, the European Commission has been seeking changes to the ETS: in 2008, it stated in a rather sophisticated impact assessment document that "the overall functioning of the Emissions Trading Scheme can be improved in a number of aspects", and that "allocating allowances for free has reduced the efficiency of the ETS".[348] However, what had already emerged in the literature is that, on efficiency grounds, an auctioning system is not always preferable to a grandfathering one. The key misunderstanding in this respect was that, given the establishment of an emission trading mechanism, the allocation of allowances is not entirely free of charge for pollution emitters, but carries an "opportunity cost", *i.e.* the cost of not trading in the market the freely allocated pollution permit. This, more simply, means that polluters virtually face a cost of retaining the permit, equal to the foregone profit of selling it on the market.

As a result, the quest for the most efficient solution is way more open that the Commission initially thought. In recent papers, such as *i.a.* Woerdman *et al.* (2008), Goeree *et al.* (2009), Botelho *et al.* (2010) and Clò (2010), the comparison between the two allocation methods has been brought back to a more economically sound framework, which denies the superior efficiency of the auctioning system *per se*, and looks at the effects that are likely to be generated by the two alternative methods on the basis of the incentives, for market players, to approximate allocative efficiency.

Against this background, several issues have to be considered before one allocation method can be seen as preferable to its alternative. First, auctioning is likely to be more expensive than grandfathering for public administrations, given the cost of organising, designing and running the auctions. At the same time, auctions can be more costly for polluters, if the competitive process that leads to the allocation of permits can drive prices above the opportunity cost of

abstract=1271843.

348 See COM(2008)16 final of 27 February 2008, and the accompanying impact assessment, http://ec.europa.eu/governance/impact/ia_carried_out/docs/ia_2008/climate_package_ia_annex.pdf.

holding a permit under grandfathering. When transaction costs are positive, this is likely to be the case, since polluters will prefer to be awarded a permit in the first place, instead of waiting for the allocation to then rely on the secondary market to secure an allowance. The ultimate impact of such a difference should be estimated depending on the expected level of transaction costs, the relative competitiveness of markets and other market features that potentially affect the result of auctions.

At the same time, auction design is essential for the final outcome, and it is a fairly difficult task. The experience with 3G auctions in telecommunications, which ended up destroying the European leadership achieved in this field during the 2G (GSM) era, is telling in this respect. If national governments are given the freedom to design the auctions, outcomes may differ so widely that the efficient reallocation of allowances in the Internal market may be jeopardized, and with it the goal of achieving allocative efficiency. One might then wonder whether there could ever be any added value from auctioning, absent a centralization of the auctioning process and design.

Moreover, a more complex set of problems may emerge since auctioning does not allow a selection of the initial allocation of rights, whereas grandfathering inevitably pre-selects initial distribution. Following the Coase theorem, the initial distribution should be essentially irrelevant for the achievement of the efficient allocation of allowances in the marketplace: however, there are very good reasons to doubt that the invariance proposition in the Coase theorem would hold in the context of environmental policy, and particularly when an auction mechanism has been put in place to determine the initial allocation of entitlements.[349]

A full treatment of the efficiency and fairness consequences of the EU ETS scheme would certainly require a dedicated volume.[350] What bears mention here, is that the costs generated by the alternative systems, the relevance of the initial allocation of rights, the likelihood that a more efficient allocation will be reached under auctioning, and the risk of failure of the auction mechanism did not play a major role in the Commission's thick impact assessment document. To the contrary, other, more stylized impacts, such as windfall profits generated by grandfathering, were given more prominence. This does not mean that the Commission made the wrong choice in selecting a gradual transition towards 100% auctioning of allowances: as a matter of fact, scholarly papers that have run experimental analysis tend to point at auctioning as potentially superior to

349 See Arcuri, A. (2005), *A Different Reason for "De-Coasing" Environmental Law and Economics*, European Journal of Law and Economics, 20: 225–246, 2005.

350 See, for an in-depth view from a law and economics perspective, Clò, S. (2010), *Economic Analysis of the European Climate Policy: the European emissions trading scheme*, http://publishing.eur.nl/ir/repub/asset/20717/Proefschrift%20Stefano%20Clo%20 BW%5Blr%5D.pdf.

grandfathering.[351] But the reasons for preferring auctioning over grandfathering (mostly, related to stability, predictability and certainty) are not the same ones quoted by the Commission in its impact assessment (efficiency-related ones): in other words, if the Commission ended up choosing the best option, this was more accidental than intentional – a good example of serendipity in policy-making. A serendipity that the impact assessment process did not manage to prevent.

In conclusion, just as in the case of spectrum allocation treated in Section 5.1 above, a more sophisticated understanding of law and economics can help policymakers design better policies: on the other hand, neoclassical law and economics can prove misleading for policymakers.

5.3. ASKING THE RIGHT QUESTIONS IN IMPACT ASSESSMENT: THE CASE OF PRIVATE ANTITRUST DAMAGES ACTIONS

A famous motto attributed to the Mandelkern report is that one of the main virtues of RIA is to help administrations "ask the right questions, at the right time, and in the right sequence".[352] However, without full support of law and economics, often RIA ends up in a "monetization craze" that bears little relevance for the purpose of legislating better.

One example in point is certainly private antitrust enforcement. A few years ago, after the Modernization of EU antitrust policy with Regulation 1/2003, the European Commission started looking at a specific problem that had emerged in the application of EU antitrust law since the Treaty of Rome that established the European Community back in 1957. As a matter of fact, even if it had always been possible for victims of antitrust infringement to sue infringers before national judges to obtain damage compensation, available evidence revealed that very few such cases had occurred, and that the number of cases that had resulted in actual compensation of damages was less than a fistful. A study carried out in

351 Botelho, A., E. Fernandes and L. Pinto (2010) conclude that "the EU ETS has the potential to reduce CO2 emissions, achieving targets considerably more restrictive than the current ones at high efficiency levels, both with auctioned and free emission permits" See Botelho *et al.* (2010), *An experimental analysis of grandfathering vs dynamic auctioning in the EU ETS*, Working Paper n. 39/2010, Núcleo de Investigação em Microeconomia Aplicada Universidade do Minho. Goeree *et al.* (2010) conclude that under grandfathering permit prices "were well above competitive (supply and demand) predictions", whereas "permit prices tended to converge to competitive levels when permits were assigned by auction". See Goeree, J.K., C.A. Holt, K. Palmer, W. Shobe and D. Burtraw (2010), *An Experimental Study of Auctions Versus Grandfathering to Assign Pollution Permits*, Journal of the European Economic Association April/May 2010, Vol. 8, No. 2–3, Pages 514–525.

352 Renda, A. *et al.* (2009), *Policymaking in the EU; achievements, challenges and proposals for reform*, Centre for European Policy Studies, Brussels.

2004 for the European Commission revealed a situation of "total underdevelopment" in private antitrust damages actions, which created a specific policy problem: if there is a right to compensation rooted in the Treaty, why was the right so under-exercised? And should something be done to ensure that the right is exercised more effectively in the future?

Since the issue was to be addressed by means of a White Paper, included in the Commission's Legislative and Work Programme, this became the subject of a Commission Impact Assessment. There, the European Commission asked a team of external consultants to help in the assessment of the potential consequences of a number of potential policy actions aimed at encouraging meritorious damages actions. I had the honor of leading that team of courageous researchers: they were all coming from a law and economics background, and due to this rather fortunate circumstance I can now tell something about using law and economics in the RIA world.

The European Commission entrusted our team with two different tasks. The first task was to assess the potential social impact of more effective private antitrust enforcement in the European Union. Already looking at this task, a major problem emerged. How can one calculate the potential impact of a "more effective private antitrust enforcement" on social welfare, if the way to achieve such result has not been identified in the first place? This is potentially a major problem in an impact assessment, since the result (especially the level of costs) depends enormously on the options chosen to achieve it. In any event, the European Commission needed that figure, *i.a.*, to show the Impact Assessment Board that they had quantified and monetized expected impacts, and that the proposed policy action would display "net benefits". At the end of our analysis, based mostly on a comparison with the US system (where private enforcement is way more developed than in Europe) we concluded that if private antitrust damages actions would not become more effective, foregone benefits for victims of antitrust infringement would range between € 5.7 billion and € 23.3 billion; at the same time, while expected costs are significant, they would never offset the corrective justice impact of enhanced private antitrust enforcement.[353]

The second task was to analyze a set of seven possible policy actions, and compare available options for each of those actions. Actions to be assessed included alternative policy options on damage compensation; on the costs and rewards of filing an private antitrust damage action; on several forms of collective actions; on ways to calculate damages; on different rules for access to evidence; on the treatment of leniency applicants as regards their exposure to liability in

353 For example, lawyers' fees and court fees, which are by far the largest portion of expected costs, would amount to approximately 15%-20% of damage recovery (this result was reached using US data as a benchmark, as no EU data were available). For a full account, see the report by Renda *et al.* (2008), *supra* note 21.

court; and on the legal approach to the so-called "passing-on defense".[354] For each of those actions, 4–5 policy options were identified, leading to an incredible number of possible scenarios – in the interim report of our Impact Assessment, we showed the Commission a table that ranked 1,728 possible policy scenarios in terms of certain categories of benefits and costs – and the "no policy action" scenario was ranking among the best!

For the purposes of this book, the most important issue to be described is that, while the European Commission was chiefly interested in producing the "figure", *i.e.* the numerical demonstration that more effective private enforcement would be needed, it was quite clear that the monetization of the overall impact on social welfare was not the most important part of that impact assessment exercise. To the contrary, what was really important was to understand whether certain legal changes would have encouraged more meritorious private antitrust damages actions, without unduly facilitating also frivolous suits by non-victims, aimed at achieving strategic advantages (*e.g.* an inefficient settlement, or the disclosure of confidential information, or merely negatively affecting the reputation of a rival). Even if this part of the analysis could not produce a final "figure" in terms of net benefits, it was a way more useful approach to enable an informed political judgment than merely imagining a world with more effective private enforcement – regardless of how this world is achieved – and then check whether this world would be better for the European society.

The two most important reasons why the European Commission (despite the fact that the team that was following the study was perhaps the most competent one I have ever worked with) was placing more emphasis on quantification of abstract impacts over the modeling of human behavior were: (i) the need to prove net benefits before the Impact Assessment Board; and (ii) the fact that modeling human behavior would have been impossible, if the Commission had relied on standard impact assessment tools such as cost-benefit analysis: in order to model human behavior, you need a law and economics approach. To put it simply, the main difference between the two approaches is that the law and economics approach, instead of providing a cost-benefit analysis upfront, assumes that players involved will adopt certain actions if a cost-benefit analysis will suggest them to do so.

We based our law and economics on two main formulas, which represented the incentives of the main players involved. First, we described the *ex ante* incentive of an undertaking that is about to decide whether to infringe competition law or not, to see whether private enforcement would add to the "deterrence" of competition law compared to the *status quo* and the baseline

354 See Renda *et al.* (2008), *supra* note 21, Section II.5.

scenarios. Second, we used a formula to describe the victim's incentive to sue for damage compensation.

As regards the incentive to infringe the law, a decisional model based on benefit-cost analysis had already been developed by many scholars, especially as regards the decision whether to form a (or join an existing) cartel. The theory of optimal fines, which can be traced back to Becker's early writings, depicts a world in which the impossibility to achieve a reasonably high probability of detection leads to the setting of too high fines, which would prove too burdensome for infringers that are actually convicted. In this respect, private enforcement effectively acts as a complement to public enforcement in a second-best context, where the optimal solution is impossible to achieve. In our impact study, we proved that private antitrust enforcement contributes to more effective deterrence by: (i) increasing the probability of detection; and (ii) increasing the infringer's prospective liability by adding expected damage awards to the prospective fines imposed by public enforcers – depending on whether a private suit is stand-alone or follow-on.

For example, a cartelist in a jurisdiction with both public and private enforcement would face the following benefit-cost calculation:

$$E(L) = p_g c_g E(F) + p_p c_p E(S) + E(R)$$

Thus, the expected liability faced *ex ante* by a cartelist is the sum of expected public penalties (*E(F)*), expected private damage settlements (*E(S)*) and expected (negative) reputational effects (*E(R)*). This also implies that if the probability of detection with private and public enforcement is greater than under pure public enforcement – and the prospective damage award is significant – then deterrence can be achieved more effectively with both private and public enforcement.

A widely acknowledged *tenet* in the literature on optimal fines is that, given the impossibility to raise fines over certain levels, *an increase in the probability of detection is more important than the increase in the amount of fines and sanctions* in order to achieve more effective deterrence of anticompetitive conduct. Absent this finding, public and private enforcement do not differ noticeably in terms of deterrence potential, and the only advantage of private over public enforcement would lie in the greater potential for corrective justice.

Several refinements are needed in order to approximate this very simple model to reality. In order to provide a more detailed assessment of the probability that a conduct is detected and the victim actually decides to sue, an additional formula had to be specified, which looked at the issue from the standpoint of the would-be claimant.

Assume that the prospective costs for a plaintiff are the opportunity cost of time spent in litigation (OC_t) or settlement (OC_s), costs of access to courts (*AC*) and – depending on the fee allocation rule chosen – legal costs for litigation (LC_t)

and settlement (LC_s). Expected rewards are the damages claimed (D), times the probability of winning at trial (w), and the expected settlement amount (S), times the probability to settle the claim before trial ($1 - p$).[355] The plaintiff will then sue whenever

$$(1) \qquad p[wD - (OC_t + LC_t + AC)] + (1 - p)[S - (OC_s + LC_s)] > 0$$

where $OC_s < OC_t$; $LC_s < LC_t$; and $S < D$.[356] In other words, the plaintiff's net expected reward from filing suit has two main components: the reward from settlement and the reward from trial. The relative weight of these two components, of course, depends on the (perceived) likelihood of settlement and trial.

Based on the formula above, we considered the impact that different procedural rules or damage multiples can exert on the plaintiff's incentive to sue. For example:

- Multiple damages increase the incentive to sue, as they increase D.
- A reversal of the burden of proof in favor of the plaintiff increases the incentives to sue, alongside with w.
- A one-way fee-shifting rule increases incentives to sue, as it removes LC_t and AC from the equation.
- All the rules that increase the probability of victory for the plaintiff (w) or increase the prospective cost of the defendant, in turn, have the effect of increasing the probability that the case will settle ($1 - p$), and also the settlement amount (S).
- All means of funding private litigation increase the probability that the plaintiff will sue, of course, as they would reduce or eliminate LC_t and AC.

The plaintiff's decision to sue depends *in primis* on her subjective perception of p, w and S. With imperfect information and behavioral bias, several cases may arise, including cases in which the plaintiff overestimates the probability of winning at trial (w), or the plaintiff mistakenly estimates the probability of settling the case ($1 - p$). The defendant's expected reaction is also important for the plaintiff's decision. If the defendant signals her nature of "tough negotiator", the plaintiff may overestimate p, and may refrain from suing in order to avoid a costly and lengthy litigation.

355 The expected reward can also be different from the damage award. For example, it could be a settlement that takes place at some time prior to the trial, or include an increase in the plaintiff's business reputation.

356 We assume that both the opportunity cost of litigation and the legal fees paid for litigating the case are greater than in the case of settlement. Consideration of time is also important, as the legal fees are to be paid upfront, whereas damages are awarded after the case has been adjudicated or settled.

Now, while the reader interested in the law and economics analysis of private antitrust enforcement is warmly invited to visit the European Commission's website where the final impact study is posted[357], in this volume I wish to focus on a tiny fraction of what we learned during that heroic effort.

Using the two formulas above and several contributions in the law and economics literature, including the literature on multi-stage litigation, on fee-shifting rules, on discovery abuse, limitation periods and many others, we could provide the policymakers with a (qualitative) indication of the expected impact of certain rules on deterrence, on corrective justice, on the risk of frivolous suits, on potential costs in terms of legal expenses, administrative burdens and even harmonization costs that would be borne by Member States in case a procedural change was introduced. We then wrapped all these results into composite scenarios, and developed methodologies to compare "bundles of options" based on a qualitative scorecard analysis, which was eventually praised by the Impact Assessment Board.[358] The discussion in the European Parliament led to an unexpected vote: a good impact assessment had significantly strengthened the persuasive power of the Commission vis-à-vis an inevitably skeptical Parliament.

Which were the real questions to be answered in the Impact Assessment on private antitrust enforcement? Not the ones that a typical US RIA would look at. It was way more useful, for a policymaker, to know which specific impacts could be expected in the incentives of individual players after the introduction of a number of legal changes, rather than knowing what the potential welfare impact of a more effective system would be. Policy action requires a direction, and whenever individual incentives are at stake, law and economics is of invaluable help to policymakers. The impact assessment on private antitrust damages actions proved exactly this: law and economics is superior to cost-benefit analysis whenever legal rules are expected to model individual behavior. The better the law and economics approach used, the more useful will the impact assessment be.

A corollary of this conclusion can also be related to our discussion of distributional impacts in Section 4 above. Given the difficulty of evaluating and aggregating individual preferences and the limits of methodological individualism in Kaldor-Hicks benefit-cost analysis, simply estimating the additional deterrence and the income transfer that would occur under more effective private enforcement says very little on the actual welfare impact of this state of the world compared to the baseline. Simply knowing what the potential magnitude of compensated damages would be is merely a communication tool,

357 See Renda *et al.* (2008), *supra* note 21.

358 The IA on private antitrust damages actions features several times in the list of best practices available at Annex 14 of the Commission's Impact Assessment guidelines. See http://ec.europa.eu/governance/impact/commission_guidelines/best_pract_lib_en.htm.

which adds very little to the soundness of the economic analysis – it would lend itself to "knowing the price of everything and the value of nothing" critique. To the contrary, knowing that (i) a combination of legal changes can increase the attractiveness of a meritorious lawsuit, thus increasing both deterrence and compensation; (ii) that frivolous lawsuits would not be significantly encouraged, and; (iii) that associated costs, including one-off costs of changing national legal rules, would not be prohibitive is exactly what political decision-makers need to convince themselves and their constituencies that moving to the new regime is worth. In our example, this meant for the European Commission the proposal of a new set of rules which entails a discretionary one-way fee-shifting rule, two forms of collective action rules (including an unprecedented "opt-out" representative action), more relaxed rules on access to evidence and provisions on limitation periods. Other scenarios were considered to be viable, but either too risky or costly, or ineffective compared to the goal set, *i.e.* making meritorious antitrust damages actions more effective in the EU.

5.4. DISTRIBUTIONAL ISSUES AND THE 2007 ROAMING REGULATION

Professors of EU law normally have a fistful of ready-made examples to show the added value of the EU Internal Market. And this happens quite often also to EU politicians, such as the President of the European Commission or the various Commissioners. Besides the simplification of cross-border bank transfers between EU member states, perhaps the only other straightforward example is the regulation of wholesale roaming tariffs, a very ambitious project of the European Commission that saw the light in 2007, with the first regulation that set a cap on both wholesale and retail tariffs applied by mobile operators in the EU27. With the "roaming regulation", European citizens are much less exposed to outrageous mobile phone bills when travelling to another Member State of the European Union.

Needless to say, such an important regulation was subject to a detailed impact assessment – one of those IAs that are quoted as "best practices" among the more than 500 IAs completed so far by the European Commission.[359] Even more importantly, the IA contained an apparently sophisticated cost-benefit analysis, which also incorporated a sensitivity analysis, *i.e.* the Commission used three possible measures of demand elasticity to calculate what the reaction of end users

359 Commission Staff Working Paper – Impact Assessment of Policy Options in Relation to a Commission Proposal for a Regulation of the European Parliament and of the Council on Roaming on Public Mobile Networks Within the Community, COM(2006) 382 final, SEC(2006) 925, Brussels, 12.7.2006.

to lower roaming tariffs would be. As a matter of fact, the Commission eventually applied a Kaldor-Hicks cost-benefit analysis and justified the adoption of a double layer of regulation – at the wholesale and retail level – by showing that net benefits would be maximized under that option compared to all alternatives.

The Commission shows the potential impact of various policy options, from the *status quo* option to the adoption of the European Home Market Approach (Commissioner Reding's initial preferred option), the regulation at wholesale level only, and the finally retained option (regulation at wholesale and retail level). The figure below reports graphically the Commission's conclusions for the retained policy options.

This description of "net benefits" portrayed by the European Commission, however, was telling only part of the story. Had the Commission fully taken into account the insights of economic theory and the law and economics approach, a number of hidden impacts might have surfaced. Below, I try to illustrate the problem shortly.

The market for international roaming featured very peculiar characteristics compared to the total mobile telecoms market: only 147 million users out of approximately 450 million European citizens were involved in that market in 2006; 75% of those users (110 million) were business customers, whose bill was most likely paid by their employers. The remaining 25% were mostly frequent leisure travelers and relatively wealthy consumers. Accordingly, the European Commission acknowledged that, with policy actions to cut roaming charges, some customers would have benefitted more than others. In other words, distributional impacts might have surfaced.

> *"Mobile services are consumed by many different types of customers. As a result of regulation, will some groups be made better off than others? Obviously, the customer segment benefiting most from a reduction in roaming charges will be high-frequency roamers. With many customers rarely or never consuming roaming services (66% of all mobile customers never roam according to A.T. Kearney), the welfare gains of high-frequency roamers would be substantial, as they would be able to reap the overwhelming part of the resulting changes in consumer surplus (see analysis of preceding sections). Other things being equal, it is to be expected that business customers who currently are not on large-scale competitive contracts (as would be the case for most SMEs), high-frequency leisure travellers and people living in border regions would profit most from a reduction in roaming charges".*[360]

[360] *Id.*, Section 4.3.3, at 53.

Figure 21. Net benefits of retail and wholesale capping

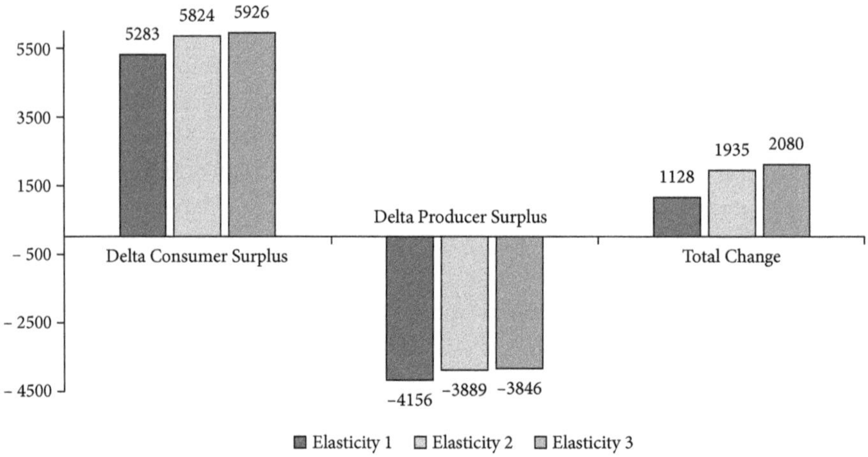

Source: Commission Impact Assessment, SEC (2006) 925, 12 July 2006.

When we look at the results of the cost-benefit analysis, are we sure that the redistribution of income from firms to consumers will be neutral from the standpoint of social welfare? And, even more importantly, are we sure that the "delta consumer surplus" does not hide income transfers between consumers?

More sound economics would have led the Commission to notice the following potential impacts. First, in the economics of mobile telephony a prominent role is played by the so-called "waterbed effect"[361]: based on this effect, mobile operators tend to redistribute revenues by setting above-cost prices for services that face a relatively rigid demand, and by setting below-cost, aggressive prices for other services where they face strong competition. Especially in the context of the EU27, where the calling-party-pays principle is applied and termination rates are everywhere regulated, mobile operators compete aggressively by trying to attract customers through generous handset subsidies and very aggressive domestic tariff plans. On the other hand they charge roamers above cost.

361 The "waterbed effect" is the effect whereby regulation of one of the prices of a multiproduct firm causes one or more of its other unregulated prices to change as a result of the firm's profit-maximizing behavior. The term "waterbed effect" was used for the first time in 1997 during an investigation of the British Monopolies and Mergers Commission, and was extensively recalled in the debate over the regulation of mobile termination rates and also during the recent debate on the regulation of wholesale and retail roaming charges in the European Union since 2007. Genakos and Valletti (2008) provide a survey of the literature and empirical data on the existence of the waterbed effect in the EU mobile industry, which they find to be strong. See Genakos, Christos and Valletti, Tommaso M., Testing the 'Waterbed' Effect in Mobile Telephony (January 2008). CEIS Working Paper No. 110.

Based on the above, one would expect that, if mobile operators compete aggressively to attract customers in EU member states, then any regulation of wholesale and retail roaming charges would lead those companies to face some loss, or to cut R&D costs, or to increase the only tariffs that are not regulated (*i.e.*, retail domestic tariffs). If this really happens, we would end up in a rather odd situation: a price regulation of roaming charges would favor business customers and rich leisure customers, but may significantly harm either mobile operators (if they sustain a loss), or end customers (if there is reduced innovation due to cuts in R&D expenditure, or even more directly if domestic prices increase).

The Commission seems to acknowledge this possibility in the Impact Assessment:

> *"To the extent that overall revenues of the mobile industry would come down as a result of regulation under some of the policy options, and to the extent that the revenue streams affected would be particularly high-margin ones, other things being equal it is reasonable to assume* some *reduction of investment ...*
> *... It is reasonable to assume that while at the margin some rebalancing of tariffs will occur, a general increase in the price level for other services, given intense competition in major markets, is highly unlikely".*[362]

Accordingly, it is fair to state that, while drafting the impact assessment document, the Commission was aware of the following facts: (i) that the mobile sector was highly competitive; (ii) that regulating roaming would create some reduction of investment in this highly dynamic sector – a key sector for the competitiveness of the EU economy; and (iii) that even some rebalancing of tariffs, with a potential increase of domestic retail tariffs, could occur, but the intense competition between mobile operators would have kept such increase at a minimum.

However, this consideration did not change the Commission's final decision as to which policy option was to be preferred. As a result, the impact assessment contained a pure resourcist cost-benefit analysis, which ignored the fact that the policy option would have favored business and rich leisure customers, potentially to the detriment of ordinary users. In this specific case, the European Commission failed to take distributional issues into due account when crafting future policy interventions: and by providing a cost-benefit analysis which looks merely at a static vision of the "size of the pie" to judge whether a policy proposal must be considered preferable to alternatives, or not. Interestingly, the consultation run by the European Commission on the 2007 Roaming regulation led to a finding that was in line with the waterbed effect: operators were relying on revenues from retail SMS tariffs to partly compensate the lost revenues in

362 Commission Impact Assessment, *supra* note 359, at 52.

voice. This led to an extension of the roaming regulation to SMS and data services in 2008: but in the new Impact Assessment, the potential negative impacts on innovation and on domestic prices are not even mentioned. A consultation was run by the Commission in 2008 to find out, *i.a.* about the possible increase in domestic prices following the 2007 roaming regulation. The result reported by the Commission was that "it would be very difficult to pinpoint any increase in domestic tariffs directly due to the introduction of the Regulation". In addition, the group of European Regulators observed that "it is unlikely that domestic mobile prices will rise, because they are the main focus of competition for consumers". Again, no mention was given to the potential impact that the regulation might exert on R&D and innovation in a sector that is considered to be highly competitive, yet is regulated with various instruments and tools and in a number of different markets.

To sum up, the roaming regulation provides a good example of cost-benefit analysis that misguides policymakers as it willingly neglects distributional issues. A closer look at the short-term and dynamic effects of the regulation might have suggested a different policy conclusion.

5.5. THE VERY STRANGE CASE OF LARGE EXPOSURE REPORTING

When, in May 2009, the European Parliament passed a legislative statement for "New rules to avoid future financial crisis" – which proposed stricter rules on large exposure reporting to save Europe from the risk of future credit crunches – many eyebrows went up in the Brussels community.[363] Such a strange destiny, that of large exposure reporting: to understand why, you have to look a couple of years back.

Large exposure reporting is a prudential measure that is in force for a compelling reason: in cases where financial institutions are widely exposed to a single client, they could incur large losses as a result of the failure of an individual client or a group of connected clients. The same can happen when banks trade their exposures between themselves: the failure of one institution can cause the failure of others. Rules on large exposure reporting were introduced in the European Union with Council Directive 92/121/EEC of 21 December 1992 on the monitoring and control of large exposures of credit institutions. Later, these rules were included in the (in)famous "Basel II" package: Art. 110 (1) of Dir. 2006/48 prescribed that a credit institution shall report every large exposure to the competent authorities; likewise, Article 30 (2) Dir 2006/49 prescribed that institutions' overall exposures to individual clients and groups of connected

363 See the Press release of the European Parliament, at www.europarl.europa.eu/sides/getDoc.do?type=IM-PRESS&reference=20090505IPR55119& language=EN.

clients calculated in accordance with paragraph 4 shall be reported in accordance with Article 110 of Directive 2006/48/EC.[364]

Back in 2004–2005, when the Basel II package was being prepared by the European Commission, EU institutions seemed to believe in the salvific virtues of large exposure reporting obligations. This, at least, is what can be inferred from the wording of the Impact Assessment on the Capital Adequacy Directive, drafted by the European Commission in support of its "Basel II" proposals in 2004.[365] There, the Commission could count on as many as three "Quantitative Impact Studies" (termed QIS1, QIS2 and QIS3 in the Impact Assessment) and one additional study by PriceWaterhouseCoopers (PWC). Compared to the former studies, the latter was more optimistic as regards the extent to which "Basel II" rules could protect Europe from future financial crises. The Commission opted for this optimistic vision and reported that "PWC's study observes that even if no regulatory regime is able to completely eliminate the possibility for banking crisis, the new framework should nevertheless help reduce the frequency of such incidents".[366]

At the same time, the industry was way more skeptical about the possibility of creating a viable system of large exposure reporting. For example, the industry-led "Counterparty Risk Management Policy Group II" (CRMPG II) Report in 2005 considered "the question of whether some form of a large-exposure regulatory reporting system directed at regulated financial institutions might play a constructive role in helping to better anticipate and mitigate systemic risks".[367] The report warned that "the members of the Policy Group are keenly aware of the formidable and practical challenges associated with designing and implementing an efficient and effective framework of large-exposure reporting requirements". Nevertheless, they concluded that "if an effective system of large-exposure reporting could be created, the potential benefits of such a system could be significant".

These were still happy days for the banking sector, and also for large exposure reporting. However, quite soon the simplification wave of the "Barroso I" Commission hit also this prudential rule. In April 2007, the European

364 Member States shall provide that reporting is to be carried out, at their discretion, in accordance with one of the following two methods: (a) reporting of all large exposures at least once a year, combined with reporting during the year of all new large exposures and any increases in existing large exposures of at least 20% with respect to the previous communication; or (b) reporting of all large exposures at least four times a year.

365 SEC (2004)921, Proposal for a Directive of the European Parliament and of the Council relating to the taking up and pursuit of the business of credit institutions (recast), 14 July 2007, http://ec.europa.eu/governance/impact/ia_carried_out/docs/ia_2004/sec_2004_0921_en.pdf.

366 Id. at 30.

367 Toward Greater Financial Stability: A Private Sector Perspective, The Report of the CRMPG II, July 27, 2005. Available online at www.isda.org/educat/pdf/CRMPGII_7-22-05_FINAL_v6_wcover.pdf.

Commission asked me to look at the administrative burdens generated by the large exposure regime as provided by Directives 48/2006 and 49/2006. They also added that the view of the banking sector was that the rule should be relaxed, if not eliminated: and the Commission was interested in exploring this avenue, since it had just promised to cut administrative burdens by 25% before the end of 2012.

So, in 2007 part of the European Commission was open to the possibility of eliminating those same rules that stood as a safeguard against the risk of future financial crises. In mid-2007, my team and I started applying the Standard Cost Model to find out about the cost of this legal provision for the banking sector.[368] This implied, *i.a.* organizing face-to-face and telephone interviews to gather information about the amount of time spent in complying with the major information obligations connected with large exposure reporting.[369] What we found was shocking. Many of the (then) bigger banks told us that the system was not working for two very simple reasons. First, the banks themselves had very limited knowledge of their overall risk exposure, since the market was not generating sufficient information on the existence of toxic assets, and they were not able to value structured financial products. Second, the banks knew that, regardless of how incomplete their information was on their own large exposure, supervisory authorities were even less aware of the level of risk exposure in their national markets: accordingly, they could report whatever they wanted, and supervisory authorities would not have been able to check.

This problem entered the public domain shortly thereafter, in the summer of 2007, when BNP Paribas froze redemptions for three investment funds, citing its inability to value structured products.[370] This led to a huge increase in counterparty risk, as testified by the soaring rates charged by banks to each other for short-term loans.[371] A few months after, the failures of European banks – starting with Northern Rock and Landesbank Sachsen – testified that something, in the European rules that should have prevented contagion, had failed. The rest is history.

---

368 For a full description of the Standard Cost Model, see Boeheim, Renda et al. (2006), *Pilot Project on Administrative Burdens*, Report for the European Commission, available at http://ec.europa.eu/enterprise/policies/better-regulation/files/pilot-study_en.pdf.

369 The information obligations identified were: (1) Reporting of large exposures to competent authorities; (2) Keeping records concerning non-/less often-reported large exposures for inspection by competent authorities; (3) Reporting of exposures exceeding large exposure limits; (4) Application for authorization to have funded credit protection recognized in the context of the limits of Art. 111; (5) Reporting on results of stress-testing to public authorities; (6) Reporting on transfers having the effect of avoiding the additional capital requirements; and (7) Reporting significant findings on possible concentrations among collateral issuers.

370 Brunnermeier, M.K. (2009). *Deciphering the Liquidity and Credit Crunch 2007–2008*, Journal of Economic Perspectives 23(1), 77–100.

371 For an illustration, see European Commission, *Economic Crisis in Europe: Causes, Consequences and Responses*, European Economy 7, 2009, at 21. Available at http://ec.europa.eu/economy_finance/publications/publication15887_en.pdf.

While performing my contractual obligations for the European Commission, I realized that there was very little that the Standard Cost Model (SCM) could do to help policymakers solve the structural failure of the EU large exposure regime, let alone the fact that the European Commission's prominent interest at that time was not to improve its functioning, but rather to repeal the system altogether (or at least, drastically simplify it).

First, the SCM only looks at certain categories of costs (administrative burdens), and does not consider benefits at all. This, in turn, means that the SCM does not provide adequate guidance on whether, in trying to reduce administrative burdens, policymakers are also achieving the highly undesirable result of cutting benefits to an even larger extent.[372] At the same time, the SCM does not help policymakers find out whether, along with a reduction in administrative burdens, a simplification proposal would also increase enforcement cost for public authorities, thus simply shifting costs from one side to the other. This would certainly have been the case of large exposure reporting obligations: if banks do not report anymore, supervisory authorities will have to collect the needed information through inspections and stronger enforcement: if they are less informed than the banks themselves, this may also represent a net additional cost for society – although banks, overall, will be left better off by the simplification of large exposure reporting, at least in the short term.

Second, there was not much the SCM could do to save European banks from the failure of the large exposure reporting system. As a matter of fact, the SCM assumes 100% compliance: even if I had collected information on the egregious lack of compliance with the requirements of the rule, I had to report the cost associated with the system *as if* all banks were fully complying with its requirements.

Was this sound policymaking? Between overly optimistic impact assessments, lack of compliance with the rules, and perhaps a bad design of the rules themselves, there was plenty for commentators and scholars to complain about. In my opinion, a more sound approach to the design and the performance of the legal provisions on large exposure reporting would have helped EU policymakers craft better rules and shield more effectively European banks from the dramatic contagion that has left many European countries in dire straits. Below, I outline some basic principles of this sound approach.

First, a legal rule is efficiently and effectively designed only if it can be efficiently and effectively enforced. This is an often ignored principle in policymaking, and this depends mostly on the fact that the implementation and enforcement phases are normally neglected *tout court* in *ex ante* impact assessment. If legislators had looked more in-depth at the incentives of the key

---

372 See Allio, L. and A. Renda, *Evaluation of Administrative Burden Reduction Programmes and their Impacts*, Report for OECD Cutting Red Tape II series, published as Annex B in OECD (2010), *Cutting Red Tape. Why is Administrative Simplification so complicated?*, PARIS: OECD Publications.

players affected by the large exposure reporting rules, they would have spotted in the first place that the asymmetric information between banks and their supervisors warranted a different treatment of large exposure, and potentially a more standardized, internationally coordinated approach to the identification of risk thresholds and capital adequacy rules that can lead to a more stable – better, a more resilient – financial infrastructure. No trace of such an approach was found in the work of major EU and US institutions before and during the crisis.

Second, instead of shopping around for simplification opportunities, the European Commission should have explored resilience opportunities. Faced with evidence of limited compliance with the system and excessive fragmentation of the legal regimes, the Commission should have first of all answered the question: why is there so limited compliance with large exposure reporting obligations? The causes of non-compliance were the same causes that led to the spread of the credit crunch in European banks. In this respect, the application of principles of "responsive regulation", as theorized by Ian Ayres and John Braithwaite, would have led to a much better and earlier understanding of where systemic weaknesses and failures lied in the European prudential regulation for the banking sector.[373]

Third, the strange case of large exposure reporting is also a case of excessive faith in the market. The idea that markets could keep risk exposure to sustainable levels, given that financial intermediaries and gatekeepers such as credit rating agencies had countervailing interests compared to more risky asset holders was fundamentally undermined by the massive use of structured finance, coupled with very badly designed governance arrangements, especially as far as rating agencies were concerned. Once and again, this was an additional proof that in some cases, the invisible hand of the market leads to very visible disasters, and that regulation, if effectively and efficiently designed to affect the incentives of key market players, is the only way to salvation. Put differently, the financial crisis of these past few years perfectly illustrates the case for public policy that departs from the mere short-term interest of affected stakeholders: if you had asked bankers what their willingness to pay would be for stricter and more effective prudential rules *before* the crisis, they would have said nil. An *ex ante* impact assessment that assessed the benefit of such an option based on stated preferences would have largely failed to spot its usefulness and efficiency. Once again, since resilience is a public good, policymakers are called to depart from the mere satisfaction of stakeholders' individual preferences when crafting future rules: as for other critical infrastructure, resilience of the financial sector is crucial to the sustainable development of our economies.[374] Current cost-benefit analysis practices are not sufficient to lead us to the most sustainable path today.

373 See Ayres and Braithwaite (1992), cit.

374 See Renda, A. (Rapporteur), *Critical Infrastructure Protection in the European Union*, CEPS Task Force Report, December 2010, available online at www.ceps.eu/book/protecting-critical-infrastructure-eu.

To get back from where I began this story, this is why eyebrows went up when the European Parliament announced a proposal for stricter large exposure reporting rules. No one questions that such rules are potentially very important to ensure the stability of EU financial markets: to the contrary, the emphasis on the need for stricter rules in this field reflects a remarkable change in the regulatory approach between pre- and post-crisis periods. But the European Parliament seemed to have passed that legislative proposal without knowing that large exposure reporting rules had been part of the EU *acquis* for seventeen years; that failure to implement them had been a major cause of the "European contagion"; and that failure to account for individual incentives had been a major cause of that problem. Looking more closely, the legislative proposal by the European Parliament simply stated that "a bank would not be able to expose more than 25% of its own funds to a client or a group of clients" and that "exceeding this threshold will only be possible for exposure between credit institutions and for not more than Euro 150 million". Is this going to save us "again" from future crises, just like the previous regime?

5.6. WHO PROTECTS CONSUMERS FROM CONSUMER PROTECTION? THE EUROPEAN COMMISSION AND RETAIL FINANCIAL SERVICES

Achieving strong consumer protection has been one of the most active policy commitments of EU institutions since the 1980s, with the debate on standard form contracts that led to the enactment of Directive 93/13 on unfair clauses in consumer contracts. In light of the evolution of the law and economics literature, the attention of policymakers around the world has shifted gradually from a formalistic approach, focused on the moment in which unfair clauses are enshrined into the final contractual document, to a more behavioral approach, aimed at capturing information manipulation by service providers to the detriment of less informed consumers. In 2005, the Directive on Unfair Commercial Practices (UCPD) focused on the pre-contractual phase and aimed at contrasting misleading and aggressive behavior that affects the formation of the consumer's will.[375] This second-generation consumer protection tried to incorporate the findings of behavioral economics, which pointed at the pre-contractual phase as the moment in which the structural asymmetries between

375 Directive 2005/29/EC of the European Parliament and of the Council of 11 May 2005 concerning unfair business-to-consumer commercial practices in the internal market and amending Council Directive 84/450/EEC, Directives 97/7/EC, 98/27/EC and 2002/65/EC of the European Parliament and of the Council and Regulation (EC) No 2006/2004 of the European Parliament and of the Council, OJ L 149, 11.6.2005, p. 22–39.

businesses and consumers could lead to sub-optimal and sometimes tragic choices on the side of consumers. This more holistic approach to consumer policy is well summarized by recent definitions, which refer to consumer policy as "preventing sellers from increasing sales by lying about their products or by engaging in unfair practices such as unilateral breach of contract or unauthorized billing"[376]; and chiefly aimed at preventing, curing or remedying: "(i) duress and undue sales pressure; (ii) information problems pre-purchase; and (iii) undue surprises post-purchase".[377]

In addition, the new wave of consumer legislation tried to adopt a wiser approach to the protection of consumers: on the one hand, the "maximum harmonization" clause aimed at the achievement of the internal market and, at the same time, the avoidance of unnecessarily strict rules in some countries[378]; on the other hand, the behavioral approach marked a departure from previous legislative initiatives, which ended up imposing additional costs on the industry and, consequently, also on final consumer prices. This, in turn, tried to remedy the concerns of several academics, who during the 1990s often repeated "who protects consumers from consumer protection?"[379]

The more behavioral economics permeated the mainstream approach to consumer protection, the more retail financial services began to appear as a peculiar policy domain, warranting *ad hoc* treatment. This was partly due to the fact that nowhere as in this field, the informational asymmetry between the financial service provider and the individual customer can determine the latter's unwanted exposure to financial risk. Given that in retail financial services, decisions under risk and ambiguity are the norm, the European Commission started to consider that a stricter approach could be warranted in this field, compared to all other fields of business-to-consumer contracts. Needless to say, the explosion of the subprime mortgage crisis confirmed the Commission's view that the retail financial services sector was a unique one, to be kept under strict supervision. Behavioral economists have gained in importance since the inception of the crisis, claiming that a more behavioral (and interventionist)

---

376 Muris, T. (2002), *The Interface of Competition and Consumer Protection*, Paper presented at Fordham Corporate Law Institute's 29th Annual Conference on International Antitrust Law and Policy, New York (Oct. 31, 2002). See also Armstrong (2008). *Interaction between Competition and Consumer Policy*, a report for the OFT, OFT 991.

377 Vickers, J. (2004), *Economics for Consumer Policy*, 125 Proc. Brit. Acad. 287–310, 289.

378 See, *i.a.*, Mak, V. (2008), *Review of the Consumer Acquis – Towards Maximum Harmonisation?*, TICOM Working Paper on Comparative and Transnational Law No. 2008/6; European Review of Private Law, 1/2009.

379 See, *i.a.*, Van den Bergh, R.J. (1997), *Wer schützt die europäischen Verbraucher vor dem Brüsseler Verbraucherschutz? Zu den möglichen adversen Effekten der europäischen Richtlinien zum Schutze des Verbrauchers'*, in C. Ott und H.-B. Schaefer (eds.) Effiziente Verhaltenssteuerung und Kooperation im Zivilrecht (Tübingen: Mohr Siebeck 1997) 77–102. A typical example is that of the Directive on the Sale of Goods and Associated Guarantees. Directive 99/44/EC of the European Parliament and of the Council of 25 May 1999 on certain aspects of the sale of consumer goods and associated guarantees.

approach would have helped avoiding the crisis altogether.[380] And even Cass Sunstein and Richard Thaler decided to add a post scriptum in their latest edition of *Nudge*, advocating a nuanced approach to consumer protection in investment decisions, based on transparency and disclosure requirements, coupled with the public provision of information.[381]

In all this, the European Commission had already paved the way for such a separate treatment. The UCPD clarified that the maximum harmonization clause applied to all economic sectors, but not to retail financial services.[382] At the same time, the Commission (DG Competition) launched a sectoral inquiry on the retail financial services sector in June 2005, pursuant to Article 17 of Regulation (EC) No 1/2003.[383] The inquiry, opened in June 2005 and closed in 2007, highlighted a low level of mobility of European customers.[384] Amongst the main factors identified as reducing customer mobility in the sector's inquiry, were the cross-selling and conditioning of banking products, which were found to be widespread across EU Member States.[385] Following the sector inquiry, a Green Paper on Retail Financial Services in the Single Market was adopted[386], accompanied by the launch of a public consultation. On the specific issue of tying, responses stressed the reduction of price transparency, making it more difficult for consumers to compare offers.[387] The overall results of this consultation were finally included in the Single Market Review adopted in November 2007.[388] The latter recalls the potential anti-competitive harm resulting from tying practices, issues raised within the sector inquiry and the

---

380 See in particular Shiller, R. (2008), *The Subprime Solution*, Princeton: Princeton University Press.

381 See Sunstein and Thaler (2008), *Nudge*, cit. *supra* note 3, at 255–260.

382 As stated in Recital 9 and prescribed in Article 3(9), specifically for financial services (and for immovable property), the UCPD is "*without prejudice to the right of Member States to go beyond its provisions to protect the economic interests of consumers*"; accordingly, "*Member States may impose requirements which are more restrictive or prescriptive than this Directive in the field which it approximates*".

383 Council Regulation (EC) No 1/2003 of 16 December 2002 on the implementation of the rules on competition laid down in Articles 81 and 82 of the Treaty, OJ L 1, 04.01.2003, p. 1–25. See Section 1.3 below for a detailed illustration of the scope and results of the sectoral inquiry.

384 Two types of indicators illustrate customer mobility. They are referred as "churn" and "longevity". See European Commission, Interim report II: Current accounts and related services, Sector Inquiry under Article 17 Regulation 1/2003 on retail banking, 17 July 2006.

385 For instance nearly two third (63%) of European banks require SMEs seeking a loan to also open a current account. See Report on the Retail Banking Sector Inquiry.

386 See European Commission, Green Paper on Retail Financial Services in the Single Market, COM(2007) 226 final, 30 April 2007.

387 See European Commission, Summary of the written contributions received on the Green Paper on retail financial services, 18 September 2007. The full text is available at http://ec.europa.eu/internal_market/finservices-retail/docs/baeg/summary_consultation_en.pdf.

388 See European Commission, Staff working document, accompanying the document 'A single market for the 21st century Europe', Initiatives in the area of retail financial services, SEC(2007) 1520, 20 November 2007.

Green Paper consultation. Several effects are likely to restrict customer choice, by altering price transparency and/or raising switching costs; in other cases, conducts may hamper competition on the market by discouraging the entry of new players.

Since then, the cross-selling ("tying") of retail financial services has become the enemy to beat. And in the middle of the financial crisis, in early 2008, the Commission launched an external study to assess the welfare impact of the persistence of tying and other "potentially unfair" commercial practices in the field of retail financial services. The objective of the Commission was essentially to verify whether the case could be made for *ad hoc* policy measures aimed at banning tying in this specific field of the economy: if the study had made such a case, then the Commission could have exploited the exception to the maximum harmonization rule in the UCPD to mandate such prohibition.

As a matter of fact, this was a rather strange policy issue. On the one hand, in the United States mainstream law and economics had led to abandoning a *per se* ban on tying in antitrust cases already in 1984, with *Jefferson Parish Hospital District*. Since 2005, the European Commission had repeatedly signaled its intention to move to a more effects-based approach to tying as a potential exclusionary abuse in antitrust: such an approach would then be formalized with the Guidance Paper on the treatment of exclusionary abuses under Article 82 EC Treaty (now 102 TFEU).[389] In other words, in antitrust, tying was being increasingly considered as a lawful conduct, to be challenged by antitrust authorities only under specific circumstances. On the other hand, the European Commission was looking at the possibility of applying a *per se* rule on tying regardless of the market power held by the financial institution that engaged in this practice. The paradoxical result would have been that what was considered in principle lawful under Community competition law would have been subject to a *per se* rule under sectoral consumer protection legislation.

As odd as it might seem, this is what happened. The study was delivered to the Commission by a group of external researchers at the end of 2009.[390] Among the main findings of the study was that tying can increase switching costs and, consequently, reduce customer mobility. This effect depends also on what products or services are included in the bundle: for example, when products have different durations, the customer may be reluctant to switch to an alternative provider of a product with a shorter duration, even if this would be easy absent the tying or pure bundling practice. The lifespan of the contractual relationship

389 See Temple Lang, J. and A. Renda (2008), *Treatment of Exclusionary Abuses under Article 82 of the EC Treaty: Comments on the European Commission's Guidance Paper*, Report of a CEPS Task Force, October 2008, at www.ceps.be/book/treatment-exclusionary-abuses-under-article-82-ec-treaty-comments-european-commissions-guidance.

390 See Renda, A. *et al.* (2009), *Tying and other potentially unfair commercial practices in the retail financial services sector*, report for the European Commission, available online at http://ec.europa.eu/internal_market/consultations/docs/2010/tying/report_en.pdf.

thus tends to become equal to that of the product or service with the longest duration. For this reason, products such as mortgage loans are often used as "gateway" products by service providers wishing to retain their customers through cross-selling strategies.

In addition, the study highlighted that the impact of tying on switching costs depends on the "thickness" of the contractual relationship[391]: once the customer has invested in a relationship with a personal banker or financial advisor, he or she may find it beneficial to enter into multiple contracts and services with the same provider: at the same time, this also means that switching would be more complicated, as it would entail losing the investment associated with building a relationship with the service provider, and having to bear the additional cost of searching for an alternative one, and testing over time the quality of the new service provider.[392]

That is, in retail financial services customers normally "love" tying. Even if it can reduce price transparency and price comparability, customers are reluctant to mix and match products by purchasing every financial service from a different provider. They hate mixing and matching. Accordingly, beyond offering better deals, competitors wishing to gain new customers would have to compensate them for the sunk, "transaction-specific" investment they have faced to enter the current contractual relationship, as well as for the risk associated with entering a new contract or set of contracts. This can represent an important obstacle to customer mobility in the market, and is a structural friction that is very difficult to overcome in the retail financial services market.

The external study also revealed that price comparability is further jeopardized by practices such as "confusopoly", *i.e.* situations where the competing offers on the marketplace are structured so differently that it is impossible for an average consumer to compare them.[393] But even in this case, reducing price transparency can help financial service providers in introducing cross-subsidies between different products, in particular in the case of add-on contracts: for example, sellers may entice customers to buy a particular product through a low "introductory" price, knowing that they will be able to sell a

391 *Id.*, In particular at Section 2.2.

392 A recent study for the European Commission by Decision Technology Ltd. conducted an online survey of 6,000 customers, which revealed that (i) consumers are often confused about the true nature of their investment; (ii) although investments are usually triggered by a change of life circumstances and not marketing, information search is very limited; (iii) Advice is ubiquitous in the retail investment market, with nearly 80% of investments made in a face-to-face setting; and (iv) trust in advisors is high – the majority of investors mostly or completely trust the advice they receive, and do not perceive their advisor to be biased. See *Consumer Decision-Making in Retail Investment Services: A Behavioural Economics Perspective*, available at http://ec.europa.eu/consumers/strategy/docs/final_report_en.pdf.

393 Gans, J. (2005), *The Road to Confusopoly*, available on the ACCC conference website (slides), www.accc.gov.au/content/index.phtml/itemId/658141/fromItemId/.

number of additional products once the customer has entered the relationship.[394] Sellers wishing to compete for only one of the bundled products may have to offer a product below their own cost in order to entice customers to switch.

At the same time, however, there is widespread consensus that tying can also bring benefits for both providers and consumers, thus potentially warranting a rule of reason approach.[395] The potential beneficial effects of tying practices include cost savings through economies of scope, more efficient pricing schemes, and "portfolio effects" or "one-stop-shop" effects for customers.

In summary, the external study found very little grounds for banning tying, as this would have meant depriving consumers of beneficial effects on price and other contractual conditions. To the contrary the study found evidence that other widespread practices, such as "churning" and "steering" had to be banned as being stereotypical cases of aggressive and misleading practices, as such falling inevitably under the scope of the UCPD.[396]

But, for the purposes of this work, the most important finding of this external study was a different one. Only partly conquered by behavioral economics, the European Commission missed the forest for the trees, and failed to see that, due to behavioral effects featured by relationship finance, banning tying would have meant nothing to customers, unless also other practices, such as mixed bundling and conditional rebates were also prohibited. Unless what occurs from a legal, contractual perspective, from a behavioral economics perspective there is almost no difference between offering a bundle of products *tout court* and offering a discount for the purchase of two combined products.[397] If the financial service

394 See Gans, J. (2005), *'Protecting consumers by protecting competition': Does behavioural economics support this contention?*, 13 Competition & Consumer Law Journal. In the literature, this has been referred to as "acquisition pricing" or "introductory pricing". See, *i.a.*, Blattberg, Getz and Thomas (2001), *Customer Equity: Building and Managing Relationships as Valuable Assets*, Harvard business publishing, at pages 47 ff.

395 For example, as recently explained by Choi (2004), "the welfare implications of tying arrangements are in general ambiguous because tying could have efficiency effects even when it has harmful exclusionary effects". See Choi, J. P. (2004), *Antitrust Analysis of Tying Arrangements*, CESifo Working Paper, N. 1336, November 2004.

396 "Churning" is a legal term used to define a practice imported from securities regulation. The Securities and Exchange Commission (SEC) defined it as an "excessive buying and selling of securities in your account by your broker, for the purpose of generating commissions and without regard to your investment objectives". See *i.a.* A.M. Pacces, *Financial intermediation in the securities markets law and economics of conduct of business regulation*, International Review of Law and Economics, Vol. 20, 2000, pp. 479–510; Walter I., "Strategies in Banking and Financial Services Firms: A Survey", December 2003, available at www.ssrn.com. "Steering", on the other hand, is a practice especially used in the mortgages market, consisting of stressing the credit risk of a potential borrower to steer him\her to higher cost loans. "Steering incentives" are officially prohibited in the US by the new Mortgage Reform and Anti-Predatory Lending Act, Sec. 103(c) H.R. 1728, May 2009.

397 The difference is mostly due to the fact that, in tying, customers can be forced to purchase products they would not have purchased otherwise. This, in any event, did not appear as a widespread problem at the time the study was conducted.

provider presents the combined offer as "standard bank policy", as is often the case *i.a.* for Payment Protection Insurance (PPI) sold together with a mortgage loan, the customer will perceive the offer almost as having binding force.

Accordingly, banning tying was simply the wrong solution. Evidence from a survey of the EU member states confirmed that, in those countries that had decided to ban tying, mixed bundling had largely replaced it; and that even where tying was in principle feasible, banks resorted more often to mixed bundling: there's no need to force customers into an unwanted tie-in, if you can nudge your customers into a more apparently spontaneous choice. In this respect, banks had invented libertarian paternalism long before Cass Sunstein.

This tortuous story bears, in my opinion, important lessons. First, behavioral law and economics can teach policymakers how to avoid meaningless and ineffective rules. Second, banning contractual behavior that can be mutually beneficial is unlikely to be an efficient solution, especially in consumer policy. Third, other remedies – coupled with rules aimed at contrasting churning, steering and similar practices – would prove way more effective, as testified by the analysis of national legislation in the EU27: for example, establishing switching facilities and web portals for customers wishing to switch to a new mortgage lender, as in the Netherlands, seems way more effective than prohibiting tying, as in France or Belgium. And more generally, increasing the "public and private" production of third-party information is a better way to break the fiduciary tie established between consumers and their counterparts, rather than imposing 20-minute questionnaires as a proof that the service provider has checked the level of financial education and overall risk attitude of his client: the latter remedy, introduced by recent financial regulation such as the Markets in Financial Instruments Directive (MiFID), are so strikingly contrary to the findings of behavioral economics that failure came as no one's surprise.

5.7. NUDGING AND ENERGY EFFICIENCY: THE BEHAVIORAL ECONOMICS OF CHEAP REFORMS

Meeting the ambitious EU goals to increase energy efficiency and tackle climate change in the years to come is increasingly recognized as a multi-stakeholder effort, requiring contributions from all the actors involved. On the supply side, discussions have revolved around reforms that are likely to be costly for society, from the imposition of taxes to the creation of primary and secondary markets for GHG allowances, to the debate on government subsidies or other supply-side incentives to simulate the transition towards climate-friendly technologies. At the same time, however, also non-price mechanisms can be put in place on the demand side to stimulate more energy-efficient behavior – an option that has been only partly explored to date, and is firmly rooted in behavioral economics.

Traditionally, attempts to induce energy-efficient behavior have been only partly successful, especially when the overall goal of policymakers was clashing with established social norms. From the need to improve buildings' insulation and persuading consumers to buy fluorescent light bulbs to more recent attempts to persuade consumers to buy hybrid cars and more energy-efficient appliances, results have always been less encouraging than politicians had hoped. Many European citizens – but results are not different in other parts of the world – have not taken any such measure to date, despite efforts at national and EU level.

Once the most straightforward possibilities have been ruled out – for example, making it mandatory for producers to adopt eco-design criteria and putting all other products out of the market – policymakers are left only with one chance: changing social norms and the context of consumption decisions to "nudge" consumers into energy-efficient behavior. The good news is that these reforms are potentially viable and entirely costless; the bad news is that no such policy has been successfully adopted to date, leading to doubts among commentators and scholars as regards the feasibility of such a behavioral approach.

Two anecdotes can illustrate the potential of nudging in achieving more energy-efficient behavior. The first is reported by Allcott and Mullainathan (2010), who describes a recent experiment run by an energy-efficiency software company called OPOWER, which presents itself as a group of "home energy gurus", able to achieve enormous savings on the energy bill.[398] OPOWER partnered with utilities in a number of states in the US and started sending energy use reports to residential electricity and natural gas consumers. These reports did not only contain data on energy consumption, but also a comparison with similar households in the same area. In addition, the bill contained energy conservation tips. When comparing trends in energy consumption of those households that had received the OPOWER bill with other households, data showed a 2% energy consumption reduction, and greater values for high-consumption households. Allcott and Mullainathan (2010) observed that, scaled nationwide, "a program like this could reduce U.S. carbon dioxide (CO2) emissions from electric power by 0.5 percent, while actually saving $165 per metric ton of reductions. This compares very favorably with other, more traditional strategies to reduce carbon emissions; wind power, carbon capture

398 See www.opower.com.

and storage added to new coal power plants, and plug-in hybrid vehicles are estimated to cost \$20, \$44, and \$15 per metric ton of CO_2 abated".[399]

Now, convincing households to behave more efficiently through social comparison and "social learning" may in principle be feasible: but how can we convince energy providers to convince their customers? Providers' incentives might be diverging from the socially optimal level of energy consumption – after all, the goal of an energy provider is to make profits, not to save the earth. This is why research on possible policy solutions that would be likely to achieve a realignment of incentives has been carried out. One possibility would be to adopt "decoupling" solutions, as was experimentally done in some US states, such as Michigan and Minnesota.[400]

The simple lesson that can be drawn from this brief anecdote is as revolutionary as it is straightforward: if one wants to fight inefficient energy consumption, one has to understand the social and behavioral factors that affect it. Awareness of the drivers of inefficient behavior is the first step towards an effective policy.[401] And social comparisons stimulate healthy virtual competition between individuals to perform better than average, and possibly better than their neighbors.

A similar story is reported by Goldstein *et al.* (2008), who describe the results of an interesting experiment: in some hotel rooms a card headlined "Help Save the Environment" was left, which urged visitors to "show your respect for nature" by reusing towels. In other rooms, a different card, "Join Your Fellow Guests in Helping to Save the Environment" was placed. Again, exposing guests to the peer pressure made them 25% more likely to reuse towels.[402]

Another experiment reported by Cialdini and Schultz (2004) and later discussed *i.a.* in Nolan *et al.* (2008) was run in San Marcos, California.[403] Five different types of hang-tags were used to encourage the community households to conserve energy. As shown below, one of the messages imposed peer pressure

---

399 See Allcott (2010), quoting McKinsey and Company (2008). *Reducing U.S. Greenhouse Gas Emissions: How Much and at What Cost?*, available online at www.mckinsey.com/clientservice/ccsi/pdf/US_ghg_final_report.pdf.

400 See www.americanprogress.org/issues/2010/08/pdf/good_jobs_new_markets.pdf; In a November 2, 2009 order for Consumers Energy, and a January 11, 2010 order for Detroit Edison, the Michigan Public Service Commission authorized these utilities to develop pilot symmetrical decoupling mechanisms in order to improve the ability of energy efficiency and distributed generation to operate within the utility environment. See also www.raponline.org/Pubs/MN-RAP_Decoupling_Rpt_6-2008.pdf.

401 Allcott and Mullainathan (2010) report that "A bill under consideration in the U.S. House of Representatives, HR 3247, would establish a program at the Department of Energy to understand behavioral factors that influence energy conservation and speed the adoption of promising initiatives".

402 www.csom.umn.edu/assets/118359.pdf.

403 Nolan, J.M., P.W. Schultz, R.B. Cialdini, N.J. Goldstein and V. Griskevicius (2008), *Normative Social Influence is Underdetected*, Personality and Social Psychology Bulletin 2008; 34; 913.

on the household by informing them implicitly that their neighbors were already adopting energy-saving behavior (*77% of your neighbors already use fans instead of air conditioning – it's your community's popular choice!*). Other messages hinted at the possibility of saving money (*save $54 a month on your utility bill!*); contributing to the preservation of the environment (*prevent the release of 262 pounds of greenhouse gases per month*); social responsibility (*It's the socially responsible thing to do!*). After four weeks, data on the relative effectiveness of the different types of messages were collected by the researchers involved. The result was that consumers presented with the "peer pressure" hang-tag reduced their energy consumption by an average of 10%, compared to 3% or less reduction in energy consumption for any of the other hang-tags.

This new wave of energy-efficiency policy has not yet reached Europe, although the bulk of European consumers still shows very little interest for energy-efficient behavior. The awareness of the importance of the message conveyed with labeling became visible in the European Commission's impact assessment on the "Proposal for a Directive of the European Parliament and of the Council on the indication by labelling and standard product information of the consumption of energy and other resources by energy-related products".[404] There, the Commission observes that "many past evaluations of labelling programs have focused on consumer awareness of the label but have not explicitly linked the label to actual behaviour (*i.e.*, to the efficiency of the appliances purchased and to the most likely purchase if there had been no label). Future evaluations should be more comprehensive than has been the case so far". However, the usefulness of peer pressure as a way to achieve more effective results has not surfaced in the debate on EU energy efficiency policy to date: given the mounting interest for nudging and behavioral economics at the European Commission, it is likely that this new approach to energy efficiency policy will soon join the roster of policy options considered by the European Commission in its Impact Assessment documents. In addition, the ongoing development of smart grids will empower administrations with the possibility to send signals on the relative energy consumption of neighboring households: within the boundaries of privacy protection, forms of peer pressure and indication of the relative consumption patterns might become a very effective way of stimulating energy efficient behavior.

---

404 SEC(2008) 2862, 13 November 2008.

Figure 22. Types of hang-tags and conservation of energy

Condition and Graphic	Doorhanger Text
Descriptive Normative Information 	**Join Your Neighbors in Conserving Energy.** Summer is here and most people in your community are finding ways to conserve energy at home. How are San Marcos residents like you conserving this summer? By using fans instead of A/C! Why? In a recent survey of households in your community, researchers at Cal State San Marcos found that ____ % of San Marcos residents often use fans instead of air conditioning to keep cool in the summer. Using fans instead of air conditioning – Your Community's Popular Choice!
Self-Interest 	**Save Money by Conserving Energy.** Summer is here and the time is right for saving money on your home energy bill. How can you save money this summer? By using fans instead of A/C! Why? According to researchers at Cal State San Marcos, you could save up to $54 per month by using fans instead of air conditioning to keep cool in the summer.
Environment 	**Protect the Environment by Conserving Energy.** Summer is here and the time is right for reducing greenhouse gases. How can you protect the environment this summer? By using fans instead of A/C! Why? According to researchers at Cal State San Marcos, you can prevent the release of up to 262 lbs of greenhouse gases per month by using fans instead of air conditioning to keep cool this summer! Using fans instead of air conditioning – the Environmental Choice.
Social Responsibility 	**Do Your Part to Conserve Energy for Future Generations.** Summer is here and we need to work together to conserve energy. How can you conserve energy for future generations? By using fans instead of A/C! Why? According to researchers at Cal State San Marcos, you can reduce your monthly demand for electricity by 29% using fans instead of air conditioning to keep cool this summer! Using fans instead of air conditioning – the Socially Responsible Choice.
Information Only	**Energy Conservation.** Summer is here and the time is right to conserve energy. How can you conserve energy this summer? By using fans instead of A/C!

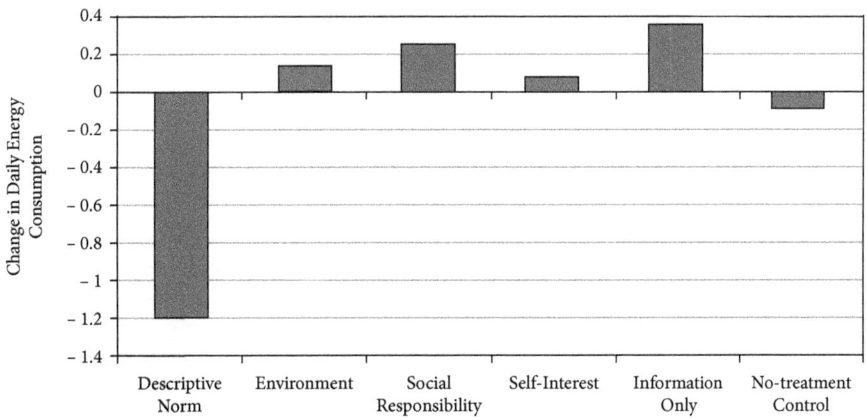

Source: Cialdini and Schultz (2004).

What lessons can be learned from these stories? First, in certain policy domains understanding the drivers and motivations underlying human behavior is essential for the design of efficient and effective policies: simply assuming that consumers will behave rationally would be very shortsighted. Second, nudging requires some independent value judgment, such as the definition of socially desirable behavior, and the recognition that social norms affect individual satisfaction – something that pure methodological individualists would never be able to accept. Third, the scope of nudging is still limited to consumer policy and the realignment of individual behavior with the need to preserve public goods such as the environment or public health. Fourth, impact assessments based on quantitative cost-benefit analysis are very unlikely to capture the need to focus on individual behavior, change social norms, use peer pressure and, ultimately, fine-tune incentives to lead people to behave in a "socially sustainable" manner.

5.8. ACHILLES AND THE TURTLE: TEN YEARS OF FAILED ATTEMPTS TO ENFORCE COPYRIGHT IN CYBERSPACE

The importance of individual incentives, social norms and the context of human behavior in determining the effectiveness of legal rules is nowhere as tangible as in the intangible world, *i.e.* as in cyberspace. The "network of networks" that today governs a growing portion of our life emerged as a sort of free zone, in which the end-to-end nature of the network and its packet-based traffic determined the impossibility for any central intelligence to detect illegal behavior in time to stop it. This is why, already at the end of the 1990s, Carol Rose defined cyberspace as unsafe as "Central Park after dark".[405] The key revolutionary potential of the Web was indeed the result of a number of concurring factors, which include the possibility to ship information in digital format (which made the copy impossible to distinguish from the original); the spread of broadband connections in e-communications; and the end-to-end architecture that researchers such as Tim Berners Lee designed for the World Wide Web, making it possible for every end user to communicate with its peers.

When the World Wide Web entered the scene, the academic and policy communities entered a phase of deep turbulence. The Web looked like a Maghreb *suq*, with sellers, magicians, shamans, prophets, gurus, each with an own, revolutionary idea on how things would develop in the years to come. For example, Stanford scholar Paul Goldstein predicted that the Internet would become like a "celestial jukebox", in which the possibility of charging users for

405 See Rose, C. (1998), *The Several Futures of Property: Of Cyberspace and Folk Tales, Emission Trades and Ecosystems*, 83 Minn. L. Rev. 129.

each and every download and access to an information good – *e.g.* a song or a movie – would finally become reality.[406] No transaction costs, monitoring or "cyberpolice" were needed on the network of networks: the same licensing mechanism that had made piano rolls and jukeboxes so popular in different epochs of the 20th Century were now to conquer the new environment of the 21st. This would have been the triumph of copyright on the Internet – a rather easy victory, after all.

But many others disagreed. For example, a former lyricist for the famous rock band "Greatful Dead", named John Perry Barlow, swiftly announced that the Internet era would have marked the death of copyright[407], and that the interests of authors and users would be assured "by the following practical values: relationship, convenience, interactivity, service, and ethics". But no copyright would be enforced in cyberspace, since the moment an information is disseminated to the public, the public can and should be able to share it and joyfully make use of it. Barlow was only the tip of an iceberg. Other authors were counting on the end of copyright, and not only in the media domain. Eric S. Raymond was working on his paper "The cathedral and the *bazaar*", in which he praised the emergence of open source licenses and "copyleft" – as opposed to copyright – as the way forward in software computing.[408]

Meanwhile, cyber gurus such as Lawrence Lessig were engaging in somewhat more sophisticated elaborations. As he stated in his enlightening book "Code", a peculiarity of cyberspace is that it is not primarily law, nor any ethical code, that defines the boundaries of possible. Code, the architecture of cyberspace, affects users' behavior more than anything else. This also meant that code is more powerful than legal rules in enforcing rights in cyberspace, and that any meaningful way of reproducing the set of entitlements people had in the "real life" would have to be translated and enforced with the help of technology to become viable in cyberspace. Lessig observed already in 1996 that

> *"Code is an efficient means of regulation. But its perfection makes it something different. One obeys these laws as code not because one should; one obeys these laws as code because one can do nothing else. There is no choice about whether to yield to the demand for a password; one complies if one wants to enter the system. In the well implemented system, there is no civil disobedience. Law as code is a start to the perfect technology of justice".*[409]

406 See Goldstein, P. (1994), *Copyright's Highway: the Law and Lore of Copyright from Gutenberg to the Celestial Jukebox*, Hill & Wang, New York, NY.

407 See, *e.g.* Barlow, J.P. (1994), *The Economy of Ideas: Selling Wine without Bottles*, 2.03 Wired 84, 1994.

408 See Raymond (2001), *The Cathedral & the Bazaar: Musings on Linux and Open Source by an Accidental Revolutionary*, O'Reilly Media.

409 Lessig, L. (1996), *The Zones of Cyberspace*, Stanford Law Review (48), p. 1408.

This meant that when traditional enforcement of legal rules is insufficient, creating structural ("architectural") constraints to user behavior is the only way of securing that laws are indeed enforced on the Web. This is not entirely a new feature: for example, if you don't want cell phones to ring loudly in an auditorium, you can post a sign telling users to switch off their mobile phones, but you can also isolate the building, so that cell phones won't work; likewise, you can count on police and legal entitlements to protect your car from thieves, but an alarm and a couple of lockers do the job more effectively in many cases. In cyberspace, the possibility of circumventing the law had become so overwhelmingly greater than the possibility to enforce legal rules, that the design and architecture of the cyber world was way more important than the mere setting of legal entitlements.

Moreover, the Web had been given an end-to-end architecture in which all bits, in principle, should be treated equally. Its creator Tim Berners Lee was so smart to devise a system in which all end users could communicate and share files with other end users, and intelligence was mostly concentrated at the edges of the network, not in the core backbone. The underlying idea was that, the more the Web acted as a "dumb pipe", the greater the network effects and the value of the network itself. A corollary of this principle was that control over the content that flowed over the Internet would have to be weak – the dumber the pipe, the freer the user.

These were some of the main voices animating the birth of the Web in the mid-1990s. A landmark example of that era is the famous cartoon posted by Peter Steiner on The New Yorker on 5 July 1993, where a dog sitting on a chair in front of a computer was enthusiastically telling a second dog sitting on the floor that "On the Internet, nobody knows you're a dog!" Freedom, anonymity, and a lot of legal uncertainty were the headlines in this rather remote story.

After more than a decade, who was right, and who was wrong?

Well, a few years after the birth of the Web, it seemed fair to state that the prophets of the "death of copyright" were right, and the advocates of the "celestial jukebox" had simply gotten it wrong. The reason was simple, and related to the combination of three different factors. First, content was flowing in digitized form over the Web, and for the first time the copy was identical to the original – some authors even started to state that on the Web, the "license is the product", meaning that access rights are what counts, and the product itself does not exist anymore. Second, the end-to-end architecture allowed end users to exchange files (regardless of whether they were copyrighted or not) without having to pass any filter, as the pipe was "dumb" and the "code" of cyberspace allowed them to do it. Third, broadband connections were becoming more widespread, and increased connectivity made it easier for end users to share content on the Web by shipping large files.

The result of all this was what we today call "file sharing". Copyright owners completely lost control of the use and distribution of their content on the Web, and cybernauts started to create a huge and uncontrollable secondary market for digital content. At the extreme, content owners would have been able to sell only one copy of their product: once sold, the digital copy could have been reproduced and shipped millions of times on the Web without significant losses in quality. Copyright enforcement as we had known it since then, in a word, had been killed by the Internet architecture. And this is why I refer to the battle that followed as the battle between architecture and control.

In policy terms, something had to be done. The music majors anticipated the "copyright problem" by extensively lobbying the US congress to form a Commission – later named the "Lehman commission" – that suggested the criminalization of all copying on the Internet.[410] But this would have meant killing the Internet architecture, as surfing requires making a copy of the web pages on the cache memory of our PCs – it would have become impractical to even think about surfing the Web. And saving control would have led to throwing the baby away with the bath water. The opposing interests found a rather unsatisfactory compromise with the *Digital Millennium Copyright Act* in 1998. The DMCA did not criminalize copying; on the other hand, it allowed whatever form of anti-circumvention technique, including technological protection measures aimed at restoring control over digital content.

But this was just the beginning. Attempts to strengthen controls have been virtually endless in those years, especially in the US. Already in 1998, the *Sonny Bono Copyright Term Extension Act* extended the validity of copyright to 70 years after the author's death. It was ironically termed the "Disney Act", as copyright law tends to be reformed in the US whenever rights on Mickey Mouse are about to expire.

These and other episodes mark an era in which the industry's response to the birth of the Web was focused mostly on lobbying for stricter rules and equally strict enforcement. But when the 20-year old Irish-American student Shawn Fanning started experimenting with Napster on the web, the majors realized that simply passing a new law would not make much sense. Napster filled the only remaining gap in the Web: even with high-speed broadband, digital content and an end-to-end architecture, users still needed a facilitator, an intermediary that could help locating "who had what" and kick-start file sharing on a large scale. Napster was simply this: a centralized directory that collected information on "who had what". But all exchanges took place between end users, eventually, so Napster was not really guilty of copyright infringement.

How to react? As users were the real infringers, initially the majors started to sue directly those who downloaded illegal content. But it was immediately clear that they could not chase each and every geek in town – famous cases include a

410 See, *i.a.*, Litman, J. (2001), *Digital Copyright*, Prometeus Books.

lawsuit against a few girl scouts, guilty of having played pirated songs while camping on a sunny afternoon.[411] That was not really a practical solution. Majors then started to look for a solution: chasing "facilitators", instead of infringers.

But copyright law, as shaped by decades of debate and case-law in the US, was not really suited to punish "facilitators", *i.e.* intermediaries. Two doctrines were available – *contributory infringement* and *vicarious liability*. But in any event, shutting down a "facilitator" would have to pass muster under a Supreme Court precedent – the 1984 decision in *Sony v. Universal Studios*.[412] Altogether, this meant that:

- Content owners could hold facilitators of infringement liable of *contributory infringement* if they proved that they had *actual knowledge* of the fact that subscribers infringed copyright, and also provided a material contribution to the infringement, for example by providing "site and facilities" for users to infringe.
- Alternatively, they could have held intermediaries *vicariously liable* if they proved that: (i) the intermediary obtained a financial benefit from the conduct; and (ii) besides having actual knowledge of the infringing conduct, it could also control such conduct, and could stop it in real time.
- In any event, to convince the judge to grant an injunction inhibiting the intermediary's conduct, content owners should have respected the 1984 *Sony* precedent, which stated that if a device or platform that facilitates infringement is also "capable of substantial non-infringing uses", then it should not be banned from the market or shut down.

This was the perimeter of the *Napster* case back in 2001. And it was quite clear from the outset that, based on these three pillars, shutting down *Napster* was impossible. As a matter of fact, Napster had no actual knowledge of the infringing conduct – it only kept a centralized directory, which provided only information, not files. In addition, it drew no financial benefit from the infringing conduct – no banners, no subscription fees. And it was heavily debated whether Napster could actually stop the infringing conduct in real time, if not shutting its server down. Moreover, Napster was capable of substantial non-infringing uses – sharing comments, preferences, old bootlegs, non-copyrighted recordings, making friends, etc. – and as such did not meet the *Sony* conditions.

But it came out that, if Napster's server had been shut down, users would not have been able to engage in massive copyright infringement. It was indeed this latter issue that led the Supreme Court to decide against Napster in the end –

---

411 See ASCAP's lawsuit against Girl Scouts. For a coment, see Lisa Bannon, *The Birds May Sing, but Campers Can't Unless They Pay Up*, Wall Street Journal, 21 agosto 1996; and Lawrence Lessig, *Free Culture*, at http://free-culture.cc/notes/.

412 *Sony Corp. of American v. Universal City Studios, Inc.*, 464 U.S. 417 (1984).

many of us remember those days in which the famous website was about to close. And it was quite clear that the decision had unacceptably stretched the *Sony* precedent and the boundaries of copyright law. But that was it. And the end of the *Napster* case was perhaps the only moment in the past few years in which content owners have thought they had won the battle.

However, as Joshua Cooper Ramo recalls in his recent *The Age of the Unthinkable*, to win the battle against revolutionaries, you have to think like one of them – and majors were not ready to go that way.[413] During 2001, I was in New York City visiting a local university, and ended up in a rather restricted workshop of quasi-hackers. There, I realized that *Napster* was only the beginning, and that the turtle had already advanced one step away from Achilles. I saw a big blackboard full of potential network architectures and each of them was scored according to a number of features: the last one indicated whether that type of network architecture was "lawsuit-proof". And some of them were.

A couple of years later, Los Angeles federal court judge Stephen Wilson opened a trial against two successors of Napster, called Grokster and Morpheus. The Hollywood Studios and the recording majors were complaining that these software platforms behaved exactly like Napster. It was thus apparently an easy case – apply the *Napster* precedent, and shut them down right away. But things were not as easy as Judge Wilson may have thought at the outset: it came out that neither Grokster nor Morpheus matched the features of the *Napster* case. In particular, Grokster was only a very light software that connected the user to a network called FastTrack, which operated independently from Grokster and linked also other services. FastTrack selected every morning some users' PCs as "supernodes", and it was supernodes that went around to look for the information to enable file-sharing, not Grokster. So, Grokster had no actual knowledge, provided no "site and facilities", had no financial benefit, etc. When it came to Morpheus, things went even worse. Morpheus was an open source software linking users to the Gnutella network – a sort of *passe-parole* between users helped identifying "who had what". Most importantly, contrary to Napster, you could have switched off Grokster and Morpheus, and the users would have continued exchanging their files.

Again, how to react? Judge Wilson took it seriously, and concluded in 2003 that

> *"[t]he Court is not blind to the possibility that Defendants may have intentionally structured their businesses to avoid secondary liability for copyright infringement... To justify a judicial remedy, however, Plaintiffs invite this Court to expand existing copyright law beyond its well-drawn boundaries."*[414]

---

413 See Cooper Ramo, J. (2009), *The Age of the Unthinkable: Why the New World Disorder Constantly Surprises Us And What We Can Do About It*, Hachette Book Group, 23 March 2009.

414 Conclusions of Judge Wilson in *MGM et al. v. Grokster et al.*, US District Court, Central District of California, judgment granted in part to defendants, 259 F. Supp. 2d 1029 (C.D. Cal. 2003).

In a nutshell, this is matter for Congress, not for a federal court judge. If majors wanted to beat Grokster, Morpheus and the dozens of their homologues, they had to lobby Congress to change the law. Absent a change in the law, the turtle could thrive.

Content owners have slowly realized that the strategy to counter peer-to-peer file sharing cannot rely only on the law. You can beat technology only with technology. There's no way to beat virus developers by simply enacting a law that states that disseminating viruses is illegal. You need anti-viruses. For file-sharing, the majors' revenge has taken different forms. The first is the development of new forms of cyber-attacks, such as "spoofing" technologies: legitimated by the DMCA, firms like Media Defender and Overpeer started using whatever means to discourage users from engaging in illegal download, including shipping viruses right to end users' PCs to "punish one, educate a hundred". And they were not garage software houses – the CEO of Media Defender was the former head of ASCAP, a well-known chap in the field.

Then came a new era of lobbying to enable technological protection measures: attempts include the *Berman Bill*[415]; the *Consumer Broadband and Digital Television Promotion Act*[416]; the *Family Entertainment and Copyright Act*[417]; and the "broadcast flag".[418]

Finally, just as Congress was debating an *Inducement Act* that would have realized the expansion of the scope of copyright protection Judge Wilson was referring to, the Supreme Court of the United States finally decided that, even without overruling *Sony v. Universal Studios*, Grokster could have been held vicariously liable anyway on the basis of an "inducement theory". And this

415 The *Berman Bill* was presented to Congress on 25 July 2002, which would have allowed content owners to block file sharing systems even absent any evidence of copyright infringement, on the basis of a mere presumption of infringing conduct, creating a "Far West" in which all means to avoid infringement were legal, as long as attacks – as they were defined – did not damage directly users' PCs; were proportionate; did not cause more than $50 damage to the intermediary for each attack; and were notified in advance to the Attorney General one week before. A proposal that Mark Lemley, one of the most authoritative experts in this field, defined simply as "a nightmare".

416 The *Consumer Broadband and Digital Television Promotion Act (CBDTPA)* was presented to the US Senate in March 2002. It banned the sale of whatever device that could support non-technologically-protected content, and punished all infringements with imprisonment for 5 to 20 years and fines between $50,000 and one million dollars.

417 The *Family Entertainment and Copyright Act* was finally approved in 2005. On the basis of this Act, those that distribute even one single non-authorized copy of a movie on the Web can be put to jail for a maximum of three years.

418 In 2005, the FCC mandated that no personal computers and digital TV recorders could be sold without carrying a "broadcast flag". The broadcast flag allowed only the reproduction of DRM-protected content on devices like PCs or the TiVo. According to the rule, hardware must "actively thwart" piracy. But the US Court of Appeals later rules that the FCC had exceeded its authority by prohibiting the manufacture of hardware without copy protection technology. But the broadcast flag came back in subsequent attempts, such as the Communications, Consumer's Choice, and Broadband Deployment Act of 2006.

because *"[n]othing in* Sony *requires courts to ignore evidence of intent to promote infringement if such evidence exists. In addition to intent ... the inducement theory requires evidence of actual infringement ... There is evidence of such infringement on a gigantic scale. Because substantial evidence supports MGM on all elements, summary judgment for respondents was error".*

With this judgment, the tide had turned. From that day, hundreds of p2p download systems have shut down, including famous ones such as WinMX, BearShare and LimeWire. And the content industry took a deep breath.

The battle was won, at the end, but the war still raged. Soon after, even more sophisticated systems such as Bit Torrent entered the stage. Torrents live a life of their own: simply, there is evidence of massive infringement, but no "facilitator" – at least not a human one: technology does it alone just as in science-fiction. No one has found a way to challenge these anonymous, amoebic, ever-changing, nomadic chains of files as belonging to anyone, at least until the Swedish *Pirate Bay* case.

As illegal file-sharing had not been fully stopped, the content industry decided to resort to another set of weapons to win the war. And they started to think like a revolutionary. To tell the truth, it was Apple, not a major recording company or one of the Hollywood studios, the first to realize that the only way to win the war against illegal downloading was not to criminalize the act of downloading, but to create room for legal downloading, and to make it enticing enough that users would decide to stop infringing copyright and convert themselves to the bright side of the Force.

In 2004, a study by INDICARE suggested that a sufficient number of users (current p2p downloaders, but also other users that were not using the internet to get music) would have started to use an online music store if the price for a single song did not exceed 1 euro. Apple decided to stick to that figure – the would-be iTunes would have never succeeded with songs sold at more than € 1. But record companies did not want to license their repertoires if not for a very high price, and only under the condition that songs could not be shared. That's why iTunes came out as it is: a system in which: (i) songs cost less than € 1; (ii) a Digital Rights Management System called Fair Play restrict the possibility of sharing the file and burn CDs[419]; and (iii) songs downloaded from iTunes can only be listened to on the iPod – Apple had to secure an additional source of revenues, as € 1 per song did not cover the cost of obtaining all the licenses.

419 DRMs are defined by the US NIST as "a system of information technology (IT) components and services along with corresponding law, policies and business models which strive to distribute and control intellectual property (IP) and its rights". More in detail, they consist of lines of code attached to individual files, which define what uses of the file are allowed; a clickwrap license signed by users, which binds them legally against any attempt to circumvent the DRM protection; and a license agreement with device producers, which again binds them legally if their devices are massively used to infringe copyright.

Since when the iTunes-iPod system entered the market, DRMs have become the "new kid in town", and potentially a panacea against the perils of enduring illegal file-sharing. In 2005 a report by an *ad hoc* High-Level Group on digital rights management appointed by the European Commission concluded that

> *"EU Institutions and Member States [must] reflect in their policy positions that copyright abuse will not be tolerated, and that protection of content delivered via DRM is the way forward".*[420]

But that, again, was only a chimera. Even the most sophisticated protection mechanism ever conceived, such as DRM, combining both technological and legal protection measures, has failed. Billions of users have bought the iPod, but they have mostly used it to listen to illegally downloaded songs. In its first years, iTunes has been a failure, and Steve Jobs himself has declared that, was it for him, he'd get rid of the DRM altogether. In an open letter dated 6 February 2007, he stated

> *"DRMs haven't worked, and may never work, to halt music piracy... Much of the concern over DRM systems has arisen in European countries. Perhaps those unhappy with the current situation should redirect their energies towards persuading the music companies to sell their music DRM-free... Convincing them to license their music to Apple and others DRM-free will create a truly interoperable music marketplace. Apple will embrace this wholeheartedly".*[421]

Now, Steve Jobs was probably right if one looks at DRMs as tools like Apple's Fair Play. I am not quite sure his statement holds if one looks at the use of technology to monitor the flow of content on the Internet, without charging for each time content is shared.

After 15 years in which the advocates of IPR control and defenders of the internet architecture have chased each other like Achilles chases the turtle in Zeno's famous paradox of motion, what have we learnt? Apparently very little, especially if one looks at recent happenings in EU countries. On the one hand, the recent *Pirate Bay* case in Sweden has marked another ephemeral victory of control over architecture. With *Pirate Bay*, Sweden has gotten as far as the US Supreme Court went in *Grokster*: it condemned the four operators of the famous website for facilitating – better, "inducing" – massive copyright infringement. And since some time has elapsed, the trial ended up capturing a technology that had been considered almost "lawsuit-proof" to date, such as the Torrent one.

---

420 See the *Final Report of the High Level Group on Digital Rights Management*, 2004, at http://ec.europa.eu/information_society/eeurope/2005/all_about/digital_rights_man/doc/040709_hlg_drm_2nd_meeting_final_report.pdf.

421 Steve Jobs, *Thoughts on Music*, at www.apple.com/hotnews/thoughtsonmusic/.

A couple of weeks later, in May 2009, France passed a controversial "content and creation" law that called for the creation of the *Haute Autorité pour la Diffusion des Oeuvres et la Protection des droits sur Internet* (HADOPI), a new agency with a mandate to sanction those accused of illegal file-sharing. The law introduced a "three strikes" rule according to which Internet Service Providers should monitor infringing conduct by their subscribers, and after two warnings put them on a black list and block their account for up to one year. The "three-strikers" would, by the way, continue to pay while being disconnected. The French government went as far as trying to include this rule in the review of the EU telecoms package – this attempt led Europe to a stall in the already quite complex negotiations for the new package. This further delay was even more paradoxical since on June 10, 2009, the Constitutional Council of France ruled against HADOPI's central provision, which allowed ISPs to impose sanctions on end users accused (even if not yet convicted) of copyright violations. The Court stated that "the Internet is a component of the freedom of expression" and that "in French law the presumption of innocence prevails". Moreover, as the Court reiterated, even in a country with a long and established tradition of administrative law like France, only a judge can impose sanctions under the law. More recently, on 22 October 2009, a "HADOPI 2" law was passed, this time with the approval of the French Constitutional Council: the new law requires judicial review before revoking a person's internet access, but otherwise keeps the original provisions contained in the first HADOPI law. The interesting fact was that, despite this unprecedentedly harsh measure, the HADOPI 2 "three-strikes" law seems to have led to an increase in illegal downloading. In March 2010, researchers at the University of Rennes found that since the HADOPI 2 law was passed, illegal downloading had grown by 3%. Those that had abandoned file-sharing had gone into streaming or direct downloads from web servers. Even if the law has been fully implemented only in October 2010, there seems to be little prospects for full compliance by end users.[422]

The French law has inspired similar initiatives in other countries, including most notably the UK, where the Digital Economy Act 2010 introduced a similar "three-strikes" rule. The Act was even subject to an impact assessment, in which the UK government explains that the new rule will lead media companies to recover £1.7 billion of displaced sales (corresponding to £200 million of annual benefits): an estimate that seems to rest on rather fragile assumptions, especially since the Impact Assessment document observes that "the measures set out in the Digital Economy Act ... were designed specifically to address the particular characteristics of unlawful P2P file-sharing but could be applied to counteract other forms of on-line copyright infringement if deemed an efficient and effective way of doing so. However, for most other forms of on-line copyright infringement

422 www.nytimes.com/2010/07/19/technology/internet/19iht-CACHE.html.

they are likely to prove less effective".[423] The available data for France reveal that the substitution effect with illegal direct downloads and streaming would be quite likely, leaving copyright owners with little improvement over the *status quo*.

Looking at the evolution of the problem in the past decade, it is fair to state that both approaches to policy, the Swedish and the French/British, seem to miss the broader picture. And the reasons are quite simple. First, technology will continue to circumvent these rules – as from Napster users moved to Grokster, and from Grokster to eMule or Pirate Bay, they'll find another, smarter technological solution to avoid being jailed and having to pay damages. If they are put on the black list by ISPs, they will use other accounts to surf the internet, and eventually disappear under anonymity. After all, it is code, not law, that defines what's possible on the Internet.

Second, it is a very well-known tenet of social sciences that only "morally acceptable" rules are likely to be complied with by their recipients.[424] And both *Pirate Bay* and the French/British "three-strikes" rule are inconsistent with the *Netiquette*, the ethical code of Internet users. They simply consider it unfair to be subject to such an aggressive dawn raid, they reject the idea of ISPs as cyber-police. And they disagree so strongly that they ended up forming a political representation, the *Piratpartiet*, that won more than 7% of the Swedish votes in the recent elections for the European Parliament, and will fight to reform (or kill) copyright in the years to come, directly from Strasbourg.

More than the underlying design of the law, it is enforcement that deserves serious reconsideration. 15 years of attempts have produced nothing: according to a recent study by Jupiter Research, for each song sold, 100 more were stolen; and 94% of online music consumers declared to be unwilling to pay for music. Against this background, current attempts such as the French "three strikes" or the US and Swedish "inducement theories" are doomed to represent mere placebos or at best temporary relief – but no long-term solution.

In order to identify some building blocks for the future, a few lessons must be kept in mind.

- *Avoid micropayments.* The Web is the domain of flat pricing, not micropayments. Users will never accept any legal download service if they know they will not be able to experiment with new content and share it with peers. So, whatever solution is found for the future, it should be such that users are left free to behave like cybernauts.

[423] See http://interactive.bis.gov.uk/digitalbritain/wp-content/uploads/2010/04/Digital-Economy-Act-IAs-final.pdf, at 56.

[424] See Christine Parker, *The Compliance Trap:; the moral message in responsive regulatory enforcement*, Law & Society Review, Volume 40, Number 3, September 2006, pp. 591–622(32).

- *Use technology to combat technology.* DRMs still have a role to play, as the only possibility to track the relative success of a piece of content over others. But DRMs must be used as an ingredient in blanket licensing systems, where flat fees are paid by users for access to a whole repertoire. DRM systems should thus not be directly linked to revenue collection, as in iTunes, but as information collectors on which authors should be remunerated, and to what extent. DRM-based, flat-fee services such as the new Napster, Qtrax, Snocap have gone this way in past years, and are likely to be followed soon by giants like Google's YouTube – especially if content majors surrender to reality, and contribute to the endeavour.
- *Empower ISPs, but not as policemen.* In the aftermath of the European debate on net neutrality, ISPs are likely to be entrusted with more powers to inspect and prioritize packets on the Internet. This will also lead us in a privileged position to detect whether illegal downloads are taking place. Blocking IP accounts is not likely to work, but a warning system and a quality of service degradation for illegal content are more likely to succeed. In a nutshell, the user experience must be significantly better in legal downloads than for illegal ones.
- *Enter the NGN era.* Content providers and ISPs should work together to make sure that in the near future, when users will be "always on", and always at high-speed, content is made available almost exclusively for streaming rather than owning or burning. In the transition from the iPod to the iPhone, this will be increasingly possible. Users will buy "access" to songs, movies, libraries and videogames, rather than owning a copy. As Bob Gomulkiewicz already stated in 1998, on the internet "The license is the product".[425] If code allows only streaming, and streaming does not lead always to additional micropayments, Cybernauts will find it "moral" to join the system. After all, on the Internet the word "free" is not intended as "free lunch", but mostly as "free speech" – users feel free when they can communicate without barriers.
- *"Hide" the cost of legal download services.* If ISPs can degrade the quality of service for illegally streamed content, DRM is used only to track content, and content is available almost exclusively for streaming in an "always on" environment, then the blanket license fees paid by users to access content can be directly included in the Internet subscription fee. Although it may seem too malicious, I am sure legal downloads can work on the Internet only if users are not constantly confronted with the fact that they are paying to access content.

If these principles are taken into account, I am sure we can soon strike a deal between the content industry and ISPs to establish a pro-copyright partnership.

[425] Gomulkiewicz, R.W. (1998), *The License Is the Product: Comments on the Promise of Article 2B for Software and Information Licensing*, 13 Berkeley Tech. L. J. 891.

And after 15 years, we will realize that almost everybody was right: Goldstein's celestial jukebox will be replaced by a big flat pricing system; Barlow's "death of copyright" will become the "death of copyright enforcement as we know it"; Lessig's "code as law" will lead to drawing new rules of the game for cybernauts; and on the Internet, nobody will know that you are a dog: after all, even Steiner's pet surfer must have paid a subscription fee at some point.

The never-ending saga of copyright protection in cyberspace highlights the impossibility of regulating against social norms, however virtual they may be. A more thorough understanding of human behavior and the patterns of social interaction in cyberspace can suggest more effective ways of regulating cyberspace, and in particular access to content. Past attempts suggest that, if social norms are not taken into account – even better, if regulation is not aimed at affecting social norms with the help of technology – even the most draconian sanctions will not scare Internet users.

5.9. CONCLUSIONS: THE MANY FACETS OF LAW AND ECONOMICS IN THE RIA WORLD

The previous pages have reported eight different stories that revolve around the problem of how to craft effective rules, and how to use law and economics in an impact assessment to inform better policy decisions. The first four stories are related to the use of law and economics in the impact assessment methodology, and spot mistakes and imperfections that have been made in the performance of an impact assessment, due to the lack of a sound law and economics approach. The spectrum allocation story revealed that sophisticated law and economics can help policymakers "think outside the box". If transaction costs, prospect theory, diverging valuations and strategic behavior are taken into account, policymakers can devise more effective rules, such as the Texas Shootout, to ensure that spectrum is not propertized, and industry players can place a value on its availability at regular intervals, thus making it possible to reallocate frequencies when they are being inefficiently used. The story about private antitrust damages actions highlighted that, when individual incentives are at stake, an impact assessment becomes more useful when it uses law and economics concepts, rather than when it attaches arbitrary values to prospective costs and benefits. The example of the roaming regulation warned against the arbitrary use of cost-benefit analysis by civil servants. Hiding distributional effects may lead to merely taking the wrong decision in an impact assessment: accordingly, this story testified of the needs for better economics in IA, and for a careful consideration of distributional effects when drafting IA documents.

The fifth story stands as a tale of the changing approach to regulation during and after the financial crisis. The story of how the approach to reporting changed over time is both sweet and sour, since it highlighted a better awareness of the importance of reporting for market surveillance purposes, but also the persisting lack of responsive regulation in investigating reasons for non-compliance.

The last three stories highlight the importance of considering both social norms and human behavior in crafting certain types of policies – indeed, an expanding portion of public policies. The case of tying in the retail financial services sector highlighted the importance of behavioral economics in the design of effective rules: trying to ban tying without expecting a rapid substitution of tying with practices with similar practices that exploit the supply-side and demand-side efficiencies generated by cross-selling is truly shortsighted policy. The energy efficiency examples are the most typical application of nudging *à la* Cass Sunstein, but also add the importance of peer pressure as an essential tool to convince individuals to adopt socially sustainable behavior. Finally, the saga of copyright in cyberspace is the most extreme case of resistant social norms: a decade of failed attempts to replace a social norm that is inconsistent with copyright law, from which policymakers and media companies still seem to have learned very little.

More stories could have been included in this section, in support of a sound use of law and economics in phases of *ex ante* impact assessment such as problem definition, identification of viable options, analysis of likely impacts, and enforcement solutions. The most important conclusion that can be drawn from the observation of current practice is in line with our conclusions in the previous Section: on the one hand, law and economics can usefully inspire the daily work of the policymaker, especially when individual incentives, human behavior and social norms are at stake; on the other hand, this requires abandoning the emphasis on Kaldor-Hicks cost-benefit analysis and exclusive reliance on methodological individualism, to embrace a more sophisticated approach to the causes and determinants of human action – in a word, the "context" in which policy outcomes materialize.

PART III
CONCLUSION:
LAW AND ECONOMICS IN THE RIA WORLD

6. THE FUTURE OF RIA – AND HOW LAW AND ECONOMICS CAN HELP

This book was essentially conceived as a tale of two crises. On the one hand, the crisis of neoclassical law and economics, attacked on many fronts by behavioral economics, neo-institutional economics and scholars in other social (and sometimes natural) sciences. On the other hand, the crisis of RIA, an *ex ante* policy appraisal tool based on neoclassical economics that is at once a great success in terms of formal adoption, and a widespread failure in terms of actual implementation. In this section, I try to answer the basic research questions outlined in the first chapter of this book, and by answering those I also address an apparently simpler question: can the combination of two crises yield a success? Or, at least, can we solve two problems with one solution – *i.e.*, improving our use of law and economics in policy?

Section 6.1 below addresses the "*an*", *i.e.* whether this research has concluded that law and economics should indeed be more integrated with RIA. Section 6.2 shows "how" this marriage can take place ("*quomodo*"). Section 6.3 discusses the potential contribution of law and economics in terms of the organization of RIA systems around the world. Section 6.4 draws more concrete policy suggestions for the US and EU systems as described in sections 2 and 3, and on the basis of the findings of Sections 4 and 5. Finally, Section 6.5 concludes by outlining future research questions and paving the way for new work that can be originated by the findings of this study.

6.1. SHOULD LAW AND ECONOMICS BE MORE INTEGRATED WITH THE PRACTICE OF *EX ANTE* IMPACT ASSESSMENT?

As shown in Sections 2 and 3, *ex ante* impact assessment often ignores the issue of individual incentives altogether. In particular, the lack of attention towards the need to consider the individual incentives to comply with legal rules is a major flaw in current IA work, especially in the European Union, and becomes almost pathologic when one looks at the Standard Cost Model, which assumes 100% compliance without spotting problems of inadequate enforcement or limited respect for the rule. The problem is more likely to emerge whenever the legal rule considered in an IA significantly depends on human behavior: absent available arrangements that would lead individuals to align with the objectives of the legal rule, choosing other alternatives – such as changing the environment in which human behavior takes place – may be preferable and more effective.

This is where law and economics can especially help *ex ante* impact assessment. The mainstream definition of law and economics, *i.e.* a discipline that treats legal rules as means to affect individual incentives, here reaches the maximum relevance: when incentives are at stake, a legal and economic analysis that shows how incentives would be affected is way more useful and important than quantitative cost-benefit analysis. Since, in any event, law and economics can encompass both types of assessment, it is fair to state that the answer to this basic research question is yes. Law and economics can and should help RIA in the years to come, but with a big *caveat*: it all depends on "which" law and economics we are talking about.

Our discussion in Section 4 highlighted that neoclassical law and economics has fully permeated RIA practice, especially in the United States, but that this type of analysis has been largely overcome by subsequent developments in social sciences: today, the most important problems legislators have to solve through *ex ante* impact assessment cannot be usefully addressed through neoclassical law and economics and Kaldor-Hicks cost-benefit analysis. The type of law and economics that RIA needs is a more refined, inter-disciplinary and context-aware version of the law and economics we have been using for years. This is why the answer to this research question can only be a "conditional yes". Law and economics can be usefully employed in support of *ex ante* impact assessment to the extent that it is able to incorporate the main insights from behavioral science, from methodological collectivism and the formulation of subjective value judgments, corresponding to long-term objectives set by politicians and policymakers. Put differently, law and economics can help RIA survive its flawed, blurred image of "number cruncher", and achieve a new role of instrument of accountability, transparency and policy coherence.

6.2. IN WHAT WAYS CAN LAW AND ECONOMICS CONTRIBUTE TO THE QUALITY, USEFULNESS AND EFFECTIVENESS OF *EX ANTE* IMPACT ASSESSMENT?

Once we have answered the previous question with a "conditional yes", answering this further question deserves a number of qualifications. In particular, Sections 4 and 5 have reached a number of findings that help addressing this question in detail. Below, I distinguish between phases of the *ex ante* impact assessment process to explain how law and economics can help.

First, law and economics can help RIA in the initial phase of problem identification. In many instances, lack of compliance is not subject to careful investigation, or is completely unknown to policymakers. My example on large exposure reporting in Section 5.5 above showed that lack of awareness of the reasons for non-compliance can lead to very serious consequences. More recent examples, such as the ongoing revision of the EU radio and telecommunications terminal equipment (R&TTE) Directive, show an equally worrying lack of attention for the causes or non-compliance.[426] Even beyond non-compliance, a refined approach to law and economics can help policymakers understand the drivers of human behavior that explain the limited success of existing policies: the example of energy efficiency in Section 5.7, as well as the story of copyright in cyberspace in Section 5.8 add more detail to this finding: identifying the problem in an *ex ante* impact assessment should mean investigating the causes and drivers of emerging (suboptimal) outcomes, and – where human behavior is a major cause – analyzing the potential behavioral biases and other market imperfections that hamper the achievement of more socially optimal results.

Second, law and economics can help policymakers in the identification of viable policy alternatives. My past experience suggests that this already occurs as a result of better problem identification. In addition, a law and economics approach can help in the assessment of the basic preconditions for seeking certain non-regulatory solutions, as well as in the identification of types of remedies and rules that have already been identified in the literature. The former case occurs whenever policymakers – as they increasingly do, especially in Brussels – explore the possibility for self- and co-regulation as possible solutions to an existing policy problem. Assessing the effectiveness and likely efficiency of those policy alternatives requires a structured analysis, aimed at verifying the extent to which the interest of private regulators would be in line with that of society as a whole; this assessment would include, *i.a.* an assessment of the governance of private regulatory arrangements, the likely effects on competition in affected markets, the representation of all interests in the activity of the private regulatory body, and the possibility of monitoring and evaluating over time the outcomes of this form of regulation.[427] In addition, as already mentioned, policymakers can use law and economics to identify otherwise unknown policy

[426] See Directive of 9 March 1999 of the European Parliament and of the Council on Radio Equipment and Telecommunications Terminal Equipment and the mutual recognition of their conformity (1999–04–07 OJ No L 91/10). A public consultation was opened by the Commission in 2010 (see http://ec.europa.eu/enterprise/sectors/rtte/public-consultation/index_en.htm) and the revision of the Directive is ongoing. The roadmap for the revision, which highlights the "low level of compliance", is available online at http://ec.europa.eu/governance/impact/planned_ia/docs/197_entr_radio_equipment_en.pdf.

[427] See, in particular on transnational private regulation, Cafaggi, F. (2010), *New Foundations for Transnational Private Regulation*, EUI Working Paper RSCAS 2010/53. See also Fuchs, D. and A. Kalfagianni (2010), *The Causes and Consequences of Private Food Governance*, Business and Politics 12(3). www.bepress.com/bap/vol12/iss3/art5/.

alternatives: my example of spectrum policy in Section 5.1 above shows how previous taxonomies identified in law and economics – from the four rules in Calabresi and Melamed (1972) to the six rules in Ayres (2005) and further optional rules in Fennell (2002), to time-shifting rules, optional law, and "pragmatically libertarian rules" – can at least propose viable alternatives, irrespective of whether such policy options will ultimately be chosen or not.

Third, what I have termed a more refined, inter-disciplinary and context-aware version of the law and economics can – or better, should – help RIA out of the tight boundaries of Neoclassical law and economics in assessing the impact of alternative policy options. This depends on several findings in this book, which suggest that Kaldor-Hicks cost-benefit analysis should be kept as only one of several criteria to be used in *ex ante* policy appraisal. Today, law and economics scholarship mostly condemns this form of cost-benefit analysis as obsolete and methodologically flawed due to the reliance on perfect rationality and methodological individualism, and due to the need to compare and aggregate individual preferences. To the contrary, the analysis of incentives, though not always conducive to a monetization of benefits and costs, can prove way more useful in guiding policymakers towards spotting the best policy decision, as our examples on private antitrust enforcement and tying of retail financial services in Sections 5.3 and 5.4 above showed.

To be sure, this requires that law and economics helps RIA deal with distributional issues, since, contrary to what Chicago economists have stated for decades, the allocation of the slices dramatically affects the size of the pie. However, I am afraid that, at this stage, the evolution of this discipline has not led to significant scientific results. As stated above, at the end of Section 4, the scientific approach that is more likely to survive the next generation is Guido Calabresi's *justice before efficiency* rather than Posner's *efficiency as justice,* also in line with developments in other social sciences, which seem to point at a broader acceptance of weak forms of paternalism in the making of public policy.

Finally, where law and economics does not help public policymakers in the *ex ante* phase is in the definition of the ultimate objectives of policy intervention. This conclusion is not straightforward, if one thinks that the main attempt of neoclassical law and economics was to suggest a single goal for public policy, *i.e.* economic efficiency and the maximization of wealth as a proxy for welfare. To the contrary, today lawyer-economists increasingly recognize that there is no such thing as a single policy goal, and that the main role of *ex ante* assessment should be that of paving the way for better policy appraisal throughout the policy process, and thus not only at the *ex ante*, but also at the *interim* and *ex post* phases of the policy cycle.

The combination of these suggestions will be seen as somewhat revolutionary by the readers that have been following the debate on RIA in the past decades. The mainstream scholarly and political approaches to RIA have so far highlighted the potential for RIA in setting objectives, at the same time downplaying the usefulness of RIA in the analysis of distributional impacts. I would argue the opposite applies: politicians should set objectives, and RIA – together with other, complementary forms of evaluations – should help achieve them.

Summing up, the answer to this research question is again mixed: as it stands, law and economics can help already understand the policy problem and identify a broader set of alternatives. Law and economics can also be of invaluable help in replacing the monetization of costs and benefits with an insightful analysis of individual incentives. In addition, law and economics should develop in a way that helps policymakers deal with distributional impacts and increasingly recognizes the importance of social norms. But law and economics should not help in the identification of broader policy objectives (if not operational objectives closely linked to the proposed policy's scope). In this respect, I fully subscribe to what Robert Pirsig stated in his highly praised "*Zen and the Art of Motorcycle Maintenance*:

> *Traditional scientific method has always been at the very best, 20–20 hindsight. It's good for seeing where you've been. It's good for testing the truth of what you think you know, but it can't tell you where you ought to go.*[428]

6.3. WHAT DOES THE LAW AND ECONOMICS LITERATURE IMPLY FOR THE DESIGN AND ORGANIZATION OF POLICY EVALUATION WITHIN GOVERNMENT?

Based on the findings of this study, it seems fair to state that the functional school of law and economics has already provided some valuable contribution to the debate on the role and function of RIA in a chain of delegation and oversight aimed at the making of efficient public policy, especially thanks to the work of Matthew Adler and Eric Posner.[429] However, there is more that law and economics can contribute to the design and organization of RIA in the years to come.

A first lesson that can be drawn, is related to the role of *ex ante* impact assessment within the overall organization of policymaking in a legal system. The view emerged in this book is that RIA should be used chiefly as an instrument of policy coherence. This means that the role of RIA should mostly revolve around the basic principle of accountability, since *ex ante* impact assessment – regardless of whether benefits and costs are quantified and monetized – illustrates the underlying rationale of policy solutions enshrined in

428 Pirsig, R. (1974), *Zen and the Art of Motorcycle Maintenance*, William Morrow & Company, New York, pt 3, ch.24.

429 See Section 4.4.1 above for a more detailed explanation.

legislative proposals. More precisely, policymakers are often elected on the basis of a given political program, which requires the setting of objectives and long-term goals: the extent to which individual legislative proposals contribute to those goals should become a key factor in future *ex ante* impact assessment. Governments elected on the basis of political agendas that devote significant attention to distributional issues will have to motivate how their policy decisions contribute to socially desirable outcomes; governments committed towards improving the environment should explain how they plan to achieve their goals through the *ex ante* impact assessment process, as well as with subsequent policy appraisal tools. Governments committed to increasing the competitiveness of certain economic sectors will explain in *ex ante* RIA what they expect to achieve with their proposals. Since most governments around the world are committed on all those fronts, *ex ante* RIA (together with a carefully planned and widely disclosed legislative planning) should incorporate an analysis of the expected outcomes of legislation, potential risks connected to unforeseen factors or unexpected behavioral responses, etc. Accountability also means that stakeholders should be able to observe how a given government agenda unfolds through individual legislative proposals, and the reason why government is proposing certain policy actions to achieve its goals: in this respect, especially in presidential democracies, RIA can serve its purpose much more effectively if it is taken as an instrument of policy coherence, rather than pure number crunching (and often, number guessing). This, in turn, forces policymakers to disclose their ultimate goals, rather than hide behind a fake representation of the ultimate objectives of their policies (economic efficiency).

That said, RIA does not only take place in governments. The issue whether independent agencies and Parliaments should undertake RIA has remained outside the scope of this study. To be sure, there seems to be no reason why more sophisticated law and economic analysis of legislation should not be used to enlighten the expected outcomes and impacts of proposed policies, also in sectoral regulation or in issues debate within Congress. Against this background, extending RIA beyond mere secondary legislation makes sense. The "RIA as policy coherence" approach fits much better the daily working of parliaments than the "RIA as efficiency" one. As is slowly happening at least in EU policymaking, the IA document can gradually become a representation of the main expectations, concerns, plans and goals that the proposing institution is attaching to a given policy proposal, incorporating over time the information provided by all stakeholders and an updated view of the effects that the policy action at hand is likely to produce in the future. Accordingly, there seems to be room for this type of RIA also in Parliaments: on the other hand, if RIA is presented as rocket science, not only the political dialogue is polluted by a distorted message (RIA is *never* rocket science), but also parliamentarians and congressmen are unlikely to welcome it, since it is proposed as a key reference that should constrain their freedom to vote.

In the case of independent (*i.e.* non-governmental) agencies, RIA is already widely used in a limited number of countries (*e.g.* the United Kingdom, but also Italy). In many cases, especially when RIA is applied to sectoral regulation, emphasis on market efficiency is likely to play a bigger role. At the same time, more socially relevant issues (*e.g.* universal service in the provision of services of general interest) should be kept in the picture as mandatory goals. Sectoral legislation normally contains already this form of political compromise: accordingly, the role of an independent sectoral regulator in performing RIA should be that of explaining to the targeted stakeholders how a given regulatory proposal is likely to contribute to the overall goals set in the framework legislation that guides the regulator's activity in that specific policy domain. Financial regulators will have the key role of developing a RIA model that accounts for impacts on financial stability, rather than mere efficiency (see the example on large exposure reporting in Section 5.5 above). Many regulators in network industries will have the key task of reconciling economic efficiency with the need to secure long-term resilience of critical infrastructure, especially if framework regulations in their sector of activity will incorporate these stances.[430]

For what concerns the issue of "nudging administrations", as illustrated in Section 4.4.1 above, the use of RIA as an instrument of policy coherence requires strong oversight at the highest political level. While, on the one hand, using Kaldor-Hicks cost-benefit analysis as a signal and a monitoring tool can distort the incentives of involved players and create equally distorted expectations on external stakeholders, a viable alternative has not been fully developed to date, and should be subject to more careful elaboration at national level, based on the specific legal and policy context featured by every country. To be sure, administrations cannot be nudged only with Kaldor-Hicks: showing net benefits is not only easy (it takes some quick manipulation of the economics), it is also useless and sometimes dangerous.

This issue brings me to three supplementary considerations, related to the role of oversight, the use of ex post evaluation and the need for additional institutional gatekeepers. As regards oversight, implementing a more sophisticated RIA system based (also) on law and economics in a government administration means that there should be a central oversight body endowed with sufficient capacity to detect the soundness of the scientific approach adopted, as well as the consistency between the impact assessment and long-term

430 For example, the EU Digital Agenda has now fully incorporated the need to protect critical infrastructure. See Actions 28–41, at http://ec.europa.eu/information_society/newsroom/cf/pillar.cfm?pillar_id=45. For a detailed overview, see Renda, A. and B. Hämmerli (2010), *Protecting Critical Infrastructure in the EU*, Centre for European Policy Studies, Brussels, December 2010.

policy goals set by the government. This implies that the central oversight body is skilled in law and economics, as well as in several technical fields of legislation (the current OIRA hosts not only economists and lawyers, but also toxicologists, environmental experts, and many other professionals). It also implies that the oversight body is rooted in the centre-of-government: an external oversight body (or a body of experts) would not be able to assess the policy coherence aspect of RIA, and would not increase the "ownership" of the policy proposal by the government itself; at the same time, an oversight body rooted in the centre of government, but unable to check the soundness of the underlying legal and economic approach to the impact assessment would simply become a club of readers, unable to provide any guidance on how to translate policy problems into political solutions.

At the same time, this emerging view of RIA as an instrument of policy coherence requires that the *interim* and the *ex post* phases of policy appraisal be strengthened. The European Commission seems to be potentially converging towards this policy coherence approach much more than the US, at least based on some recent developments in the EU better regulation agenda. Policy coherence must be checked along the implementation phases of the policy cycle, and be translated into feedback for future regulatory initiatives. Behavioral effects and the evolution of social norms must be monitored over time to ensure the effectiveness of policy decisions, and evaluated *ex post* to ensure that policy learning takes place. That said, the current evaluation practice mostly looks at another aspect of policy: whether the quantification and monetization of benefits and costs was correct. This is, in my opinion, a futile exercise, since the *ex ante* estimates are unlikely to be precise. What really counts is assessing if those estimates led to adopting a wise policy option, and whether the current policy in place is helping the achievement of policy goals.

For what concerns the role of additional institutional gatekeepers, the "RIA as policy coherence" approach might make it more difficult to challenge RIA in court on the basis of failure to perform full-fledged cost-benefit analysis. At the same time, judicial oversight could be introduced for the mere failure to perform impact assessment. In addition, the need to create forms of external *ex post* oversight of the soundness of the regulatory appraisal process leaves room for the Courts of Auditors, external expert groups representing various stakeholders, competition authorities and groups of academic advisors to act as gatekeepers of the system, helping a more constructive dialogue through an analysis of the impact assessments performed in support of policy decisions.

Finally, as I observed in Section 4 above, it is important to provide a clear answer to the question "if" and "when" policymakers should engage in RIA for a given policy proposal. My "meta-RIA" approach as illustrated in Section 4.4.1 above led to concluding that the principle of proportionate analysis should be better qualified: depending on the stage of the policy process, the questions to be addressed should differ, and the extent to which certain answers are delegated to the *ex post* phase should be addressed more carefully, in order to enable a more efficient use of resources to be allocated to the policy appraisal process. I will get back to this issue in the next section, especially looking at the future of the EU impact assessment system.

6.4. WHAT WOULD A STRONGER INTEGRATION BETWEEN LAW AND ECONOMICS AND RIA MEAN FOR THE US AND EU IMPACT ASSESSMENT SYSTEMS?

The two RIA systems analyzed in Sections 2 and 3 – the US and EU – are radically different in scope, purpose, methodology, number of analyses, oversight and also overall "success" – defined as the extent to which the system is mainstreamed in the policy process. Accordingly, the conclusions drawn in this study cannot be said to potentially affect the two systems in one and the same way. To the contrary, the lessons that can be drawn for the US system are to a large extent different from those that can be addressed to the EU system. Below, I discuss briefly the potential lesson for the United States, and focus more on the European Union, a system that I have gotten to know more directly in the past few years.

The US RIA system is currently under attack for at least three different reasons: its scope, its methodology, and the use of nudging. As regards the first two, they seem to be intimately related: the exclusive application of RIA to secondary legislation makes it easier to use Kaldor-Hicks cost-benefit analysis as a reference methodology, under the assumption that such methodology is a viable tool to enable principal-agent monitoring. However, two important *caveats* much be spelled out. First, in certain fields secondary legislation poses important distributional issues, as well as problems with social norms and public goods; when these problems are at hand, the use of neoclassical economics as a theoretical framework seems likely to hamper the effectiveness of the principal-agent scheme that underlies US RIA. Put differently, controlling the Environmental Protection Agency by simply checking that rules have satisfied Kaldor-Hicks does not ensure that the need to preserve the environment of biodiversity has been fully taken into account; controlling the Occupational Safety and Health Administration in this way does not sufficiently guarantee safety. Accordingly, this book leads to concluding that the Kaldor-Hicks cost-benefit analysis should be replaced with a more refined and updated methodology also in the US RIA system.

Moreover, we also concluded that (a more sophisticated version of) RIA can be usefully implemented also outside the rather narrow scope of secondary legislation, and permeate parliaments and independent agencies. If this were the case in the United States, then the current version of RIA, tailored for government agencies, could not be usefully transplanted. Major changes are needed to make RIA useful and compatible with the context of independent agencies and (even more importantly) parliaments: without those changes, the transplant would lead to an immediate, inevitable rejection. The changes that would be needed imply, alas, abandoning the current emphasis on cost-benefit analysis, and embracing a more useful concept of policy coherence, as well as openness to stakeholder opinions and interests.

Finally, as regards the use of nudging techniques, my impression is that this use of "gentle push" can be interpreted in at least two different ways. If we are simply referring to nudging as the attempt to inspire individual behavior by showing citizens which courses of action would be good "for themselves" at the moment of choosing, then the application of nudging is likely to be very narrow in scope, and confined to all those case in which systematic behavioral biases lead consumers to make undesired mistakes, which they will regret afterwards. However, if nudging means a more aggressive form of libertarian paternalism, this may mean that, while preserving the possibility for individuals or businesses to choose whatever course of conduct, the government will take action to persuade them to adopt a socially sustainable behavior, *i.e.* what would be "good for society", rather than "good for themselves". This latter version is of course much more debatable in political terms: not only it implies a potentially more intrusive role of the state in individual decisions; it also implies that governments formulate independent value judgments, and use those judgments to steer individual behavior. I do not disagree with this view, and am confident in stating that the need for such value judgments to orient also *ex ante* policy appraisal is supported by recent developments in social sciences. At the same time, I am also aware that different political views can lead to widely diverging opinions on the extent to which the visible hand of the government can and should interfere with the invisible hand of individual freedom.

The potential consequences of this book's findings for the EU Impact Assessment system and overall smart regulation agenda are more far-reaching. Policy recommendations can be drawn as regards many aspects of the current EU system, including; (i) the overall approach to IA; (ii) the scope of the analysis; (iii) the principle of proportionate analysis; (iv) the methodology used; (v) the most appropriate forms of oversight; (vi) the IA activity in the European Parliament and in the Council; (vii) the role of indicators and *ex post* evaluation; and (viii) the need to create a multi-level chain of impact assessments, which involves also Member States of the European union in a quest for enhanced policy coherence in the EU. Below, I briefly comment on each of those eight fronts.

First, as regards the overall approach to Impact Assessment, the European Commission rightly decided to depart from exclusive reliance on quantitative cost-benefit analysis when introducing the system back in 2002, also based on the wise indications of the Mandelkern report. At the same time, the Commission seems to be getting it right when it announces that, in the future, more attention will be dedicated to *ex post* evaluation in order to "close" the policy cycle. However, the good news end here. A look at the practice of impact assessment in Brussels reveals a persisting and still stunning lack of skills, a growing emphasis towards administrative burdens reductions, and no interest whatsoever for the analysis of incentives as opposed to the quantification of impacts. Even the new Communication on Smart Regulation adopted in October 2010, though emphasizing the need for more *ex post* evaluation, relates this change mostly to the need to "identify new opportunities to simplify legislation and reduce administrative burdens".[431] Accordingly, the EU impact assessment system remains suspended in a sort of political limb, with weak emphasis on quantification of impacts, but also weak relation to high-level political goals, as also observed by authoritative commentators. This book suggests that, of the two opposite directions, the European Commission should move towards a better link between overarching policy goals (politically set and monitored over time), and the methodology chosen to achieve them (adopted in the *ex ante* impact assessment). In this respect, recent calls for stronger involvement of the European Parliament and the Council in the decisions of which proposals should undertake IA would enhance the role of IA as a tool that supports high quality policy proposals within a principal-agent mechanisms, where the Commission is the agent and the politically elected bodies the principal.[432]

Second, for what concerns the scope of the analysis, the EU system made a very ambitious, but also encouraging step in the direction of a more pervasive RIA system, by getting rid of the "R" in RIA and creating an impact assessment system that applies to binding and non-binding policy documents, and to primary as well as secondary legislation. At the same time, this decision was not accompanied by sufficient arrangements aimed at diversifying the type of analysis needed, the types of questions asked at each stage of the policy process, as well as making the Commission accountable for deciding to undertake IA or not on a policy proposal. This is why the decision on the scope of IA in the European Union has remained orphan of accompanying measures.

Third, the previous paragraph leads to further reflection, in particular as regards the use of the principle of proportionate analysis and the need to "ask the right questions, at the right time and in the right sequence". As already recalled,

431 See the Communication from the Commission to the European Parliament, the Council, the European Economic and Social Committee and the Committee of the Regions, *Smart Regulation in the European Union*, COM(2010)543, 8 October 2010, at 2.1.

432 Renda, A. *et al.* (2009), *Policymaking in the EU; achievements, challenges and proposals for reform*, Centre for European Policy Studies, Brussels.

the EU better regulation agenda contemplates a chain of IAs over the policy cycle, from the initial stage of broad strategic document to subsequent stages, in which the policy initiative is translated into a legislative document. This feature of the IA in Brussels calls for a careful application of the principle of proportionality, as well as of the selection of methodologies that are more appropriate at each step of the policy process. In particular, a "policy cycle" approach to the selection of the "right questions" to be addressed at each policy stage is needed in order to ensure that resources are correctly allocated. Against this background, using IA efficiently means investing effort and resources in *ex ante* appraisal up to the point where the input provided by the IA allows the decision-maker to make "the right choice", or at least a reasonably educated guess. A useful example is the impact assessment performed on White Papers, such as the one illustrated in our example on private antitrust enforcement in Section 5.3 above. As these documents normally contain an indication of the direction the Commission has decided to undertake in order to address a specific policy problem, the key issues that should be tackled at this stage certainly include a thorough assessment of the need to intervene, and to do it at EU level. Thus, the subsidiarity test and the analysis of the zero option should play a paramount role in these IAs; in addition, a scenario analysis corresponding to alternative policy choices is certainly helpful to justify a specific approach the Commission considers to be preferable over alternative policy choices. Failing to assess the impact of the zero option and to perform the subsidiarity test at an early stage of the policy process can lead to undesirable results in terms of the efficiency of the overall process: what happens if, after an IA on a broad strategy document, in the IA on the final legislative document the analysis of the zero option (or, also, the subsidiarity test) shows that the proposal is a dead end, at least in cost-benefit terms? Many resources would have been invested in vain.[433] A possible way to approach the problem of timing and efficient use of resources

433 Conversely, investing too much effort in quantifying the impact of specific policy measures already at the White Paper stage makes little sense from an economic perspective, as the final policy choice will be taken only after a new legislative document, at least two rounds of consultation, the opinions of a number of EU institutions (EESC, CoR, etc.) and the input of Parliament and Council. Currently, many IAs performed by the Commission carry an in-depth analysis of options that are not translated into final policy choices at the end of the legislative *iter*. For example, the IA on the proposed "Directive on the cross-border transfer of registered office" in 2007 concluded that it was "not clear that adopting a directive would represent the least onerous way of achieving the objectives set", and that it would be "more appropriate to wait until the impacts of those developments can be fully assessed and the need and scope for any EU action better defined". However desirable this result may appear, it must also be noticed that it was reached after two rounds of consultation (1997 and 2002), the work performed by a high-level group and a constant involvement of stakeholders before the IA was finally performed on the proposed directive. Part of this effort could have been avoided, had the IA been carried out at an earlier stage with a specific focus on the "zero option", subsidiarity and proportionality. The same can be said of other IAs, such as the IA on the "Proportionality between Capital and Control in Listed Companies".

is to revisit the IA guidelines by creating an "incremental" or "staged" approach to IA, such as the simple one reported below, in Figure 23.[434] As shown in the Figure, after the Green Paper stage, the first IA is normally performed on the way towards the White Paper or a Communication. In this phase, the key questions to be addressed are: is there a problem? Is action at EU level needed? What alternative policy options may be envisaged? These questions should ideally be addressed from a law and economics perspective, aimed at identifying the causes and drivers of emerging policy problems. Needless to say, if these questions are answered negatively, the IA would indicate a "dead end". Once the White Paper sets the general approach that can be undertaken by the Commission, a consultation process leads to the refinement of such approach, and its translation into concrete policy proposals. This is the stage at which more in-depth analyses such as cost-benefit analysis (CBA), cost-effectiveness analysis (CEA) or in-depth law and economics analysis must be undertaken. Finally, as will be clarified in the next pages, the IA should be updated to reflect the amendments introduced by the Parliament and the Council during co-decision.

Figure 23. An example of "Staged approach" to Impact Assessment

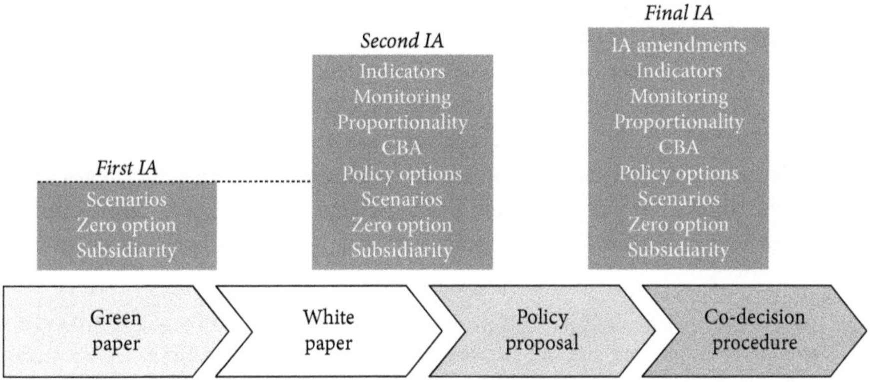

Fourth, the methodology to be used in Impact Assessment must be chosen with due care, especially in a system with a very broad scope such as the EU impact assessment system. This book suggests that mainstream cost-benefit analysis can be useful only in a very narrow subset of the policy problems addressed by the European Commission in its impact assessments. To the contrary, especially

434 I proposed one such system in an earlier paper, back in 2008: the proposal was later taken on board by the European Court of Auditors in the draft version of its report on the EU Impact Assessment System, but not included in the final version of the report. See European Court of Auditors, *Impact Assessments in the EU institutions: do they support decision-making?*, Special Report no. 3, 2010, available online at http://eca.europa.eu/portal/pls/portal/docs/1/5412743.PDF. The draft version of the Report was much longer and way more critical, but was ultimately shortened and cut after bilateral exchanges with the European Commission.

whenever individual incentives, compliance and enforcement are at stake, a refined version of law and economics can help policymakers take informed decisions. In all other cases, a qualitative indication of the pros and cons of different policy options, such as a scorecard exercise, can prove useful. The decision about the right methodology must be taken by the central oversight body in charge of the impact assessment system, together with the proposing administration, at the beginning of the impact assessment process. Currently, no such decision is taken, which weakens the role of the oversight body and its capacity to monitor and support in due time the impact assessment work being carried out by the administration.

Fifth, the problem of strengthening oversight to improve the quality of IAs has long been discussed in Brussels. As I reported in other publications, since the end of the 1990s the issue whether a dedicated, external oversight body should be created to oversee the better regulation agenda was always hot at the EU level. Since 2003, several authors – including myself – have advocated stronger oversight of Commission IAs, which led the European Commission to appoint the Impact Assessment Board. Today, several options are still on the table, including: (i) strengthening the IAB with more resources and support staff; (ii) enhancing/institutionalizing the role of existing networks such as the HLG of national regulatory experts and the HLG of independent stakeholders[435]; (iii) mandating consultation on draft IAs; (iv) creating a new agency in charge of oversight; (v) providing for *ex post* scrutiny of a sample of IAs by the European Court of Auditors[436]; or (vi) creating a representation of businesses within the Commission Secretariat General, along the lines of the UK Risk and Regulation Advisory Council (formerly "Better Regulation Task Force" and "Better Regulation Commission"). In previous research, I have advocated for public

435 For example, *ex post* oversight could be strengthened by mandating that existing High Level Groups (HLGs) dealing with IA-related issues review a sample of Commission IAs every year and issue suggestions for improvement. The HLGs at hand would be the HLG of national regulatory experts and the HLG of independent stakeholders (for issues concerning the measurement of administrative burdens). This option would provide a rather "soft" solution to the need for increased accountability of the Commission's work on IA, providing for an "institutionalization" of existing expert groups. This would be particularly welcome in case the EU agenda heads towards some form of convergence between the IA system and methodology at EU and national level, in line with one of the issues identified by the Commission in the Communication on the second strategic review of better regulation in the EU.

436 In the UK, the National Audit Office reviews a sample of RIAs carried out by UK departments every year, highlights best and worst practices and issues recommendations. The replicability of the "NAO review" in Brussels is however difficult, as the ECA would have to be empowered with a function that is quite far from its current mission and competences. If the IA system at EU level were more explicitly targeted towards an efficient use of Commission resources, then the ECA could be given a broader role of ensuring that the Commission has spent its budget for IAs properly: but the ECA will hardly be able to comment on the quality of economic analysis contained in a sample of Commission IAs. In short, this option would require the creation of an additional unit within the ECA, which would remain rather separate from the mission of the institution.

consultation on draft Impact Assessments as the most viable way of ensuring that administrations think outside the box, consider all possible options and provide all needed data for a comprehensive analysis of the policy problem. At the same time, only relying on stronger public consultation would create risks of capture of the European Commission, and does not guarantee a sound law and economics approach such as the one advocated in this book. To achieve the latter result, a stronger Impact Assessment Board, with the participation of experts in inter-disciplinary analysis and behavioral sciences should be created – possibly with the participation of experts from the rather idle Bureau of Economic Policy Advisors of the European Commission, adequately re-staffed.

Sixth, no reform of the EU impact assessment model would lead anywhere if IAs keep being so short-lived. At the same time, there seem to be little prospects for fulfilling the original promises carved in stone by the Inter-Institutional Agreement on Better Lawmaking and by the Common Approach to Impact Assessment. If the EU impact assessment system will remain as it is, with no real tie with long-term EU policy goals, the involvement of the European Parliament and the Council in the drafting of Impact Assessments is unlikely to materialize. To the contrary, the European Commission could assist the Parliament and the Council in drafting IAs on their own amendments, just as in the US the OIRA has been offering advice to the Congressional Budget Office for the drafting of certain *ad hoc* policy evaluations. For strategic Commission initiatives included in the policy agenda, the need to update the IA document during the co-decision procedure is almost a "must": without a fully updated impact assessment document, closing the policy cycle and involving other EU institutions and Member States would simply be impossible – this, in turn, would mean that also the current objectives of the EU smart regulation agenda would not be achieved. In summary, a strong central body in the Commission, supported by economic advisors skilled in law and economics, should select together with the European Parliament and the Council the strategic initiatives that should undergo in-depth Impact Assessment in the Commission's yearly agenda; depending on the stage of the policy cycle at which the proposal can be located, the key questions to be answered should be selected by the central oversight body; there should be consultation on draft IAs, and update of those IAs during co-decision. All the analytical work should be performed by the European Commission.

Seventh, the need to update the IA document overtime becomes stronger as the European Commission has expressed its desire to "close the policy cycle" by expanding the use of *ex post* evaluation, and making such evaluation a mandatory step before any new *ex ante* Impact Assessment is performed. In this respect, it must be observed that Commission IAs almost increasingly feature a choice of indicators that will enable monitoring and evaluation over time, even though these indicators are not always properly chosen, and no one can assure they will be applied. In the future, a number of refinements should be introduced: (i) indicators should be chosen based on the specific objectives of the policy proposal, as specified in the introductory sections of the Impact Assessment; (ii) indicators should also reflect the policy coherence between the objectives of the specific policy proposal and the longer-term objectives of the European Union in the specific policy domain in which the proposal can be located; (iii) indicators should be revised during co-decision; and (iv) the same indicators should become the basis for tracking progress in the implementation of the policy action in Member States, as well as collecting data on the performance of the policy over time. This, and only this, means having a chance to close the policy cycle.

Eight, there is a need for a coordinated action of the EU and member states in order to achieve multi-level convergence in the use of Impact Assessment tools. This has proven to be prohibitively difficult in the past years, also due to the fact that the Commission was expecting from Member States a mirror image of its own impact assessment system. To the contrary, the European Commission should involve Member States in the performance of key IA steps in the monitoring of the implementation and enforcement phases of the adopted policy action. This would help Commission policies keep their relation with the ultimate policy goals the Commission intended to pursue at the very beginning: the same goals that are currently lost very quickly, if not instantaneously, in the policy process of the European Union.

Summing up, insights from law and economics suggest that the EU Impact Assessment system should be substantially reformed. This would lead to a system in which the democratically elected EU bodies – the European Parliament and the Council – act as principals in the policy process, choosing which proposals would deserve Impact Assessment (on the basis of clear-cut criteria) and delegating all IA activity to the European Commission, including the update of the IA document during co-decision. A system in which the Commission performs Impact Assessment based on more flexible methodologies, fine-tuned both on the basis of the specific stage of the policy process at which the proposal is located, and on the IA techniques that fits best the specifics of the policy problem. An IA system in which incentives play a more important role, and are always considered, especially when public goods and long-term objectives of EU policies are at stake. And a system in which Member States contribute to tracking the progress and performance of EU policies through the provision of data and a virtuous market for ideas and policy suggestions. Finally, a system in which *ex ante* policy appraisal is only a piece of a more complex puzzle, in which some issues are addressed at the *ex post* evaluation phase, rather than uselessly subject to in-depth analysis *ex ante*.

But most importantly, the EU Impact Assessment should become an instrument of policy coherence. In particular, coherence with the long term goals of the European Union, as enshrined in the EU Treaty, but also in the articulated long-term strategies of the European Union, including, most notably, the EU2020 strategy, its ambition to pursue smart, sustainable and inclusive growth, and the many indicators that are being developed under the umbrellas of its seven flagship initiatives. Since the European Commission is known as being the "guardian of the Treaty" in the European Union, it should also act as the ultimate guardian of the long-term policy objectives that have been agreed upon by political consensus of the 27 Member States of the European Union. Once these objectives have been identified, the Commission will have a set of goals to pursue with its proposed policies, and will have to address the issue whether command and control policies, self-regulatory policies, nudging or other forms of regulatory intervention are the most suited to effectively achieve these goals in the years to come. This is what I mean by policy coherence: linking the *ex ante* and *ex post* evaluation of EU policies to the promises made at EU level, and using the IA system to avoid that politically set goals are then easily lost in the day-to-day policy jungle of co-decision procedures.

6.5. AGENDA FOR FUTURE RESEARCH

This book is an attempt to lay the first stone of what should, in my opinion, become a much more sophisticated dialogue in the years to come. Below, I outline some of the most promising avenues for future research I have identified during the drafting of this work. I start from individual research paths in law and economics and in policy appraisal, and then explore new research directions on the integration between the two disciplines.

As far as law and economics is concerned, this book has argued that more research would be needed on the incorporation of independent value judgments and on the treatment of distributional issues in cost-benefit analysis. At the same time, scholars in this field should seek to find ways to re-build the prescriptive power of law and economics after the advent of behavioral law and economics, which destroyed most of the self-confidence exhibited by neoclassical lawyer-economists in the past years. In this respect, asymmetric or libertarian paternalism do not seem to have substantially addressed the current lack of normative guidance from law and economics. Moreover, research on how to overcome methodological individualism in law and economics would help building a bridge between this and other, equally enlightening social sciences, such as positive political theory, moral philosophy, psychology and sociology, which can help policymakers understand the causes of social actions and the mechanisms underlying public policymaking: the inspiring contributions of scholars such as Herbert Hovenkamp back in the mid-1990s has been almost neglected in recent years, and this study attempted a rediscovery that I hope will trigger more research in the future. Finally, research on possible taxonomies of legal intervention and alternative forms of regulation would preserve the usefulness of law and economics scholarship for policymaking purposes.

For what concerns the RIA world, this book has argued that the international regulatory reform community should take a deep breath and reflect further, before proposing models of RIA in developed and developing countries. This comment is mostly addressed to the OECD and the World Bank, which sponsor RIA worldwide, often without placing it in the national context and ignoring the treatment of distributional issues in RIA. The main reasons for the huge adoption-implementation gap already denounced by authoritative scholars in the field can partly be related to the fact that the usefulness of the RIA model sponsored so far at the international level hardly justifies the skills and resources needed to put it in place. A more open approach to possible methodologies for *ex ante* impact assessment, including the use of behavioral sciences and the departure from methodological individualism, would certainly contribute to a more coherent use of RIA within the policy process adopted by national governments. Likewise, this book has highlighted the need for more research on the "staged approach" to impact assessment, as well as on the allocation of resources between (different phases of) *ex ante* and (various stages of) *ex post* policy appraisal as ways to really close the policy cycle. This would also lead to a different view of cornerstones of regulatory reform, such as the principle of proportionate analysis and the interaction between the analysis of the stock (including the administrative burdens it generates) and the appraisal of the flow of legislation. Finally, this book has also argued in favor of more research on indicators: this can be applied both at the systemic level (*i.e.* better ways of tracking the implementation of RIA in the policy process); at the individual IA level (*i.e.* comparing the relative quality of different IA documents); and at the individual policy level (*i.e.* developing indicators to enable monitoring and evaluation of individual policies).

To the extent that readers will find the scientific angle adopted in this research a promising one, more research will be needed to assess the extent to which law and economics, in the refined version advocated here, can find citizenship in the RIA world. This implies that the modeling of incentives, the assessment of patterns of compliance, the development of more advanced criteria to determine efficiency, fairness and justice impacts of alternative policy options would be needed in the years to come in order to inspire better impact assessment and policy evaluation work. Likewise, the study of social norms and how to change them to trigger more socially and environmentally sustainable behavior; the analysis of optimal incentives to use public goods; the assessment of the effectiveness of private and public regulation; and the possible uses of nudging and asymmetric paternalism in the context of *ex ante* policy appraisal will constitute each an equally promising research avenue. If researchers will decide to advance in these directions, we may soon be able to announce that law and economics and RIA are not anymore twins separated at birth, but mutually supportive disciplines in the restless search for better lawmaking.

Finally, and perhaps most importantly, future research is likely to shed more light on the possibility for all social sciences to more usefully contribute to the relatively isolated science of policy formulation. The brief account of recent theories of justice given in Section 4.3.3.2 above is perhaps the most revealing. There is little doubt that economics has in the past decades departed from the enlightening foundations laid by Adam Smith, David Hume and some of their inspired successors; similarly, there is no doubt that moral philosophy has had limited impact on policy studies because its prescriptions have remained so far tied to the definition of ideal states of the world, rather than to the reality that policymakers have to face every day. Bringing economics back to its methodological holism, and moral philosophy down to reality are two very promising ways to lay the foundations for a better society, and to bring all social sciences "in the RIA world". For this reason, the interaction between theories of justice, efficiency and fairness should be subject to extensive future research, to which I myself plan to contribute.

SELECTED REFERENCES

Ackerman, F. and L. Heinzerling (2004), *Priceless: On Knowing the Price of Everything and the Value of Nothing*, The New Press.

Ackerman, F., L. Heinzerling and R. Massey (2004), *Applying Cost-Benefit to Past Decisions: Was environmental protection ever a good idea?*, Georgetown Public Law Research Paper No. 576161.

Adler, M. and E.A. Posner (2007), *Happiness Research and Cost-Benefit Analysis*, U of Penn, Inst for Law & Econ Research Paper No. 07–15; U of Penn Law School, Public Law Research Paper No. 07–29; U of Chicago Law & Economics, Olin Working Paper No. 345. Available at SSRN: http://ssrn.com/abstract=999928.

Adler, M.D. (2000), *Beyond Efficiency and Procedure: a Welfarist Theory of Regulation*, 28 Florida State Univ. L. R.

Adler, M.D. (2003), *The Puzzle of "Ex Ante Efficiency": Does Rational Approvability Have Moral Weight?*, 151 U. PA. L. REV. 1255 (2003).

Adler, M.D. (2008), *Risk Equity: A New Proposal*, 32 HARV. ENVTL. L. REV. 1, 27.

Adler, M.D. and C.W. Sanchirico (2006), *Inequality and Uncertainty: Theory and Legal Applications*. University of Pennsylvania Law Review, Vol. 155, p. 279.

Adler, M.D. and E.A. Posner (1999), *Rethinking Cost-Benefit Analysis* (April 1999), University of Chicago Law School, John M. Olin Law & Economics Working Paper No. 72.

Adler, M.D. and E.A. Posner (2000), *Implementing Cost-Benefit Analysis when Preferences are Distorted*, Journal of Legal Studies, vol. 29, issue 2, pages 1105–47.

Adler, M.D. and E.A. Posner (2001), *Cost-Benefit Analysis: Legal, Economic, and Philosophical Perspectives*, Chicago, IL: University of Chicago Press, 2001.

Adler, M.D. and E.A. Posner (2006), *New Foundations of Cost-Benefit Analysis*, Harvard University Press.

Ahdieh, R.B. (2004), *Law's Signal: A Cueing Theory of Law in Market Transition*, 77 Southern California Law Rev. 215.

Ahdieh, R.B. (2009), *Beyond Individualism in Law and Economics*. Emory Public Law Research Paper No. 9–78, Emory Law and Economics Research Paper No. 09–48.

Allais, M. (1952), *Traité d'Economie Pure*, Paris: Impr. Nationale. Translated and edited by Maurice Allais and Ole Hagen as "The Foundations of a Positive Theory of Choice Involving Risk and a Criticism of the Postulates and Axioms of the American School," in Expected Utility Hypotheses and the Allais Paradox: Contemporary Discussions of Decisions Under Uncertainty, 27–145 (Dordrecht, Holland: D. Reidel Publishing, 1979).

Allcott, H. and S. Mullainathan (2010), *Behavior and Energy Policy*. Science. 327(5970): 1204 - 1205

Allio, L. (2008), *The emergence of better regulation in the European Union.* King's college. University of London, London.
Allio, L. and A. Renda (2011), *Evaluation of Administrative Burden Reduction Programmes and their Impacts*, Report for OECD Cutting Red Tape II series, published as Annex B in OECD (2010), *Cutting Red Tape. Why is Administrative Simplification so Complicated?*, PARIS: OECD Publications.
Ambler T. and F. Chittenden. (2009), *Worlds Apart: The EU and British Regulatory Systems*, British Chamber of Commerce.
Andeweg, R. and G.A. Irwin (2009), *Governance and Politics of the Netherlands*, Houndsmill: Palgrave-MacMillan, 3rd edition.
Arcuri, A. (2005), *A Different Reason for de-Coasing Environmental Law and Economics*, European Journal of Law and Economics, Volume 20, Number 2, 225–246.
Arcuri, A. (2008), *Eclecticism in Law and Economics.* Erasmus Law Review, Vol. 1, No. 3.
Arkes, H.R., D. Faust, T.J. Guilmette and K. Hart (1988), *Eliminating the Hindsight Bias*, Journal of Applied Psychology, 73:305–07.
Armstrong, M.A. (2008), *Interaction between Competition and Consumer Policy,* a report for the OFT, OFT 991.
Arnould, R.J. and H. Grabowski (1981), *Auto Safety Regulation: An Analysis of Market Failure*, Bell Journal of Economics, 12:27–48.
Arrow, K.J., Cropper, M.L., Eads, G.C., Hahn, R.W., Lave, L.B., Noll, R.G., *et al.* (eds.). (1996), *Benefit-Cost Analysis in Environmental, Health, and Safety Regulation*, Washington DC: American Enterprise Institute.
Arrow, K.J. *et al.* (1996), *Is There a Role for Benefit-Cost Analysis in Environmental, Health, and Safety Regulation?*, 272 Science 221, 222
Autor, D. and M. Duggan (2003), *The Rise in the Disability Rolls and the Decline in Unemployment*, Quarterly Journal of Economics, 118:157–206.
Ayres, I. (2005), *Optional Law. The Structure of Legal Entitlements*, University of Chicago Press.
Ayres, I. and E. Talley (1995), *Distinguishing between Consensual and Nonconsensual Advantages of Liability Rules*, Yale Law Journal 105 (1):235–53
Ayres, I. and E. Talley (1995), *Solomonic Bargaining: Dividing a Legal Entitlement to Facilitate Coasean Trade*, Yale Law Journal 104 (5):1027–1117
Ayres, I. and J. Braithwaite (1992), *Responsive Regulation: Transcending the Deregulation Debate*, New York: Oxford Univ. Press.
Ayres, I. and J.M. Balkin (1996), *Legal Entitlements as Auctions: Property Rules, Liability Rules, and Beyond*, Yale Law Journal 106 (3):703–50.
Ayres, I. and P.M. Goldbart (2001), *Optimal Delegation and Decoupling in the Design of Liability Rules*, Michigan Law Review 100 (1):1–79
Ayres, I. and P.M. Goldbart (2003), *Correlated Values in the Theory of Property and Liability Rules*, Journal of Legal Studies 32 (1):121–51.
Babcock, L., G. Loewenstein and S. Issacharoff (1997), *Creating Convergence: Debiasing Biased Litigants*, Law and Social Inquiry, 22:913–26.
Babcock, L., X. Wang and G. Loewenstein (1996), *Choosing the Wrong Pond: Social Comparisons in Negotiations that Reflect a Self-Serving Bias*, Quarterly Journal of Economics, 111:1–19.

Bagley, N. and R.L. Revesz (2006), *Centralized Oversight of the Regulatory State*, Columbia L. Rev. Vol. 106, 1260–1329.

Baldwin, R. (2005), *Is better regulation smarter regulation?*, Public Law (Autumn), 485–511.

Baldwin, R. and C. McCrudden (1987), *Regulation and Public Law*, London: Weidenfeld and Nicolson.

Baldwin, R. and J. Black (2007), *Really Responsive Regulation*, LSE Law, Economy and Society working Papers 15/2007.

Barberis, N. and R. Thaler (2002), *A Survey of Behavioral Finance*, available at http://ssrn.com/abstract=327880 or doi:10.2139/ssrn.327880

Bar-Gill, O. and O. Ben-Shahar (2003), *Threatening an 'Irrational' Breach of Contract*, Supreme Court Economic Review, 11:143–70.

Barlow, J.P. (1994), *The Economy of Ideas: Selling Wine without Bottles*, 2.03 Wired 84, 1994.

Barzelay, M. (2007), *Learning from Second-Hand Experience: Methodology for Extrapolation-Oriented Case Research*, Governance 20 (3): 521–543.

Bebchuk, L.A. (1980), *The Pursuit of a Bigger Pie: Can Everyone Expect a Bigger Slice?*, in Symposium on Efficiency as a Legal Concern, 8 Hofstra Law Review 671–709.

Bebchuk, L.A. (1998), *Negative Expected Value Suits*, NBER Working Paper No. W6474.

Becker, G.S. (1968), *Crime and Punishment: An Economic Approach*, Journal of Political Economy, Vol. 76, 169–217.

Becker, G.S. (2000), *A Comment on the Conference on Cost-Benefit Analysis*, 29 J Legal Stud 1151–52.

Becker, G.S. and G.J. Stigler (1977), *De Gustibus Non Est Disputandum*, The American Economic Review Vol. 67, No. 2 (Mar., 1977), 76–90

Becker, G.S. and G.J. Stigler (1974), *Law Enforcement, Malfeasance and Compensation of Enforcers*, Journal of Legal Studies, Vol. 3, 1–18.

Bertelsmann Foundation (2009), *Regulierungskostenmessung, Thesenpapier.* Available at: www.bertelsmann-stiftung.de/cps/rde/xchg/SID-6861EAEB-F8F97DD9/bst/hs.xsl/93908_93969.htm.

Biegelbauer, P. and S. Mayer (2007), *RIA or no RIA: the Dialogue Between Policymakers and Stakeholders in the Regulatory Process in Austria*, ENBR Working Paper No. 10.

Biegelbauer, P. and S. Mayer (2008), *Regulatory Impact Assessment in Austria: Promising Regulations, Disappointing Practices*, in: Critical Policy Analysis 2(2), 118–142.

Black, J. and S. Jacobzone (2009), *Tools for Regulatory Quality and Financial Sector Regulation: A Cross-Country Perspective, OECD Working Papers on Public Governance*, No. 16, OECD Publishing, © OECD. doi:10.1787/218772641848

Blattberg, R.C., G. Getz and J. S. Thomas (2001), *Customer Equity: Building and Managing Relationships as Valuable Assets*, Harvard business publishing.

Blumstein, J.F. (2001), *Regulatory review by the executive office of the President: An overview and policy analysis of current issues*, Duke Law Journal 51(December): 851–899.

Boardman, A.E. (1997), *Cost-benefit Analysis: Concepts and Practice*, Upper Saddle River, NJ: Prentice Hall.

Boden R., J. Froud, A. Ogus and P. Stubbs (1998), *Controlling the Regulators*, London: MacMillan Press.

Böheim, M., A. Renda *et al.* (2006), *Pilot Project on Administrative Burdens*, Report for the European Commission, DG Enterprise, at http://ec.europa.eu/enterprise/policies/better-regulation/files/pilot-study_en.pdf.

Bohlin, E., C. Blackman, S. Forge and A. Renda (2008), *A Common European Spectrum Policy: barriers and prospects*, study for the European Parliament, ITRE Committee, January 2008, available at www.europarl.europa.eu/meetdocs/2004_2009/documents/dv/itre_st_2007_spectrum_poli/ITRE_ST_2007_SPECTRUM_POLICY.pdf

Bosanquet, N. (1983), *Sir Keith's Reading List*, Political Quarterly, 52(3): 324–341.

Bossaerts, P.L. (2009), *What Decision Neuroscience Teaches Us About Financial Decision Making*, Annual Rev. Fin. Econ. 2009, 1:383–404

Botelho *et al.* (2010), *An experimental analysis of grandfathering vs dynamic auctioning in the EU ETS*, Working Paper n. 39/2010, Núcleo de Investigação em Microeconomia Aplicada Universidade do Minho.

Bovens, M. (2006), *Analysing and assessing public accountability: A conceptual framework*, European Law Journal, *13*(4), 447–468.

Bovens, M., Schillemans, T. and T'Hart, P. (2008), *Does public accountability work? An assessment tool*, Public Administration, 86(1), 225–242.

Braithwaite, J. (2002), *Rewards and Regulation*, Journal of Law and Society, Volume 29, Issue 1, 12–26.

Breyer, S. (1990), *Regulation and Deregulation in the United States*, in G. Majone (ed.), *De-regulation or Re-regulation? Regulatory Reform in Europe and the United States*, London: Pinter Publishers.

Bronsteen *et al.* (2010), *Welfare as Happiness*, Georgetown L.J., Vol. 98, 1583.

Brunnermeier, M.K. (2009), *Deciphering the Liquidity and Credit Crunch 2007–2008*, Journal of Economic Perspectives 23(1), 77–100.

Brunsson, N. (1989), *The Organization of Hypocrisy: Talk, Decisions and Actions in Organizations*, Chirchester and New York: John Wiley and Sons.

Buchanan, J. and G. Tullock (1962), *The Calculus of Consent*, Ann Arbor, University of Michigan Press.

Bundestag Economics and Technology Committee (2009), *Schwerpunktsetzung beim Bürokratieabbau ist erfoigreich*, 21 April.

Calabrese E.J. and L.A. Baldwin (2001), *The frequency of U-shaped dose responses in the toxicological literature*, Toxicol. Sci. 2001, 62(2):330–338.

Calabrese E.J. and L.A. Baldwin (2003a), *Hormesis: the dose-response revolution*, Annual Rev. Pharmacol. Toxicol. 2003, 43:175–197.

Calabrese E.J. and L.A. Baldwin (2003b), *Peptides and hormesis*, Crit. Rev. Toxicol. 2003, 33(3–4):355–405.

Calabresi, G. (1970), *The Costs of Accidents. A Legal and Economic Analysis*, New Haven: Yale University Press.

Calabresi, G. (1991), *The Pointlessness of Pareto: Carrying Coase Further*, 100 Yale Law Journal, 1211–1237.

Calabresi, G. and A. Douglas Melamed (1972), *Property Rules, Liability Rules, and Inalienability: One View of the Cathedral*, 85 HARV. L. REV., 1089.

Camerer, C.F. (2008), *The Case for Mindful Economics*, in Caplin, A. and Schotter, A. (ed.), Foundations of Positive and Normative Economics, New York: Oxford University Press, 2008.

Camerer, C.F., G. Loewenstein, and D. Prelec (2004), *Neuroeconomics: Why Economics Needs Brains*, Scandinavian Journal of Economics, 2004, 106(3), 555–579.

Camerer, C.F., S. Issacharoff, G. Loewenstein, T. O'Donoghue and M. Rabin (2003), *Regulation for Conservatives: Behavioral Economics and the Case for 'Asymmetric Paternalism,'* in Symposium: Preferences and Rational Choice: New Perspectives and Legal Implications, University of Pennsylvania Law Review, 151:1211–54.

Camerer, C.F. and H. Kunreuther (1989), *Decision Processes for Low Probability Events: Policy Implications*, Journal of Policy Analysis & Management, 8:565–92.

Camerer, C.F.; G. Loewenstein, and D. Prelec (2005), *Neuroeconomics: How Neuroscience Can Inform Economics*, Journal of Economic Literature, 2005, 43, 9–64.

Campbell, D. (1994), *Ayres versus Coase: An Attempt to Recover the Issue of Equality in Law and Economics*, Journal of Law and Society, Vol. 21, No. 4, 434–463.

Castro, R.J. (2010), *Ex Post Liability Rules in Modern Patent Law*, Intersentia European Law and Economics Series.

Cecot, C., R.W. Hahn, A. Renda and L.S. Schrefler (2007), *An Evaluation of the Quality of Impact Assessment in the European Union with Lessons for the U.S. and the EU*, AEI-Brookings Joint Center Working Paper No. 07–09.

Chang, H.F. (2000a), *A Liberal Theory of Social Welfare: Fairness, Utility, and the Pareto Principle*, 110 Yale L.J. 173.

Chang, H.F. (2000b), *The Possibility of a Fair Paretian*, 110 Yale L.J.251.

Choi, J.P. (2004), *Antitrust Analysis of Tying Arrangements*, CESifo Working Paper, N. 1336, November 2004.

Christensen, T. and Laegreid, P. (eds.) (2001), *New Public Management: The Transformation of Ideas and Practice*, Aldershot: Ashgate.

Clò, S. (2010), *Economic Analysis of the European Climate Policy: the European emissions trading scheme*, http://publishing.eur.nl/ir/repub/asset/20717/Proefschrift%20Stefano%20Clo%20BW%5Blr%5D.pdf

Coase, R.H. (1960), *The Problem of Social Cost*, Journal of Law and Economics, 3:1–44.

Coase, R.H. (1993), *Law and Economics at Chicago*, 36 Journal of Law and Economics 239.

Coleman, J. (2003), *The Grounds of Welfare*, Review of the article "Fairness versus Welfare by Kaplow, L. and S. Shavell, The Yale Law Journal Vol. 112, No. 6 (Apr. 2003), 1511–1543.

Cooper Ramo, J. (2009), *The Age of the Unthinkable: Why the New World Disorder Constantly Surprises Us And What We Can Do About It*, Hachette Book Group, 23 March 2009.

Cooter, R. and T. Ulen (2004), *Law and Economics*, 4th edn, Addison-Wesley Longman.

Cooter, R.D. (1996), *Decentralized Law for a Complex Economy: The Structural Approach to Adjudicating the New Law Merchant*, 144 University of Pennsylvania Law Review 1643–1696.

Cooter, R.D. (2000), *Three effects of social norms*, Oregon Law Review Vol. 79.

Craswell, R. (1991), *Passing On the Costs of Legal Rules: Efficiency and Distribution in Buyer-Seller Relationships*, Stanford Law Review, 1991, Vol. 43, 361.

Cutler, D. and J. Gruber (1996), *Does Public Insurance Crowd Out Private Insurance?*, Quarterly Journal of Economics, 111:391–430.

Darby, M.R. and E. Karni (1973), *Free Competition and the Optimal Amount of Fraud*, Journal of Law and Economics, 16 (April), 67–88.

Dasgupta, N. and A.G. Greenwald (2001), *On the Malleability of Automatic Attitudes: Combating Automatic Prejudice With Images of Admired and Disliked Individuals*, Journal of Personality and Social Psychology, 81:800–14.

De Francesco, F. (2008), *Prerequisites of adoption and patterns of diffusion: the Case of regulatory impact analysis in European Union and OECD member states*, Paper presented at the 58th Political Studies Association Annual Conference Democracy, Governance and Conflict: Dilemmas of Theory and Practice, Panel on EU External Relations and Regional Development, 1–3 April, Swansea University.

DEBR (2003), ad hoc Group of Directors and Experts on Better Regulation, *Report to the Ministers responsible for Public Administration in the EU member states on the progress of the implementation of the Mandelkern Report's Action Plan on Better Regulation*, Athens, 2003.

Decision Technology Ltd. (2010), *Consumer Decision-Making in Retail Investment Services: A Behavioural Economics Perspective*, available at http://ec.europa.eu/consumers/strategy/docs/final_report_en.pdf.

DeJoy, D.M. (1989), *The Optimism Bias and Traffic Accident Risk Perception*, Accident Analysis and Prevention, 21:333–40.

Doern, B. (2007), *Red Tape-Red Flags: Regulation in the Innovation Age*, Conference Board of Canada CIBC Scholar-in Residence Lecture, Ottawa.

Donev, G. (2004), *Methodology for Regulatory Impact Assessment Related to Occupational Safety and Health*, paper presented at the International Seminar on Implementation of Regulatory Impact Assessment: Best Practices in Europe, 8–11 June, AUBG, Blagoevgrad, Bulgaria.

Donohue, J.J. III and J. Heckman (1991), *Continuous versus Episodic Change: The Impact of Civil Rights Policy on the Economic Status of Blacks*, Journal of Economic Literature, 29:1603–43.

Dorff, M.B. (2002), *Why Welfare Depends on Fairness: a Reply to Kaplow and Shavell*, 75 S. Cal. L. Rev. 847.

Dovidio, J.F., K. Kawakami and S.L. Gaertner (2002), *Implicit and Explicit Prejudice and Interracial Interaction*, Journal of Personality and Social Psychology, 82:62–68.

Driesen, D. (2006), *Is Cost-Benefit Analysis Neutral?*, College of Law Faculty Scholarship, Paper 17.

Dudley, S.E. and A. Antonelli (1997), *Congress and the Clinton OMB: Unwilling Partners in Regulatory Oversight?*, Regulation, Fall 1997, 17–18.

Dworkin, R. (1981a), *What is Equality? Part 1: Equality of Resources*, Philosophy and Public Affairs, 10: 185–246.

Dworkin, R. (1981b), *What is Equality? Part 2: Equality of Welfare*, Philosophy and Public Affairs, 10: 283–345.

Easterlin, R.A. (1995), *Will Raising the Income of All Increase the Happiness of All?*, 27 J. ECON. BEHAV. & ORG. 35, 39.

Easterlin, R.A. (2004), *Diminishing Marginal Utility of Income? A Caveat*. Social Indicators Research, available at SSRN: http://ssrn.com/abstract=539262.

Ehrlich, I. and R.A. Posner (1974), *An Economic Analysis of Legal Rulemaking*, Journal of Legal Studies, 3 (1), 257–286.

Ellsberg, Daniel (1961), *Risk, Ambiguity, and the Savage Axioms*, Quarterly Journal of Economics, 75:643–69.

Elster, J. (1979), *Ulysses and the Sirens: Studies in Rationality and Irrationality*, New York: Cambridge University Press.

Epstein, D. and S. O'Halloran (1999), *Delegating Powers. A Transaction Cost Politics Approach to Policymaking under Separate Powers*, Cambridge University Press.

Epstein, R.A. (1997), *A Clear View of The Cathedral: The Dominance of Property Rules*, Yale Law Journal 106 (7):2091–2120.

Epstein, R.A. (1998), *Protecting Property Rights with Legal Remedies: A Common Sense Reply to Professor Ayres*, Val. University Law Review 32:833.

European Commission (1996), Communication of 6 November 1996, COM(96)559 (Report of the Commission on the SLIM Pilot Project), 1996 (available at http://europa.eu.int/comm/internal_market/simplification/docs/com1996-559/com1996-559_en.pdf).

European Commission (2001), White Paper on European Governance, COM(2001)727, 25 July 2001.

European Commission (2002), *Action Plan on Simplifying and improving the regulatory environment* (COM(2002) 278).

European Commission (2002), *Better Regulation Action Plan*, COM(2002)278, 5 June 2002.

European Commission (2002), BIA Final Report, *Lessons Learned and the Way Forward*, Enterprise Paper No. 9, 2002 (available at http://europa.eu.int/comm/enterprise/library/enterprise-papers/pdf/enterprise_paper_09_2002.pdf).

European Commission (2002), Communication from the Commission to the European parliament, the Council, the Economic and Social Committee and the Committee of the Regions, *Towards a Global Partnership for Sustainable Development*, COM(2002)82, 12 February 2002.

European Commission (2002), Communication on better monitoring of the application of community law (COM(2002) 725).

European Commission (2002), Communication on framework for target-based tripartite contracts (COM(2002) 709).

European Commission (2002), Communication on general principles and minimum standards for consultation (COM(2002)704).

European Commission (2002), Communication on impact assessment (COM(2002) 276), including internal *Guidelines*.

European Commission (2002), Communication on operating framework for the European Regulatory Agencies (COM(2002) 718).

European Commission (2002), Communication on proposal for a new comitology decision (COM(2002) 719).

European Commission (2002), Communication on Simplifying and improving the regulatory environment (COM(2002) 278).

European Commission (2002), Communication on the collection and use of expertise (COM(2002) 713).

European Commission (2002), Preparatory Work for the White Paper, 2002.

European Commission (2002), *Recommendations for Actions to Member States for Inclusion in their Lisbon Programmes*, COM(2005)24, companion document, 3 February 2005.
European Commission (2002), Report "Better Lawmaking 2004", COM(2005)98, 21 March 2005 ("Simplification of the *acquis* remains a top priority, in particular for the Lisbon strategy").
European Commission (2002), reports on the SLIM project, 2005 (available at http://europa.eu.int/comm/internal_market/simplification/index_en.htm#slim).
European Commission (2004), *Annual Evaluation Review 2004 – Overview of the Commission's Findings and Activities*, SEC(2005)587, 2005.
European Commission (2004), Staff Working Paper, *Impact Assessment: Next Steps – In Support of Competitiveness and Sustainable Development*, SEC(2004)1377, 2004.
European Commission (2005), *A Handbook for Impact Assessment in the Commission – How to do an Impact Assessment*, 2005.
European Commission (2005), *Better Regulation for Growth and Jobs in the European Union*, COM(2005)97, 16 March 2005.
European Commission (2005), Communication on the Outcome of the screening of legislative proposals pending before the legislator, COM(2005)462, 27 September 2005.
European Commission (2005), Communication to the Spring European Council on "Working together for Growth and Jobs – A New Start for the Lisbon Strategy", COM(2005)24, 2 February 2005.
European Commission (2005), Enterprise DG, Final Report of the Pilot Project "Ex-Post Evaluation of EC Legislation and its Burden on Business", 2005.
European Commission (2005), Impact Assessment Guidelines, SEC(2005)971, 15 June 2005.
European Commission (2005), Staff Working Paper, Annex to the 2005 Communication on Better Regulation for Growth and Jobs in the European Union, *Minimizing Administrative Costs Imposed by Legislation, Detailed Outline of a Possible EU Net Administrative Cost Model*, SEC(2005)175, 16 March 2005.
European Commission (2005), Staff Working Paper, *The Economic Costs of Non-Lisbon*, SEC(2005)385, 15 March 2005.
European Commission (2009), *Economic Crisis in Europe: Causes, Consequences and Responses*, European Economy 7, 2009, at 21. Available at http://ec.europa.eu/economy_finance/publications/publication15887_en.pdf.
European Commission (2010), Communication on "Smart Regulation in the European Union", COM(2010)543, 11 October 2010.
European Court of Auditors (2010), *Impact Assessment in the EU Institutions: do they support decision-making?*, Special Report 3/2010.
European Parliament (2001), *Report on the Commission White Paper on European Governance*, A5-0399/2001, adopted by the European Parliament on 29 November 2001, OJ C 153E, 27 June 2002, pp. 314–322.
European Parliament (2004), "Protocol on the application of the principles of subsidiarity and proportionality", OJ C310/207, 16 December 2004.
European Parliament (2004), Resolution 2004/A5-0221, 24 March 2004.

Everson, M., G. Majone, L. Metcalfe and A. Schout (1999), *The Role of Specialised Agencies in Decentralising EU Governance*, Report to the Commission, 1999 (available at http://europa.eu.int/comm/governance/areas/group6/index_en.htm).

EVIA (2008), *Final report* – Project leader: Dr Klaus Jacob, Free University, Berlin.

Farber, D.A. (1999), *Taking Slippage Seriously: Noncompliance and Creative Compliance in Environmental Law*, 23 Harv. Envtl. L. Rev. 297, 301–11 (1999).

Farnsworth, W. (1999), *Do Parties to Nuisance Cases Bargain after Judgment? A Glimpse inside the Cathedral*. The University of Chicago Law Review 66 (2):373–436.

Farnsworth, W. (2003), *The Legal Regulation of Self-Serving Bias*, U.C. Davis Law Review, 37:567–603.

Fennell, L.A. (2005), *Revealing Options*, Harvard Law Review 118 (5):1401–1488

Ferrell, A. (2007), *Mandatory Disclosure and Stock Returns: Evidence from the Over-the-Counter Market*, Journal of Legal Studies, vol. 36.

Fischhoff, B. (1982), *Debiasing*, in Judgment under Uncertainty: Heuristics and Biases, ed. Daniel Kahneman, Paul Slovic and Amos Tversky, 422–44 (New York: Cambridge University Press).

Foka-Kavalieraki, Yulie and Hatzis, Aristides N. (2010), *Rational After All: Toward an Improved Model of Rationality in Economics*. Available at SSRN: http://ssrn.com/abstract=1692441

Fontaine, P. (2001), *The changing place of empathy in welfare economics*. Hist. Polit. Econ. 33, 387–409.

Fontaine, P. (2007), *From Philanthropy to Altruism: Incorporating Unselfish Behavior into Economics*, 1961–1975, History of Political Economy 2007 39(1):1–46.

Formez – Centro di Formazione e Studi (2004), *A comparative analysis of regulatory impact assessment in ten EU countries*, a report prepared for the EU Directors of Better Regulation Group, Dublin.

Frank, R.H. (2000), *Why Is Cost-Benefit Analysis So Controversial?*, 29 J. Legal Stud. 913, 917

Friedman, B.D. (1995), *Regulation in the Reagan-Bush Era: The Eruption of Presidential Influence*, Pittsburgh: Pittsburgh University Press

Friedman, D. D. (1984), *Efficient Institutions for the Private Enforcement of Law*, Journal of Legal Studies, Vol. 13, 379–397.

Frontier Economics, *Bulletin, Wrong Numbers – Difficulties in Estimating the Welfare Gains from Regulation*, June 2005.

Froud, J., Boden, R., Ogus, A. and Stubbs, P. (1998), *Controlling the Regulators*, Basingstoke, Hampshire: Macmillan.

Fuchs, D. and A. Kalfagianni (2010), *The Causes and Consequences of Private Food Governance*, Business and Politics 12(3), www.bepress.com/bap/vol12/iss3/art5/.

Gaebler, T., J. Blackman, L. Blessing, R. Bruce, W. Keene and P. Smith (1999), *Positive Outcomes: Raising the Bar on Government Reinvention*, Chatelaine Press.

Gaertner, S.L. and J.P. McLaughlin (1983), *Racial Stereotypes: Associations and Ascriptions of Positive and Negative Characteristics*, Social Psychology, 46:23–30.

Galligan, D. (2003), *The Failure of Law in Post-Communist Countries: A Study of Law and Social Norms*, in Galligan and Kurkchiyan (eds.), Law and Informal Practices in Post-Communist Societies (Oxford UP, 2003).

Gans, J. (2005), *'Protecting consumers by protecting competition': Does behavioural economics support this contention?*, 13 Competition & Consumer Law Journal.

Gans, J. (2005), *The Road to Confusopoly*, available on the ACCC conference website (slides), www.accc.gov.au/content/index. phtml/itemId/658141/fromItemId/

Garoupa, N. and G. Vasconcelos Vilaça (2007), *The Practice And Discourse of Legislative Evaluation in Portugal*, ENBR working paper 12/2007.

Gattuso, J.L. (2004), *What is the Bush Administration's Record on Regulatory Reform?*, testimony before the Subcommittee on Energy Policy, Natural Resources and Regulatory Affairs Committee on Government Reform, US House of Representatives, 17 November 2004.

Genakos, C. and T.M. Valletti (2008), *Testing the 'Waterbed' Effect in Mobile Telephony*, CEIS Working Paper No. 110.

Gewertz, K. (2003), *Adding Some Color to Harvard Portraits*, Harvard University Gazette (May 1):11.

Goeree, J.K., C.A. Holt, K. Palmer, W. Shobe and D. Burtraw (2010), *An Experimental Study of Auctions Versus Grandfathering to Assign Pollution Permits*, Journal of the European Economic Association April/May 2010, Vol. 8, No. 2–3, Pages 514–525.

Goldstein, P. (1994), *Copyright's Highway: the Law and Lore of Copyright from Gutenberg to the Celestial Jukebox*, Hill & Wang, New York, NY.

Gompers, Paul A., J.L. Ishii and A. Metrick (2003), *Corporate Governance and Equity Prices*, Quarterly Journal of Economics, 118:107–55.

Gomulkiewicz R.W. (1998), *The License Is the Product: Comments on the Promise of Article 2B for Software and Information Licensing*, 13 Berkeley Tech. L. J. 891.

Gore, A. (1993), *From Red Tape to Results: Creating a Government that Works Better and Costs Less*, Report of the National Performance Review, 1993.

Graham, J.D. (2007), *Saving Lives through Administrative Law and Economics*, University of Pennsylvania Law Review, Vol. 157: 395.

Graham, J.D. (2007), *The Evolving Regulatory Role of the U.S. Office of Management and Budget*, Review of Environmental Economics and Policy, No. 1: 171–191.

Graham, J.D. and Wiener, J.B. (1995), *Risk versus Risk. Trade-offs in Protecting Health and Environment*, Cambridge, Harvard University Press.

Greenfield, K. (2002), *Using Behavioral Economics to Show the Power and Efficiency of Corporate Law as Regulatory Tool*, in Symposium: Corporations Theory and Corporate Governance Law, U.C. Davis Law Review, 25:581–644.

Greenstone, M., P. Oyer and A. Vissing-Jorgensen (2006), *Mandated Disclosure, Stock Returns, and the 1964 Securities Acts Amendments*," Quarterly Journal of Economics (forthcoming).

Greenwald, A.G., D.E. McGhee and J.L.K. Schwartz (1998), *Measuring Individual Differences in Implicit Cognition: The Implicit Association Test*, Journal of Personality and Social Psychology, 74:1464–80.

Grembi, V. (2005), *Guido Calabresi e L'Analisi Economica del Diritto*, Siena Memos and Papers in Law and Economics, 41/05, at www.unisi.it/lawandeconomics/simple/041_Grembi.pdf.

Grossman, S.J. and O.D. Hart (1986), *The Costs and Benefits of Ownership: A Theory of Vertical and Lateral Integration*, Journal of Political Economy, XCIV (1986), 691–719.

Gruber, J. (1994), *The Incidence of Mandated Maternity Benefits*, American Economic Review, 84:622–41.

Gualmini, E. (2008), *Restructuring Weberian Bureaucracy: Comparing Managerial Reforms in Europe and the United States*. Public Administration, 86(1), 75–94.

Gulati, M. and M. Yelnosky (2006), *Behavioral Analyses of Workplace Discrimination* (Dordrecht, Holland: Kluwer Academic Publishers, forthcoming).

Guppy, A. (1993), *Subjective Probability of Accident and Apprehension in Relation to Self-Other Bias, Age, and Reported Behavior*, Accident Analysis and Prevention, 25:375–82.

Guth, W., R. Schmittberger and B. Schwarze (1982), *An Experimental Analysis of Ultimatum Bargaining*, Journal of Economic Behavior and Organization, 3:367–88.

Guthrie, C. (2003), *Prospect Theory, Risk Preference, and the Law*, in Symposium: Empirical Legal Realism: A New Social Scientific Assessment of Law and Human Behavior, Northwestern University Law Review, 97:1115–63.

Hagerup, B. (2002), *Business Impact Assessment – The Danish Model*, paper presented at the Seminar on Regulatory Transparency: The Use of Public Consultation to Improve the Investment Climate, Thessaloniki, Greece (at www.oecd.org/dataoecd/58/39/2410437.pdf).

Hahn, R.W. and R.E. Litan (2005), *Counting Regulatory Benefits and Costs: Lessons for the US and Europe, Journal of International Economic Law*, Oxford University Press, vol. 8(2), pages 473–508, June

Hahn, R.W. (1999), *Regulatory Reform: Assessing the Government's Numbers*, AEI-Brookings Center for Regulatory Studies, Working Paper No. 99–06, American Enterprise Institute and Brookings Institute, Washington, D.C.

Hahn, R.W. (2005), *In Defense of the Economic Analysis of Regulation*, American Enterprise Institute, Washington, D.C., 2005.

Hahn, R.W. (2008), *Designing Smarter Regulation with Improved Benefit-Cost Analysis*, Reg-Markets Center Working Paper No. 08–20.

Hahn, R.W. and C.R. Sunstein (2001), *Regulatory Oversight Takes Exciting New Tack*, AEI-Brookings Joint Center Policy Matters 01–25, American Enterprise Institute and Brookings Institute, Washington, D.C.

Hahn, R.W. and C.S. Sunstein (2002), *New Executive Order For Improving Federal Regulation? Deeper And Wider Cost-Benefit Analysis*, University of Pennsylvania Law Review, Vol. 150, No. 1489

Hahn, R.W. and M.B. Muething (2003), *The Grand Experiment in Regulatory Reporting*, Administrative Law Review, 2003, Vol. 55, No. 3, 607–642.

Hahn, R.W. and P. Dudley (2004), *How well Does the Government Do Cost-Benefit Analysis?*, AEI-Brookings Joint Center for Regulatory Studies, Working Paper 04–01, American Enterprise Institute and Brookings Institute, Washington, D.C., 2004.

Hahn, R.W. and P. Tetlock (2008), *Has Economic Analysis Improved Regulatory Decisions?*, Journal of Economic Perspectives, Volume 22, Number 1, Winter 2008, 67–84.

Hahn, R.W. and R. Litan (2000), *An Analysis of the Third Government Report on the Benefits and Costs of Federal Regulation*, AEI-Brookings Joint Center for Regulatory Studies, 2000

Hahn, R.W., J. Burnett, Chan Yee-Ho, E. Mader and P. Moyle (2000), *Assessing Regulatory Impact Analysis: the Failure of Agencies to Comply with Executive Order 12866*, Harvard Journal of Law and Policy, 2000, Vol. 23, No. 3.

Hampton, P. (2005), *Reducing administrative burdens: Effective inspection and enforcement*, London, www.berr.gov.uk/files/file22988.pdf.

Harnay, A. and S. Marciano (2009), *Posner, Economics and the Law: from Law and Economics to an Economic Analysis of Law*, Journal of the History of Economic Thought, Volume 31, Issue 2, 215–232.

Harrington W. *et al.* (2009), *Controversies surrounding Regulatory Impact Analysis*, in Harrington *et al.* (eds.), Reforming Regulatory Impact Analysis, 10–20. Washington, D.C.: Resources for the Future.

Harrington, W. (2004), *RIA Assessment Methods*, paper prepared for the OECD project on *ex post* evaluation of regulatory tools and institutions, OECD, Paris.

Harrington, W. and R.D. Morgenstern (2003), *Evaluating Regulatory Impact Analyses*, paper prepared for the OECD project on *ex post* evaluation of regulatory tools and institutions, OECD, Paris.

Harrington, W., L. Heinzerling and R. Morgenstern (2009), *Reforming Regulatory Impact Analysis*, Resources for the Future Report, Washington D.C.

Harrington, W., R.D. Morgenstern, and P. Nelson (2000), *On the Accuracy of Regulatory Cost Estimates*', Journal of Policy Analysis and Management 19(2):297–322, 314.

Harsanyi, J.C. (1955), *Cardinal Welfare, Individualistic Ethics, and Interpersonal Comparisons of Utility*, 63 J. Pol. Econ. 309.

Hatzis, A.N. and S. Nalpantidou (2007), *From Nothing to Too Much: Regulatory Reform in Greece*, available at SSRN: http://ssrn.com/abstract=1075963

Hayden, G.M. and S.E. Ellis (2007), *Law and Economics After Behavioral Economics*, University of Kansas Law Review, 55:3 (April 2007): 629–675.

Hazlett, T. (2001), *The Wireless Craze, the Unlimited Bandwidth Myth, the Spectrum Auction Faux Pas, and the Punchline to Ronald Coase's "Big Jokes": An Essay on Airwave Allocation Policy*, Harvard J. Law & Tech, 14(2), Spring, 335–545.

Hazlett, T. (2002), *Washington Wireless Wars*, Washington Institute Forum, August 2002, available online at www.manhattan-institute.org/pdf/mif2.pdf.

Heckman, J.J. and B.S. Payner (1989), *Determining the Impact of Federal Antidiscrimination Policy on the Economic Status of Blacks: A Study of South Carolina*, American Economic Review, 79:138–77.

Hedström, P. (2005), *Dissecting the Social. On the Principles of Analytical Sociology*, Cambridge: Cambridge University Press.

Hedström, P. and R. Swedberg (1998) (eds.), *Social Mechanisms: An Analytical Approach to Social Theory*, Cambridge, Cambridge University Press.

Heinzerling, L. and Frank Ackerman (2007), *Wasting Away in Paretoville*, 1 Harv. L. & Pol'y Rev., 363–370.

Hertin, J., Pesch, U. and Jacob (2007), *The production and use of knowledge in Regulatory Impact Assessment – an empirical analysis*, ECPR General Conference Pisa, 6–8 September 2007.

Herzel, L. (1951), *"Public Interest" and the Market in Color Television Regulation*, 18 Univ. Chi. L. Rev. 802.

Hicks, J.R. (1939), *The Foundations of Welfare Economics*, 49 ECON. J. 696

Hoffman, E. and M. Spitzer (1982), *The Coase Theorem: Some Experimental Tests*, Journal of Law and Economics, 25:73–98.

Hoffman, E. and M. Spitzer (1986), *Experimental Tests of the Coase Theorem with Large Bargaining Groups*, Journal of Legal Studies, 15:149–71.

Hood, C. and G. Peters (2004), *The middle aging of new public management: Into the age of paradox?*, Journal of Public Administration Research and Theory, 14(3), 267–282.

Hovenkamp, H. (1994), *The Limits of Preference-Based Legal Policy*, 89 Northwestern University Law Review 4.

Hylton, K.N. (2004), *Calabresi and the Intellectual History of Law and Economics*, Working Paper Series Law and Economics 04–04, Boston University, School of Law (2004).

Irish, Dutch, Luxembourg, UK, Austrian and Finnish Presidencies of the European Union, *Joint statement on Advancing Regulatory Reform in Europe*, 7 December 2004 (available at www.hm-treasury.gov.uk/media/95A/52/6presidencies.pdf).

Issacharoff, S. and G. Loewenstein (1995), *Unintended Consequences of Mandatory Disclosure*, Texas Law Review, 73:753–86.

Itoh, H. (2004), *Moral Hazard and Other-regarding Preferences* (2004).

Jacob, K., J. Hertin, P. Hjerp, C.M. Radaelli *et al.* (2008), *Improving the practice of impact assessment*, Berlin, EVIA consortium.

Jacobs, S. (2006a), *Current Trends in Regulatory Impact Analysis: The Challenges of Mainstreaming RIA into Policy-making*, Jacobs & Associates, Washington.

Jacobs, S. (2006b), *Regulatory Impact Analysis in Regulatory Process, Method, and Co-operation: Lessons for Canada from International Trends*, Washington, D.C.

Jalilian, H., Kirkpatrick, C. and D. Parker (2007), *The impact of regulation on economic growth in developing countries: A cross-country analysis*, World Development, 35(1): 87–103.

James, O. and N. Manning (1996), *Public management: A Global perspective*, Politics, *16*(3), 143–149.

James, W. (1890), *The Principles of Psychology*, available online at http://psychclassics.yorku.ca/James/Principles/.

Jolls, C. (1997), *Contracts as Bilateral Commitments: A New Perspective on Contract Modification*, Journal of Legal Studies, 26:203–37.

Jolls, C. (1998), *Behavioral Economic Analysis of Redistributive Legal Rules*, in Symposium: The Legal Implications of Psychology: Human Behavior, Behavioral Economics, and the Law, Vanderbilt Law Review, 51:1653–77.

Jolls, C. (2002), *Fairness, Minimum Wage Law, and Employee Benefits*, in Symposium: Research Conference on Behavioral Law and Economics in the Workplace, New York University Law Review, 77:47–70.

Jolls, C. (2004), *Identifying the Effects of the Americans with Disabilities Act Using State-Law Variation: Preliminary Evidence on Educational Participation Effects*, American Economic Review (Papers and Proceedings), 94:447–53.

Jolls, C. (2004), *On Law Enforcement With Boundedly Rational Actors*, Harvard L&E Discussion paper No. 494

Jolls, C. (2006), *Antidiscrimination Law's Effects on Implicit Bias*, in Behavioral Analyses of Workplace Discrimination, ed. Mitu Gulati and Michael Yelnosky (Dordrecht, Holland: Kluwer Academic Publishers, forthcoming).

Jolls, C. (2007), *Behavioral law and economics,* Chapter 4 in Diamond, Hannu Vartiainen and Yrjö Jahnssonin säätiö (eds.), *Behavioral economics and its applications,* Princeton, N.J.: Princeton University Press, at 34–35.

Jolls, C. (2010), *Governing America: the Emerging of Behavioral Law and Economics.*

Jolls, C. and C.R. Sunstein (2006), *Debiasing through Law,* Journal of Legal Studies, Vol. 35, 1.

Jolls, C. and C.R. Sunstein (2006), *Debiasing Through Law,* Journal of Legal Studies, 35:199–241.

Jolls, C. and C.R. Sunstein (2006), *The Law of Implicit Bias,* Cal. L. Rev., 94, 969–996.

Jolls, C., C.R. Sunstein and R. Thaler (1998), *A Behavioral Approach to Law and Economics,* Stanford Law Review, 50:1471–1550.

Jordan, A., Wurzel, R., Zito, A.R. and Bruckner, L. (2003), *European governance and the transfer of 'new' environmental policy instruments (NEPIs) in the European Union,* Public Administration, 81(3), 555–574.

Kagan, E. (2001), *Presidential administration,* Harvard Law Review 114: 2245–2385.

Kahneman, D. and A. Tversky (1979), *Prospect Theory: An Analysis of Decision Under Risk,* Econometrica, 47:263–91.

Kahneman, D. and S. Frederick (2002), *Representativeness Revisited: Attribute Substitution in Intuitive Judgment,* in Heuristics and Biases: The Psychology of Intuitive Judgment, ed. Thomas Gilovich, Dale Griffin and Daniel Kahneman, 49–81 (New York: Cambridge University Press).

Kahneman, D. *et al.* (2006), *Would You Be Happier if You Were Richer? A Focusing Illusion,* 312 Science 1908.

Kahneman, D., A.B. Krueger, D.A. Schkade, N. Schwarz and A.A. Stone (2006), *Would You Be Happier If You Were Richer? A Focusing Illusion,* Science 312, 1908–1910. And Kahneman, D. and A. B. Krueger (2006), *Developments in the Measurement of Subjective Well-Being,* Journal of Economic Perspectives 20, 3–24.

Kahneman, D., J.L. Knetsch and R.H. Thaler (1986), *Fairness as a Constraint on Profit Seeking: Entitlements in the Market,* American Economic Review, 76:728-

Kaldor, N. (1939), *Welfare Propositions of Economics and Interpersonal Comparisons of Utility,* 49 ECON. J. 549.

Kamensky, J. (1997), *The US Reform Experience: The National Performance Review,* paper presented at the Conference on Civil Service Systems in Comparative Perspectives, Indiana University, Bloomington, IN, 6 April 1997 (available from the US Government archive at http://govinfo.library.unt.edu/npr/library/papers/bkgrd/kamensky.html).

Kaplow, L. and S. Shavell (1994), *Why the Legal System is Less Efficient Than the Income Tax in Redistributing Income,* Journal of Legal Studies, 23:667–81.

Kaplow, L. and S. Shavell (1996), *Property Rules versus Liability Rules,* Harvard Law Review 109:713.

Kaplow, L. and S. Shavell (2002), *Fairness versus Welfare,* Cambridge, Mass.: Harvard University Press.

Karapanou, V. and L.T. Visscher (2010), *Quality Adjusted Life Years as a Way Out of the Impasse between Prevention Theory and Insurance Theory*, Rotterdam Institute of Law and Economics (RILE) Working Paper No. 2010/06.

Katz, L.F. and B. Meyer (1990), *Unemployment Insurance, Recall Expectations, and Unemployment Outcomes*, Quarterly Journal of Economics, 105:973–1002.

Katzen, S. (2007), Testimony before the House Committee on Science and Technology, Subcommittee on investigation and oversight.

Kau, J.B. and P.H. Rubin (1982), *Congressmen, Constituents and Contributors*, Boston: Martinus Nijoff.

Kelly J. (1988), *Social Choice Theory: an Introduction*, Springer.

Kelman, M. (1979), *Consumption Theory, Production Theory, and Ideology in the Coase Theorem*, Southern California Law Review, 52:669–98.

Khalil, E. (2007), *The Mirror-Neuron Paradox: How Far is Sympathy from Compassion, Indulgence, and Adulation?*, MPRA Paper No. 3961.

Kirman A. and M. Techl (2010), *Selfish or selfless? The role of empathy in economics*, Phil. Trans. R. Soc. B 2010 365, 303–317.

Klein, B., R.G. Crawford, and A.A. Alchian (1978), *Vertical Integration, Appropriable Rents, and the Competitive Contracting Process*, Journal of Law and Economics, XXI, 297–326.

Kleinertova, J. (2004), "Specifics and Problems of RIA in Transition Economics and How to Overcome Them", paper presented at the International Seminar on "Implementation of Regulatory Impact Assessment. Best Practices in Europe", 8–11 June, AUBG, Blagoevgrad, Bulgaria, 2004.

Klick, J. and F. Parisi (2003), *Functional Law and Economics: The Search for Value-Neutral Principles of Lawmaking*, George Mason University Law and Economics Working Paper Series, 03–39.

Konvitz, J. (2004), *The Institutional Context for Better Regulation*, paper presented at the Conference on Simple is Better: Effective Regulation for a More Competitive Europe, Amsterdam, 7–8 October 2004.

Kornhauser, L.A. (1986), *An Introduction to the Economic Analysis of Contract Remedies.* University of Colorado Law Review 57 (4):683–725.

Kornhauser, L.A. (2000), *On Justifying Cost-Benefit Analysis*, 29 J. Legal Stud. 1037, 1054 (2000)

Korobkin, R. (1998), *The Status Quo Bias and Contract Default Rules*, Cornell Law Review, 83:608–87.

Korobkin, R. (2003), *The Endowment Effect and Legal Analysis*, in Symposium: Empirical Legal Realism: A New Social Scientific Assessment of Law and Human Behavior, Northwestern University Law Review, 97:1227–93.

Korobkin, R.B. (2009), *A 'Traditional' and 'Behavioral' Law-and-Economics Analysis of Williams v. Walker-Thomas Furniture Company.* University of Hawaii Law Review, Vol. 26, 441, 2004; UCLA School of Law, Law & Econ. Research Paper No. 03–24.

Korobkin, R.B. (2009), *Libertarian Welfarism.* California Law Review, Vol. 97, No. 6, 2009; UCLA School of Law, Law-Econ Research Paper No. 09–09.

Korobkin, R.B. and T.S. Ulen (2000), *Law and Behavioral Science: Removing the Rationality Assumption from Law and Economics.* California Law Review, Vol. 88, at 1102 ff.

Krier, J.E., and S.J. Schwab (1995), *Property Rules and Liability Rules: The cathedral in another light*. New York University Law Review 70 (May):440.

Krier, J.E., and S.J. Schwab (1997), *The Cathedral at Twenty-Five: Citations and Impressions*. Yale Law Journal 106 (7):2121–47.

Krugman, P. (2009), *The Return of Depression Economics and the Crisis of 2008*, W.W. Norton & Company, New York.

Kuran, T. and C.R. Sunstein (1999), *Availability Cascades and Risk Regulation*, Stanford Law Review, 51:683–768.

Laffont, J.J. and D. Martimort (2002), *The Theory of Incentives: The Principal-Agent Model*, Princeton, NJ: Princeton University Press, 2002.

Laibson, D. (1997), *Golden Eggs and Hyperbolic Discounting*, Quarterly Journal of Economics, 112:443–77.

Landes, W.M. and R.A. Posner (1975), *The Private Enforcement of Law*, Journal of Legal Studies, Vol. 4. Pages 1–46.

Lane, J.E. (2000), *New Public Management*, London: Routledge, 2000.

Layard, R. (2005), *Happiness: Lessons From A New Science*, The Penguin Press, at 122.

Lazer, D., *Regulatory Review: Presidential Control through Selective Communication and Institutionalized Conflict*, 1998 (available at www.ksg.harvard.edu/prg/lazer/control.pdf).

Lee, N. and C. Kirkpatrick (2004), *A Pilot Study of the Quality of European Commission Extended Impact Assessments*, IARC Working Paper Series No. 8, 2004, p. 27.

Lenschow, A., P. Graef, K. Kurze and K. Rottmann (2008), *Exploring the German RIA-Puzzle*, ENBR Working Paper 20/2008.

Leonard, H.B. and R.J. Zeckhauser (1986), *Cost-Benefit Analysis Applied to Risks: Its Philosophy and Legitimacy*, in VALUES AT RISK 31, 47–48 (Douglas MacLean ed., 1986).

Lessig, L. (1996), *The Zones of Cyberspace*, Stanford Law Review (48), 1408.

Licht, A. (2008), *Social Norms and the Law. Why Peoples Obey the Law*, Review of Law and Economics, 4:3, 715.

Lichtenstein, S., P. Slovic, B. Fischhoff, M. Layman and B. Combs (1978), *Judged Frequency of Lethal Events*, Journal of Experimental Psychology: Human Learning and Memory, 4:551–78.

Litman, J. (2001), *Digital Copyright*, Prometeus Books.

Lo, A.W. and M.T. Mueller (2010), *Warning: Physics Envy May be Hazardous to Your Wealth!* (March 12, 2010), available at SSRN: http://ssrn.com/abstract=1563882.

Loewenstein, G. and D.A. Moore (2004), *When Ignorance Is Bliss: Information Exchange and Inefficiency in Bargaining*, Journal of Legal Studies, 33:37–58.

Loewenstein, G., S. Issacharoff, C. Camerer and L. Babcock (1993), *Self-Serving Assessments of Fairness and Pretrial Bargaining*, Journal of Legal Studies, 22:135–59.

Löfstedt, R. (2007), *The 'Plateau-ing' of the European Better Regulation Agenda: An Analysis of Activities Carried out by the Barroso Commission*, Journal of Risk Research, vol. 10 (4), 423–447.

Lukes, S. (1973), *Individualism*, reprinted by ECPR Press, Colchester, 2006.

Lussis, B. (2004), *EU Extended Impact Assessment Review*, Institut pour un Développement Durable Working Paper, 9 December 2004 (available at HTTP://USERS.SKYNET.BE/IDD/DOCUMENTS/EIDDD/WP01.PDF).

Lutter, R. (2001), *Economic Analysis of Regulation in the U.S.: What Lessons for the European Commission?*, AEI-Brookings Joint Center for Regulatory Studies, American Enterprise Institute and Brookings Institute, Washington, D.C., 2001.

Macaulay, S. (1963), *Non-Contractual Relations in Business: A Preliminary Study*. 28 American Sociological Review 1963, pp. 55–67.

MacKaay, E. (2000), *History of Law and Economics*, 1 Encyclopedia of Law and Economics (Cheltenham, U.K.: Edward Elgar Publishing).

Macrae, C. Neil, G.V. Bodenhausen and A.B. Milne (1995), *The Dissection of Selection in Person Perception: Inhibitory Processes in Social Stereotyping*, Journal of Personality and Social Psychology, 69:397–407.

Majone, G.D. (1989), *Evidence, Argument and Persuasion in the Policy Process* (1st ed.). New Haven and London: Yale University Press.

Majone, G.D. (1996), *Regulating Europe*, London: Routledge.

Majone, G.D. (1999), *Regulation in comparative perspective*, Journal of Comparative Policy Analysis, 1(3), 309–324.

Majone, G.D. (2002), *What Price Safety? The Precautionary Principle and its Policy Implications*, Journal of Common Market Studies, *40*(1), 89–109.

Mak, V. (2008), *Review of the Consumer Acquis – Towards Maximum Harmonisation?*, TICOM Working Paper on Comparative and Transnational Law No. 2008/6; European Review of Private Law, 1/2009.

Mandelkern Group, Final Report, 2001 (available at http://europa.eu.int/comm/secretariat_general/impact/docs/mandelkern.pdf).

Manne, H.G. and J.D. Wright (2008), *The Future of Law and Economics: a Discussion*, George Mason University Law and Economics Research Paper Series n. 08–35.

Marcos Fernandez, F., J. Santaló Mediavilla and A. Sanchez Graells (2007), *Decentralisation, Regulatory Burden And Economic Development In Spain*, ENBR Working Paper 05/2007.

Masur, J.S. and Posner, Eric A. (2010), *Against Feasibility Analysis*, University of Chicago Law Review, Forthcoming; University of Chicago Law & Economics, Olin Working Paper No. 480; University of Chicago, Public Law Working Paper No. 274. Available at SSRN: http://ssrn.com/abstract=1452984.

Matthew D., Roger G. Noll, and Barry R. Weingast (1987), Administrative Procedures as Instruments of Political Control, 3 J L, Econ & Org 243, 246.

Maynard Smith, J. and G.R. Price (1973), *The Logic of Animal Conflict*, Nature 246, 15–18.

McAdam, D., Tarrow, S. and C. Tilly (2001), *Dynamics of Contention*, Cambridge, Cambridge University Press.

McAdams, R.H. and T.S. Ulen (2008), *Behavioral Criminal Law and Economics*, U of Chicago Law & Economics, Olin Working Paper No. 440; U of Chicago, Public Law Working Paper No. 244; U Illinois Law & Economics Research Paper No. LE08–035. Available at SSRN: http://ssrn.com/abstract=1299963.

McConnell, R. Allen and J.M. Leibold (2001), *Relations Among the Implicit Association Test, Discriminatory Behavior, and Explicit Measure of Racial Attitudes*, Journal of Experimental Social Psychology, 37:435–42.

McCormick, R.E. and R.D. Tollison (1981), *Politicians, Legislation and the Economy. An Inquiry into the Interest-Group Theory of Government*, Boston: Martinus Nijoff.

McCubbins, M.D., Noll, R.G. and Weingast, B.R. (1987), *Administrative procedures as instruments of political control*, Journal of Law, Economics, and Organization, *3*(2), 243–277.

McCubbins, M.D., Noll, R.G. and Weingast, B.R. (1989), *Structure and process, politics and policy: administrative arrangements and the political control of agencies*, Virginia Law Review, 431–482.

McGarity, T.O. (1991), *Reinventing Rationality The Role of Regulatory Analysis in the Federal Bureaucracy*, Cambridge: Cambridge University Press.

McGarity, T.O. (1998), *A Cost-Benefit State*, 50 ADMIN. L. REV. 7

McGarity, T.O. (1987), *Regulatory Analysis and Regulatory Reform*, Texas Law Review, Vol. 65, No. 1243.

McGarity, T.O. (1992), *Some Thoughts on "Deossifying" the Rulemaking Process*, 41 DUKE L.J. 1385, 1385–86.

McGarity, T.O. (1997), *The Courts and the Ossification of Rulemaking: A Response to Professor Seidenfeld*, 75 TEX. L. REV. 525, 528–36

McKinsey and Company (2008), *Reducing U.S. Greenhouse Gas Emissions: How Much and at What Cost?*, available online at www.mckinsey.com/clientservice/ccsi/pdf/US_ghg_final_report.pdf

Medema, S.G. (2010), *From Dismal to Dominance? Law and Economics and the Values of Imperial Science*, in Hatzis, A. (ed.), *Norms and Values in Law and Economics*, London: Routledge, forthcoming 2011.

Merges, R.P. (1996), *Contracting into Liability Rules: Intellectual Property Rights and Collective Rights Organizations*, California Law Review, Vol. 84, No. 5.

Meuwese, A.C.M. (2007), *Inter-institutionalising EU Impact Assessment*, In S. Weatherill (ed.), *Better Regulation* (287–309). Oxford: Hart Publishing.

Meuwese, A.C.M. (2008), *Impact assessment in EU law-making*, Alphen aan den Rijn: Kluwer Law International.

Moe, T. (1982), *Regulatory performance and presidential administration*, American Journal of Political Science, 26(2), 197–224

Moe, T. (1984), *The new economics of organization*, American Journal of Political Science, Vol. 28, n. 4, 739–777.

Moe, T. (1985), *Control and feedback in economic regulation: The case of the NLRB*, American Political Science Review, 79, 1094–1016.

Moe, T. and S. A. Wilson (1994), *Presidents and the politics of structure*, Law and Contemporary Problems 57(2, Spring): 1–44.

Moran, M. (2003), *The British Regulatory State: High Modernism and Hyper-Innovation*, Oxford: Oxford University Press.

Morgenstern, R.D. (1997), *Economic Analysis at EPA: Assessing Regulatory Impact.* Washington, D.C.: Resources for the Future.

Morgenstern, R.D., W.A. Pizer and Jhih-Shyang Shih (2001), *The Cost of Environmental Protection*, The Review of Economics and Statistics, 83(4): 732–738.

Morrall III, J. (1997), *An Assessment of the U.S. Regulatory Impact Assessment Program*, in Best Practices in the Main OECD Countries, OECD, Paris, 1997.

Morrall III, J. (2001), *Ebbs and Flows in the Quality of Regulatory Analysis*, speech at the Weidenbaum Center Forum on "Executive Regulatory Analysis: Surveying the Record, Making It Work", National Press Club, Washington, D.C., 17 December 2001.

Morrison, A. (1986), *OMB Interference with Agency Rulemaking: The Wrong Way to Write a Regulation*, 99 Harvard Law Review 1059.

Munger, M. (2000), *Analyzing Policy; Choices, Conflicts and Practices*, W.W. Norton & Co., 2000.

Munnich, N. (2004), *The Regulatory Burdens and Administrative Compliance Costs for Companies*, survey by the Confederation of Swedish Enterprise, Brussels Office, 2004.

Muris, T. (2002), *The Interface of Competition and Consumer Protection*, Paper presented at Fordham Corporate Law Institute's 29th Annual Conference on International Antitrust Law and Policy, New York.

Nelson, P. (1970), *Information and Consumer Behavior*, Journal of Political Economy, 78 - (March-April), 311–29.

Nelson, P. (1974), *Advertising as Information*, Journal of Political Economy, 83 (July-August), 729–54.

Nilsson, M. *et al.* (2008), *The use and non-use of policy appraisal in public policy making: an analysis of three European countries and the European Union*, Policy Sciences, 41, 335–355.

Niskanen, W.A. (1971), *Bureaucracy and Representative Government*, Chicago, IL: Aldine, 1971.

Niskanen, W.A. (1988), *The Weak Fourth Leg of Reaganomics*, Wall Street Journal, 30 June 1988.

Nolan, J.M., P.W. Schultz, R.B. Cialdini, N.J. Goldstein and V. Griskevicius (2008), *Normative Social Influence is Underdetected*, Personality and Social Psychology Bulletin 2008; 34; 913.

North, D. (1990), *Institutions, Institutional Change, and Economics Performance*, Cambridge University Press, Cambridge.

Nosek, B.A., M.R. Banaji and A.G. Greenwald (2002), *Harvesting Implicit Group Attitudes and Beliefs from a Demonstration Website*, Group Dynamics: Theory, Research, and Practice, 6:101–15.

OECD (1997), *Regulatory Impact Analysis: Best Practice in OECD Countries*, Paris: OECD Publications.

OECD (1999), *Regulatory Reform in the United States: Government Capacity to Ensure High-Quality Regulation*, Paris: OECD Publications.

OECD (2002), *Regulatory policies in OECD countries: from interventionism to regulatory governance*, Paris: OECD Publications.

OECD (2003), *From Red Tape to Smart Tape. Administrative Simplification in OECD Countries*, Paris: OECD Publications.

OECD (2004), "Regulatory Impact Analysis (RIA) Inventory", note by the Secretariat, 29th Session of the OECD Public Governance Committee, International Energy Agency, Paris: OECD Publications.

OECD (2004), *Economic Survey of the United Kingdom*, Paris: OECD.

OECD (2004), *Regulatory Performance: Ex-Post Evaluation of Regulatory Tools and Institutions*, Paris: OECD Publications.

OECD (2005), "Designing Independent and Accountable Regulatory Authorities for High-Quality Regulation", proceedings of the OECD Working Party on Regulatory Management and Reform, London, 10–11 January 2005 (available at www.oecd.org/dataoecd/15/28/35028836.pdf).

OECD (2005), *Modernising Government: The Way Forward*, Paris: OECD Publications.

OECD (2008), *Building and Institutional Framework for Regulatory Impact Analysis: Guidance for Policy Makers*. Paris: OECD Publications.

OECD (2002), *Regulatory reform in Canada. Government capacity to assure high quality regulation*, Paris: OECD Publications.

OECD (2006), *Determinants of Quality in Regulatory Impact Analysis*, Paris: OECD Publications.

OECD (2007), *Comparing Administrative Burdens Across Countries*, Paris: OECD Publications.

OECD (2007), *Government capacity to assure high quality regulation in Sweden*, Paris: Organisation for Economic Cooperation and Development.

OECD (2007), *Methodological Guidance and Frameworks for RIA*, Paris: OECD Publications.

OECD (2009), *Better Regulation in the Netherlands*, Paris: OECD Publications.

OECD (2009), *Better regulation in the United Kingdom*, Paris: OECD Publications.

OECD (2009), *Regulatory Impact Analysis: A Tool for Policy Coherence*, Paris: OECD Publications.

Oehler, A. and D. Kohlert (2009), *Financial Advice Giving and Taking – Where are the Market's Self-healing Powers and a Functioning Legal Framework When We Need Them?*, Journal of Consumer Policy 32: 91–116., 103.

Ogus, A. (1998), *Regulatory Appraisal: A Neglected Opportunity for Law and Economics*, European Journal of Law and Economics, Volume 6, Number 1, July 1998, 53–68(16).

Opoku, C. and A. Jordan (2004), *Impact Assessment in the EU: A Global Sustainable Development Perspective*, paper presented at the Berlin Conference on the Human Dimension of Global Environmental Change, 3–4 December 2004 (available at www.fu-berlin.de/ffu/akumwelt/bc2004/download/opoku_jordan_f.pdf).

Osborne, D. and T. Gaebler (1992), *Reinventing Government: How the Entrepreneurial Spirit is Transforming the Public Sector*, Addison-Wesley Co., 1992.

Pacces, A. M. (2000), *Financial intermediation in the securities markets law and economics of conduct of business regulation*, International Review of Law and Economics, Vol. 20, 2000, pp. 479–510

Padilla, A.J. and D.S. Evans (2005), *Designing Antitrust Rules for Assessing Unilateral Practices: A Neo-Chicago Approach*, University of Chicago Law Review, Vol. 72.

Parisi, F. (2004), *Positive, Normative and Functional Schools in Law and Economics*, European Journal of Law and Economics, Vol. 18, No. 3, 259–272.

Parisi, F. and J. Klick (2004), "Functional Law and Economics: The Search for Value-Neutral Principles of Lawmaking", 79 *Chicago-Kent Law Review*, 2004, 431–450.

Parker, C. (2006), *The Compliance Trap: The Moral Message in Responsive Regulatory Enforcement*, U. of Melbourne Legal Studies Research Paper No. 163.

Parker, R. (2003), *Grading the Government*, University of Chicago Law Review, 70: 1346, 2003.

Parker, W.D. (2006), *Methodological Individualism vs. Methodological Holism: Neoclassicism, Institutionalism and Socionomic Theory*", Paper presented at the joint annual congress of the International Association for Research in Economic Psychology (IAREP) and the Society for the Advancement of Behavioral Economics (SABE), University of Paris (Sorbonne), Paris, France, July 5–8, 2006.

Pearce, D.W. and R.K. Turner (1990), *Economics of Natural Resources and the Environment,* Hemel Hempstead: Harvester Wheatsheaf.

Pelkmans, J., S. Labory and G. Majone (2000), *Better EU Regulatory Quality: Assessing Current Initiatives and New Proposals,* in G. Galli and J. Pelkmans (eds.), "Regulatory Reform and Competitiveness in Europe", Cheltenham: Edward Elgar, Vol. 1.

Peltzman, S. (1984), *Constituent Interest and Congressional Voting,* Journal of Law and Economics 27, 181–210.

Pierce, Jr., R.J. (1991), *The Unintended Effects of Judicial Review of Agency Rules: How Federal Courts Have Contributed to the Electricity Crisis of the 1990s,* Administrative Law Review 43:7.

Pierce, Jr., R.J. (1995), *Seven Ways to Deossify Agency Rulemaking,* 47 ADMIN. L. REV. 59, 60–62.

Pildes, R.H. and Sunstein, C.R. (1995), *Reinventing the Regulatory State,* The University of Chicago Law Review 62: 1–129.

Pirsig, R. (1974), *Zen and the Art of Motorcycle Maintenance,* William Morrow & Company, New York, pt. 3, ch. 24.

Plott, Charles R. and Kathryn Zeiler (2005), *The Willingness to Pay–Willingness to Accept Gap, the 'Endowment Effect,' Subject Misconceptions, and Experimental Procedures for Eliciting Valuations,* American Economic Review, 95:530–45.

Polanyi, K. (1944) *The Great Transformation,* New York: Farrar & Rinehart.

Polinsky, A.M. and S. Shavell (1999), *The Economic Theory of Public Enforcement of Law,* Journal of Economic Literature, Journal of Economic Literature 38, 45–76.

Pollitt, C. and G. Bouckaert (2002), *Public Management Reform. A Comparative Analysis,* Oxford: Oxford University Press.

Posner, E.A. (1995), *Contract Law in the Welfare State: A Defense of the Unconscionability Doctrine, Usury Laws, and Related Limitations on the Freedom to Contract,* Journal of Legal Studies, 24:283–319.

Posner, E.A. (2001), *Controlling Agencies with Cost-benefit Analysis. A Positive Political Theory Perspective,* University of Chicago Law Review, Vol. 68, 2001.

Posner, R.A. (1979), *Utilitarianism, Economics, and Legal Theory,* Journal of Legal Studies, 8:103–40.

Posner, R.A. (1981), *The Economics Of Justice,* Harvard University Press.

Posner, R.A. (1992), *Economic Analysis of Law,* 4th ed. (Boston: Little Brown).

Posner, R.A. (1997), *Are We One Self or Multiple Selves? Implications for Law and Public Policy,* in Legal Theory, 3, pp. 23–35.

Posner, R.A. (2005), *The Law and Economics Movement: From Bentham to Becker,* in F. Parisi and C.K. Rowley (eds.) The Origins of Law and Economics: Essays by the Founding Fathers (Cheltenham, U.K. and Northampton, MA: Elgar 2005), 328.

Posner, R.A. (1980), *The Ethical and Political Basis of the Efficiency Norm in Common Law Adjudication*, 8 Hofstra L. Rev. 487.

Posner, R.A. (2009), *A Failure of Capitalism. The Crisis of '08 and the Descent into Depression*, Harvard University Press.

Power, M. (1999), *The Audit Society: Rituals of Verification*, Oxford: Oxford University Press – 2nd edition.

Priest, G.L. (1977), *The Common Law Process and the Selection of Efficient Rules*, 6 Journal of Legal Studies 65–82 (1977).

Priest, G.L. (2006), *The Rise of Law and Economics: A Memoir of the Early Years*, in The Origins of Law And Economics: Essays By The Founding Fathers, Francesco Parisi and Charles K. Rowley (eds), Cheltenham, Edwad Elgar, chapter 14.

Rabin, M. (1993), *Incorporating Fairness into Game Theory and Economics*, American Economic Review, 83:1281–1302.

Rachlinski, J.J. (1998), *A Positive Psychological Theory of Judging in Hindsight*, University of Chicago Law Review, 65:571–625.

Rachlinski, J.J. (2000), *The "New" Law and Psychology: A Reply to Critics, Skeptics and Cautious Supporters*, 85 Cornell L. Rev. 739.

Rachlinski, J.J. (2003). *The Uncertain Psychological Case for Paternalism*, in Symposium: Empirical Legal Realism: A New Social Scientific Assessment of Law and Human Behavior, Northwestern University Law Review, 97:1165–1225.

Radaelli, C.M. (2004), *The diffusion of regulatory impact analysis: Best-practice or lesson drawing?* European Journal of Political Research, 43(5), 723–747.

Radaelli, C.M. (2005), *What does regulatory impact assessment mean in Europe?* Washington D.C. AEI-Brookings Joint Center for Regulatory Studies.

Radaelli, C.M. (2005). *Diffusion without convergence: How political context shapes the adoption of regulatory impact assessment,* Journal of European Public Policy, 12(5), 924–943.

Radaelli, C.M. (2009), *Desperately seeking regulatory impact assessments: Diary of a reflective researcher,* Evaluation, 15(1), 31–48.

Radaelli, C.M. and A. Meuwese (2009), *Better Regulation in Europe: between Public Management and Regulatory Reform*, Public Administration, Volume 87, Issue 3, 639–654.

Radaelli, C.M. and De Francesco, F. (2007), *Regulatory Quality in Europe: Concepts, Measures, and Policy Processes*, Manchester: Manchester University Press.

Radaelli, C.M., L. Allio, A. Renda and L. Schrefler (2010), *How to Learn From International Experience: Impact Assessment in the Netherlands*, study for the Dutch government, available at www.eerstekamer.nl/behandeling/20100527/how_to_learn_from_the/f=/vifklgll6miz.pdf.

Radaelli, C., (2005) *How Context Matters: Regulatory Quality in the European Union*, Journal of European Public Policy, 12, 5, 924-943.

Radaelli, C., (2004), *The Diffusion of Regulatory Impact Analysis in OECD Countries: Best Practices or Lesson-drawing?*, European Journal of Political Research, 43(5): 723–747, 2004.

Radaelli, C.M. and Meuwese, A.C.M. (2010), *Hard questions and equally hard solutions? The choice for proceduralization in EU impact assessment*, West European Politics, 33(1): 136–153.

Radaelli, C.M. (2010), *Rationality, power, management and symbols: Four images of regulatory impact assessment*, Scandinavian Political Studies, 33(2).

Radaelli, C.M., F. De Francesco and V.E. Troeger (2007), *The implementation of Regulatory Impact Assessment in Europe*, Paper presented at the European Network for Better Regulation, Workshop on Regulatory Quality: Developing tools, approaches and sources for research on impact assessment, University of Exeter, Exeter 27 and 28 March 2007.

Rajdlova, J. (2004), *Impact Assessment in a Country of Reforms – Slovak Experience*, paper presented at the International Seminar on Implementation of Regulatory Impact Assessment: Best Practices in Europe, 8–11 June, AUBG, Blagoevgrad, Bulgaria, 2004.

Rasmusen, E. (2008), *Internalities and Paternalism. Applying the Compensation Criterion to Multiple Selves across Time*, Indiana University, Kelley School of Business, Department of Business Economics and Public Policy Working Paper No 2008–13.

Raymond, E. (2001), *The Cathedral & the Bazaar: Musings on Linux and Open Source by an Accidental Revolutionary*, O'Reilly Media.

Renda, A. (2006) *Impact assessment in the EU. The State of the Art and the Art of the States*, Centre for European Policy Studies, Brussels, 2006.

Renda, A. (2006), *L'Importanza di Essere Onesto. Come Trasformare un Benthamiano in un Rawlsiano*, Rivista della Scuola Superiore dell'Economia e delle Finanze, 2006, Issue 3, at 175.

Renda, A. (2008), *Law and Economics in the RIA World*. Available at SSRN: http://ssrn.com/abstract=1291032.

Renda, A. (2008), *Advancing the EU better regulation agenda: Selected Challenges for Europe*, Paper presented at the Bertelsmann Foundation's High Level Colloquium on Better Regulation, Brussels, 10–11 September 2008. At http://papers.ssrn.com/sol3/papers.cfm? abstract_id=1291030.

Renda, A. (2009), *Achilles and the Turtle (Akilles och sköldpaddan)*, in "Gratis? Om kvalitet, pengar och skapandets villkor" (ed. Strömbäck, Per), Stockholm: Volante QNB, 2009). (in Swedish language). Information available at http://bokengratis.se/utdrag-andrea-renda/.

Renda, A. (2010), *The Development of RIA in the European Union*, paper presented at the World Bank Regulatory Reform Conference in Belgrade (Serbia), 13–14 September 2010.

Renda, A. and B. Hämmerli (2010), *Protecting Critical Infrastructure in the EU*, Centre for European Policy Studies, Brussels, December 2010.

Renda, A. *et al.*, (2009), *Tying and other potentially unfair commercial practices in retail financial services*, final report for the European Commission, Dg internal Market and Services, available online at http://ec.europa.eu/internal_market/consultations/docs/2010/tying/report_en.pdf.

Renda, A., A. Riley. J. Peysner, R. Van Den Bergh, S. Keske, R. Pardolesi, P. Caprile, E. L. Camilli (2008), *Making Antitrust Damages Actions More Effective in the EU*, Report for the European Commission, at http://ec.europa.eu/competition/antitrust/actionsdamages/files_white_paper/impact_study.pdf.

Renda, A., S. Kurpas, P. M. Kaczyński, L. Montoya and L. Schrefler (2009), *Policy-Making in the EU: Achievements, Challenges and Proposals for Reform*, Centre for European Policy Studies, 2009. Available at SSRN: http://ssrn.com/abstract=1417390.

Rizzo, M.J. (1980), *The Mirage of Efficiency*, 8 Hofstra L. Rev., 641.

Robbins, L. (1932), *An Essay on the Nature and Significance of Economic Science*, (holding that economists, as scientists, could say nothing about the relative pleasures of a Brahmin and an untouchable).

Rodriguez, L. (1988), *Constitutional and Statutory Limits for Cost-Benefit Analysis Pursuant to Executive Orders 12291 and 12498*, Environmental Affairs Law Review, 1988, Vol. 15, No. 505, p. 512.

Rogowski, W. and W. Szpringer (2007), *Methodological Problems Of The Polish System Of Regulation Impact Assessment*, ENBR Working Paper 04/2007, at www.enbr.org/public/ENBR%20WP%20042007.pdf.

Rohlfs, J. (1974), *A Theory of Interdependent Demand for a Communications Service*, Bell Journal of Economics 5, 16–37.

Rose, C. (1998), *The Several Futures of Property: Of Cyberspace and Folk Tales, Emission Trades and Ecosystems*, 83 Minn. L. Rev. 129.

Rubin, P.H. (1977), *Why is the Common Law Efficient?*, 6 Journal of Legal Studies 51–63.

Sanchirico, C.W. (2001), *Deconstructing the New Efficiency Rationale*, Cornell Law Review 86(6): 1003–1089.

Schelling, T.C. (1984), *The Intimate Contest for Self-Command*, in Choice and Consequence Cambridge, MA: Harvard University Press.

Schmidtchen, D. *et al.* (2008), *The Internalisation of External Costs in Transport: From the Polluter Pays to the Cheapest Cost Avoider Principle*, German Working Papers in Law and Economics, Paper 1.

Schumpeter, J. (1909), *On the Concept of Social Value*, 23 Q.J. ECON. 213, 231 (1909).

Schwab, S. (1988), *A Coasean Experiment on Contract Presumptions*, Journal of Legal Studies, 17:237–68.

Scitovsky, T. (1941), *A Note on Welfare Propositions in Economics*, 9 REV. ECON. STUD. 77 (1941);

Scott, R.E. (2000), *The Limits of Behavioral Theories of Law and Social Norms*, 86 Virginia Law Review 1603–1647.

Seidenfeld, M. (1997), *Demystifying Deossification: Rethinking Recent Proposals to Modify Judicial Review of Notice and Comment Rulemaking*, 75 TEX. L. REV. 483, 483–90.

Sen, A.K. (1987), *On Ethics and Economics*, Basil Blackwell Oxford, 32.

Sen, A.K. (2009), *The Idea of Justice*, the Belknap Press of Harvard University Press, Cambridge, MA.

Shavell, S. (1981), *A Note on Efficiency vs. Distributional Equity in Legal Rulemaking: Should Distributional Equity Matter Given Optimal Income Taxation?*, American Economic Review, 71:414–18.

Shavell, S. (2004), *Foundations of Economic Analysis of Law*, Cambridge, Mass.: Belknap Press of Harvard University Press.

Shiller, R. (2008), *The Subprime Solution*, Princeton: Princeton University Press.

Simon, H.A. (1956), *Rational Choice and the Structure of the Environment*, Psychological Review, Vol. 63 No. 2, 129–138.

Sinden, A. (2004), *Cass Sunstein's Cost-Benefit Lite: Economics for Liberals*, 29 Colum. J. Envtl. L. 191, 239.

Staronova, K. (2003), *Analysis of the Policy-making Process in Slovakia*, (at www.policy.hu/staronova/FinalResearch.pdf).

Staronova, K. (2010), *Regulatory Impact Assessment: Formal Institutionalization and Practice*, Journal of Public Policy, 30, 1, 117–136.

Stigler, G.J. (1971), *The Theory of Economic Regulation*, Bell Journal of Economics and Management Science, 2:3–21.

Stigler, G.J. and G.S. Becker (1977), *De Gustibus Non Est Disputandum*, American Economic Review, March 1977, 67:1, 76–90.

Stiglitz, J.E. (1987), *Pareto Efficient and Optimal Taxation and the New Welfare Economics*, in Handbook of Public Economics, ed. Alan Auerbach and Martin Feldstein, 2:991–1042, Amsterdam: Elsevier Science Publishers.

Stiglitz, J.E. *et al.* (2010), *The Stiglitz report: Reforming the World Economy in the Wake of the Global Crisis*, The New Press, New York.

Stolberg, S.G. (2003), *Face Value at the Capitol: Senator Wants to 'Promote Some Diversity' in Congressional Artwork*, New York Times (Aug. 13):E1.

Strøm, K., W.C. Müller and T. Bergman (eds.) (2003), *Delegation and Accountability in Parliamentary Democracies*, Oxford: Oxford University Press.

Strotz, R.H. (1955–56), *Myopia and Inconsistency in Dynamic Utility Maximization*, Review of Economic Studies, 23:165–80.

Sugden, R. (2002), *Beyond Sympathy and Empathy: Adam Smith's Concept of Fellow-Feeling*, Economics and Philosophy, 18:1, 63–87.

Sunstein, C.R. (1996), *Congress, Constitutional Moments, and the Cost-Benefit State*, 48 STAN. L. REV. 247, 255.

Sunstein, C.R. (2000), *Cognition and Cost-Benefit Analysis*, 29 J Legal Stud 1059, 1060–61.

Sunstein, C.R. (2001), *Cost-Benefit Default Principles*, 99 MICH. L. REV. 1651.

Sunstein, C.R. (2007) *Willingness to Pay vs. Welfare*, 1 Harv. L. & Pol'y Rev. 303, 304 (2007).

Sunstein, C.R. (2007), *On Fairy Tales*, 1 Harv. L. & Pol'y Rev. 371–374.

Sunstein, C.R. and R.H. Thaler (2008), *Nudge: Improving Decisions about Health, Wealth, and Happiness*, Yale University Press.

Sunstein, C.R. and R.H. Thaler (2003), *Libertarian Paternalism Is Not an Oxymoron*, University of Chicago Law Review, 70:1159–1202.

Sunstein, C.R., D. Kahneman, D. Schkade and I. Ritov (2002), *Predictably Incoherent Judgments*, Stan. L. Rev. 54, 1153

Sunstein, C.R., D. Schkade and D. Kahneman (1999), *Do People Want Optimal Deterrence?*, University of Chicago Law School, John M. Olin Law & Economics Working Paper No. 77.

Sunstein, C.R. (2002), *Risk and Reason. Safety, Law and the Environment*, Cambridge: Cambridge University Press.

Sunstein, C.R. (1996), *The Cost-Benefit State*, University of Chicago Law School, John M. Olin Law & Economics, Working Paper No. 39.

Svenson, O., B. Fischhoff and D. MacGregor (1985), *Perceived Driving Safety and Seatbelt Usage*, Accident Analysis & Prevention, 17:119–33.

Temple Lang, J. and A. Renda (2008), *Treatment of Exclusionary Abuses under Article 82 of the EC Treaty: Comments on the European Commission's Guidance Paper*, Report of a CEPS Task Force, October 2008.

Thaler, R.H. (1980), *Toward a positive theory of consumer choice*, Journal of Economic Behavior and Organization, 1, 39–60.

Thaler, R.H. (1996), *Doing Economics Without Homo Economicus*, in "Foundations of Research in Economics: How Do Economists Do Economics?", ed. Steven G. Medema and Warren J. Samuels, 227–37, Brookfield, VT: Edward Elgar Publishing Company.

Thaler, R.H. and R.M. Dawes (1992), *Cooperation*, in R.H. Thaler, "The Winner's Curse: Paradoxes and Anomalies of Economic Life", 6–20, New York: The Free Press.

The Evaluation Partnership-TEP (2007), *Evaluation of the European Commission Impact Assessment System*. Available at: http://ec.europa.eu/governance/impact/key_docs/key_docs_en.htm

Tilman, R. (1990), *New Light on John Dewey, Clarence Ayres, and the Development of Evolutionary Economics*, Journal of Economic Issues Vol. 24, No. 4 (Dec., 1990), 963–979.

Timmermans, A. and Andeweg, R. (2003), *The Netherlands: Rules and Mores in Delegation and Accountability Relationships*. In K. Strøm, W. C. Müller and T. Bergman (eds.), *Delegation and Accountability in Parliamentary Democracies*, Oxford: Oxford University Press.

Toth, F.L. (2001), *Participatory integrated assessment methods – An assessment of their usefulness to the European Environmental Agency*, EEA Technical Report No. 64, European Environment Agency, 2001.

Tversky, A. and D. Kahneman (1973), *Availability: A Heuristic for Judging Frequency and Probability*, Cognitive Psychology 5:207–32.

Udehn, L. (2002), *The Changing Face of Methodological Individualism*, 28 Annual Review of Sociology 479, 484.

UK House of Commons, Regulatory Reform Committee (2008), *Getting Results: The Better Regulation Executive and the Impact of the Regulatory Reform Agenda*. London: The Stationery Office Limited.

UK National Audit Office (2009), *Delivering high quality impact assessment*, London: NAO publications.

UK Presidency of the European Union, *Prospects for the EU in 2005 – The UK Presidency of the European Union*, presented to Parliament by the Secretary of State for Foreign and Commonwealth Affairs by Command of Her Majesty, June 2005.

Ulen, T.S. and N.M. Garoupa (2007), *The Market for Legal Innovation: Law and Economics in Europe and the United States*, University of Illinois Law and Economics Research Paper No. LE07-009. Available at SSRN: http://ssrn.com/abstract=972360.

US General Accounting Office (2003), *OMB's Role in the Reviews of Agencies' Draft Rules and the Transparency of these Reviews*, US Government, Washington, D.C., 2003.

Van den Bergh, R.J. (1997), *Wer schützt die europäischen Verbraucher vor dem Brüsseler Verbraucherschutz? Zu den möglichen adversen Effekten der europäischen Richtlinien zum Schutze des Verbrauchers*', in C. Ott und H.-B. Schaefer (eds.)

Effiziente Verhaltenssteuerung und Kooperation im Zivilrecht (Tübingen: Mohr Siebeck 1997) 77–102.
Van Den Bergh, R.J. (2005), *Towards Efficient Self-Regulation in Markets for Professional Services*, (at www.hertig.ethz.ch/LE_2005_files/Papers).
Veljanosky, C. (1982), *The new law-and-economics: a research review*, Oxford: Centre for Socio-Legal Studies.
Vibert, F. (2004), *The EU's New System of Regulatory Impact Assessment – A Scorecard*, European Policy Forum, London.
Vibert, F. (2007), *The Rise of the Unelected: Democracy and the New Separation of Powers* Cambridge: Cambridge University Press.
Vickers, J. (2004), *Economics for Consumer Policy*, 125 Proc. Brit. Acad. 287–310, 289.
Viscusi, K., Vernon, J.M. and Harrington, J.E. (1995), *Economics of Regulation and Anti-Trust*, Cambridge, MA: MIT Press.
Vogel, D. (2003), *The Hare and the Tortoise Revisited: The New Politics of Consumer and Environmental Regulation in Europe*, British Journal of Political Science, *33*, 557–580.
Volkery, A. and K. Ehrhardt (2004), *Sustainability and Regulatory Impact Assessment in the Netherlands*, Berlin: Environmental Policy Research Centre.
Wallace-Wells, B. (2010), *Cass Sunstein wants to nudge us*, New York Times, 16 May 2010.
Walter I. (2003), *Strategies in Banking and Financial Services Firms: A Survey*, NYU Working Paper No. FIN-03-050.
Weick, K. (1976), *Educational organizations as loosely coupled systems.* Administrative Science Quarterly, 21, 1–19.
Weidenbaum, M. (2000), *Regulatory Process Reform from Ford to Clinton*, The CATO Institute, 2000 (available at www.cato.org/pubs/regulation/regv20n1/reg20n1a.html).
Weigel, W. (2008), *The Standard Cost Model – A Critical Appraisal*, 25th Annual Conference of the European Association of Law and Economics, 2008. Available at SSRN: http://ssrn.com/abstract=1295861.
Weinstein, N.D. (1980), *Unrealistic Optimism About Future Life Events*, Journal of Personality and Social Psychology, 39:806–20.
Weinstein, N.D. and W.M. Klein (2002), *Resistance of Personal Risk Perceptions to Debiasing Interventions*, in Heuristics and Biases: The Psychology of Intuitive Judgment, ed. Thomas Gilovich, Dale Griffin and Daniel Kahneman, 313–23, New York: Cambridge University Press.
Weiser, P. (2007), *Should Property or Liability Rules Govern Information?*. Texas Law Review, Vol. 85, 783.
Weiss, C.H. (1979), *The Many Meanings of Research Utilization*, Public Administration Review, *39*(5), 426–431.
Weiss, D.M. (1991), *Paternalistic Pension Policy: Psychological Evidence and Economic Theory*, University of Chicago Law Review, 58:1275–1319.
West, W.F. (2005), *The institutionalization of regulatory review: Organizational stability and responsive competence at OIRA*, Presidential Studies Quarterly, 35(1), 76–93.
Wiener, J.B. (2004), *Hormesis, hotspots and emissions trading*, Human & Experimental Toxicology 23: 289–301.
Wiener, J.B. (2008), *Best Cass Scenario*, Tulsa L. Rev., Vol. 43, 933–946.

Wiener, J.B. and A. Alemanno (2010), *Comparing Regulatory Oversight Bodies Across the Atlantic: The Office of Information and Regulatory Affairs in the US and the Impact Assessment Board in the EU,* in Rose-Ackerman, S. and Peter Lindseth, eds., "Comparative Administrative Law", Edward Elgar.

Wiener, J.B. and B.D. Richman (2009), *Mechanism Choice*, Public Choice and Public Law, Daniel A. Farber and Anne Joseph O'Connell, eds., Forthcoming; Duke Law School Public Law & Legal Theory Paper No. 250. Available at SSRN: http://ssrn.com/abstract=1408163.

Williamson, O.E. (1979), *Transaction Cost Economics: The Governance of Contractual Relations,* Journal of Law and Economics, XXII, 233–261

Williamson, O.E. (1985), *The Economic Institutions of Capitalism* (New York: The Free Press).

Williamson, O.E. (1999), *Public and Private Bureaucracies: A Transaction Cost Economics Perspective,* 15 J.L. Econ & Org. 306.

Winn, J.K. (1994), *Relational Practices and the Marginalization of Law: Informal Financial Practices of Small Businesses in Taiwan.* 28 Law and Society Review 1994, 193–241.

Woerdman, E., A. Arcuri and S. Clò (2007), *Emissions Trading and the Polluter-Pays Principle: Do Polluters Pay under Grandfathering,* Available at SSRN: http://ssrn.com/abstract=1271843.

Woodward, B. and D.S. Broder (1992), *Quayle's Quest: Curb Rules, Leave 'No Fingerprints',* Washington Post, 9 January 1992.

Zerbe Jr., R.O. (1998), *Is Cost-Benefit Analysis Legal? Three Rules,* Journal of Policy Analysis and Management, Vol. 17, 419–456.

Zerbe Jr., R.O., Y. Bauman and A. Finkle (2007), *An Aggregate Measure for Benefit–Cost Analysis,* in Richard Zerbe, John Kirkwood (ed.), Research in Law and Economics, Research in Law and Economics, Volume 23, Emerald Group Publishing Limited, 223–245.

European Studies in Law and Economics

The *European Studies in Law and Economics* Series is an initiative of the board of the EDLE programme. It is a peer-reviewed book series for a wide audience, including policy makers, legislators, economists, lawyers and judges. The books in the series cover a very broad range of topics. They all treat the effects of laws and regulation on people's behaviour, thus providing the tools to understand their impact on the economic system.

The European Doctorate in Law and Economics (EDLE) is the academic response to the increasing importance of the economic analysis of law in Europe. It is an excellence programme offered by the Universities of Bologna, Hamburg and Rotterdam and sponsored by the European Commission under the Erasmus Mundus scheme. It offers the unique opportunity to study Law and Economics on a PhD level in three different countries. The programme prepares economists and lawyers of high promise for an academic career in a research field of growing importance or for responsible positions in government, research organizations and international consulting groups.

For further information: www.edle-phd.eu.

www.ingramcontent.com/pod-product-compliance
Ingram Content Group UK Ltd.
Pitfield, Milton Keynes, MK11 3LW, UK
UKHW051921100926
8556IPUK00021B/1306

9 781780 680231